Hans Dieter Schaal
Landscape Architecture
Landschaftsarchitektur

Hans Dieter Schaal

Landscape Architecture
Landschaftsarchitektur

with a preface by
mit einem Vorwort von
Frank R. Werner

and photographs by
und Photographien von
Peter C. Horn

Edition Axel Menges

ISBN 978-3-86905-003-4

Printing and binding / Druck und Bindearbeiten: Graspo CZ, a.s., Zlín, Czech Republic / Tschechische Republik

Translation into English / Übersetzung ins Englische: Alison Kirkland
Book design / Buchgestaltung: Axel Menges

Picture on the backside of the jacket / Bild auf der Rückseite des Umschlags: Hans Dieter Schaal, 2017. (Photo: Verena Schaal.)

Frank Rolf Werner

Some remarks on the scenographic landscape spaces of Hans Dieter Schaal

»A garden is not simply pure gratification of the external senses, but an inner true illumination of the soul, an enriching of the imagination, a refinement of the feelings, expanding the field for taste and art, the human creative spirit concerning itself with a place where it had not previously been scarcely active, the ennobling of the works of nature and the beautifying of the earth which is, for a time, our home.«
(Christian Cay Lorenz Hirschfeld, *Theorie der Gartenkunst*, *Volume I*, Leipzig 1779)

If there is a plateau that continuously unites Hans Dieter Schaal's numerous artistic fields of activity – a kind of fundamental level – then it is surely that of landscape architecture. Landscape motifs are as convincingly present in his stage sets as they are in his installations, his exhibition architectures, his texts, and, naturally, also his park and garden designs.

Hans Dieter Schaal has been on the track of the fascination of landscapes since the 1960s. He systematically researches European topographies, to which he was initially primarily attracted by authentic »primal landscapes« such as the Norwegian fjords. He used his cine-camera to film and to edit semi-professional films, which exclusively reflected abstract manifestations of landscape configurations. For him, encountering the parterre or »carpet patterns« of the baroque Herrenhäuser Gärten in Hannover was a key experience. This was followed by an intensive study of the early landscape gardens of Great Britain, the park complexes of the Romantics and the Enlightenment in Weimar, Wörlitz, and Muskau, and by studies of the garden art ideas and philosophical implications that underpinned each of them. Rather like Oswald Mathias Ungers, Hans Dieter Schaal looked particularly intensively at Karl Friedrich Schinkel and Peter Joseph Lenné's artistic transformations of the sandy Mark soil. Above all, he was interested in the staging methods and artifice used to reshape formless surfaces into the unique landscapes and architectonic features of a unified artwork such as the »Athens on the Spree«. As a twice-over »Artist-in-Residence« at the Villa Massimo, Hans Dieter Schaal was also able to absorb the whole cosmos of Italian garden and park planning, from the Renaissance to the present day.

All of this swiftly expressed itself in a flood of drawings and paintings that aimed to use artistic methods to analytically explore archaic landscape manifestations. In the early 1970s, Schaal began to present his own landscape designs in texts, images, plans, and models that received much attention: initially based on challenges he imposed on himself, and later for specific landscape design competitions. The timing could hardly have been better. At the time, landscape had dwindled into »remnant green spaces« for which barely anyone felt responsible, at least in the cities and on their peripheries. On the one hand, this circumstance favoured postmodernism – first proclaimed a short time afterward – although this had little relevance to Hans Dieter Schaal. From a standing start, as it were, he focused on the public spaces, with their rudimentary green spaces. On the other hand, the ways of thought of a newly keen ecological consciousness were changing attitudes to »open spaces«. Lastly, movements in art and architecture were increasingly becoming more emancipated, more critical in their attitude, and more didactic in their exploration of new forms of expression, and were increasingly asserting their right to a say in public design projects.

Sceptical about every form of updating – and thus with a retrospective orientation – the trivial and vulgar currents in post-modernism tried to begin where the tradition of public »thought spaces« had broken off, as they were supposed to have done in the early 19th century. However, instead of picking up the central thread from those times and creatively extending it, these trends laboured the subject of strategic requirements such as beautification and suppression, thus sweeping clear conflicts under the proverbial carpet. With its so-called reconstructions of public »free spaces«, this side of post-modernism was taking refuge either in the healthy preindustrial world of restoration, or in the non-binding scenery worlds of »beautiful seemings«. They still exist today, these »taking-refuge« models that attempt to regenerate urban spaces primarily through the tools of yesterday as walled-off pseudo-regionalistic illusory worlds catering to the demands of the sophisticated. It is no accident that, today, we still have (as can be seen in Frankfurt and elsewhere) whole city centres reverted to the conditions of the past, with »déja vu« for the city's past experiencing a positive Renaissance.

The serious ecologists of the early 1970s, on the other hand, wanted to see their thinking used as a learning model for experiencing a new kind of urban and natural reality. They looked to users of open spaces with a close-to-nature design and hoped that, as regained learning or self-experiencing spaces, these would contribute to a changed relationship between human beings and nature. In an increasingly denatured and high-tech interconnected environment, it was believed that this relationship would provide people with a new orientation.

However, it would without doubt be too simplistic to reduce the 60s and 70s solely to restorative postmodern beautification efforts with no bearing on society, or to progressive ecological self-experiencing programmes. After all, very different activities for reclaiming »thought spaces« were gaining in significance at the time. These activities were focused almost entirely on the space between an artistic searching-for-traces strategy, landscape design, and architecture. I am thinking of the magnificent achievements of »Land Art«, and also of the pioneering projects of Hans Hollein, Haus-Rucker-Co, Archigram, Future Systems, Superstudio, Archizoom, and Site, and the ecological »operations« performed by Hermann de Vries and others; »operations« that aspired to the status of art. Since the universalist philosophy of Joseph Beuys (if not before), no clear dividing line can be drawn between art, nature, the city, and the whole of the ecology. At the time, the approaches to projects resulting from this really did generate new »thought spaces« and »thought places«. This is because they forced viewers and users to once again think about a specific place. The degree of thought required exploded all conventions: past events, literary footnotes on the place or on a spiritually related place, juxtapositions of historic developments, fictional archaeologies, questions about »what might have happened here«, and interruptions of reality in favour of flung-out or cast-aside design commentary. Incidentally, these rarely enter the schemata of post-modern »embellissements«; after all, they almost always involve a certain subliminal element of pressure and challenge, sometimes causing gooseflesh, but generally allowing one to exhale in a liberating way.

Today, Hans Dieter Schaal is still one of the most significant pioneers of such »thought spaces« and »thought places« analogous to landscapes. A kind of prelude was provided by the »Ulm neu« project, developed in 1975/76, but in that project, the landscape/architectonic links still played a secondary role. Even so, the first emergence of those artistically staged landscape zones enriched with alienating materials that Schaal was to go on to develop can be seen here.

He subsequently designed antithetical gardens in stone, metal, glass, and organic refuse materials. In simply endless series of graphical experiments – now on display worldwide in many prominent museums – Schaal's theme was »green fittings« for artful paradises, poetically-charged road and path spaces, and never-before-seen architecture/garden combinations. The resulting visionary places were dreamlike presentations of metaphysical city/land configurations.

In 1977, Schaal and a number of friends took part in a major competition relating to the Bundesgartenschau (federal garden show) of 1985, narrowly missing out on winning first prize. Because his design was too provocative, he had to be content with a special prize equivalent to first prize. It was simply that Schaal had not accepted without criticism the specified programme for the garden and architectonic features. Instead, he looked for an entirely different way to respond to this programme. He was primarily interested in the paired concepts that offered themselves: »natural nature/artificial nature« or »natural art/tectonic art«. Furthermore, he exchanged the expected petty bourgeois/populist style of the conventional garden show for a »hard« didactic structure that did not shrink from offering »fields« full of TV sets and antennae, petrified meadows with grazing cows made from plastic, and wildly romantic, exaggerated culture film landscapes. Behind all this was an attempt to unmask the false, degenerate concept of nature in the late 20th century, and to generate new antithetical reifications of the qualities of the urban landscape. Since the media stirred up a full-blown campaign against this project, this extensive design sadly remained, as it were, on the shelf. With hindsight, this can be seen as a stroke of luck, since it meant that Schaal's design was never exposed »in statu nascendi« to the torturous business of looking for lazy compromises. It is significantly owing to this that, today, this piece of work has gone down in the relevant literature as a kind of European key project for a fundamental paradigm shift in the postmodern perception of nature, and a corresponding cultural history »shift« in the treatment of urban nature. Without the Berlin project, avant-garde thinking and practical approaches such as those ingeniously pursued today by prominent landscape designer Adriaan Geuze (born 1960) and his firm West 8 Urban Design & Landscape Architecture B.V. would be virtually unthinkable.

In 1978, Schaal published his first book, entitled *Wege und Wegräume* (Paths and Passages). Today, it can be described as a true classic. Less an artist book in the traditional sense than a heartily refreshing creative continuation of Pückler-Muskau's *Andeutungen über Landschaftsgärtnerei* (1834). *Wege und Wegräume* has since become required reading, and has become an artistic leitmotif for generations of landscape designers and architects.

Further non-realised competition proposals followed, including one in 1983 (once again for Berlin). This highly complex collage of designs was awarded second prize. I am referring to the Görlitzer Park design. For this design, Schaal developed a consistent concept – which, however, did not triumph. Given the negative developments to which the actually implemented project by the first-prize-winner was subjected, which ranged from destruction by vandals to the complete elimination of all hedges and walls, Hans Dieter Schaal can today be happy that he did not receive the planning commission. It appears clear that contemporary landscape architects with genuine artistic qualities can only unfold their full potential within the protected territories of the »Hortus conclusus« garden type.

This makes it all the more important that Schaal did receive a specific commission during the 1983 to 1986 period. The town of Singen asked him to create a concept for a cemetery for the interment of urns, to include an open space design. The complex that was built became, for Schaal, a kind of three-dimensional interim evaluation of the themes »architecture – garden – place«. Protection and openness, finitude and endlessness, organic growth and artificiality appear to come together here, after centuries of graphical exploration, in an interplay that is at once full of exciting contrasts and highly dialectical, with nothing too overt or interchangeably fashionable. To this day, this place of remembrance exudes an effortless dignity and appeal.

In the absence of further projects ready for implementation, Hans Dieter Schaal focused on »follies« (large and small), and was actually able to realise a large number of these. »Folly« is a word of English origin; in French, the term is »folie«. Both refer to small buildings that are not primarily required to be usable, but simply to be surprising and to evoke shivers, merriment, contemplation, enlightenment, or dreams, depending upon the nature of the viewer. Thus »follies« or »folies« were an established part of architectonic discourse long before Bernard Tschumi's Paris Parc de la Villette. They had been rediscovered, long before this, in the Italian Renaissance, not just at Bomarzo, but in almost every grand garden of that period. The baroque-era gardens adopted »follies«, and tried to give them a greater significance. The mosque in the baroque castle park at Schwetzingen provides a beautiful example of a »folly's« many-layered reception across time and space. Originally planned as an exotic »eye-catcher« and a reminiscence of Middle Eastern and Far Eastern yearnings, it was occupied and used as a canteen by American officers after the Second World War, who regarded it as a Disneyland product. Until the first Turkish guest workers arrived in the young Federal Republic; they naturally regarded the Schwetzingen mosque as a sacred place. When, in fact, it had never been any such thing.

Hans Dieter Schaal's contributions to the »folly« theme are far more diverse than Bernard Tschumi's »folies« in Paris, which also spring from very different intellectual principles and design paradigms. Whilst the serially arranged Paris »folies«, painted bright red, are the result of highly complex processes of »decomposition« and »deconstruction«, Schaal develops his »follies« based on the real existing site. For this reason, no project of his – and no design approach – is like the previous one. The prelude was provided by a contemplative wooden Laubenhaus (arbor house) in Stuttgart (1978), now long since fallen victim to vandalism. In 1986, this was followed by the striking entrance ensemble for the Freiburg Landesgartenschau (regional garden show) held in that year, which combined a »motorway gate« with other elements. Originally conceived as a temporary wooden installation, this weathered ensemble is now a familiar landmark to many of the people of Freiburg. Notwithstanding this, it will probably soon have to make way for new urban plans.

Additionally, there is the extensive body of large format by-hand drawings that Hans Dieter Schaal has created in parallel with his other work, in which he engages with practically any and all life situations, but above all with buried cultural, ritual, and mythological implications. Installations that resemble Far East observatories play a role, but so do his choreographed reservations for close-to-nature activities, such as hunting, sports, games, bathing, tents, and gardening. The more trivial the engagement with nature appears, the more intensively Schaal seems to pursue it, after the fashion of an ethnologist searching for traces. This initially takes place auto-reflexively, and is then deepened on the graphical and analytical levels. Schaal's ability to review stored literary references and image elements in his unconscious until a daring but internally coherent chain of association emerges is still surprising today. This ability is of course also useful to Schaal when composing overviews of his own work and insights.

His engagement with the archetypes of house and home has produced significant books such as *Architektonische Situationen* (1980) and *Denkgebäude* (1983). Both anthologies represent such widely informed and subjectively founded design repertories, incorporating every conceivable aspect of landscapes, that Schaal's stage sets, installations, scenographies, memorials, and garden projects are still drawn from this cosmos or fund of virtual image or interpretation worlds. Additionally, both books have served generations of designers as regular »quarries« and inexhaustible sources of inspiration.

In 1994, a fourth Hans Dieter Schaal key work appeared, under the rather terse title *Neue Landschaftsarchitektur*. It proved to be one of the most comprehensive studies sui generis of matters pertaining to landscapes and their handling by a designer for the late 20th century. This pioneering collection of material on the theme of landscape architecture is neither a historiography of landscape design nor a »hortulus animae« for the training of disorientated agronomists, gardeners, and urban planners. Instead, this new standard work by Schaal encourages us to complete an existential subjective excursus into all those spheres that are inscribed into landscape, including those outside of the mainstream, and those that are sublimated. Today, more than ever, *Neue Landschafsarchitektur* is considered to be among recent decades' most comprehensive encyclopaedias on the subject.

Thanks to support from the gifted garden architect Hans Luz, the art coordinator of the time succeeded in making Hans Dieter Schaal responsible for two of the most important follies to be built on the U-shaped garden show site for the Internationale Gartenbauausstellung Stuttgart 1993, for which Luz created the concept. The first of these was concerned with the theme of coming into being and passing away. Above the wildly overgrown remains of the foundations of the former factory owner's villa Moser-Leibfried, forgotten since the end of the war, Schaal erected a complex system of seemingly floating walkways and stairs. By standing on these, one could view the ruins without setting foot on them. Added new architectural elements, such as the suggestion of a front drive and steps to the entrance and an entrance gate shaped like an arbour, new viewing pavilions, birdhouses, and stairs descending into the villa's former garden, came together to form a decomposed »thought building« that related directly to the former villa's invisible, virtual volumes. The result looks as though nature had generated the new architectonic superstructure of its own accord, as a kind of interface. Today, this »folly« is languishing virtually forgotten, badly damaged by vandals and overgrown – a ruin, as it were, amid the ruins. On the other hand, the second »folly« – the »Stangenwald« (forest of stakes) marks a prominent plaza, from which 67 white concrete pillars rise in a regular grid formation. Six further pillars lie scattered on the periphery like forgotten, tumbled spoil. Depending upon mood and light, the composition as a whole (which is still fairly well preserved) looks today like a ruined ancient temple that has lost its roof, or a pure white pergola, open to the sky, whose regular geometry appears to be waiting to be overgrown – a transitional zone between tectonics and nature, between heaven and earth.

In 1996, Schaal built the famous (or »notorious«) white landscape wave for Germany's contribution to the Architecture Biennale in Venice. Projects from Karl Ganser's IBA Emscher Park were to be exhibited in the German Pavilion. Schaal's original concept of a wave of coke and briquettes was rejected. The wishes expressed resulted in the clinical, pure white wave for which Schaal was later berated by a number of his contemporaries. Things were a great deal worse for his wonderful contribution »Reisigstadt« (brushwood city), created in collaboration with Christof Luz in the same year for the Landesgartenschau Böblingen. Owing to a shortage of time and materials, the project was so badly ruined during implementation that Schaal and Luz had to publically distance themselves from it. Matters went significantly better with another »folly«, the Monopteros which was built in 1998 in the Hohenheimer Gärten. To this day, its hill base and its striking domeless silhouette represent an immovable »point de vue« in the former Hohenheim garden area.

In the early 1990s, Schaal took part in a variety of working groups competing in numerous international competitions with a landscape element. These projects included the Berlin Memorial for the Murdered Jews of Germany (1995), the competition for the outside areas of Berlin's Adlershof science city (2003), for the T4-memorial site in Berlin (2012), for the Mühldorfer Hart location on a commission from the Dachau concentration camp memorial site (2014), and the »Trauerweg« (path of mourning) for the city cemetery at Celle (2013/14). Every one of these competition entries deserved to be implemented owing to its wealth of ideas and its innovative force, but in many cases this was prevented by timidity or fear of negative reactions to innovative, unconventional solutions. It is small comfort that Hans Dieter Schaal's »wasted« proposals can number themselves among a long and honourable line of landscapes and pieces of architecture that were never built. In any case, he was able to rescue a part of all these ideas in his realised concentration camp memorials and other memorial sites.

In the years between 1998 and 2003, however a kind of miraculous liberating stroke took place (surely not for the last time). During this period, Schaal was able to realise, for the first time, an original concept of his own for a garden and park on a large scale – his Biberach Wielandpark – largely without needing to consider other persons who might have doubts. This is the place where, for the first time, masses of earth were actually moved, trees planted, and expanses of water laid out according to Schaal's ideas. The land that was made available was located in immediate proximity to the well preserved little garden house where the Swabian poet Christoph Martin Wieland worked on his texts in the 1760s. In his design for the park, Schaal used filmic methods. He wrote a kind of script for a fictional encounter between the French Enlightenment thinker Jean-Jacques Rousseau (1712–1778) and the German poet Christoph Martin Wieland (1733–1813). The plot sees Schaal considering what these two very different personalities might have had to say to one another; the exchanges between them concerning their notions of Enlightenment landscapes, and where they might have strolled during their fictional Biberach encounter. Based on this interplay of thoughts, Hans Dieter Schaal designed a film-ready set, or, more specifically, a stage set full of staged allusions and associative references. In this way, he juxtaposes Wieland's little house with the pathos of Rousseau's poplar island in Ermenonville, which he sets amid his large new lake. Additionally, he builds an artificial ruin – a fictional critique of the Romantic in Wieland. Additionally, he places stones chiselled with quotes from the Enlightenment figure Rousseau and the poet Wieland by the sides of paths and on the island. An arbour offers itself for intensive contemplation or communication.

In the Wielandpark, ordered garden spaces are juxtaposed with sections of free-growing landscape, reinforcing the conflict between the social conventions of the collective and the free development of the individual. Additionally, the whole of the park is »infiltrated« by a subsidiary weave or substructure of associative, intricate elements and symbols, which have the task of prompting empathetic feelings, and sometimes a liberating laugh, from the viewer. It is true that this fragile unified art-work, which is unprotected and open to public use and abuse, is now badly in need of a great deal of care. Here, also, vandalism has left the first traces of destruction. If further measures are not taken to transform the park into a »hortus conclusus« (at least at night), its future does not look good.

The fascination of Schaal's Wielandpark rests upon an exceptionally delicately balanced fluid equilibrium of diverging psychographic fields of force and the narrative messages attached to them. If this equilibrium is wilfully disturbed, this would, it seems, mean the end of the park. Regardless of this, the landscape and architectonic and mental layout of this park also embodies the distilled essence of decades of working with the nature-attuned bridle paths of the psyche. Anyone willing to engage in an unprejudiced way with the texts and subtexts of this place will inevitably see analogies with Jan Hamilton Finlay's »Little Sparta«, near the Scottish locality of Dansyre. Jan Hamilton Finlay (1925–2006) worked on this, his private »world garden«, from 1966 until his death. Unlike Schaal, Finlay was a born sculptor. He created sculptural projects all over the globe, even though he suffered all his life from a phobia of travelling. Thus, he never saw the places where his artworks stood, hence his efforts to inextinguishably inscribe the great narratives and ideas of the wider world into his own private ground. This idea ultimately gave birth to a highly complex, labyrinthine system of poetically charged places, complete with corresponding messages. These messages are encoded in chiselled form in stones and objects, which are embedded piece by piece, »primal landscape« fashion, in groves. In Finlay's own words:

»Usually each area gets a small artefact, which reigns like a small deity or spirit of place. My understanding is that the work is the whole composition – the arte-fact in its context. The work is not an isolated object, but an object with flowers, plants, trees, water and so on.«

Now globally recognised as a significant work of contemporary Scottish art, Finlay's extensive garden world continues to exercise an enormous suggestive power upon visitors today. Admittedly, comparing a private garden with a public park is problematic. But a similar deep fascination is exuded by Schaal's Wielandpark and by Schaal's other efforts to reify the past and the future in an expert symbiosis of landscape and architecture. »Little Sparta« and the Wielandpark are two unequal but intensely spiritually connected highlights of contemporary European landscape architecture.

In contrast to Jan Hamilton Finlay, Hans Dieter Schaal is a polyglot traveller who, in his own opinion, has seen and experienced more gardens and parks than most of his contemporaries. Thus, he knows how to evaluate the works of other transgressors of boundaries and other landscape designers, both affirmatively and critically. He is also familiar with the relevant international discourses. Thus, he is very much conscious of his own special position, and even appears to make creative capital out of it. The realised part of his garden œuvre is comparatively small, but his body of drawings is enormous. Strictly speaking, Schaal is not a »native« landscape architect. He does not feel himself to be a part of the social revolutionary tradition of Fritz Schumacher, Lebrecht Migge, and Harry Maasz, or owe anything to the notions of Roberto Burle Marx, Hermann Mattern, and Louis le Roy. On the other hand, he values the garden work of Hans Luz, with whom he has worked over an extended period with exceptional success. Of course, he also looks at the works of Dieter Kienast, Hans Peter Latz, and other professional landscape designers.

Certainly, landscape architects think primarily in terms of open spaces, botanical categories, and growth cycles. They have to design green spaces that, in many cases, will only grow into the form originally envisaged decades later (if they do so at all). Schaal's landscapes, on the other hand, have long since left Lenné, Sckell, and Pückler-Muskau's »Old Master« precepts behind. Schaal does not just set the scene for landscapes in a Romantic or Enlightenment manner, and does not just supplement his landscapes with architectonic systems of symbols. He unmistakably calls upon viewers and users to walk the tightrope of his bridle paths of the psyche; without a net and with a double floor. In a striking manner, the fields through which Schaal's »dérive« takes us recurringly resemble the fields described so impressively as »smooth« and »grooved« action and reference levels by Gilles Deleuze and Felix Guattari in their brilliant cultural criticism anthology *Mille Plateaux* from 1980. And, after all, didn't Siegfried Kracauer remark in the 1920s, with wise foresight, that: »The insight into cities is linked to the decoding of their dreamlike evoked images.« If one were permitted to replace Kracauer's »insight into cities« with the term »insight into city landscapes«, then Kracauer's phrase could also be taken to apply, without restriction, to Schaal's œuvre – it might even apply especially to Schaal's œuvre.

In an analogous way, Schaal has confronted us, for several decades now, with powerful three-dimensional »mental mappings«, which embody an entirely new psychography of landscapes. Probably, this is where Schaal's real achievement and significance to many of the relevant discourses lies. For that reason, in this text, I will venture the hypothesis that such pioneering manifestos of architecture theory as Tschumi's *Manhattan Transcripts* (1976–1981), in spite of their completely different provenance, would be unthinkable without the foundation provided by the work of Hans Dieter Schaal. In his psychographies of landscapes, Hans Dieter Schaal created truly pioneering work, and he has surely made history.

If only very simple subjective feelings might be permitted to be overlaid on these insights, such as the aura of artificial nature and the fragrance of natural nature, or the sense of lingering, of losing oneself, of travelling in lines, in serpentine and circular shapes, the traces of turbulences and rhythms, the yearning for melodies, the rippling of water, dancing in a rain of light, the gentle whispering of the trees, the flying of hair in the wind – or just the sense of letting oneself fall unconditionally, becoming incorporated into dreamed-of landscapes. Then we, also, would be »initially confused, but later be charmed and finally – who knows – curiously inspired«, just as Geoffrey Jellicoe so inimitably put it when speaking of Schaal's landscapes.

Frank Rolf Werner

Anmerkungen zu den inszenierten Landschaftsräumen von Hans Dieter Schaal

»Ein Garten ist nicht bloße Belustigung des äußeren Sinnes, sondern innere wahre Aufhellung der Seele, Bereicherung der Phantasie, Verfeinerung der Gefühle; Erweiterung des Bezirks für Geschmack und Kunst; Beschäftigung des menschlichen Schöpfungsgeistes mit einem Platze, worauf er noch wenig wirksam war; Veredelung der Werke der Natur und Verschönerung einer Erde, die auf eine Zeit unsere Wohnung ist.«
(Christian Cay Lorenz Hirschfeld, *Theorie der Gartenkunst, Band I*, Leipzig 1779)

Wenn es ein Plateau gibt, das die zahlreichen künstlerischen Betätigungsfelder Hans Dieter Schaals gleichsam als fundierende Schicht durchgängig miteinander verbindet, dann sicher das der Landschaftsarchitektur. Denn landschaftliche Motive lassen sich in seinen Bühnenbildern gleichermaßen wirkmächtig nachweisen wie in seinen Installationen, Ausstellungsarchitekturen, Texten und selbstredend auch in seinen Park- und Gartenentwürfen.

Dabei ist Hans Dieter Schaal dem Faszinosum des Landschaftlichen schon seit den 1960er Jahren auf der Spur. Systematisch erforscht er europäische Topographien, wobei es ihm anfänglich vor allem unverfälschte »Urlandschaften« wie die norwegischen Fjorde angetan haben. Mit seiner Schmalfilmkamera dreht und schneidet er semiprofessionelle Filme, welche ausschließlich abstrahierte Erscheinungsformen landschaftlicher Konfigurationen reflektieren. Ein Schlüsselerlebnis ist für ihn die Begegnung mit den Parterre- oder »Teppichmustern« der barocken Herrenhäuser Gärten in Hannover. Es folgen intensive Beschäftigungen mit den frühen Landschaftsgärten Großbritanniens, den Parkanlagen der Romantik und Aufklärung in Weimar, Wörlitz und Muskau sowie Studien der ihnen jeweils zugrundeliegenden gartenkünstlerischen Ideen und philosophischen Implikationen. Ähnlich wie Oswald Mathias Ungers setzt sich Hans Dieter Schaal besonders intensiv mit Karl Friedrich Schinkels und Peter Joseph Lennés künstlerischen Transformationen märkischer Sandböden auseinander. Wobei ihn vor allem die inszenatorischen Methoden und Kunstgriffe bei der Umformung gestaltloser Flächen zu landschaftlich und architektonisch einzigartigen Gesamtkunstwerken wie »Spree-Athen« interessieren. Als zweimaliger »Artist-in-Residence« in der Villa Massimo kann sich Hans Dieter Schaal zudem auch den ganzen Kosmos italienischer Garten- und Parkplanungen von der Renaissance bis zur Gegenwart einverleiben.

All dies schlägt sich bei ihm alsbald in einer regelrechten Flut von Zeichnungen und Gemälden nieder, die archaische landschaftliche Erscheinungsformen mit künstlerischen Mitteln analytisch auszuloten suchen. Anfang der 1970er Jahre beginnt Schaal in Texten, Bildern, Plänen und Modellen dann aber auch eigene, aufsehenerregende Landschaftsentwürfe vorzustellen; zunächst für selbst gestellte Aufgaben, später für konkrete landschaftsgestalterische Wettbewerbe. Der Zeitpunkt dafür könnte kaum günstiger sein. Denn das Landschaftliche ist seinerzeit, zumindest in den Städten und an ihren Peripherien, zum »Restgrün« verkümmert, für das sich kaum noch jemand verantwortlich fühlt. Dieser Umstand begünstigt zum einen die kurz darauf proklamierte, Hans Dieter Schaal freilich wenig tangierende Postmoderne. Letztere fokussiert sich gleichsam aus dem Stand heraus auf die öffentlichen Räume mit ihren rudimentären Grünflächen. Zum anderen verändern aber auch die Denkweisen eines neu geschärften ökologischen Bewußtseins die Einstellung zu städtischen »Freiräumen«. Und schließlich reklamieren zunehmend emanzipierende, kritisch eingestellte und didaktisch neue Ausdrucksformen auslotende Kunst- und Architekturströmungen das ihnen zustehende Mitspracherecht an öffentlichen Gestaltungsaufgaben.

Skeptisch eingestellt gegenüber jeder Form von Vergegenwärtigung und daher retrospektiv orientiert, versuchen die trivial-vulgären Strömungen der Postmoderne dort anzuknüpfen, wo die Tradition öffentlicher »Denkräume« abgebrochen ist, soll heißen im frühen 19. Jahrhundert. Anstatt jedoch den roten Faden von damals aufzugreifen und kreativ weiterzuspinnen, pochen sie auf strategische Forderungen wie Behübschung oder Verdrängung, um offensichtliche Konflikte unter den sprichwörtlichen Teppich zu kehren. Somit flüchtet sich diese Seite der Postmoderne mit ihren vermeintlichen Rekonstruktionen öffentlicher »Freiräume« entweder in die heile vorindustrielle Welt der Restauration oder in die unverbindlichen Kulissenwelten des »schönen Scheins«. Es gibt sie heute übrigens immer noch, jene Fluchtmodelle, die städtische Räume vornehmlich mit den Mitteln von gestern als ausgegrenzte pseudo-regionalistische Scheinwelten für gehobene Ansprüche zu regenerieren versuchen. Nicht von ungefähr werden noch heute, wie derzeit nicht nur in Frankfurt zu beobachten ist, ganze Stadtzentren in den Zustand von vorgestern zurückversetzt, erlebt das »Déja vu« städtischer Vergangenheiten eine regelrechte Renaissance.

Seröse Ökologen hingegen wollen ihr Gedankengut mit Beginn der 1970er Jahre als Lernmodell zur Erfahrung einer neuen Art von Stadt- und Naturwirklichkeit eingesetzt wissen. Unter Einbeziehung der Nutzer naturnah gestalteter Freiflächen dienen ihnen dabei wiedergewonnene Schulungs- oder Selbsterfahrungsräume für eine veränderte Mensch-Natur-Relation. In einer zunehmend denaturierten und hochtechnologisch vernetzten Umwelt soll diese Relation Orientierungshilfe leisten.

Doch wäre es zweifellos viel zu einfach, die 1970er und 1980er Jahre allein auf restaurative postmoderne Behübschungsversuche ohne Gesellschaftsbezug oder progressive ökologische Selbsterfahrungsprogramme reduzieren zu wollen. Denn schließlich gewinnen seinerzeit ganz andere Aktivitäten zur Rückgewinnung von »Denkräumen« an Bedeutung. Aktivitäten, die fast allesamt im Grenzbereich zwischen künstlerischer Spurensuche, Landschaftsgestaltung und Architektur angesiedelt sind. Ich denke da an die großartigen Leistungen der »Land Art«. Oder an wegweisende Projekte von Hans Hollein, Haus-Rucker-Co, Archigram, Future Systems, Superstudio, Archizoom, Site oder auch an die ökologischen »Operationen« eines Hermann de Vries und anderer; an »Operationen« mit künstlerischem Anspruch also. Spätestens seit dem Universalisten Joseph Beuys ist ja auch keine Trennungslinie mehr zu ziehen zwischen Kunst, Natur, Stadt und deren aller Ökologie. Die seinerzeit daraus resultierenden Projektansätze generieren in der Tat wirklich neue »Denkräume« oder »Denkorte«. Sie zwingen die jeweiligen Bertrachter und Benutzer nämlich, wieder über einen spezifischen Ort nachzudenken. Wobei das geforderte Maß des Nachdenkens alle Konventionen sprengt: gewesene Ereignisse, literarische Fußnoten zu diesem oder einem wesensverwandten Ort, Juxtapositionen historischer Entwicklungen, fiktive Archäologien, Fragen nach dem, »was hier alles hätte stattfinden können«, und immer wieder Brechungen der Realität zugunsten ge- oder verworfener gestalterischer Kommentare. Beiläufig gesagt, passen diese seinerzeit wie heute nur selten in die Schemata postmoderner »Embellissements«, sind sie doch unterschwellig fast immer bedrängend, herausfordernd, verursachen sie manchmal Gänsehaut, meist aber befreiendes Aufatmen.

Hans Dieter Schaal ist bis heute einer der prägendsten Wegbereiter solcher landschaftsanaloger »Denkräume« und »Denkorte« geblieben. Eine Art von Vorlauf verkörpert das 1975/76 entwickelte Projekt »Ulm neu«, bei dem landschaftsarchitektonische Bezüge allerdings noch eine untergeordnete Rolle spielen. Freilich sind bereits hier ansatzweise jene künstlich inszenierten und mit verfremdeten Materialien angereicherten Landschaftszonen zu erkennen, an denen Schaal weiter arbeiten wird.

In der Folge entwirft er antithetische Gärten aus Stein, Metall, Glas oder organischen Abfällen. In schier endlosen zeichnerischen Versuchsanordnungen, die mittlerweile in vielen bedeutenden Museen hängen, thematisiert Schaal die »Grünausstattung« künstlicher Paradiese, poetisch aufgeladene Straßen- und Wegräume sowie nie zuvor gesehene Architektur-Garten-Konstellationen. Daraus resultieren visionäre Plätze als traumhafte Inszenierungen metaphysischer Stadt-Land-Konfigurationen.

Im Jahr 1977 nimmt Schaal mit Freunden an einem großen Wettbewerb für die Bundesgartenschau 1985 in Berlin teil und gewinnt beinahe den ersten Preis. Weil sein Entwurf zu provokant ist, muß er sich jedoch mit einem gleichrangigen 1. Sonderpreis zufrieden geben. Dabei hat Schaal lediglich die vorgegebenen gärtnerischen und architektonischen Programme nicht einfach kritiklos hingenommen. Statt dessen sucht er diese Programme ganz andersartig zu beantworten. Sein Interesse gilt nämlich vorrangig disponiblen Begriffspaaren wie »natürliche Natur/künstliche Natur« oder »natürliche Kunst/tektonische Kunst«. Des weiteren vertauscht er den erwarteten, kleinbürgerlichen bis populistischen Habitus konventioneller Gartenschauen gegen ein »hartes« didaktisches Gefüge, das nicht davor zurückschreckt, »Felder« voller Fernsehapparate und Antennen, versteinerte Wiesen mit Weidevieh aus Kunststoff, aber auch wildromantisch überzeichnete Kulturfilmlandschaften anzubieten. Dahinter verbirgt sich der Versuch, den unaufrichtigen, degenerierten Naturbegriff des späten 20. Jahrhunderts zu enttarnen und antithetisch neue Vergegenwärtigungsformen des Stadtlandschaftlichen zu generieren. Da die Medien eine regelrechte Kampagne gegen dieses Projekt entfachen, bleiben die umfänglichen Entwurfsarbeiten leider in den sprichwörtlichen Schubladen. Wobei dies in der Nachschau als Glücksfall erscheint, da Schaals Entwurf im »Status nascendi« nie der qualvollen Suche nach faulen Kompromissen ausgesetzt gewesen ist. Nicht zuletzt deshalb gilt diese Arbeit in der einschlägigen Literatur noch heute als eine Art europäisches Schlüsselprojekt für einen grundlegenden Paradigmenwechsel nachmoderner Naturwahrnehmung und als kulturgeschichtliche »Umschaltung« im Umgang mit städtischer Natur. Ohne das Berliner Projekt wären avantgardistische Denk- und Handlungsansätze, wie sie etwa von dem erst 1960 geborenen, prominenten Landschaftsgestalter Adriaan Geuze und seinem Büro, West 8 Urban Design & Landscape Architecture B.V., heute ingeniös verfolgt werden, praktisch undenkbar.

1978 publiziert Schaal unter dem Titel *Wege und Wegräume* sein erstes Buch, das man heute schon als regelrechten »Klassiker« bezeichnen darf, weil es sich dabei weniger um ein Künstlerbuch im traditionellen Sinne handelt als vielmehr um eine herzerfrischend kreative Fortschreibung von Pückler-Muskaus *Andeutungen über Landschaftsgärtnerei* (1834). *Wege und Wegräume* ist seitdem Pflichtlektüre und künstlerischer Leitfaden für Generationen von Landschaftsgestaltern und Architekten geworden.

Es folgen weitere nicht realisierte Wettbewerbsvorschläge, darunter im Jahre 1983 eine wiederum für Berlin geschaffene, hochkomplexe entwerferische Collage, die mit einem zweiten Preis ausgezeichnet wird. Gemeint ist der Görlitzer Park. Schaal entwickelt für ihn ein stringentes Konzept, das sich freilich nicht durchsetzen kann. In Anbetracht der negativen Entwicklungen, denen das tatsächlich ausgeführte Projekt des 1. Preisträgers im Zuge vandalistischer Zerstörungen bis hin zur vollständigen Eliminierung aller Hecken und Mauern später ausgesetzt ist, kann Hans Dieter Schaal heute froh sein, daß er seinerzeit keinen Planungsauftrag erhalten hat. Zeitgenössische Landschaftsarchitekturen mit unverstelltem künstlerischem Anspruch scheinen sich offensichtlich nur noch auf den geschützten Territorien der Gattung »Hortus conclusus« entfalten zu können.

Um so wichtiger ist es, daß Schaal in den Jahren 1983 bis 1986 dann doch einen konkreten Auftrag erhält. Er soll für die Stadt Singen am Hohentwiel einen Friedhof für Urnenbestattungen inklusive der dazu erforderlichen Freiraumgestaltung konzipieren. Der ausgeführte Komplex wird für Schaal eine Art von dreidimensionaler Zwischenbilanz zum Themenbereich »Architektur – Garten – Ort«. Geborgenheit und Offenheit, Endlichkeit und Unendlichkeit, Gewachsenes und Künstliches scheinen sich hier nach jahrzehntelangen zeichnerischen Explorationen zu einem gleichermaßen spannungsreichen wie hoch dialektischen Wechselspiel zu verdichten, dem nichts Vordergründiges, modisch Austauschbares anhaftet. Bis heute strahlt dieser Ort des Gedenkens eine unangestrengte Würde und Anmut aus.

In Ermangelung weiterer ausführungsreifer Projekte fokussiert sich Hans Dieter Schaal auf kleinere und größere »Follies«, von denen er eine stattliche Anzahl tatsächlich realisieren kann. Die Bezeichnung »Folly« stammt aus England, in Frankreich benutzt man den Begriff »Folie«. In beiden Fällen sind damit kleinere Gebäude gemeint, die keinem unmittelbaren Nutzungszwang unterliegen, sondern allein überraschen und, entsprechend der Verfassung des jeweiligen Betrachters, Erschauern, Heiterkeit, Kontemplation, Aufklärung oder Träume hervorrufen sollen. »Follies« oder »Folies« sind daher nicht erst seit Bernard Tschumis Pariser Parc de la Villette ein fester Begriff in architektonischen Diskursen. Sie sind schon lange vorher in der italienischen Renaissance wiederentdeckt worden und nicht nur in Bomarzo, sondern in fast jedem repräsentativen Garten jener Zeit anzutreffen. Die Gärten der Barockzeit übernehmen die »Follies« und versuchen deren Bedeutung noch einmal zu steigern. Ein schönes Beispiel für die Zeit und Raum übergreifende vielschichtige Rezeption einer »Folly« ist die Moschee im barocken Schloßpark von Schwetzingen. Ursprünglich als exotischer »Eyecatcher« und Reminiszenz an nah- und fernöstliche Sehnsüchte geplant, wird sie nach dem Zweiten Weltkrieg von amerikanischen Offizieren als vermeintliches Disneyland-Produkt okkupiert und für Kasinozwecke genutzt. Bis die ersten türkischen Gastarbeiter in der jungen Bundesrepublik eintreffen und die Schwetzinger Moschee wie selbstverständlich als geheiligten Ort begreifen. Faktisch ist er das freilich nie gewesen.

Hans Dieter Schaals Beiträge zum Thema »Folly« sehen weitaus vielfältiger aus als Bernard Tschumis »Follies« in Paris, die sich zudem aus ganz anderen intellektuellen Prämissen und entwerferischen Paradigmen herleiten. Während die seriell angeordneten, feuerrot lackierten Pariser »Folies« das Resultat hochkomplexer Vorgänge des »Dekomponierens« und »Dekonstruierens« sind, entwickelt Schaal seine »Follies« stets aus dem jeweils vorgefundenen Ort heraus. Weshalb kein Projekt dem anderen, kein entwerferischer Ansatz dem nächsten gleicht. Den Auftakt macht ein kontemplatives hölzernes Laubenhaus in Stuttgart (1978), das längst dem Vandalismus zum Opfer gefallen ist. 1986 folgt das markante, mit einem »Autobahntor« und weiteren Elementen kombinierte Eingangsensemble zur damaligen Freiburger Landesgartenschau. Ursprünglich als vergängliche hölzerne Installation aus Holz konzipiert, ist das verwitterte Ensemble für viele Freiburger längst zu einer vertrauten Landmarke geworden. Gleichwohl wird es demnächst wohl neuen urbanen Planungen weichen müssen.

Parallel hierzu entstehen weiterhin umfängliche Konvolute großformatiger Handzeichnungen, in denen sich Hans Dieter Schaal mit nahezu allen Situationen des Lebens, vor allem aber mit ihren verschütteten kulturellen, rituellen und mythologischen Implikationen auseinandersetzt. Installationen, die an fernöstliche Observatorien erinnern, spielen dabei eine Rolle, aber auch inszenierte Reservate für naturnahe Tätigkeiten, wie Jagen, Sport betreiben, Spielen, Baden, Zelten oder Gärtnern. Je trivialer die jeweilige Beschäftigung mit der Natur erscheint, desto intensiver scheint ihr Schaal nach Art eines spurensuchenden Ethnologen auf den Grund zu gehen. Dies geschieht zunächst autoreflexiv, um dann auf zeichnerisch-analytischen Ebenen vertieft zu werden. Die Fähigkeit, abgespeicherte Literaturbezüge und Bildelemente so lange im Unterbewußtsein Revue passieren zu lassen, bis jede noch so wagemutige Assoziationskette in sich stimmig wird, verblüfft bis heute. Diese Fähigkeit kommt Schaal selbstredend auch bei der Zusammenstellung seiner eigenen Werkübersichten und Einsichten zugute.

Aus der Beschäftigung mit den Archetypen des Hausens und Behausens gehen so wichtige Bücher hervor wie *Architektonische Situationen* (1980) und *Denkgebäude* (1983). Beide Anthologien stellen unter Einbeziehung aller nur denkbaren landschaftlichen Aspekte so breit angelegte und subjektiv fundierte gestalterische Repertorien dar, daß sich Schaals Bühnenbilder, Installationen, Szenographien, Gedenkstätten oder Gartenprojekte bis heute aus diesem Kosmos oder Fundus virtueller Bild- und Deutungswelten speisen. Darüber hinaus dienen beide Bücher Generationen von Gestaltern als regelrechte »Steinbrüche«, sprich unerschöpfliche Quelle der Inspiration.

Im Jahr 1994 erscheint unter dem eher lapidaren Titel *Neue Landschaftsarchitektur* ein viertes Grundlagenwerk Hans Dieter Schaals, das sich seinerzeit als eine der umfassendsten Studien des ausgehenden 20. Jahrhunderts über Landschaftliches sui generis sowie den gestalterischen Umgang mit ihm erweist. Dabei verkörpert diese bahnbrechende Materialsammlung zum Thema Landschaftsarchitektur weder eine Historiographie der Landschaftsgestaltung noch ein »hortulus animae« zur Ertüchtigung desorientierter Agronomen, Gärtner oder Städtebauer. Statt dessen regt Schaals neues Standardwerk zum Nachvollzug existenzieller subjektiver Exkurse in all jene Sphären an, die dem Landschaftlichen auch jenseits des Mainstreams eingeschrieben sind; inklusive derer, die von ihm sublimiert werden. Heute gilt die *Neue Landschafsarchitektur* mehr denn je als eine der umfassendsten einschlägigen Enzyclopädien der letzten Jahrzehnte.

Mit Unterstützung des begnadeten Gartenarchitekten Hans Luz gelingt es dem damaligem Kunstkoordinator, Hans Dieter Schaal im Kontext der von Luz konzipierten »Internationalen Gartenbauausstellung Stuttgart 1993« für zwei der wichtigsten »Follies« auf dem U-förmigen Gartenschaugelände zu verpflichten. Das erste beschäftigt sich mit dem Thema Werden und Vergehen. Über den seit Kriegsende in Vergessenheit geratenen, wild überwucherten Fundamentresten der ehemaligen Fabrikantenvilla Moser-Leibfried errichtet Schaal ein komplexes System aus schwebend wirkenden Stegen und Treppen. Von dort aus läßt sich die Ruine betrachten, ohne sie zu betreten. Additiv hinzugefügte neue Architekturelemente, wie eine angedeutete Vorfahrt und Eingangstreppe, ein als Laube ausgebildetes Eingangstor, neue Aussichtpavillons, Vogelhäuser oder Treppenabgänge in den ehemaligen Villengarten, konstituieren sich zu einem dekomponierten »Denkgebäude« mit direktem Bezug zum unsichtbaren virtuellen Volumen der ehemaligen Villa. Das Resultat wirkt geradezu so, als habe die Natur den neuen architektonischen Überbau als eine Art von Schnittstelle wie beiläufig aus sich selbst generiert. Heute dämmert dieses »Folly«, von Vandalen schwer beschädigt und zugewachsen, gleichsam als Ruine in der Ruine nahezu vergessen vor sich hin. Das zweite »Folly«, der sogenannte »Stangenwald«, markiert hingegen einen repräsentativen Platz, auf dem sich in einem strengen Raster 67 weiße Betonsäulen erheben. Sechs weitere Säulen liegen wie vergessene, übereinandergefallene Spolien am Rande verstreut. Je nach Stimmung und Tageslicht wirkt das bis heute leidlich erhaltene Ganze wie eine archaische, ihres Daches beraubte Tempelruine oder eine himmelwärts offene, makellos weiße Pergola, deren strenge Geometrie geradewegs auf Überwucherung zu warten scheint, eine transitorische Zone zwischen Tektonik und Natur, zwischen Himmel und Erde.

Im Jahr 1996 baut Schaal die berühmt »berüchtigte« weiße Landschaftswelle für den deutschen Beitrag auf der Architektur-Biennale Venedig. Im deutschen Pavillon sollen Projekte von Karl Gansers IBA Emscher Park gezeigt werden. Mit seinem ursprünglichen Konzept einer Welle aus Koks und Briketts kann sich Schaal nicht durchsetzen. Was, wie gewünscht, jene klinisch reine weiße Welle zur Folge hat, für die Schaal später von einigen Zeitgenossen gescholten wird. Weitaus übler ergeht es seinem wunderbaren Beitrag »Reisigstadt«, den er in Zusammenarbeit mit Christof Luz im gleichen Jahr für die Landesgartenschau Böblingen ausführt. Aus Geld- und Materialmangel wird das Projekt während der Umsetzung so verhunzt, daß sich Schaal und Luz öffentlich von ihm distanzieren müssen. Da geht es einem anderen »Folly«, dem 1998 errichteten Monopteros in den Hohenheimer Gärten weitaus besser. Sein hügeliger Unterbau und seine markante kuppellose Silhouette verorten bis heute einen unverrückbaren »point de vu« im ehemaligen Hohenheimer Gartenreich.

Mit Beginn der 1990er Jahre nimmt Schaal in wechselnden Arbeitsgemeinschaften an zahlreichen internationalen Wettbewerben mit Landschaftsbezug teil. Zum Beispiel um das Berliner Denkmal für die ermordeten Juden Europas (1995), für die Außenräume der Berliner Wissenschaftsstadt Adlershof (2003), für den T4-Gedenkplatz in Berlin (2012), für den Mühldorfer Hart im Auftrag der KZ-Gedenkstätte Dachau (2014) oder den »Trauerweg« des Stadtfriedhofs Celle (2013/14). Obwohl es jeder dieser Wettbewerbsbeiträge aufgrund seines Ideenreichtums und seiner Innovationskraft verdient hätte, verwirklicht zu werden, haben in vielen Fällen Kleinmut oder Angst vor negativen Reaktionen auf innovative unkonventionelle Lösungen genau das verhindert. Da mag es lediglich ein kleiner Trost sein, daß sich Hans Dieter Schaal mit seinen »vergeudeten« Vorschlägen in eine äußerst prominent besetzte Ahnenreihe nicht gebauter Landschaften und Architekturen einreihen kann. Immerhin kann er einen Teil all dieser Ideen in seine realisierten KZ-Gedenkstätten und andere Gedenkorte hinüberretten.

In den Jahren 1998 bis 2003 ist es dann aber doch noch zu einer Art von Wunder in Gestalt eines Befreiungsschlages gekommen, der sicher nicht der letzte sein wird. In dieser Zeitspanne kann Schaal nämlich mit seinem Biberacher Wielandpark erstmals ureigene Garten- und Parkvorstellungen in einem größeren Maßstab und weitestgehend ohne Rücksichtnahme auf mögliche Bedenkenträger realisieren. Hier ist der Ort, an dem nach seinen Vorstellungen nun wirklich erstmals Erdmassen bewegt, Bäume gepflanzt und Wasserflächen angelegt werden. Das zur Verfügung stehende Gelände befindet sich in unmittelbarer Nachbarschaft jenes wohlerhaltenen Gartenhäuschens, in dem der schwäbische Dichter Christoph Martin Wieland in den 1760er Jahren an seinen Texten arbeitete. Bei der Ausgestaltung des Parks bedient sich Schaal filmischer Mittel. So schreibt er eine Art Drehbuch zu einer fiktiven Begegnung zwischen dem französischen Aufklärer Jean-Jaques Rousseau (1712–1778) und dem deutschen Dichter Christoph Martin Wieland (1733–1813). In dem Plot sinniert Schaal darüber, was sich die beiden so gegensätzlichen Persönlichkeiten wohl zu sagen gehabt hätten; wie sie ihre kontroversen Vorstellungen von aufklärerischen Landschaften wohl untereinander ausgetauscht hätten, wo sie bei ihrer fiktiven Biberacher Begegnung wohl lustgewandelt wären. Aus diesem Gedankenspiel heraus entwirft Hans Dieter Schaal ein filmreifes Set, genauer gesagt ein Bühnenbild voller inszenierter Andeutungen und assoziativer Anspielungen. Dabei konfrontiert er das kleine Wieland-Häuschen mit Rousseaus pathetischer Pappelinsel aus Ermenonville, die er in seinem großen neuen See treiben läßt. Dazu baut er eine künstliche Ruine, als fiktive Kritik der Romantiker an Wieland. Zusätzlich legt er Steine mit eingemeißelten Zitaten des Aufklärers Rousseau und des Dichters Wieland an Wegränder und auf die Insel. Eine Laube lädt zur intensiver Kontemplation oder Kommunikation ein.

Im Wielandpark stehen sich strenge Gartenräume und frei wachsende Landschaftspartien gegenüber, die den Konflikt zwischen gesellschaftlichen Konventionen des Kollektivs und der freien Entfaltung des Individuums verdeutlichen. Zusätzlich wird das ganze Parkgelände von einem subsidiären Geflecht bzw. einer Substruktur assoziativer kleinteiliger Elemente und Zeichen »unterwandert«, denen die Aufgabe zukommt, Betrachter zu empathischen Gefühlen anzuregen, mitunter sogar zum befreienden Lachen zu verleiten. Freilich bedarf auch dieses fragile, schutzlos öffentlichem Ge- und Verbrauch ausgelieferte Gesamtkunstwerk längst einer intensiver Fürsorge. Denn auch hier hat der Vandalismus bereits erste Spuren der Zerstörung hinterlassen. Sollte sich der Park nicht durch welche Maßnahmen auch immer wenigstens nachtsüber in einen »Hortus conclusus« verwandeln lassen, wäre es vermutlich nicht gut um seine Zukunft bestellt.

Die von Schaals Wielandpark ausgehende Faszination beruht nämlich auf einem äußerst fragil austarierten Fließgleichgewicht divergierender psychographischer Kraftfelder und der mit ihnen verknüpften narrativen Botschaften. Würde diese Gleichgewicht mutwillig gestört, würde das vermutlich das Ende des Parks bedeuten. Dessen ungeachtet verkörpert das landschaftliche, architektonische und gedankliche Layout dieses Parks aber auch die Quintessenz einer jahrzehntelangen Beschäftigung mit den naturbezogenen Saumpfaden der Psyche. Demjenigen, der bereit ist, sich unvoreingenommen auf die Texte und Subtexte dieses Ortes einzulassen, dem drängen sich unwillkürlich Analogien zu Jan Hamilton Finlays »Little Sparta« in der Nähe der schottischen Ortschaft Dansyre auf. Von 1966 bis zu seinem Tod hat Jan Hamilton Finlay (1925–2006) an seinem privaten »Weltgarten« gearbeitet. Anders als Schaal war Finlay von Hause aus Bildhauer. Er hat weltweit Skulpturenprojekte realisiert, obwohl er lebenslang unter einer Reisephobie litt. Daher hat er die Orte, an denen seine Kunstwerke stehen, nie gesehen, weshalb er versuchte, die großen Erzählungen und Ideen der Welt da draußen seinem privaten Grund und Boden unauslöschbar einzuschreiben. Aus dieser Idee ist letztendlich ein hochkomplexes, labyrinthisch verschachteltes System poetisch aufgeladener Orte inklusive entsprechender Botschaften entstanden. Letztere sind verschlüsselt in Steine und Objekte eingemeißelt, die Stück für Stück »urlandschaftlich« in Haine eingebettet sind. Finlay hat das selbst mit den Worten kommentiert:

»Usually each area gets a small artefact, which reigns like a small deity or spirit of place. My understanding is that the work is the whole composition – the artefact in its context. The work is not an isolated object, but an object with flowers, plants, trees, water and so on.«

Inzwischen weltweit längst als bedeutendstes Werk zeitgenössischer schottischer Kunst anerkannt, strahlt die weitläufige Gartenwelt Finlays bis heute eine enorme Suggestivkraft auf ihre Besucher aus. Ein privater Garten läßt sich schwerlich mit einem öffentlichen Park vergleichen. Aber eine ähnlich tiefe Faszination geht auch von Schaals Wielandpark und anderen Versuchen aus, Gewesenes und Künftiges in beredten Symbiosen aus Landschaft und Architektur zu vergegenwärtigen. »Little Sparta« und der Wielandpark, das sind zwei ungleiche aber doch zutiefst wesensverwandte Höhepunkte zeitgenössischer europäischer Landschaftsarchitektur.

Im Gegensatz zu Jan Hamilton Finlay ist Hans Dieter Schaal ein polyglotter Reisender, der aus eigener Anschauung mehr Gärten und Parks gesehen und erlebt hat als die meisten seiner Zeitgenossen. Deshalb weiß er die Arbeiten anderer Grenzgänger und Landschaftsgestalter affirmativ wie kritisch einzuschätzen. Und er kennt die einschlägigen internationalen Diskurse. Dabei ist er sich seiner eigenen Sonderstellung durchaus bewußt, ja er scheint daraus sogar kreatives Kapital zu schlagen. Sein realisiertes Gartenœuvre ist vergleichsweise klein, sein gezeichnetes hingegen riesig. Schaal ist wohlgemerkt kein »nativer« Landschaftsarchitekt. Er fühlt sich weder in der sozialrevolutionären Tradition eines Fritz Schumacher, Lebrecht Migge oder Harry Maasz stehend, noch den Vorstellungen eines Roberto Burle Marx, Hermann Mattern oder Louis le Roy verpflichtet. Hingegen schätzt er das gärtnerische Werk von Hans Luz, mit dem er lange Zeit außerordentlich erfolgreich zusammengearbeitet hat. Natürlich setzt er sich auch mit den Arbeiten von Dieter Kienast, Hans Peter Latz und anderen professionellen Landschaftsgestaltern auseinander.

Landschaftsarchitekten denken freilich vorrangig in offenen Räumen, botanischen Kategorien oder Wachstumszyklen. Sie müssen Grünräume konzipieren, die häufig erst Jahrzehnte später zu dem heranwachsen (oder auch nicht), was sie sich ursprünglich einmal vorgestellt hatten. Schaals Landschaften hingegen haben Lennés, Sckells oder Pückler-Muskaus altmeisterliche Anweisungen schon vor langer Zeit hinter sich gelassen. Schaal setzt Landschaften nicht nur romantisch oder aufklärerisch in Szene, er reichert seine Landschaften nicht nur mit architektonischen Zeichensystemen an, sondern er fordert Betrachter wie Nutzer unmißverständlich zu Gratwanderungen auf seinen Saumpfaden der Psyche auf; ohne Netz und doppelten Boden. Auf frappierende Weise ähneln die Felder, auf die uns das Schaalsche »dérive« immer wieder führt, denjenigen, die uns Gilles Deleuze und Felix Guattari in ihrer fulminanten kulturkritischen Anthologie *Mille Plateaux* aus dem Jahr 1980 so einprägsam als »glatte« und »gekerbte« Handlungs- und Bezugsebene vorgestellt haben. Und hatte nicht Siegfried Kracauer schon in den 1920er Jahren des vergangenen Jahrhunderts in weiser Voraussicht festgestellt: »Die Erkenntnis der Städte ist an die Entzifferung ihrer traumhaft hingesagten Bilder geknüpft.« Dürfte man Kracauers »Erkenntnis der Städte« durch den Terminus »Erkenntnis der Stadtlandschaften« ersetzen, dann könnte Kracauers Satz auch oder gerade auf Schaals Œuvre uneingeschränkt zutreffen.

Auf analoge Weise konfrontiert uns Schaal nunmehr schon seit vielen Jahrzehnten mit kraftvollen dreidimensionalen »mental mappings«, die eine gänzlich neue Psychographie des Landschaftlichen verkörpern. Vermutlich liegt darin Schaals eigentliche Leistung und Bedeutung für viele einschlägige Diskurse. Deshalb sei an dieser Stelle die Hypothese gewagt, daß so wegweisende architekturtheoretische Manifeste wie etwa Tschumis *Manhattan Transcripts* (1976–1981), ungeachtet ihrer völlig anders herzuleitenden Provenienz, ohne die Grundlagenarbeit Hans Dieter Schaals eigentlich undenkbar wären. Mit seinen Psychographien des Landschaftlichen hat Hans Dieter Schaal wirklich Pionierarbeit geleistet, und er hat damit sicher schon Geschichte geschrieben.

Wenn sich über diese Einsichten auch noch ganz einfache subjektive Empfindungen legen dürfen, wie etwa der Glanz künstlicher Natur und der Duft natürlicher Natur oder das Bleiben, das Sich-Verlieren, Gehen in Linien, Serpentinen und Kreisen, das Spüren von Verwirbelungen und Rhythmen, die Sehnsucht nach Melodien, das Kräuseln des Wassers, das Tanzen im fallenden Lichterregen, das sanfte Wispern der Bäume, das Wirbeln der Haare im Wind – oder einfach nur das bedingungslose Sich-Fallen-Lassen und Einverleiben in erträumte Landschaften, dann wären auch wir, so wie Geoffrey Jellicoe Schaals Landschaften unnachahmlich beschrieben hat, »zunächst verwirrt, dann entzückt und schließlich – wer weiß! – auf unerklärliche Weise inspiriert«.

Drawings and photo collages, 1970–1976

The paired terms »artificial – natural« are the central theme of my 1970–1975 images, drawings, and photo collages. What interested me in the landscape, the horizon-wide »outside« of our lives, was, in particular, the edges and transitional zones between the constructed city and the areas used for agriculture and forestry. I asked myself: are these the sites of injuries, of wounds that cannot be healed, or is what we observe here rather to be welcomed, as a civilised technological act of progress against a chaotic nature that is hostile to human beings, against the threatening, overwhelming power of nature's primal jungle? Should we regard the open spaces wrested from the forest – the land cleared for use, the planting lines and geometric field structures created by farmers and gardeners, the severely regular plantations of forestry managers, the asphalt and concrete surfaces of road engineers and architects – as pure destruction of landscape and nature, or should we see them as success stories, both in productive economic terms and in aesthetic terms?

In all ages, the wildness of untamed nature has awakened fear, foreboding, curiosity, reverence, and respect – human reactions expressed in every mythology and religion. Ancient stones and trees were (and perhaps still are?) revered like sacred entities; faced with these things, the brief span of human life shrinks into a fleeting, momentary existence. Oceans, deserts, mountains, and frozen landscapes had to be outwitted by brave, inquisitive, and adventurous researchers with a thirst for knowledge. Even in the 18th century, passengers in mail coaches would cover the windows when they passed through forests and through mountain ravines. Not until the Romantic era did artists discover beautiful transitional zones between the ego, the world, and metaphysical zones in wild rock formations and in radically empty oceans.

My works from this phase do not offer concrete answers, instead encapsulating these processes in image form, and sometimes taking the situations they represent into the realms of utopian science-fiction.

Zeichnungen und Photocollagen, 1970–1976

Das zentrale Thema, um das meine Bilder, Zeichnungen und Photocollagen in den Jahren 1970 bis 1975 kreisten, war das Begriffspaar »künstlich – natürlich«. Mich interessierten in der Landschaft, dem horizontweiten »Draußen« unseres Lebens, die Ränder und Übergangszonen zwischen gebauter Stadt und land- und forstwirtschaftlich genutzten Bereichen besonders. Ich fragte mich: Entstehen hier Verletzungen, unheilbare Wunden, oder sind hier mehr erfreuliche zivilisatorisch-technische Fortschritte gegen das menschenfeindliche Natur-Chaos, den drohenden, übermächtigen Natur-Urwald zu beobachten? Sollten wir die erkämpften freien Flächen, die nutzbaren Lichtungen, die Pflanzlinien und geometrischen Feldstrukturen der Landwirte und Gärtner, die strengen Plantagen der Forstwirte, die Asphalt- und Betonflächen der Straßenbau-Ingenieure und Architekten als reine Landschafts- und Naturdestruktionen betrachten oder darin eher Erfolge im produktiv-wirtschaftlichen wie im ästhetischen Sinn erkennen?

Die Wildheit der ungezähmten Natur erweckte zu allen Zeiten Furcht, Angst, Neugier, Achtung und Respekt – menschliche Reaktionen, die sich in allen Mythologien und Religionen niederschlagen. Uralte Steine und Bäume wurden (und werden?) verehrt wie Heilige. Das kurze menschliche Leben verkümmert davor zu einem flüchtigen Augenblicksdasein. Meere, Wüsten, Gebirge und Eislandschaften mußten beim Erforschen von mutigen, neugierigen, wissensdurstigen und abenteuerlustigen Menschen überlistet werden. Postkutschen-Reisende verhängten noch im 18. Jahrhundert bei Durchquerung von Wäldern und Gebirgsschluchten die Fenster. Erst mit der Romantik entdeckten Künstler in wilden Gebirgsformationen und radikal leeren Meeransichten schöne Übergangszonen zwischen Ich, Welt und metaphysischen Zonen.

Meine Arbeiten aus dieser Phase geben keine konkreten Anworten, sie spitzen die Vorgänge bildlich zu und treiben die dargestellten Zustände manchmal ins Utopisch-Science-fictionhafte.

1. Drawing on the subject of »artificial – natural«: The furrows are as exactly ploughed, as if a solar field were being laid out here. 1971.
2. Photo collage featuring a massively large, mirrored skyscraper block: A high-rise apartment block? A solar facility? A cloud power station? 1972.

1. Zeichnung zum Thema »künstlich – natürlich«: Die Ackerfurchen sind so exakt gezogen, als würde hier ein Solarfeld angelegt. 1971.
2. Photocollage mit einem gewaltig großen, verspiegelten Wolkenkratzer-Block: Wohn-Hochhaus? Solar-Anlage? Wolken-Kraftwerk? 1972.

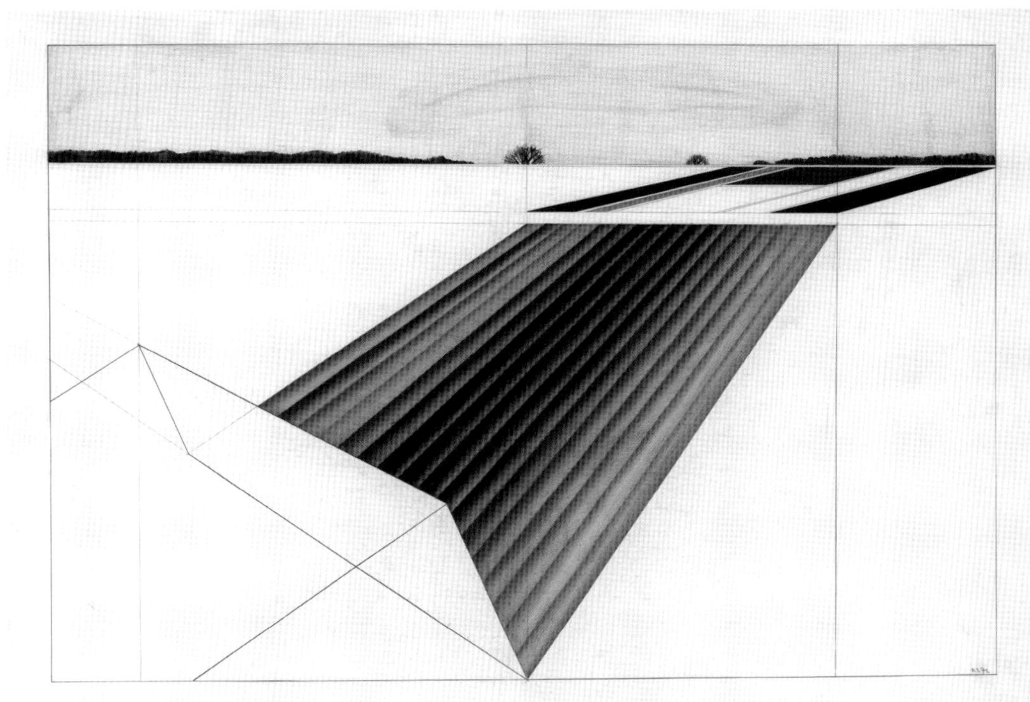

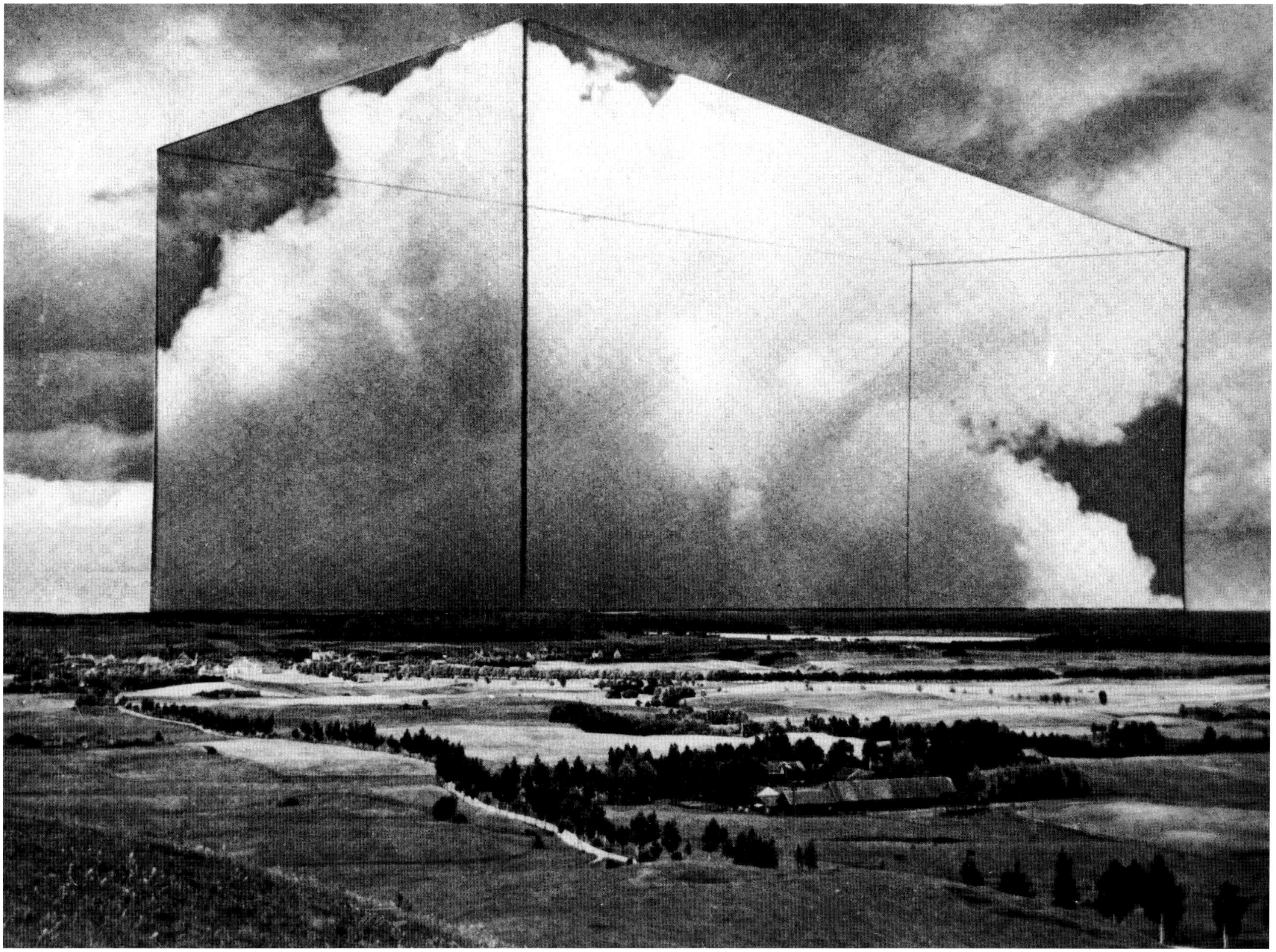

3, 4. I looked for motifs that could be integrated into my future landscape parks and scenic gardens. I was thinking of recreational natural spaces open to the public, with paths and with quiet areas, where I would try to invent new, poetic/surreal narratives by means of art elements and »wrongly positioned everyday fragments«. The historically-formed and all-too-well-known park and landscape pictures are infiltrated by museum showcases, walkways, film sets, stage sets, and fragments of tourist dream landscapes. Here and there, the modern-day goddesses and gods of film appear before visitors, between tree trunks, in clearings, and on rock escarpments, either as media projections or in concrete, marble – or sometimes plastic – form. With or without music. 1974–1976.

3, 4. Ich suchte nach Motiven, die in meine zukünftigen Landschaftsparks und szenischen Gärten integriert werden könnten. Dabei dachte ich an öffentlich zugängliche Natur-Erholungsorte mit Wegen und Ruhezonen, die durch Kunstelemente und »falsch eingesetzte Alltagsfragmente« versuchen, neue, poetisch-surreale Erzählungen zu erfinden. Die historisch gewachsenen und allzu bekannten Park- und Landschaftsbilder werden unterwandert von Museumsvitrinen, Laufstegen, Film-Sets, Bühnenbildern und Fragmenten touristischer Traumlandschaften. Ab und zu tauchen zwischen Baumstämmen in Lichtungen und auf Felsvorsprüngen aktuelle Film-Göttinnen und Film-Götter auf. Entweder sie werden medial projiziert, oder sie stehen konkret aus Marmor – manchmal auch aus Kunststoff – geformt vor den Besuchern. Mit und ohne Musik. 1974–1976.

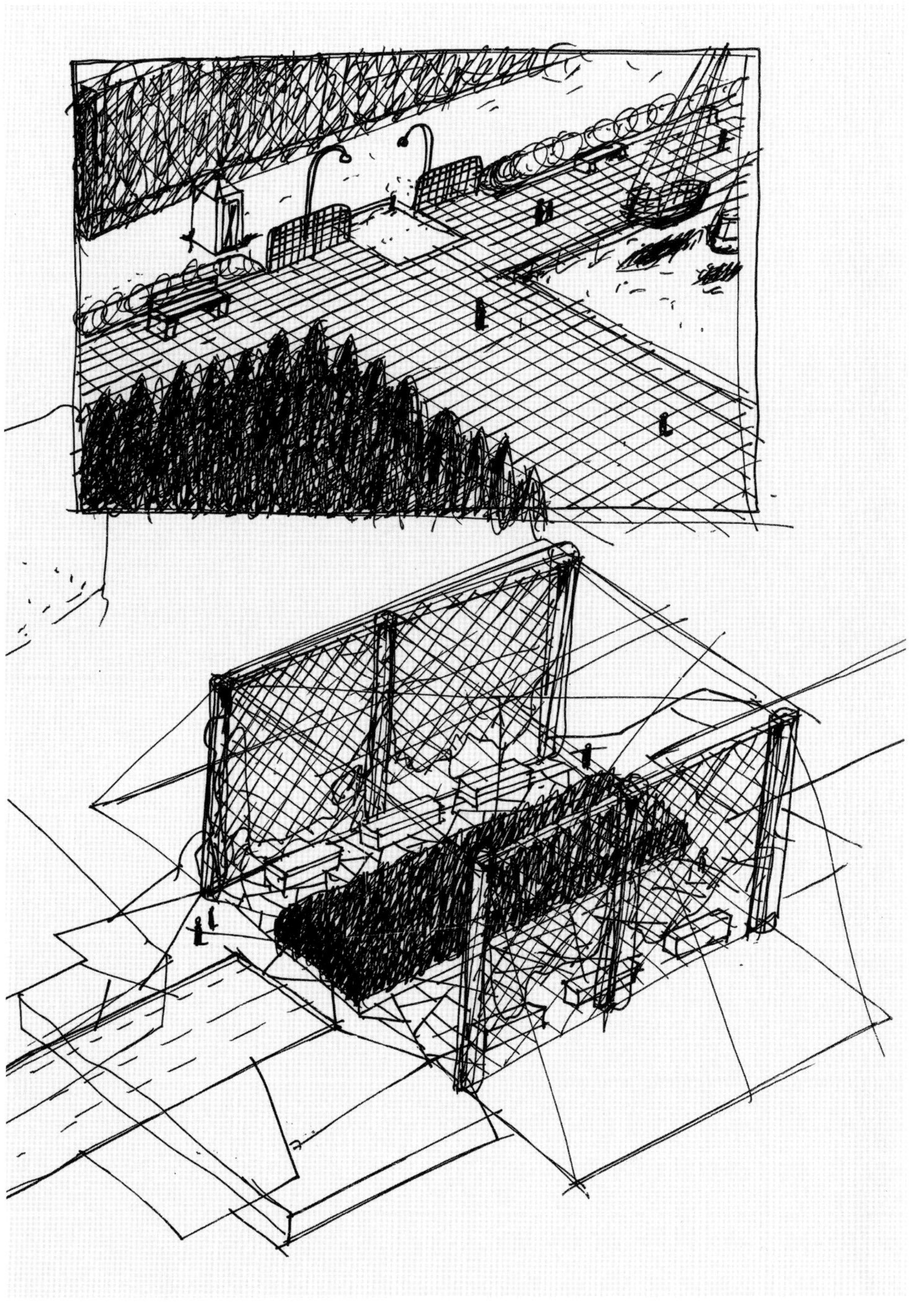

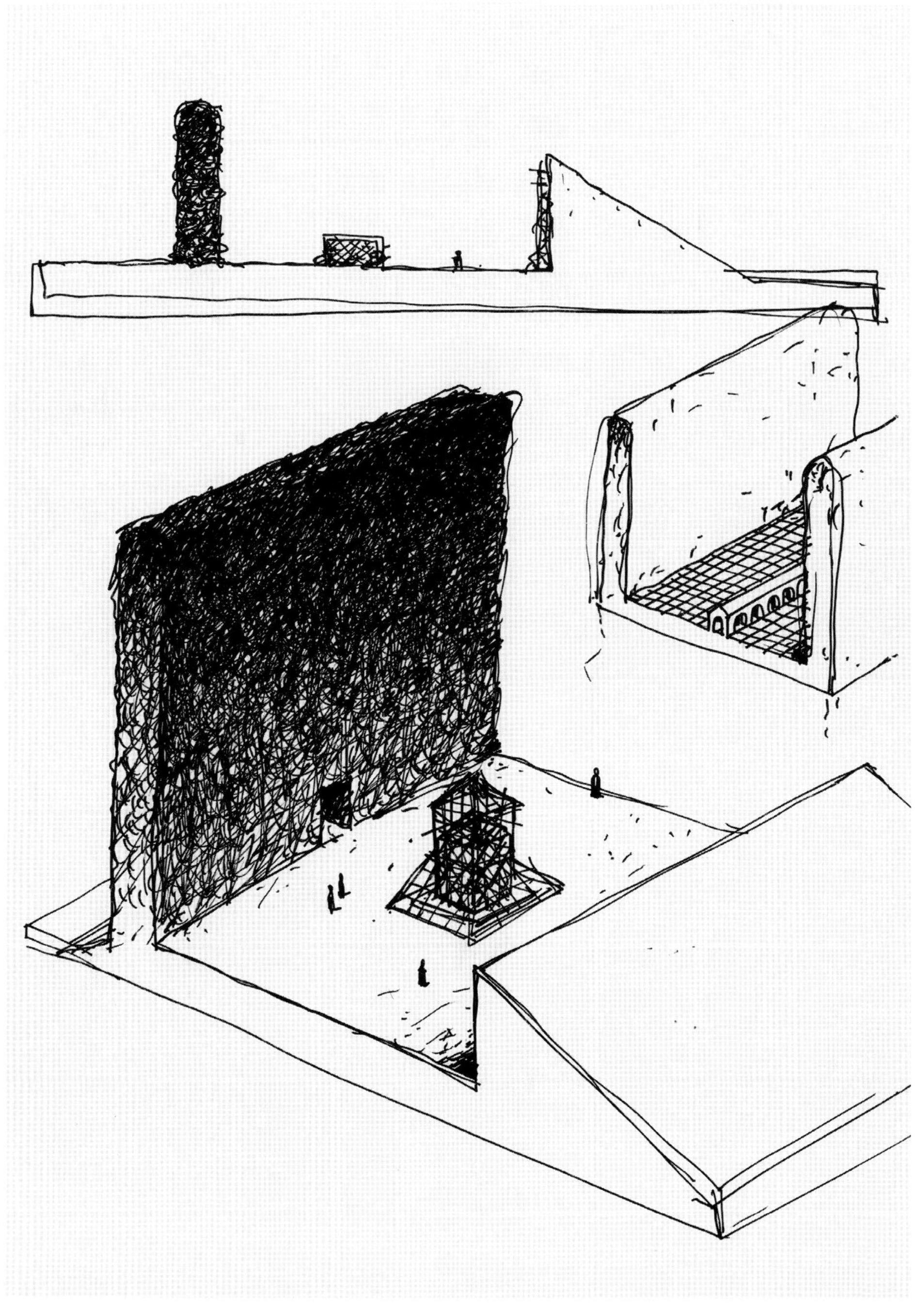

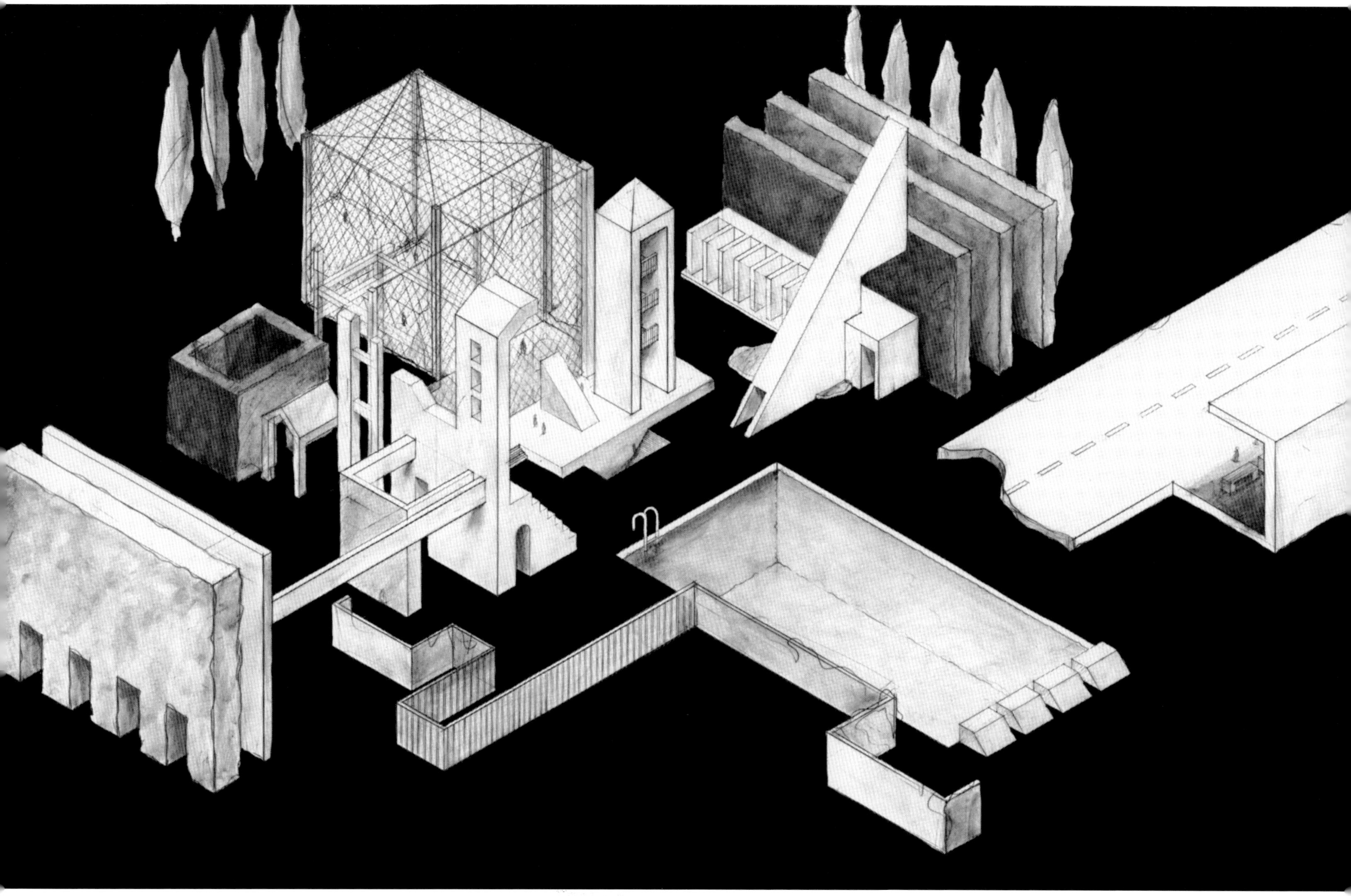

5. A park seen by night. I wanted to use enigmas and artistic/romanticising features (without a commercial aspect) to disrupt any association with pleasure parks and Disney Worlds. I envisioned a perfectly new magical atmosphere, of the type that would otherwise arise only in the reading of poetic/exciting books or when watching films (crime thrillers, melodramas, adventure and horror films, witty satirical films and romantic films with a happy ending). Anyone who visited these art-park gardens and scenic landscapes – alone, in company, or with family – was to be transformed into a dreamer, moving beyond everyday/egoistic rivalries, bellicose civil war situations, and media babble. Close to nature and its silent activities, and also close to literature, to theatre, to opera, to Hollywood, and to one's own inner longings. 1975.

5. Nächtliche Parksituation. Die Nähe zu Vergnügungsparks und Disney-Worlds wollte ich durch Verrätselung und Kunst-Romantisierung (ohne kommerzielle Aspekte) brechen. Mir schwebte eine vollkommen neue Zauberstimmung vor, die sich sonst nur beim Lesen von poetisch-spannenden Büchern oder beim Filmeschauen (Krimis, Melos, Abenteuer- und Horrorfilme, witzig-satirische Filme oder Liebesfilme mit Happy-End) einstellt. Jeder, der diese Kunst-Parkgärten und szenischen Landschaften – allein, zu zweit oder mit Familie – besucht, sollte verwandelt werden in einen Träumer, jenseits alltäglich-egoistischer Rivalitäten, bösartiger Bürgerkriegssituationen und medialem Geplapper. Nahe der Natur, ihrem schweigenden Wirken, nahe auch der Literatur, dem Theater, der Oper, Hollywood und den eigenen, innersten Sehnsüchten. 1975.

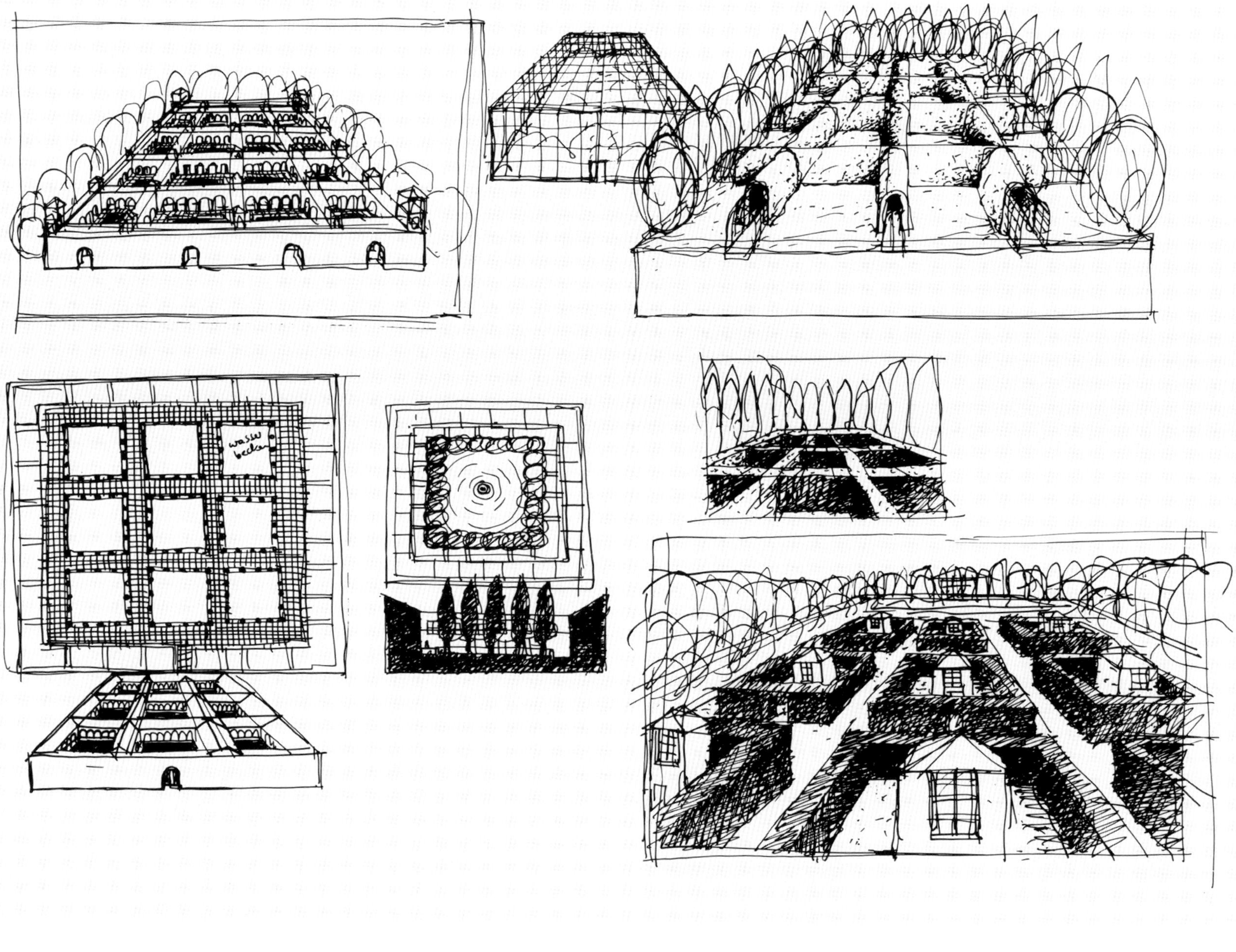
wasser
becken

6. In 1976, I made my first extended visit to Rome (at the Villa Massimo). Roman gardens influenced my thinking in designing landscapes, parks, and gardens. I recognised how lovely it can be to live and work within garden walls and fragrant, geometrically clipped laurel hedges, in the shade of cypresses and pines. In the distance is the tinkling sound of fountains. Among the arbours, shady peace prevails. 1976.

7. After I returned to Germany, I drew and experimented with natural stone, earth and straw houses. All of these were surrounded by a climate-controlled residential glass house. This was my effort to master three-dimensionality, and possibly also the realities of the home. Examples of the straw houses were exhibited as art objects in Ulm (studio f, 1979) and Berlin (Galerie Aedes, 1980). I was never able to realise actual homes of this type.

6. 1976 hielt ich mich zum ersten Mal länger in Rom (Villa Massimo) auf. Römische Gärten beeinflußten mein entwerfendes Landschafts-, Park- und Garten-Denken. Ich erkannte, wie schön es sein kann, innerhalb von Gartenmauern und duftenden, geometrisch beschnittenen Lorbeerhecken, im Schatten von Zypressen und Pinien zu wohnen und zu arbeiten. In der Ferne plätscherten Brunnen. Unter Arkadengängen herrschte schattige Ruhe. 1976.

7. Zurückgekehrt nach Deutschland, zeichnete und experimentierte ich mit Naturstein-, Erd- und Strohhäusern. Sie alle umschlossen ein klimatisiertes Wohn-Glashaus. Damit versuchte ich für mich, die Dreidimensionalität, möglichst auch die Wohnrealität zu erobern. Exemplare der Strohhäuser waren als Kunstobjekte in Ulm (studio f, 1979) und Berlin (Galerie Aedes, 1980) ausgestellt. Tatsächliche Wohnhäuser in dieser Art konnte ich nie realisieren.

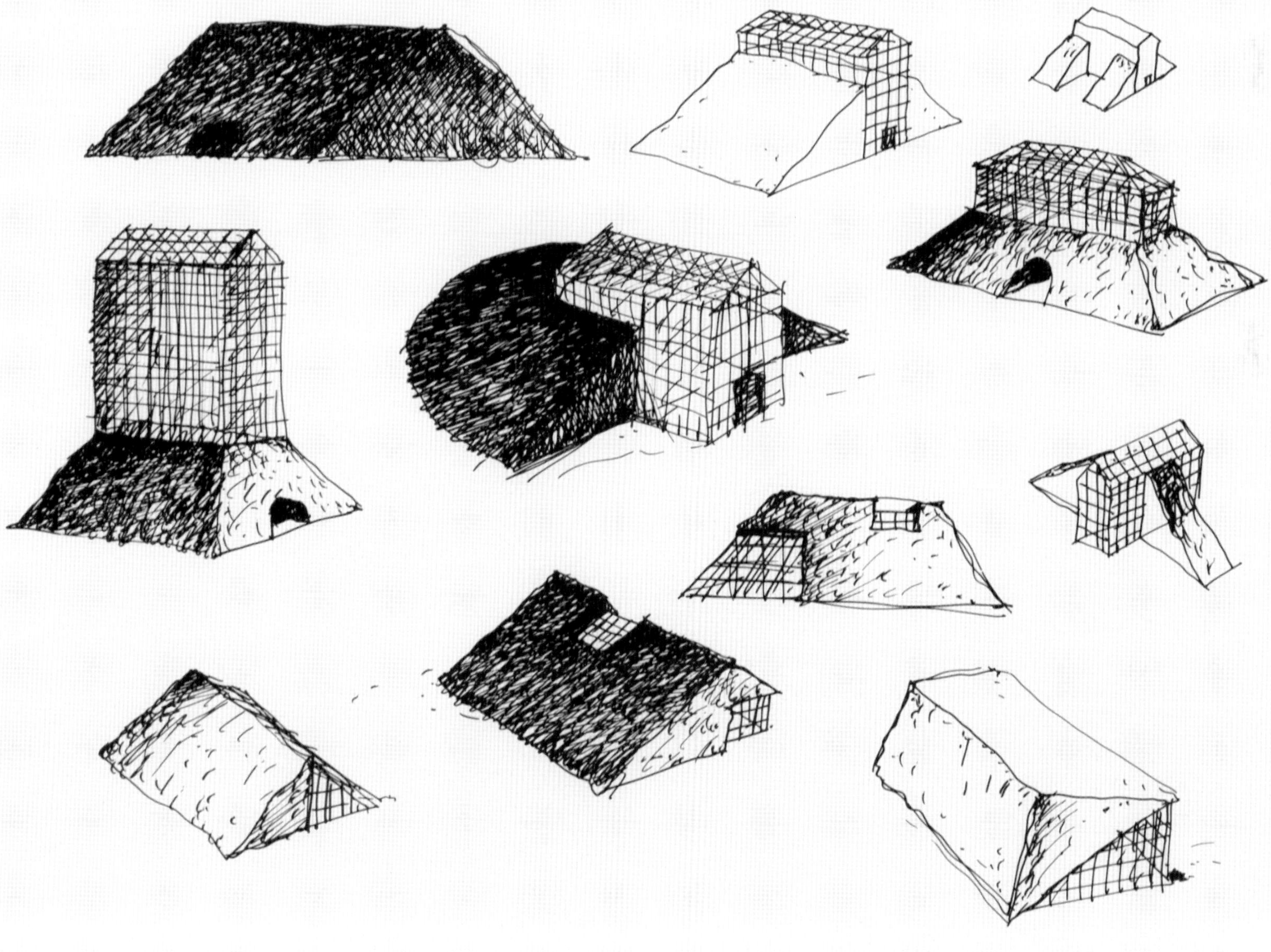

»Ulm neu«, 1975/1976

Garden and park designs played only a secondary role in the design project »Ulm neu« (new Ulm), which I developed jointly with the designer Frank Hess (with no commission).

The central axis of our plans for the environs of Ulm's Münster, which began at the plaza in front of the highest church spire in the world and ends at the choir of the Gothic church, was accompanied by artificial rocks, meadow fragments, a dawn redwood tree, and a mirrored cavern tunnel. The axis reached its provocative culmination in the mediaeval choir area.

In our design, we proposed filling the whole choir area with sand, so that the heads of the famous Syrlin choir stalls (in contrast to the main altar, these survived the iconoclasm of the Reformation) would still be visible. We wished to present the very pragmatic secularisation of the notion of paradise today: for most educated persons of today, the pinnacle of happiness in life is to spend their annual holiday – and perhaps their retirement – on a picturesque South Sea beach, alone, with a partner, or with their family, with lots of sun and shady palms, with pleasant music, good food, and cool drinks. To misquote Heinrich Heine, they prefer to leave heaven to the sparrows, seagulls, clouds, astronauts, and stars.

»Ulm neu«, 1975/1976

Bei dem Entwurfsprojekt »Ulm neu«, das ich zusammen mit dem Designer Frank Hess ohne Auftrag entwickelte, spielten Garten- und Parkentwürfe nur eine Nebenrolle. Die zentrale Achse unseres Münsterumfeldplanes, die auf dem Platz vor dem höchsten Kirchturm der Welt begann und im Chor der gotischen Kirche endete, wurde begleitet von künstlichen Felsen, Wiesenfragmenten, einer Wassertanne und einem verspiegelten Höhlen-Tunnel. Den provozierenden Höhepunkt erreichte die Achse im mittelalterlichen Chorbereich.

Hier schlugen wir in unserem Entwurf vor, den gesamten Chorbereich mit Sand zu füllen und zwar so hoch, daß die Köpfe des berühmten Syrlin-Chorgestühls (sie hatten – im Gegensatz zum Hauptaltar – den Bildersturm der Reformation überlebt) noch zu sehen waren. Damit wollten wir die heutige, sehr pragmatische Verweltlichung der Paradiesvorstellung inszenieren: Der Gipfel des Lebensglücks besteht für die meisten aufgeklärten Menschen heute darin, ihren Jahresurlaub – vielleicht auch ihr Rentnerleben – allein, zu zweit oder mit Familie an einem malerischen Südseestrand mit viel Sonne und Palmenschatten, mit angenehmer Musik, gutem Essen und kühlen Drinks zu verbringen. Den Himmel überlassen sie, frei nach Heinrich Heine, lieber den Spatzen, Möwen, Wolken, Flugzeugen, Astronauten und Sternen.

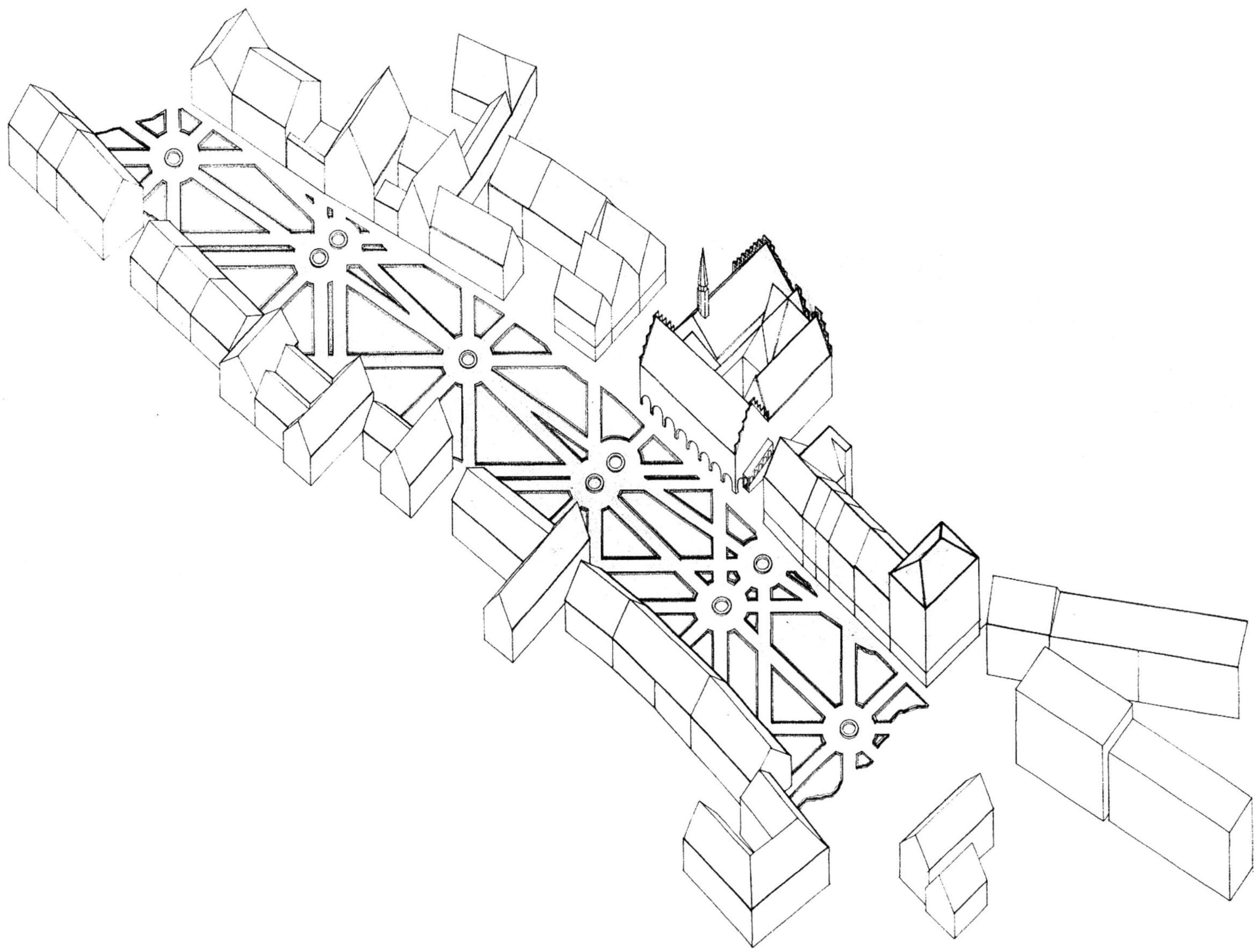

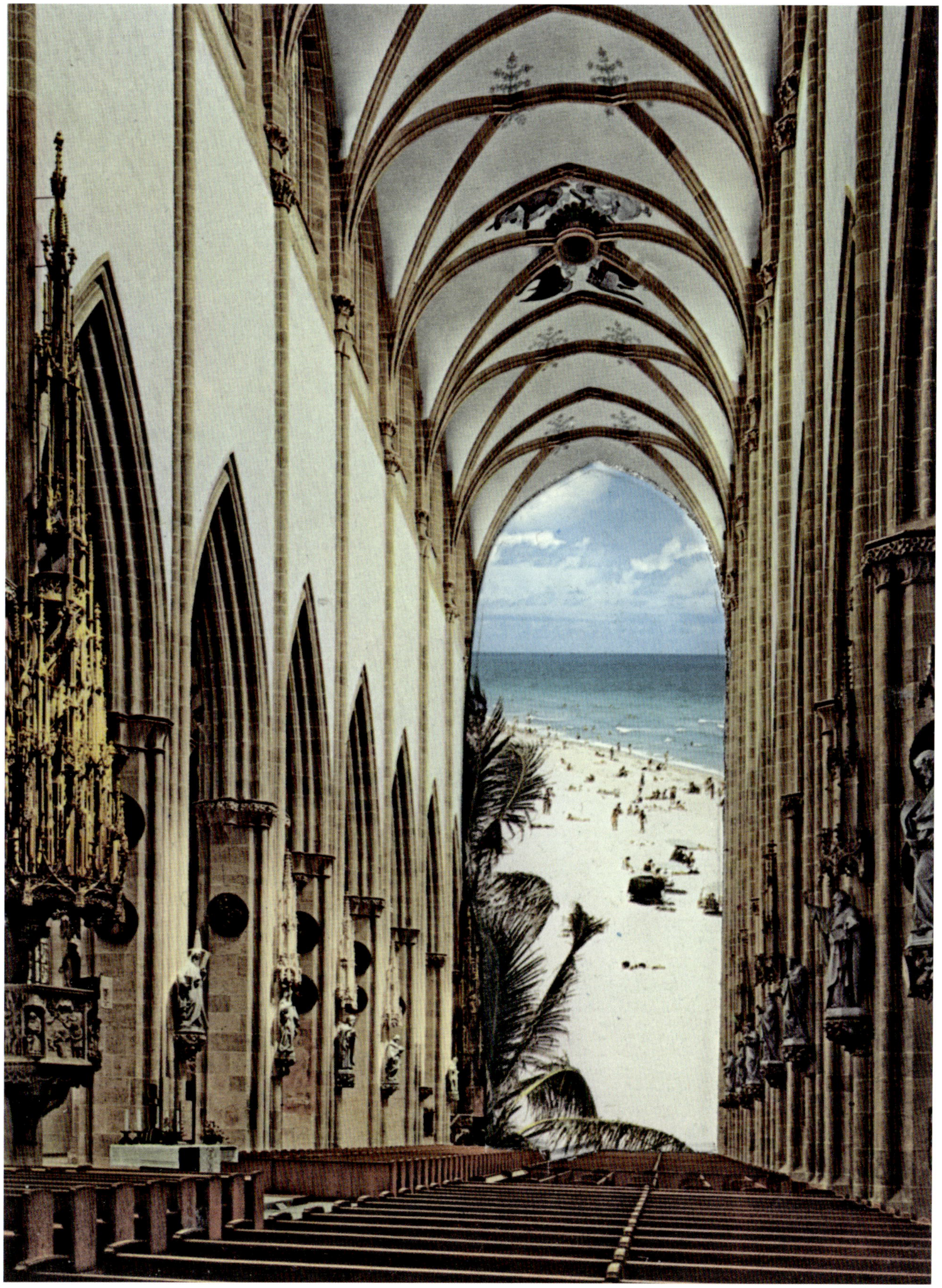

1. On the open space of the then undeveloped Neue Straße, which, as a traffic lane, disrupted the inner city pedestrian paradise), we proposed a number of provocative landscape installations, whose alien materials make them clearly recognisable as artistically staged landscape zones. These are artistic stage sets that can be entered and used freely, without commercial pressures.
2. South Sea paradise in Ulm's Münster choir. Postcard collage.

1. Auf der Freifläche der damals noch unbebauten Neuen Straße, die als Verkehrsschneise das Fußgänger-Paradies Innenstadt störte, schlugen wir einige provokante Landschaftseinbauten vor, die durch ihre verfremdende Materialität eindeutig als künstlich inszenierte Landschaftszonen zu erkennen waren. Frei begeh- und benutzbare Kunst-Bühnenbilder mit Naturaspekten, ohne Kommerzwang.
2. Südseeparadies im Ulmer Münsterchor. Postkartencollage.

Bundesgartenschau 1985, Berlin (Britz, Bukow, Mariendorf), 1977, competition contribution, special first prize, developed jointly with Peter Klingemann, Rolf-Reiner Maria Borchard, Goetz Lehder, and Uwe Nagel

This was the first competition in which I took part. I wanted to use it to transfer as many as possible of the landscape, park, and garden ideas I had so far developed into reality.

At the time, West Berlin was still an enclosed city whose inhabitants dreamed of a blossoming, joyously beautiful garden show to banish their thoughts of being in a prison. It is therefore only too easy to understand that the jury members found themselves faced with a dilemma: they wanted to initiate and create something very special for their at one time free, metropolitan, tolerant, and sometimes even avant-garde city. However, at the same time, they also had to think of Berlin's numerous allotment gardens. For this reason, they were able to award us only a special price (equivalent to the first prize), whilst recommending the implementation of nice normal garden show designs.

We had, in fact, proposed a very utopian/provocative concept. The theme »artificial – natural« played a major role. There were artificial fields and rocks, flowers and carols, but also water areas designed in naturalistic way, with Romantic, reed-covered banks, and wild nature meadows and forests. In the centre, we planned a giant, round glass house, with a tropical forest with waterfalls, lakes, and beachfront cafes to delight visitors (including allotment gardeners).

When they got to hear about our design, many Berlin citizens were outraged, as were most of the journalists. After an initial glimmer of hope, a campaign of persecution by the *Bild* newspaper, with angry letters from the allotment gardeners of the Britzer-Garten (as the park is known today) finally put paid to our design, which they derided as a »Horror-Park«.

The concept by the »normal first prize winner« was not realised. Instead, a mixture of the second and fifth prize designs was used. The result is still worth seeing today; well tended, hedged, and fenced, it unfolds a harmonious landscape magic with no thorny presentations, poetic surrealisms or critical undertones!

Astonishingly, our design, having been published and discussed worldwide, even reached Hollywood eventually. In October 1992, in Attenweiler, I received a Fedex letter from Universal Studios. This letter read:

»This is to request your consent to allow us to use the drawing of the ›Recreation park at the Massiner Weg, Berlin‹ for Steven Spielberg's new film *Jurassic Park* …«

Steven Spielberg (or rather his set designers) wanted to use the design for his new film. The floor plan was to appear in the background during a discussion. I gave my consent, but it did not appear in the final version of the film. Not until *Jurassic Park II* did a model appear with formal – but only very, very distant – similarities.

Bundesgartenschau 1985, Berlin (Britz, Bukow, Mariendorf), 1977, Wettbewerbsbeitrag, erster Sonderpreis, gemeinsam erarbeitet mit Peter Klingemann, Rolf-Reiner Maria Borchard, Goetz Lehder und Uwe Nagel

Es war der erste Wettbewerb, an dem ich teilnahm. Damit wollte ich möglichst viele meiner bisher entwickelten Landschafts-, Park- und Garten-Ideen in die Realtät übertragen.

West-Berlin war damals noch eine eingeschlossene Stadt, deren Bewohner von einer erfreulich-schönen, blühenden Gartenschau träumten, die ihre Gefängnisgedanken vertreiben sollte. Es ist deswegen nur zu gut verständlich, daß sich alle Jury-Mitglieder in einem Zwiespalt befanden: Sie wollten etwas ganz Besonderes für ihre einst freie, weltoffene, tolerante und manchmal sogar avantgardistische Stadt anstoßen und schaffen, gleichzeitig mußten sie jedoch auch an die zahlreichen ortsansässigen Schrebergärtner denken. Aus diesem Grund konnten sie uns nur einen Sonderpreis (dem ersten Preis gleichrangig) zusprechen und für die Realisierung brav-normale Gartenschau-Entwürfe empfehlen.

Wir hatten tatsächlich ein sehr utopisch-provozierendes Konzept vorgeschlagen. Das Thema »künstlich – natürlich« spielte eine große Rolle. Es gab künstliche Felder und Felsen, Blumen und Kühe, aber auch naturhaft gestaltete Wasserzonen mit romantischen, schilfbewachsenen Ufern, dazu wilde, naturbelassene Wiesen und Wälder. Im Zentrum planten wir ein riesiges, rundes Glashaus, in dem ein Tropenwald mit Wasserfällen, Seen und Strand-Cafés die Besucher (auch die Schrebergärtner) begeistern sollten.

Mit dem Bekanntwerden unseres Entwurfs waren nicht nur viele Berliner Bürger empört, sondern auch die meisten Journalisten. Nach anfänglichem Hoffnungsschimmer machte eine Hetzkampagne der *Bild*-Zeitung mit bösen Zuschriften der am Britzer-Garten (so der heutige Name des Parks) ansässigen Schrebergärtner unserem Entwurf, diffamiert als »Horror-Park«, endgültig den Garaus.

Realisiert wurde nicht das Konzept des »normalen ersten Preisträgers«, sondern eine Mischung aus zweitem und fünftem Preis. Das Ergebnis ist auch heute noch sehenswert und entfaltet, wohl gepflegt, gehegt und umzäunt, einen harmonischen Landschaftszauber ohne Inszenierungswiderhaken, poetische Surrealismen und kritische Untertöne!

Erstaunlich, daß unser weltweit veröffentlichter und diskutierter Entwurf sogar irgendwann Hollywood erreichte. Im Oktober 1992 kam bei mir in Attenweiler ein Fedex-Brief der Universal Studios an. Darin war zu lesen:

»This is to request your consent to allow us to use the drawing of the ›Recreation park at the Massiner Weg, Berlin‹ for Steven Spielbergs new film *Jurassic Park* …«

Steven Spielberg (besser: sein Set-Designer) wollte den Entwurf für seinen neuen Film verwenden. Der Grundrißplan sollte während einer Diskussion im Hintergrund erscheinen. Obwohl ich meine Zustimmung gab, war davon nichts in der Film-Endfassung zu sehen. Erst im *Jurassic Park II* tauchten in einem Modell formale Ähnlichkeiten auf. Aber nur sehr, sehr entfernte.

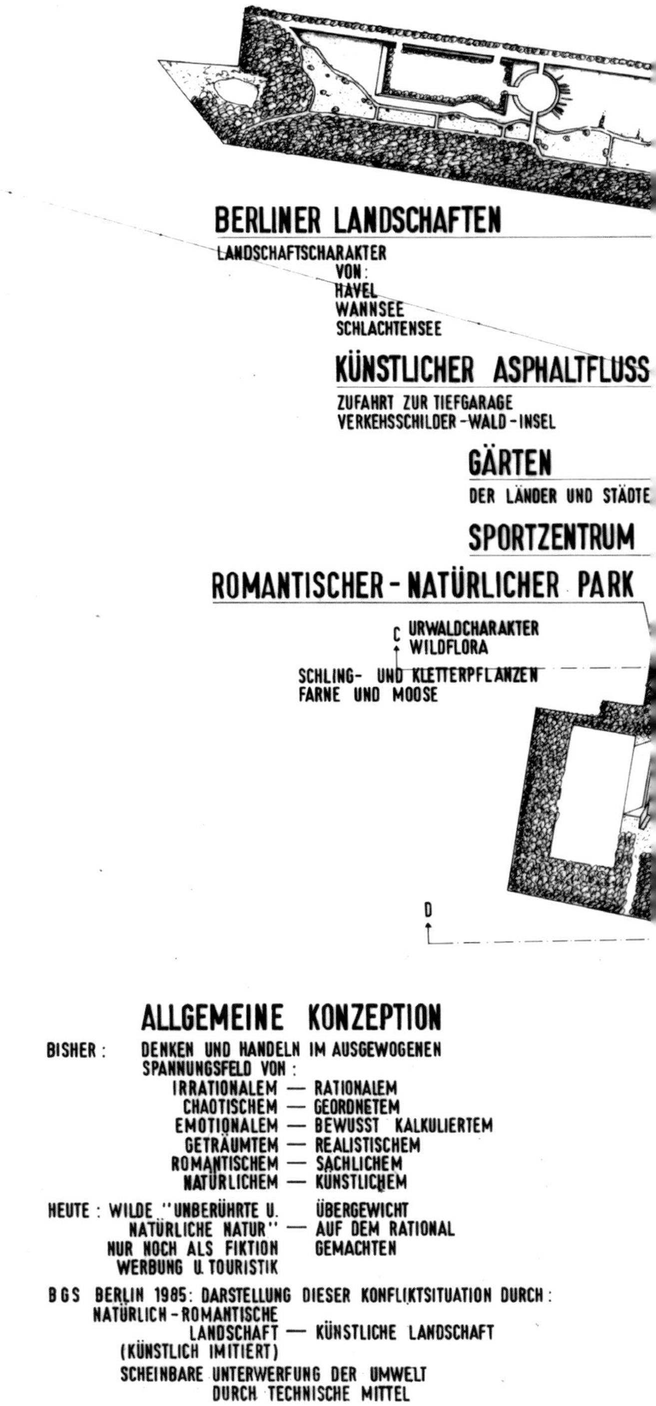

1. Overall plan of the Massiner Weg recreational park. 1. Gesamtplan des Erholungsparks Massiner Weg.

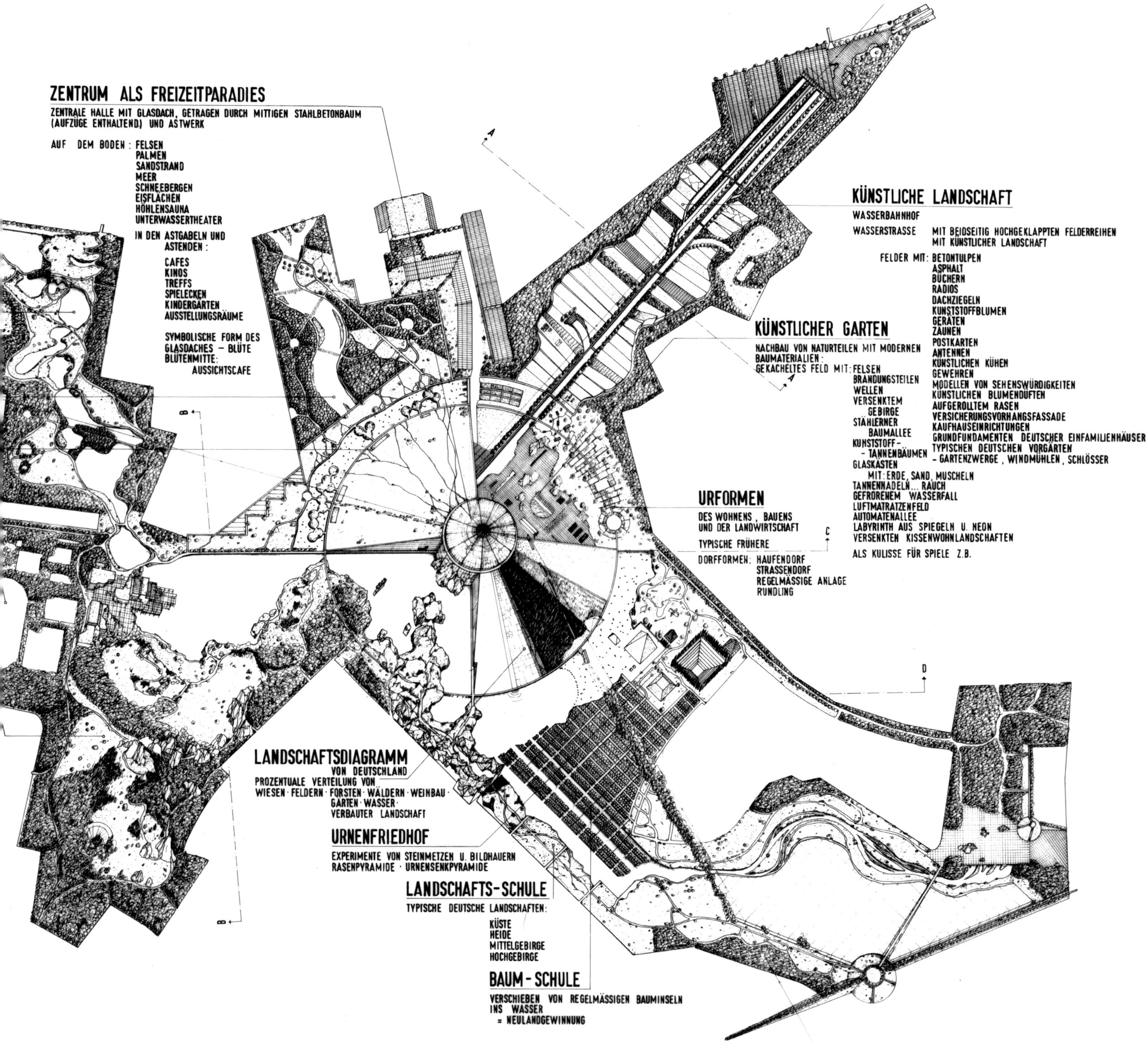

2, 3. Model photo und Isometric view of the recreational park Massiner Weg.

2, 3. Modellphoto und Isometrie des Erholungsparks Massiner Weg.

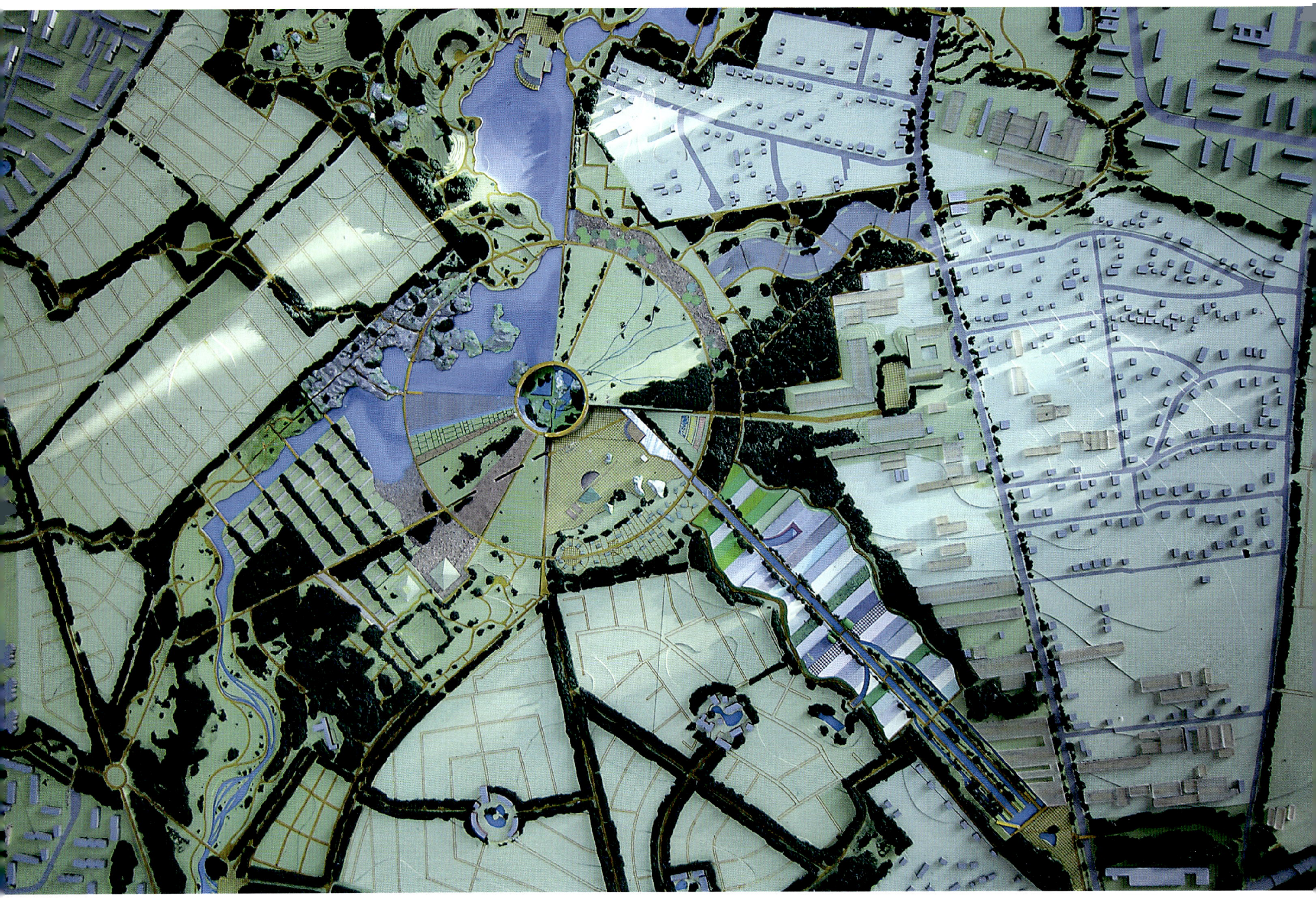

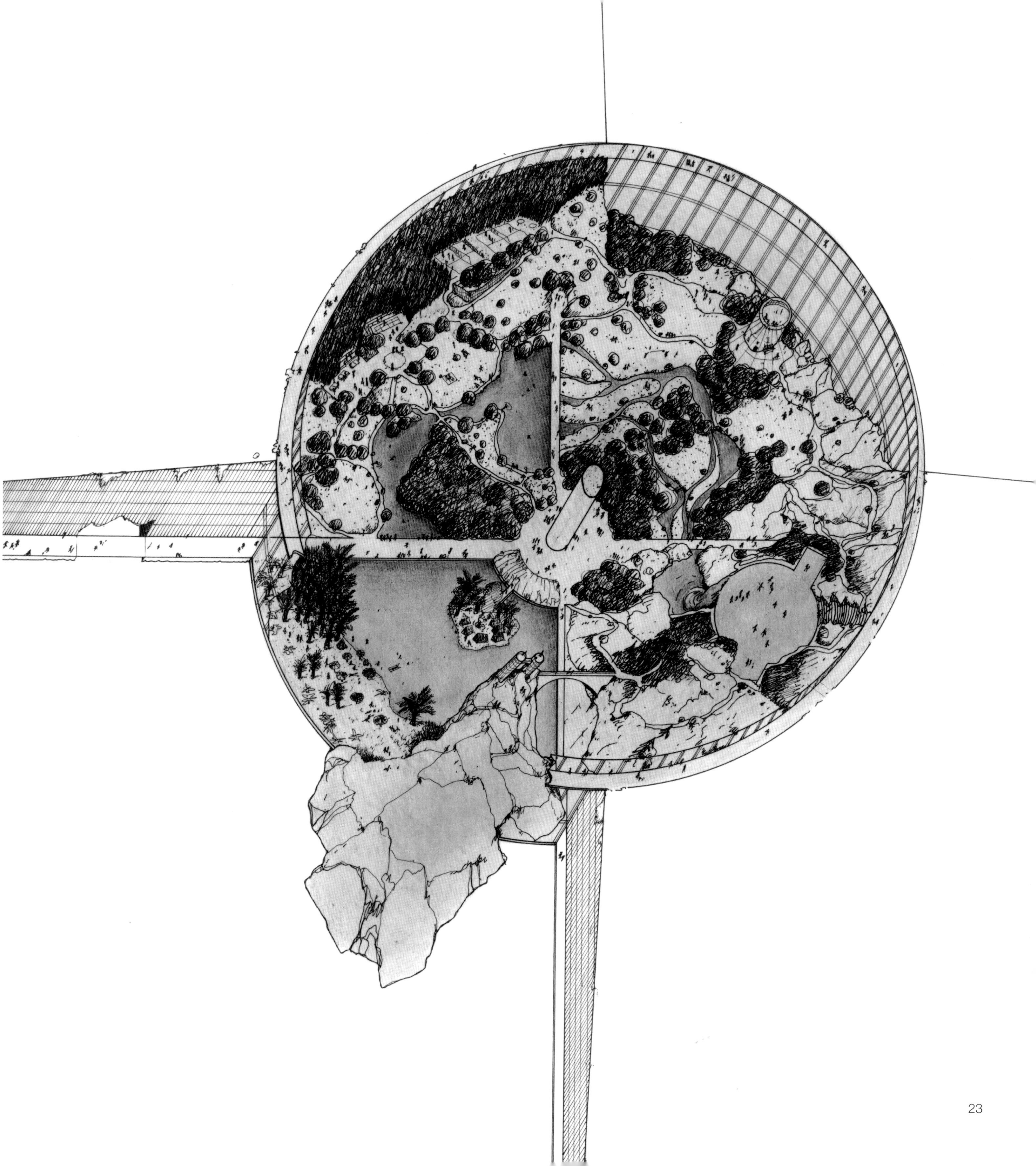

Wege und Wegräume (paths and passages), 1978

With this book, I returned once again to the realm of pure drawing, investigating my previous landscape and garden ideas from a new angle. Instead of beginning with a tendency to remain static or circle within the here and now in a garden or park, I began with the state of being under way in the real or invented landscape. The path spaces that emerged and then disappeared again had garden-like tendencies, but continued to be transitional zones with subjectively viewed and experienced image elements taken from the reality of cities, houses, and landscapes. The central focus was always provided by the I, with its stream of consciousness, its memory associations, and its fantasy islands.

I understood space, time, and consciousness as something unified, living, flowing, constantly changing, and thus flickering and spooling past in a filmic fashion. At the time, I wrote in the foreword that:

»I pass through cities and landscapes, through conversations and books. Everything that plays out in time and in space, I understand as a path. I represent time-space as real space. The path is thus made into the central medium for experiencing the world, and thus a synonym for life.

The visible landscape and the intellectual landscape are shot through with paths and roads: road atlases and books. Every path is a pre-prepared passage; a guidance system within which one generally moves unnoticed. Only a narrow strip of consciousness moves with you …

Passing freely through trackless territory is dangerous, and thus rare. One must determine one's own direction, and one may change it at any moment. However, one is always in danger of going astray …«

The book was initially self-published. It achieved widespread national and later international attention owing to a strongly positive article by Manfred Sack in *Zeit*. A second edition was brought out by Moos-Verlag in Munich. In the 1980s, the Berlin publishing house Ernst & Sohn took over publication, getting the text translated into English and releasing 3rd, 4th, and 5th editions for the global market.

Wege und Wegräume, 1978

Mit diesem Buch kehrte ich noch einmal zurück in den Bereich der reinen Zeichnung und untersuchte meine bisherigen Landschafts- und Gartenideen unter einem neuen Aspekt. Ich ging jetzt nicht mehr von der Tendenz eines statischen Bleibens oder Kreisens im Hier und Jetzt eines Gartens oder Parks aus, sondern von einem Unterwegssein in der realen oder erfundenen Landschaft. Die auf- und abtauchenden Wegräume hatten zwar Gartentendenzen, blieben jedoch Durchgangszonen mit subjektiv gesehenen und erlebten Bildelementen aus der Realität von Städten, Häusern und Landschaften. Im Zentrum stand immer das Ich mit seinem Bewußtseinsstrom, seinen Erinnerungsassoziationen und Phantasieinseln. Eine Art neue Bild-Philosophie entstand.

Raum, Zeit und Bewußtsein faßte ich als etwas Einheitliches, Lebendiges, Fließendes, Sich-ständig-Veränderndes und damit auch filmhaft Vorbeiziehendes auf. Im Vorwort schrieb ich damals:

»Ich gehe durch Städte und Landschaften, durch Gespräche und Bücher. Alles, was sich in der Zeit und im Raum abspielt, fasse ich als Weg auf. Den Zeitraum stelle ich als realen Raum dar. Der Weg wird so zum zentralen Medium der Welterfahrung und damit zum Synonym von Leben.

Die sichtbare Landschaft und die geistige Landschaft sind überzogen mit Wegen und Straßen: Straßenkarten und Bücher. Jeder Weg ist vorgefertigtes Gehen; ein Leitsystem, in das man sich meist unbemerkt begibt. Nur ein schmaler Bewußtseinsstreifen läuft mit …

Das freie Gehen durch wegloses Gelände ist gefährlich und daher selten. Man muß die Richtung selbst bestimmen und kann sie in jedem Augenblick ändern, allerdings läuft man immer Gefahr, sich zu verirren …«

Das Buch erschien zunächst im Eigenverlag und erreichte durch einen sehr positiven Artikel von Manfred Sack in der *Zeit* große nationale, später auch internationale Aufmerksamkeit. Eine zweite Auflage brachte der Moos-Verlag in München heraus. In den 1980er Jahren übernahm der Berliner Verlag Ernst & Sohn die Veröffentlichung, ließ die Texte ins Englische übersetzen und zielte mit dritten, vierten und fünften Auflagen auf den Weltmarkt.

1. Picture caption in the book: »Path system as reference system, with things and wishes. One imagines the daily paths of the individual cartographed, and then overlays them with the paths of the inhabitants of a house, a street, a whole city. As a map: a map of all paths ever travelled by human beings.«

1. Bildunterschrift im Buch: »Wegsystem als Bezugssystem mit Dingen und Wünschen. Man stelle sich die täglichen Wege der Einzelnen kartographiert vor und überlagere sie dann mit den Wegen der Bewohner eines Hauses, einer Straße, einer ganzen Stadt. Als Karte: alle Wege, die jemals von Menschen zurückgelegt worden sind.«.

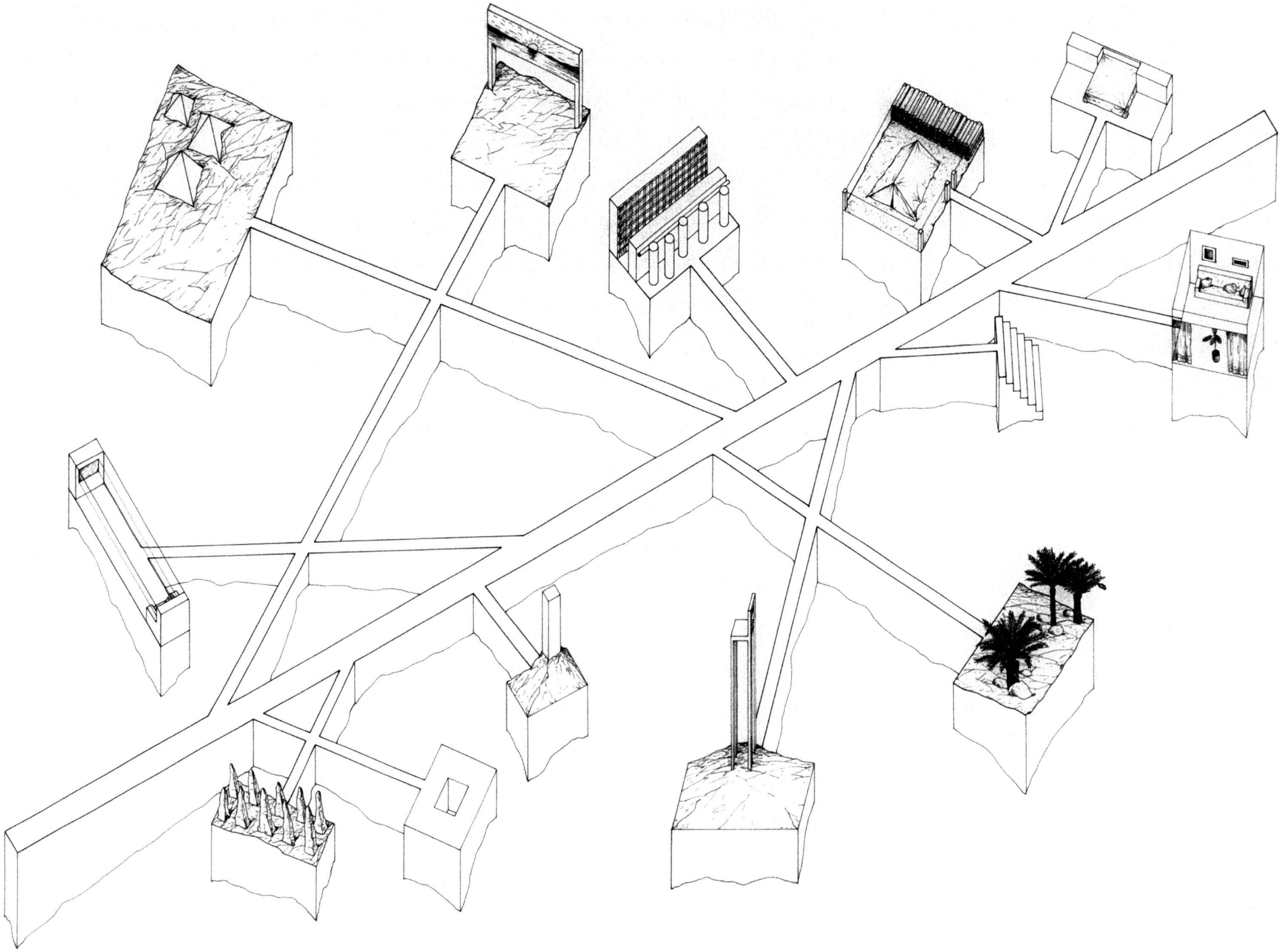

»Laubenhaus« (arbor house) on the Stuttgart University grounds in Stuttgart-Vaihingen, 1979

In this project, a Kunst-am-Bau (art for buildings) competition success, I implemented my first »house« in a green context, with a small front garden and tree plantings.

I proposed a wooden simple gable house, with a split south façade and with visitors and passers-by able to walk into this opening day and night. Aside from its nonfunctionality in living terms, the house's unconventional nature was owing to the fact that the roof zone was also constructed from a framework with a timber grid structure. This meant that the inside of the house offered no real protection from rain, snow, and other adverse weather conditions, and thus had only a symbolic character.

Perhaps this was a mere sketch of a dream house, of the kind that one dreams of as a student? A house advertisement? An advert for a building society? An advert for home insurance? A house in itself? An ideal house? Or a house that should never have been built in this way? So, is it a cautionary example? A piece of artistic bad planning on the university campus, and thus in the public space?

In the left half of the house (with slight ironic exaggeration) a kind of living room has been set up, with a wooden sofa, four wooden armchairs, and a coffee table (complete with table lamp). A distant reminder of allotment garden houses and airy living in a green setting. In the right half of the house there are four high seats, thus making the house into an absurd surreal construction that does not open itself up to the »normal people and students«, who believe only in absolutely necessary, scientifically founded functional sequences and buildings. A lonely midday sleep, up high and cosy? Associations with hunters on the university campus? A standard act of provocation by modern art?

The idea was that, over the years, wild vines and ivy would transform the whole wooden construction into a natural structure, and thus – perhaps – transform sober matter-of-fact students into lesser – or greater – nature Romantics. However, some kind of malign influence appeared to hover over this installation. The front garden, with its low fence, its flowers, its berry bushes, a lilac bush, its bench for sitting on, its army of garden gnomes, and its model-sized imitation of the Romantic fairytale castle of Lichtenstein on the Swabian Alps was destroyed on the very first night by persons unknown. The second version, with a new Lichtenstein model, met with a similar fate.

In the years that followed, this unsecured installation was subjected to numerous further attacks involving vandalism and spray paint. No-one was sure whether it was a case of an alcohol-fuelled student prank, senseless destructive attacks, or even political acts (from which side?). No witnesses came forward, and there was no CCTV footage, and thus no proof. At some point, the university building authority lost interest in renovation (it was also too expensive!), and, in the year 2000, finally decided to have the unloved, half-overgrown and half-destroyed object demolished and removed.

»Laubenhaus« auf dem Universitätsgelände in Stuttgart-Vaihingen, 1979

Mit diesem Projekt, ein Kunst-am-Bau-Wettbewerbserfolg, realisierte ich mein erstes »Haus« im Grünen, mit kleinem Vorgarten und Baumpflanzungen.

Ich hatte ein hölzernes Giebeleinfachhaus vorgeschlagen, dessen Südfassade aufgespalten war. Durch diese Öffnung konnten Besucher und Passanten das Haus Tag und Nacht betreten. Die Ungewöhnlichkeit des Hauses bestand – neben der Funktionslosigkeit in Sachen Wohnen – darin, daß auch die Dachzone aus Fachwerk mit Holzgitterstruktur gebaut war. Deswegen bot das Hausinnere keinen wirklichen Schutz vor Regen, Schnee und anderen Wetterangriffen und hatte damit nur einen symbolischen Charakter.

Vielleicht ein angedeutetes Traumhaus, wovon man als Student oder Studentin träumt? Eine Hausreklame? Eine Bausparkassenreklame? Eine Hausversicherungsreklame? Ein Haus an sich? Ein Ideal-Haus? Oder ein Haus, das man so nie bauen sollte? Demnach ein abschreckendes Beispiel? Eine surreale Kunst-Fehlplanung auf dem Universitätsgelände und damit im öffentlichen Raum?

In der linken Haushälfte hatte ich, leicht ironisch überhöht, eine Art Wohnzimmer eingerichtet, mit Holzsofa, vier Holzsesseln und einem Couchtisch, einschließlich Tischlampe. Ferne Erinnerung an Schrebergartenhäuser und luftiges Wohnen im Grünen. In der rechten Haushälfte standen vier Hochsitze und machten das Haus damit zu einer absurd-surrealen Konstruktion, die sich dem normalen Menschen und Studenten, der nur an absolut notwendige, wissenschaftlich begründbare Funktionsabläufe und -bauten glaubt, nicht erschloß. Einsamer Mittagsschlaf in lauschigen Höhen? Jägerassoziationen auf dem Universitätsgelände? Eine der üblichen Moderne-Kunst-Irritationen?

Wilder Wein und Efeu sollte die gesamte Holz-Konstruktion im Laufe der Jahre zu einem Naturgebilde umformen und damit – vielleicht – aus sachlich-nüchternen Studenten kleine oder große Naturromantiker machen. Aber es schwebte ein gewisses Unheil über der Anlage. Denn bereits der Vorgarten mit niedrigem Zaun, Blumen, Beerenstauden, einem Fliederbusch, Sitzbank, einer Gartenzwergarmee und einer modellgroßen Nachbildung des romantischen Märchenschlosses Lichtenstein auf der Schwäbischen Alb aus farbigem Beton wurde in der ersten Nacht von unbekannten Tätern zerstört. Auch einer zweiten Fassung mit neuem Lichtenstein-Modell erging es nicht viel besser.

In den Jahren danach war die ungesicherte Anlage zahlreichen weiteren Attacken von Sprayern und Vandalen ausgeliefert. Niemand wußte, ob es sich dabei um alkoholisierten Studentenulk, sinnlose Zerstörungsangriffe oder gar um politische Anschläge (von welcher Seite?) handelte. Es gab keine Zeugen, die sich meldeten oder gar Video-Überwachungsaufzeichnungen und damit keine Beweise. Das Universitätsbauamt verlor irgendwann die Lust am Renovieren (war ja auch zu teuer!) und entschloß sich im Jahr 2000 dazu, das ungeliebte, halb eingewachsene und halb zerstörte Objekt endgültig abreißen und entsorgen zu lassen.

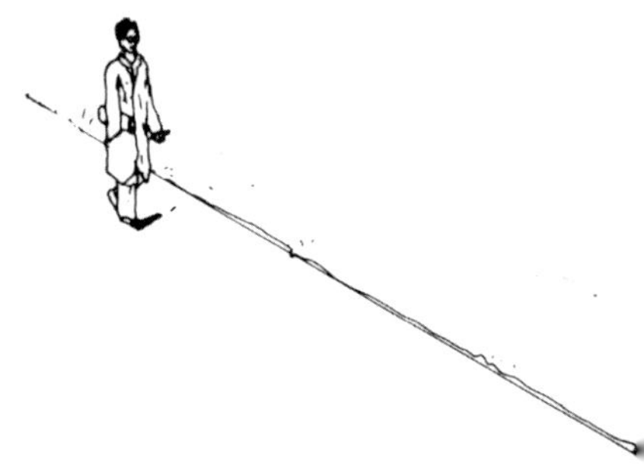

1. A perspective drawing of the »Laubenhaus« (arbor house) with its entrance cleft. In the front garden is the model of the fairytale castle of Lichtenstein and a garden-gnome army.

1. Perspektivische Zeichnung des »Laubenhauses« mit Eingangsspalt. Im Vorgarten das Modell des Märchenschlosses Lichtenstein und eine Gartenzwergarmee.

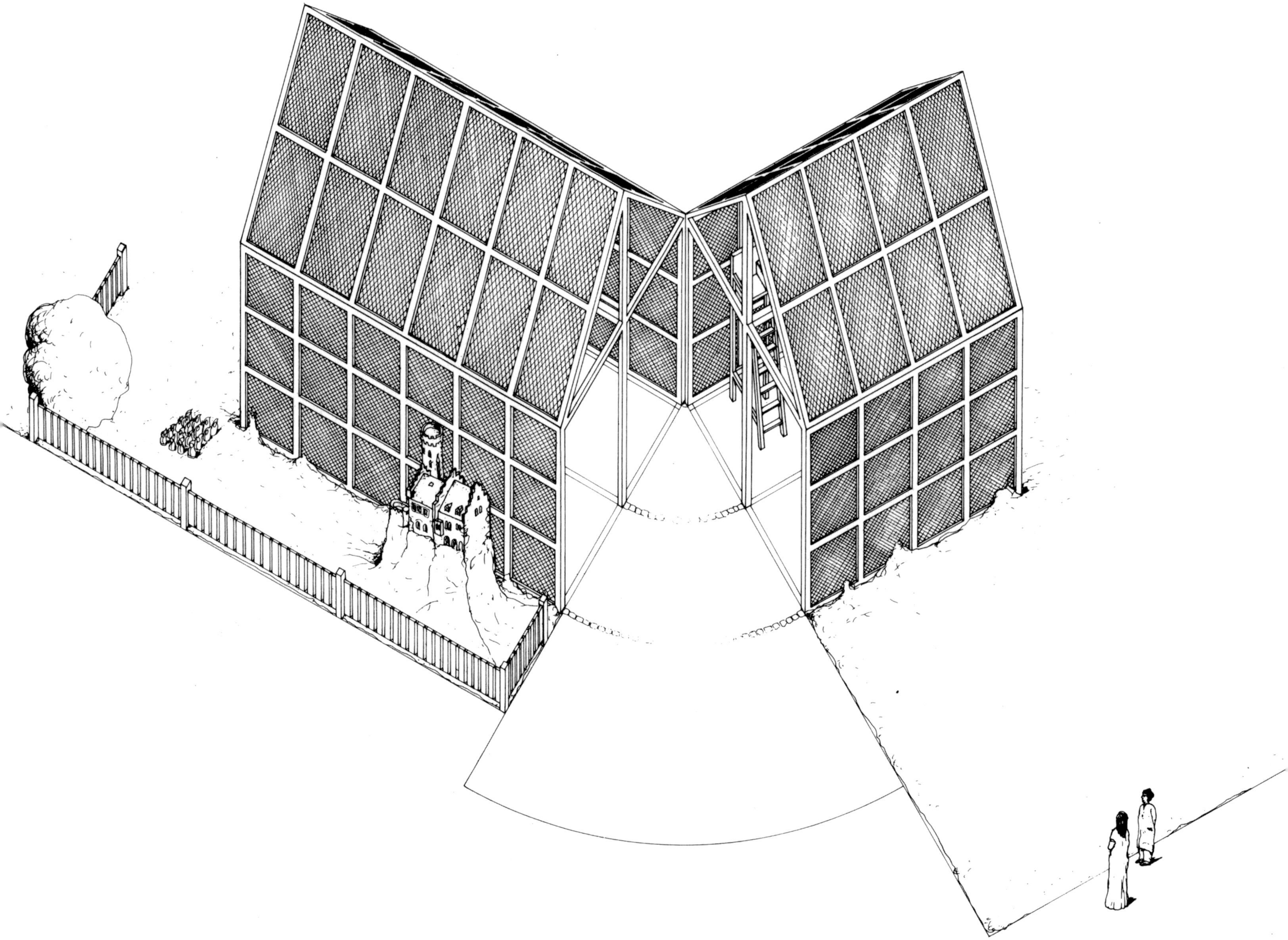

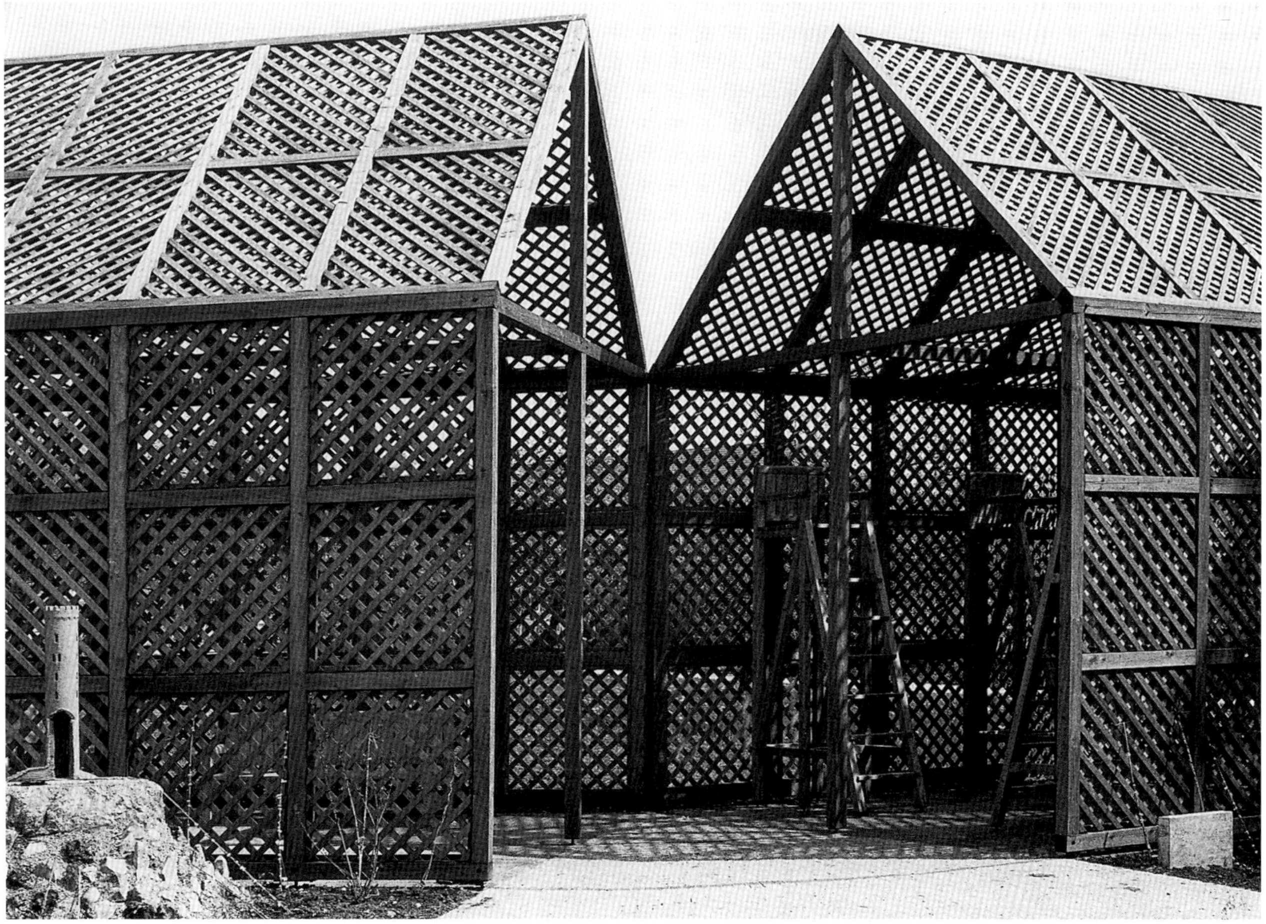

2, 3. Front and back view of the »Laubenhaus«.
(Photo: Hans Dieter Schaal, 1979.)

2. Vorder- und Rückansicht des »Laubenhauses«.
(Photo: Hans Dieter Schaal, 1979.)

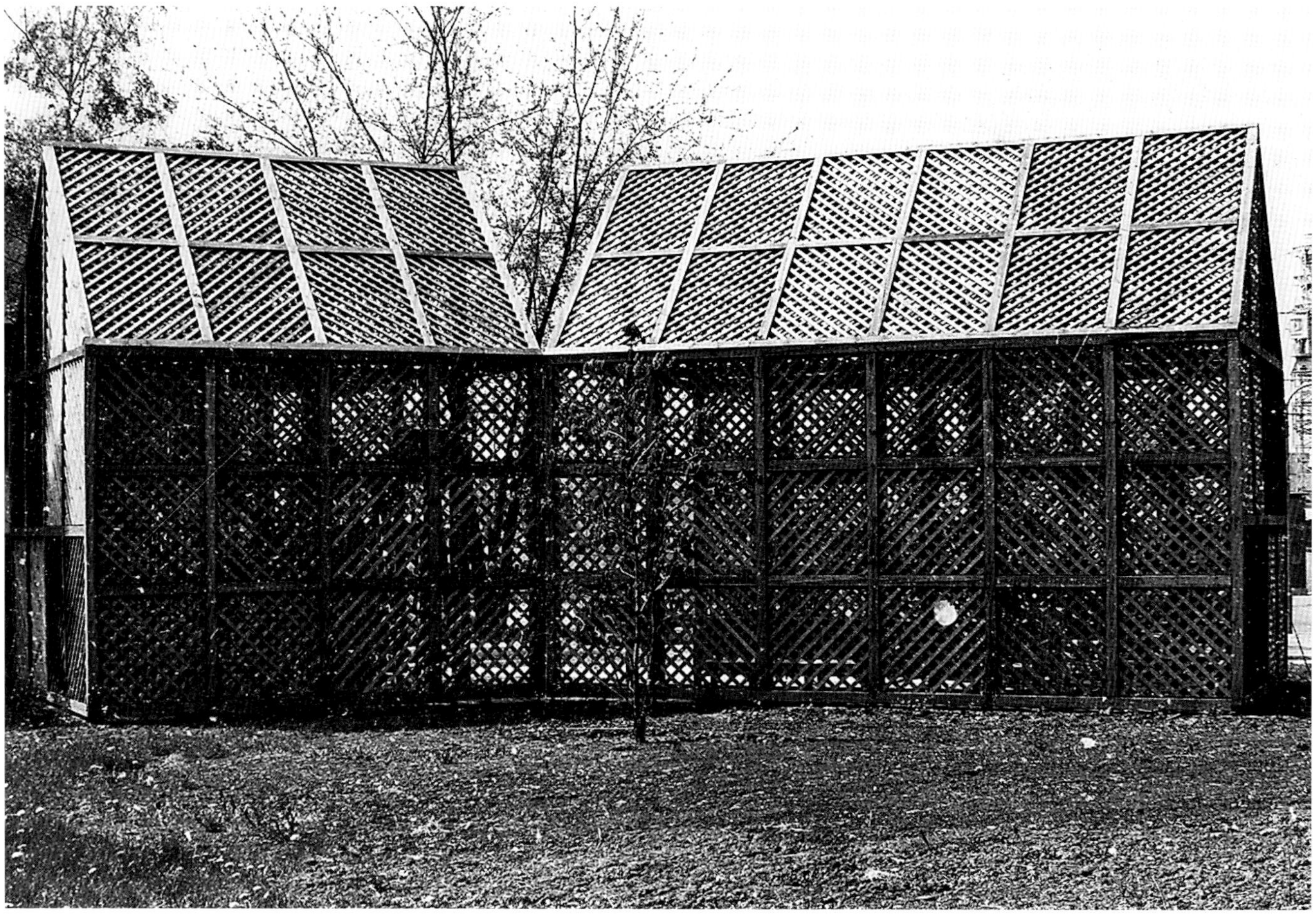

Romantic student café, 1981

In 1981, I designed a Romantic student café in a fictional, new-build castle tower built of coarse natural stone for the flat meadow area behind the »Laubenhaus« (arbor house). I worked without a commission (and without garden gnomes). With a decayed, crumbling ruined wall and sloping meadow around, I wanted to create an architectonic structure that looked as though it had formed naturally. The presence of coffee-drinking students would also have meant that my »Laubenhaus« would be better protected, at least during the day.

My café idea was discussed for a while by the University building authority. Following my bad experience with the »Laubenhaus«, the Lichtenstein castle and the garden gnome army, however, the plans soon ended up in the wastepaper basket.

In reality, one would have to think in terms of a larger garden with a secure fence. In today's reality, with its ever more reckless vandalism (culminating in the Stuttgart-21 demonstrations), buildings like my »Laubenhaus« and the student café cannot survive unprotected. This is the bitter realisation that has been deepened and confirmed over past decades.

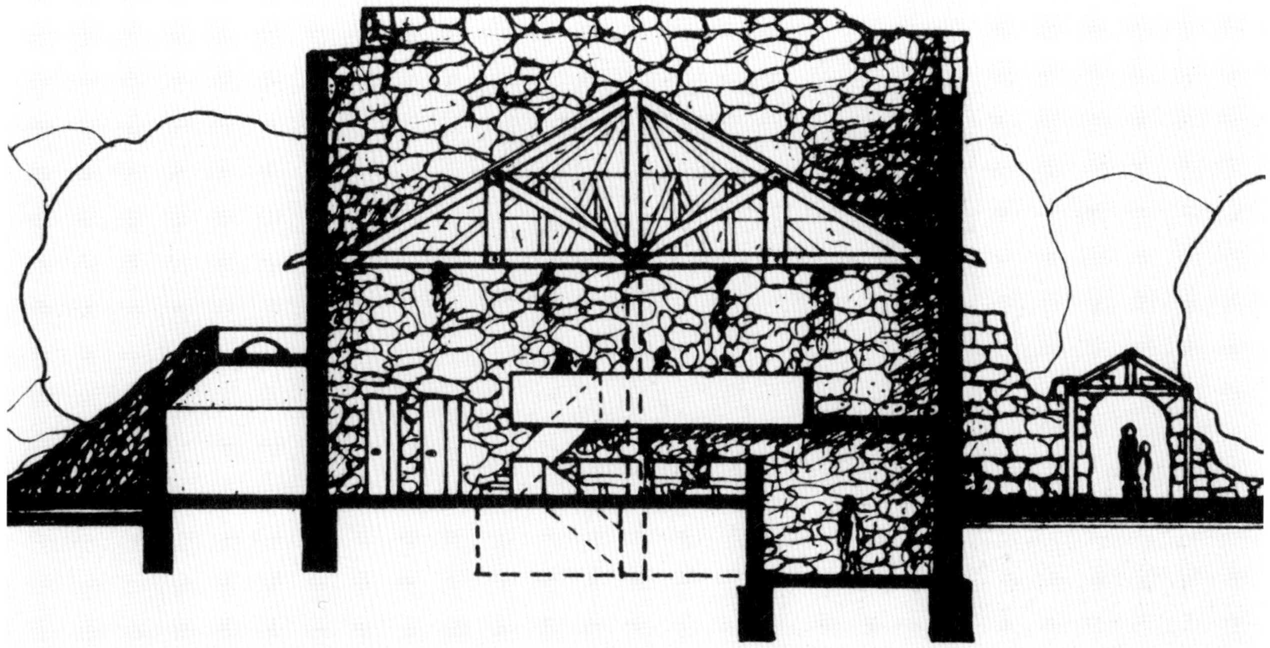

Romantisches Studentencafé, 1981

Für den flachen Wiesenbereich hinter dem »Laubenhaus« entwarf ich 1981 ohne Auftrag (und ohne Gartenzwerge) ein romantisches Studentencafé in einem fiktiven, neu gebauten Burgturm aus groben Natursteinen. Mit einer ruinös-abgebrochenen Ruinenmauer und angeböschter Wiese ringsum wollte ich ein architektonisches Gebilde schaffen, das wie naturhaft gewachsen aussieht. Durch die Anwesenheit von kaffeetrinkenden Studenten wäre mein »Laubenhaus«, zumindest tagsüber, auch besser geschützt gewesen.

Eine Zeitlang wurde im Universitätsbauamt über meine Café-Idee diskutiert. Nach den schlechten Erfahrungen mit dem »Laubenhaus«, dem Schloß Lichtenstein und der Gartenzwergarmee landeten die Pläne jedoch bald im Papierkorb.

In Wirklichkeit hätte über einen größeren Garten mit sicherer Umzäunung gesprochen werden müssen. Gebäude wie mein »Laubenhaus« und das Studentencafé haben ungeschützt in der heutigen, immer rücksichtsloser werdenden Vandalen-Realität (bis hin zu den Stuttgart-21-Demonstrationen) keine Chance zum Überleben mehr. Das war die bittere Erkenntnis, die sich im Laufe der letzten Jahrzehnte noch weiter vertieft und bestätigt hat.

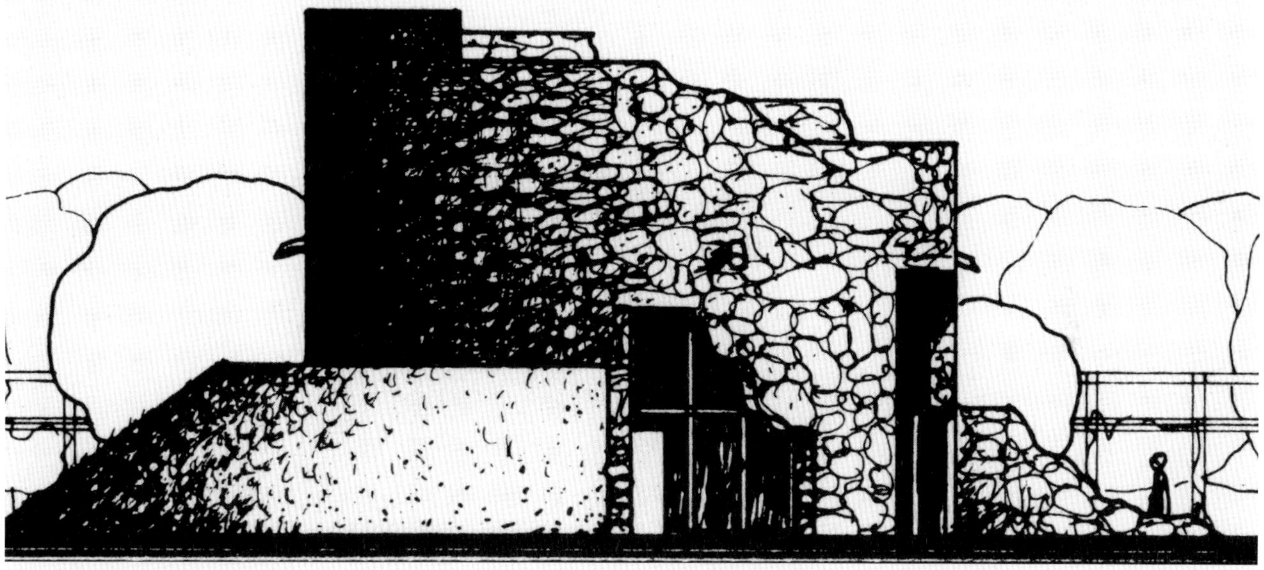

1, 2. Student café. Section and elevation.

1, 2. Studentencafé. Schnitt und Ansicht.

Congress-hall project, Berlin, 1980. Architecture art project, inspired by Kristin Feireiss, Galerie Aedes, Berlin

Ever since 1957, the Berliner Kongreßhalle, which was designed by one-time assistant to Gropius Hugh Stubbins, has been considered a historic piece of daring avant-garde West Berlin architecture.

This unconventional construction, however, was not built entirely according to the Americans precepts. German construction regulations, false safety precautions, and material fatigue led to the collapse of the south roof arch on the 21st of May 1980, injuring five people, one of whom died. West Berlin's Senate debated at some length whether the remains of the dangerous building should be demolished or should be rebuilt.

Shortly after this catastrophe to the building, Kristin Feireiss (at the time still Riedemann-Feireiss) and her fellow gallery founder Helga Retzer (who, only a short time later, suffered a lethal motor accident) invited a number of internationally active artist-architects to create imaginative, more-or-less realistic planning proposals for the continued use of the damaged structure. From his chosen home in New Zealand, Friedensreich Hundertwasser sent one of his famous pamphlets, in which he stated:

»The partial collapse of the Kongreßhalle and the resulting God-willed world of forms is a gift that we accept with gratitude. My proposal: support the ruins with pillars and allow a forest to grow over the roof.«

Other artist-architects – such as the Belgian Paul von Rafelghem – piled up earth, envisioning the growth of grass and moss.

Looked at in this way, I was not isolated in my proposal to construct a great earth and glass pyramid over the ruins. I wanted the preserved halls to be visible as artificially illuminated caverns. In order to ameliorate the depressing death-related aspect, I intended to have an elevator installed to take people to the top of the pyramid, with a cafe with a panoramic view in a glass crystal on top.

Partly out of consideration for the Americans, the Berlin Senate decided to have the congress hall renovated and modernised at a cost of several millions. Today, it is no longer a utopian propaganda building in defiance of »backward GDR functionaries and GDR citizens«; it is instead the new Haus der Kulturen, a venue for international exhibitions, theatre events, and music festivals.

Kongreßhallenprojekt, Berlin, 1980. Architektur-Kunstprojekt, angeregt von Kristin Feireiss, Galerie Aedes, Berlin

Seit 1957 galt die Berliner Kongreßhalle, die vom einstigen Gropius-Assistenten Hugh Stubbins entworfen wurde, als avantgardistisch gewagtes Baumonument West-Berlins.

Allerdings war die ungewöhnliche Konstruktion nicht ganz nach den Vorgaben des Amerikaners ausgeführt worden. Deutsche Bauvorschriften, falsche Sicherheitsvorkehrungen und Materialermüdung hatten dazu geführt, daß am 21. Mai 1980 der südliche Dachbogen einstürzte und dabei fünf Menschen verletzt wurden. Einer von ihnen starb. Der West-Berliner Senat diskutierte lange darüber, ob die gefährliche Bauruine abgerissen oder wieder aufgebaut werden soll.

Kurz nach der Baukatastrophe luden Kristin Feireiss (damals noch Riedemann-Feireiss) und ihre Galerie-Mitbegründerin Helga Retzer (sie verunglückte in jener Zeit bei einem Autounfall tödlich) einige international tätige Künstler-Architekten dazu ein, phantasievolle, mehr oder weniger realistische Planungsvorschläge für die Weiternutzung des verletzten Bauwerks zu machen. Friedensreich Hundertwasser schickte aus seiner Wahlheimat Neuseeland eines seiner berühmten Pamphlete, in dem er formulierte: »Das teilweise Zusammenfallen der Kongreßhalle und die dadurch entstandene gottgewollte Formenwelt ist ein Geschenk, das wir mit Dankbarkeit akzeptieren. Mein Vorschlag: die Ruine mit Säulen stützen und das Dach von einem Wald überwuchern lassen.«

Auch andere Künstler-Architekten – wie der Belgier Paul von Rafelghem – schütteten Erde darüber und ließen in Gedanken Gras und Moos wachsen.

So gesehen, stand ich mit meinem Vorschlag, eine große Erd-Gras-Pyramide darüber zu bauen, nicht alleine da. Ich wollte, daß die erhaltenen Säle als künstlich beleuchtete Höhlen zu besichtigen sind. Um den deprimierenden Totenaspekt zu mildern, dachte ich an einen Aufzug zur Pyramidenspitze und an ein Aussichtscafé in einem Glaskristall.

Der Berliner Senat entschied sich dazu (schon aus Rücksicht gegenüber den Amerikanern), die Kongreßhalle für viele Millionen renovieren und modernisieren zu lassen. Sie dient heute nicht mehr als utopischer Propagandabau gegenüber den »rückständigen DDR-Funktionären und DDR-Bürgern«, sondern dem neu gegründeten Haus der Kulturen als Ort von internationalen Ausstellungen, Theater-Veranstaltungen und Musik-Festivals.

1. Earth-grass pyramid over the congress hall ruins. With no panorama café in the top of the pyramid.

1. Erd-Gras-Pyramide über der Kongreßhallenruine. Ohne Aussichtscafé in der Pyramidenspitze.

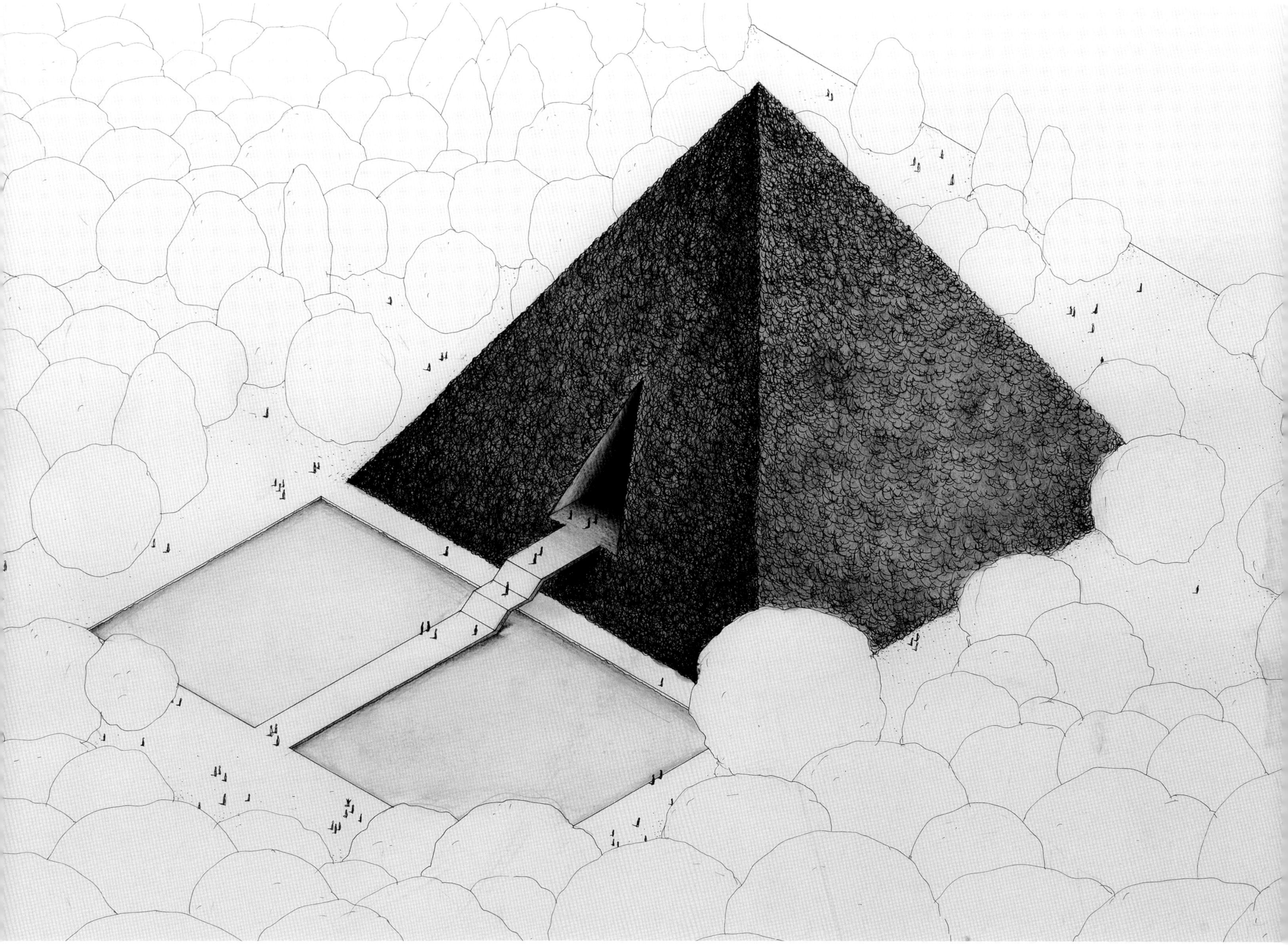

Königsplatz project, Kassel, 1981/1982

A design proposal for the Königsplatz in Kassel, a circular area much frequented by traffic. Created in connection with the »documenta urbana«.

Between 1980 and 1982, Lucius Burckhardt invited 15 internationally active artist-architects to develop unusual and original design ideas incorporating garden and park aspects for the inner-city area. Over the previous years, the »documenta urbana« housing projects that he had initiated, which had since been implemented, had been subjected to criticism. Thus, he was now searching for new, greener ways out of the problematic situation, which, in addition to handling the urban environment creatively, would also have to engage with landscape and nature. None of these projects ever found their way to becoming a reality.

Königsplatzprojekt, Kassel, 1981/1982

Vorschlag für die Gestaltung des kreisrunden, verkehrsreichen Königsplatzes in Kassel. Entstanden im Rahmen der »documenta urbana«.

Lucius Burckhardt hatte in den Jahren 1980 bis 1982 fünfzehn international tätige Künstler-Architekten eingeladen, für den Innenstadtbereich ungewöhnlich-originelle Gestaltungsideen mit Garten- und Parktendenzen zu entwickeln. In den Jahren zuvor waren die von ihm initiierten, inzwischen realisierten Wohnungsbauprojekte der »documenta urbana« in die Kritik geraten. Jetzt suchte er nach neuen, grüneren Wegen aus der Misere, die sich nicht nur kreativ mit dem urbanen Umfeld, sondern auch mit Landschaft und Natur auseinandersetzen sollten. Den Weg in die Realität fand kein einziges dieser Projekte.

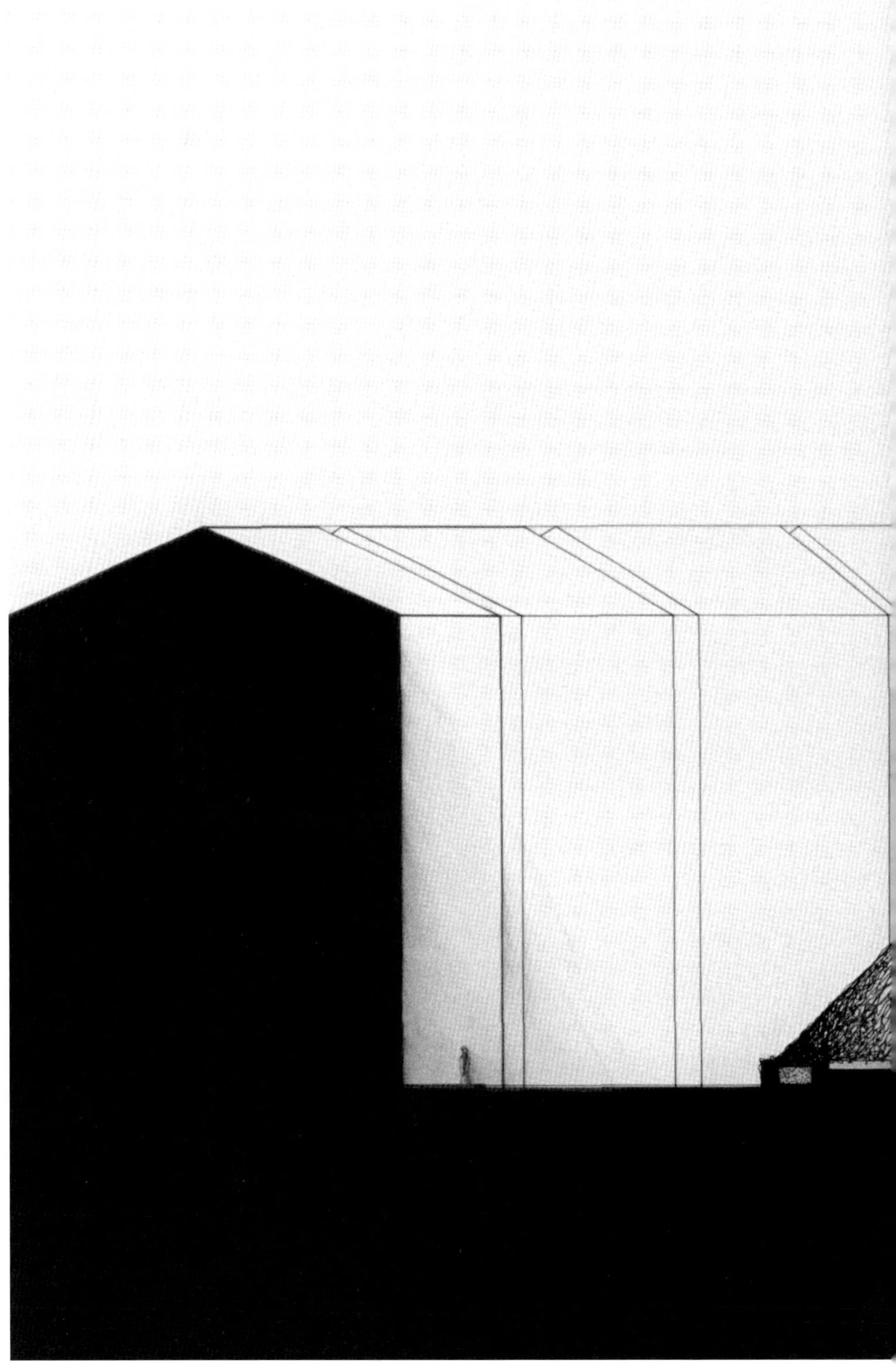

1. Ansicht/Schnitt.

1. Elevation/section.

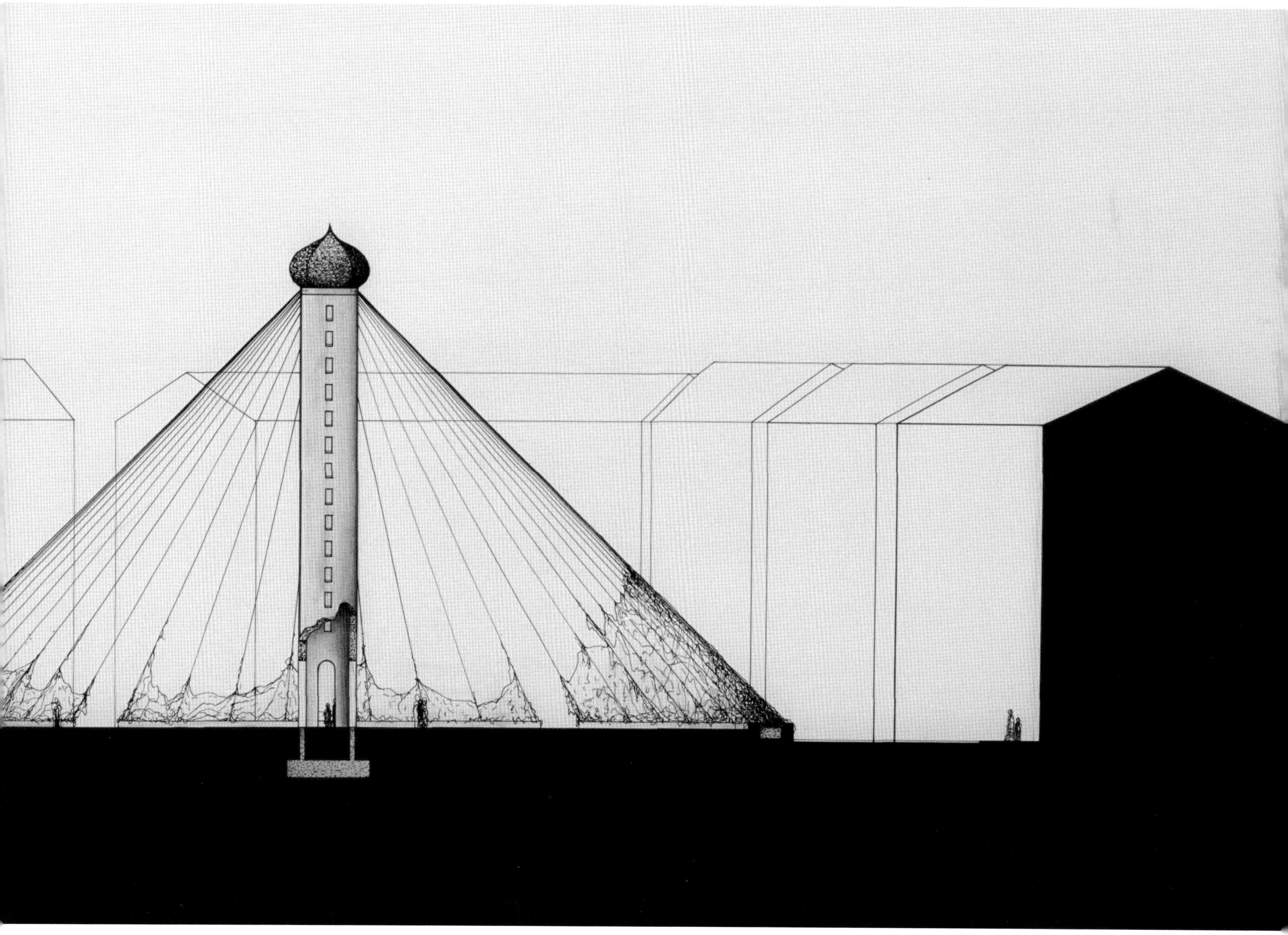

Görlitzer Park, Berlin. Competition entry, developed jointly with Pfrommer, Lehnhoff und Partner, Stuttgart, 1983. Second prize

A further attempt to intervene in the concrete landscape design of a large city. The fact that the project was rejected in favour of the first-prize-winning Freie Planungsgruppe Berlin was – looking back from today's vantage point – no bad thing, since the Kreuzberg city zone, where the one kilometre long and 200 meter wide park is located, is no simpler as a location today.

In addition to the required sport and games fields, we had proposed a far-too-complex landscape programme. Garden poetry with imitations of Tahiti and Capri, the Canale Grande, a fountain plaza, arcade walks, and a bathing lake would probably not have survived the nightly chaos and vandal attacks. Only stress-resistant meadows for ball games and barbecues, a children's farm, a road practice area and areas for skaters, with the addition of few robust trees, stood a real chance in the harsh everyday realities of Kreuzberg.

In the years following its completion, »Görli«, as the park is affectionately known to residents, became a dangerous zone in the city's landscape, where attacks and murders were not uncommon, since it was unfenced and open day and night. In particular, drug dealers were causing the police problems. For this reason, the relevant officials from the city's green spaces authority decided to have all the low vegetation – bushes, hedges, shrubs – removed from the park. The idea was to eliminate hiding places.

Additionally, an art project for the entrance area of the Görlitzer Park that began hopefully – the »Pamukkale-Brunnen« – ended in tragedy for the Berlin sculptor Wigand Wittig (married to the actress Angela Winkler). Because of the high Turkish population in Kreuzberg, the artist proposed to create a fountain composition that imitated the famous Turkish sinter terrace landscape, but chose a non-frost-resistant Portuguese limestone which broke in the first winter. He was sued by the Berlin Senate for damages of more than one million Euros. After a number of legal proceedings, this judgement was ultimately upheld in November 2008.

Görlitzer Park, Berlin. Wettbewerbsentwurf, erarbeitet zusammen mit Pfrommer, Lehnhoff und Partner, Stuttgart, 1983. Zweiter Preis

Wieder der Versuch, in die konkrete Landschaftsgestaltung einer großen Stadt einzugreifen. Daß das Projekt abgelehnt wurde und an den ersten Preisträger, die Freie Planungsgruppe Berlin fiel, ist – von heute aus gesehen – nicht unerfreulich, denn die Stadtzone Kreuzberg, in dem der einen Kilometer lange und 200 Meter breite Park liegt, ist bis heute nicht einfacher geworden.

Wir hatten, neben den geforderten Sport- und Spielfeldern, ein viel zu komplexes Landschaftsprogramm vorgeschlagen. Garten-Poesie mit Tahiti- und Capri-Nachbildungen, Canale Grande, Fontänenplatz, Laubengänge und Badesee hätten hier wahrscheinlich die nächtlichen Chaotenspiele und Vandalenattacken nicht überleben können. Nur strapazierfähige Wiesen zum Ballspielen und Grillen, ein Kinderbauernhof, ein Verkehrsübungsplatz und Flächen für Skater, dazu wenige robuste Bäume, hatten eine reale Chance im harten Kreuzberger Alltag.

In den Jahren nach der Fertigstellung entwickelte sich der nicht eingezäunte, Tag und Nacht offene »Görli«, wie der Park liebevoll von den Anwohner genannt

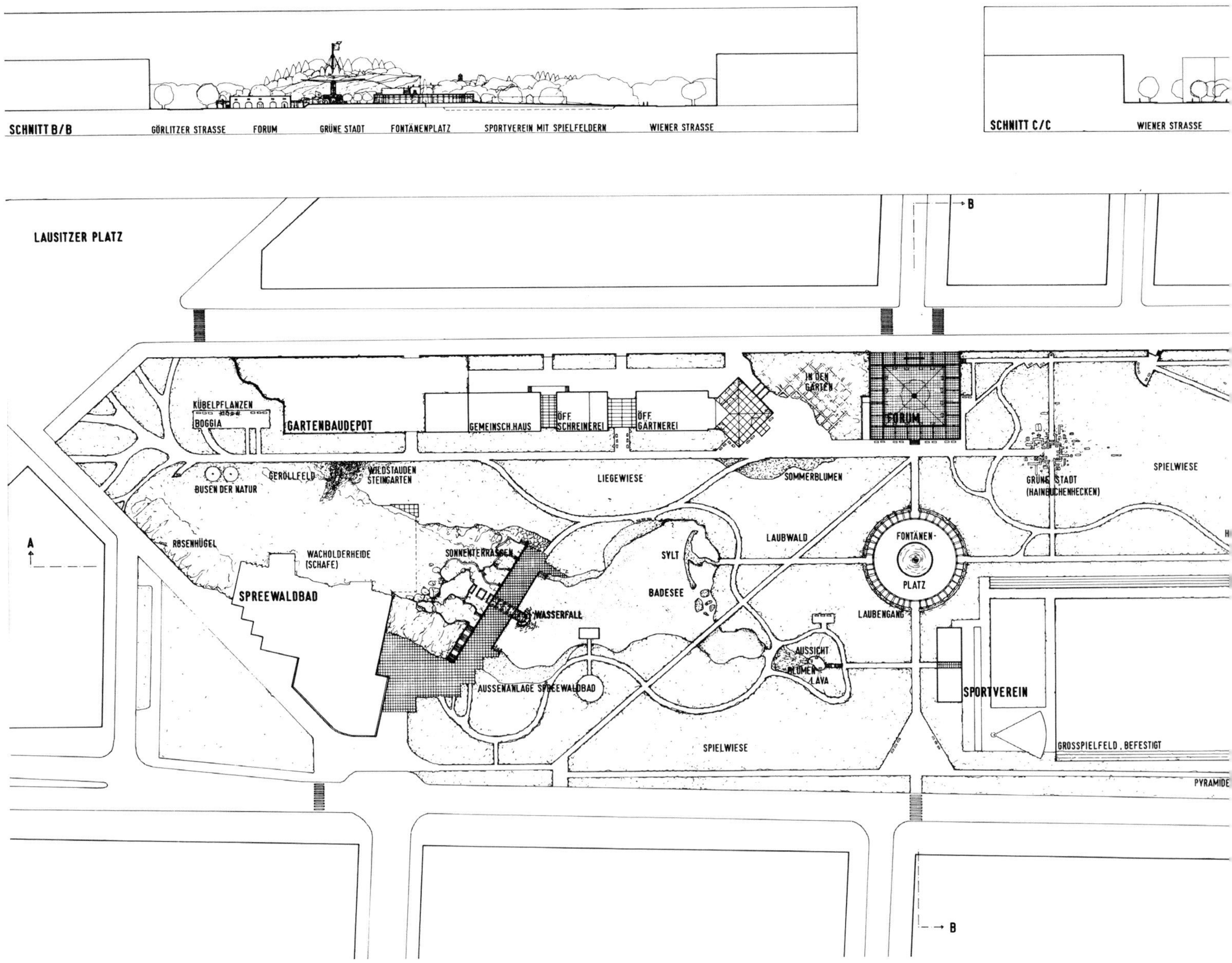

wird, in eine gefährliche Stadtlandschaftszone, wo Überfälle und Morde nichts Ungewöhnliches sind. Besonders die Rauschgifthändler machen der Polizei Probleme. Deswegen beschlossen die zuständigen Beamten des städtischen Grünamtes, die gesamte niedrige Vegetation – Büsche, Hecken, Stauden – aus dem Park entfernen zu lassen. Man will keine Versteckssituationen mehr bieten.

Daneben hat sich ein hoffnungsvoll begonnenes Kunst-Projekt – der »Pamukkale-Brunnen« – im Zugangsbreich des Görlitzer Parks für den Berliner Bildhauer Wigand Wittig (der mit der Schauspielerin Angela Winkler verheiratet ist) zur Tragödie entwickelt. Wegen der türkischen Bewohnerdichte in Kreuzberg schlug der Künstler vor, die berühmte türkische Sinterterrassenlandschaft in seiner Brunnenkomposition nachzubilden. Da er sich für einen frostunbeständigen Kalkstein aus Portugal entschied, zerbrach das Gestein bereits im ersten Winter. Er wurde vom Berliner Senat zu einem Schadenersatz von über einer Million Euro verklagt. Nach mehreren Prozessen erhielt das Urteil im November 2008 in letzter Instanz Rechtsgültigkeit.

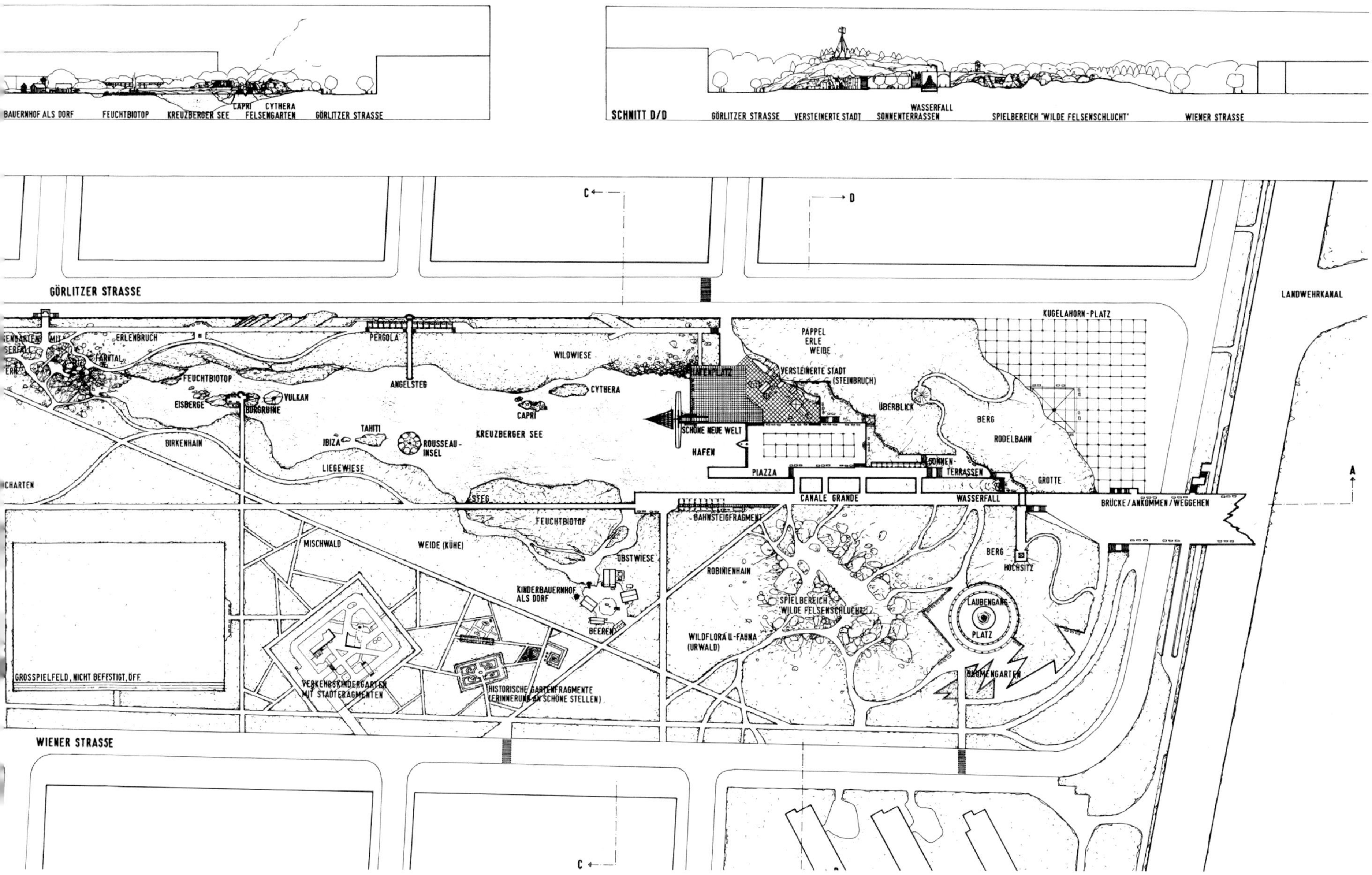

1. Overall plan.

1. Gesamtplan.

Urn complex. An urban cemetery in Singen am Hohentwiel, 1984/1985. Construction management: Hochbauamt Singen. The complex was renovated in 2015 by the Hochbauamt Singen

Unlike the Stuttgart »Laubenhaus« (arbor house), this urn complex is still standing today. Since it is embedded in a gentle hill in the urban cemetery at Singen, provided with old trees, it could justifiably be described as landscape architecture or as an architectural landscape. This complex was well received by the citizens of Singen. All of the urn compartments were »spoken for« within a few years.

In 1990, Frank R. Werner wrote the following text on the subject:

»An avenue of oaks leads from a side entrance of the old Singen woodland cemetery to a slightly raised hall of committal, rendered superfluous by the building of a new modern hall on another site. The urgently needed new urn complex was to be created here. Schaal retained the existing entrance axis. He used it to divide the newly laid out ›cloister courtyard‹ below the old hall into two halves.

Through the ›cleft‹ thus created, one enters the cloister, a space which is enclosed by pillars and arches. Urn chambers are set into the outer walls.

One reaches the higher level by means of an axially arranged staircase. Here, the old hall of committal has largely been demolished and reshaped into the adyton of a ›temple of rest‹. An artificially fragmented pillar portico with an ›urn tympanum‹ lying behind it centres the frontage onto the neighbouring field of grave plots. In the interior of the ›temple of rest‹ is a marble ›spring fountain‹ symbolising ›birth‹. The water is constantly overflowing and flowing through an open channel set into the stair axis – symbolising ›the course of life‹ – into a round central basin in the centre of the ›cloister courtyard‹. At the bottom of this dark basin of water, the ruins of a model city can be seen. This archaeological fiction of a sunken city is a visual metaphor for ›impermanence‹ and ›death‹, shimmering out of the unfathomable depths of this ritual pool.«

Urnenanlage, Stadtfriedhof in Singen am Hohentwiel, 1984/1985. Bauleitung: Hochbauamt Singen. Die Anlage wurde 2015 durch das Hochbauamt Singen renoviert

Im Gegensatz zum Stuttgarter »Laubenhaus« steht diese Urnenanlage heute immer noch. Da sie in einen sanften Hügel des Stadtfriedhofs von Singen mit alter Baumsubstanz eingebettet ist, kann man hier zu Recht von Landschaftsarchitektur oder Architekturlandschaft sprechen. Die Anlage fand bei den Singener Bürgern viel Anklang. Nach wenigen Jahren waren alle Urnenfächer »belegt«.

1990 schrieb Frank R. Werner folgenden Text darüber:

»Eine Eichenallee führte von einem Nebeneingang des alten Singener Waldfriedhofs zu einer leicht erhöhten Aussegnungshalle, die durch den Neubau einer modernen Halle an anderer Stelle überflüssig geworden war. Hier sollte die dringend benötigte neue Urnenanlage geschaffen werden. Schaal behielt die bestehende Eingangsachse bei. Mit ihr spaltete er den neu angelegten ›Klosterhof‹ unterhalb der alten Halle in zwei Hälften.

Durch den so geschaffenen ›Spalt‹ betritt man den Kreuzgang, der von Pfeilern und Bögen räumlich gefaßt wird. In die Umfassungswände sind Urnenkammern eingelassen.

Über eine axial angeordnete Treppe erreicht man das höher gelegene Niveau. Hier wurde die alte Aussegnungshalle größtenteils demoliert und zum Adyton eines ›Resttempels‹ umgeformt. Ein künstlich fragmentierter Säulenportikus mit einem dahinter liegenden ›Urnen-Tympanon‹ zentriert die Front zum angrenzenden Gräberfeld. Im Inneren des ›Resttempels‹ befindet sich ein marmorgefaßter, die ›Geburt‹ symbolisierender ›Quellbrunnen‹. Dessen stetig überlaufendes Wasser fließt über eine offene, in die Treppenachse eingelassene und den ›Lebenslauf‹ verkörpernde Rinne in ein zentrales Rundbecken in der Mitte des ›Klosterhofs‹. Am Grund dieses dunklen Wasserbassins sind die Ruinen einer Modellstadt zu erkennen. Mit dieser archäologischen Fiktion einer versunkenen Stadt schimmert eine anschauliche Metapher für ›Vergänglichkeit‹ und ›Tod‹ aus der unergründlichen Tiefe dieses Kultbeckens herauf.«

1. A view of the avenue of common oaks at the entrance to the urn complex.

1. Blick durch die Stieleichenallee zum Eingang der Urnenanlage.

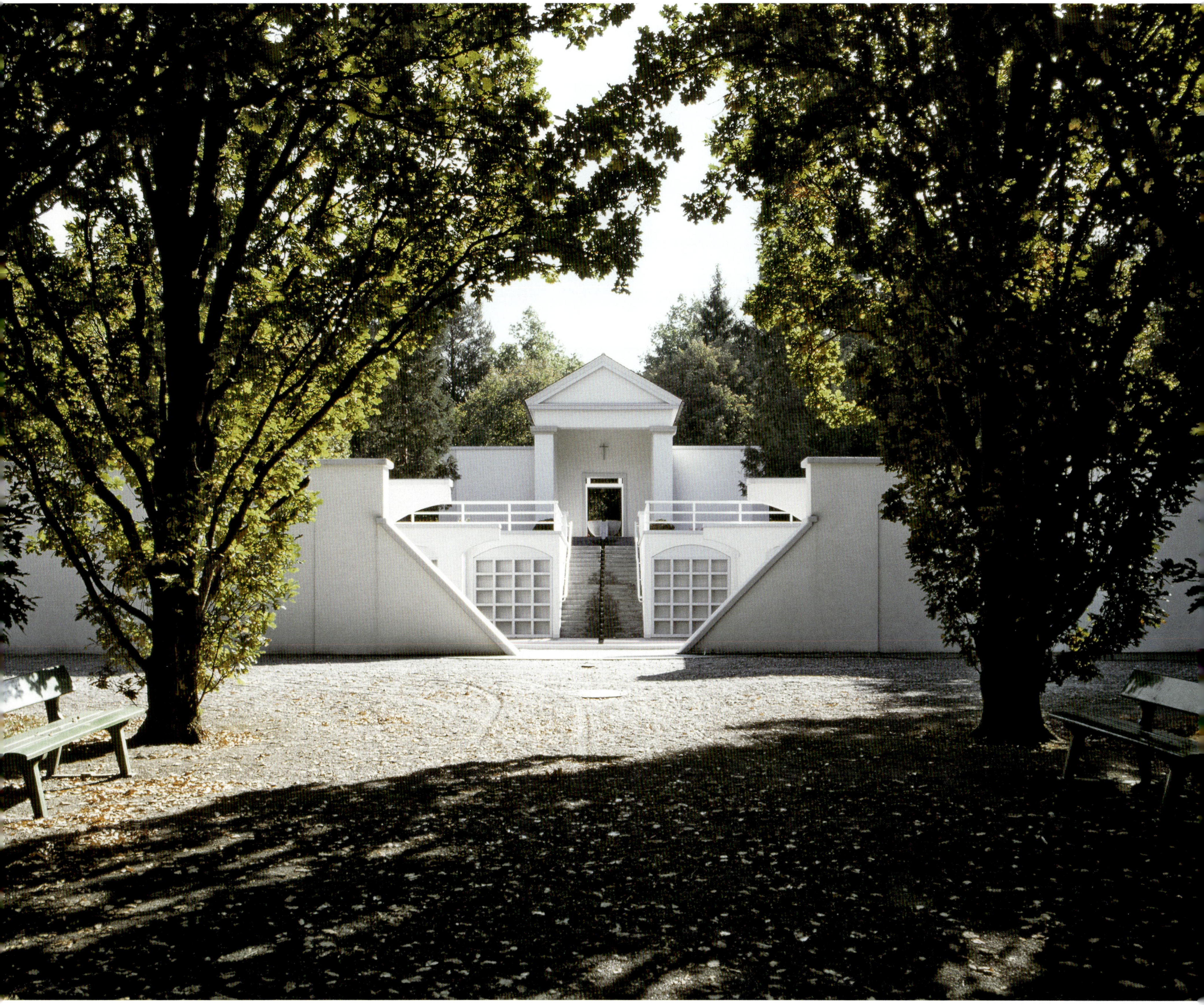

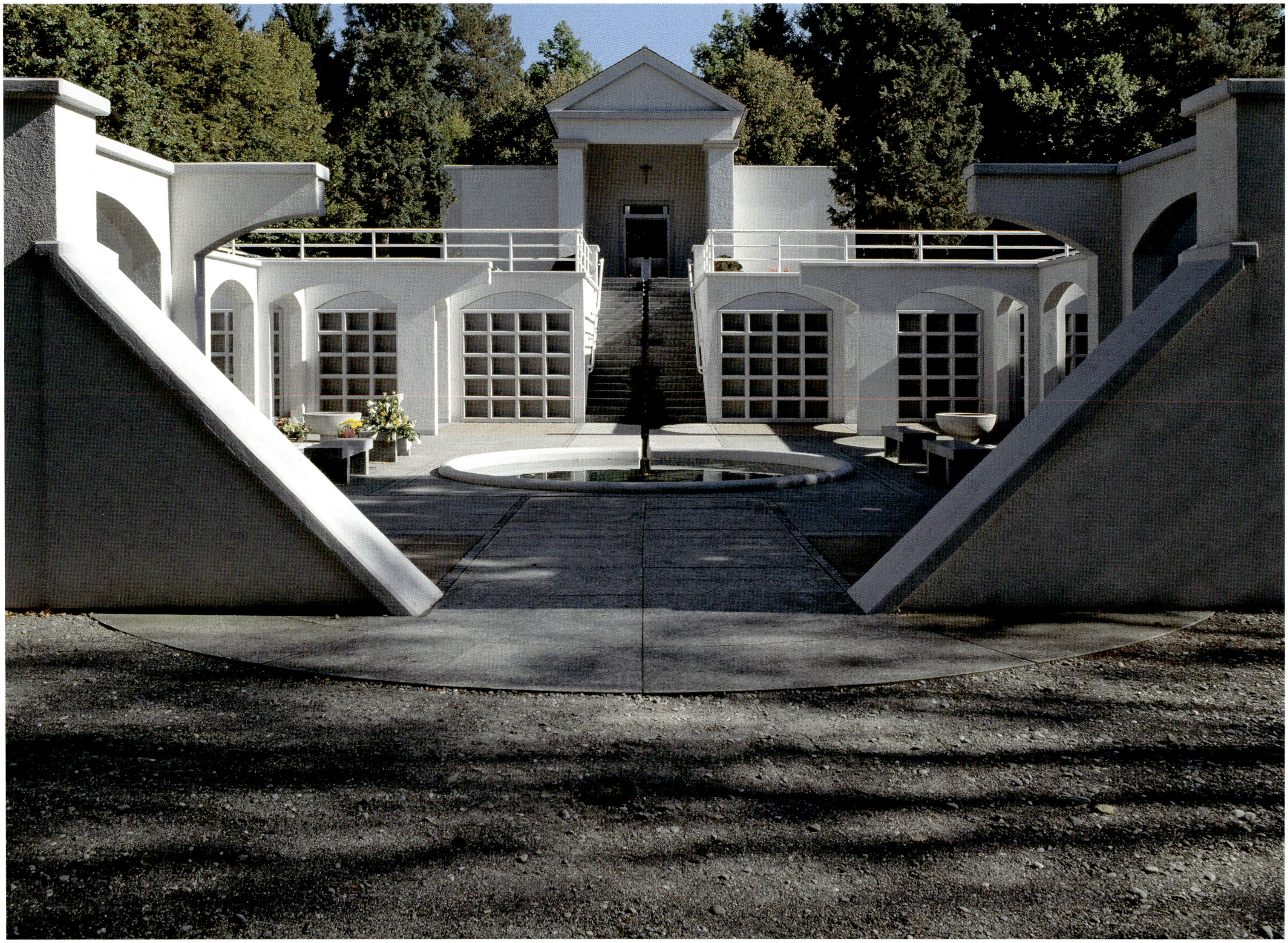

2. Entrance to the urn complex.
3. The central fountain pool in the cloister courtyard. The suggestion of a ruined city can be seen beneath the water.

2. Eingang in die Urnenanlage.
3. Das zentrale Brunnenbecken im Klosterhof. Unter Wasser ist eine angedeutete Ruinenstadt zu erkennen.

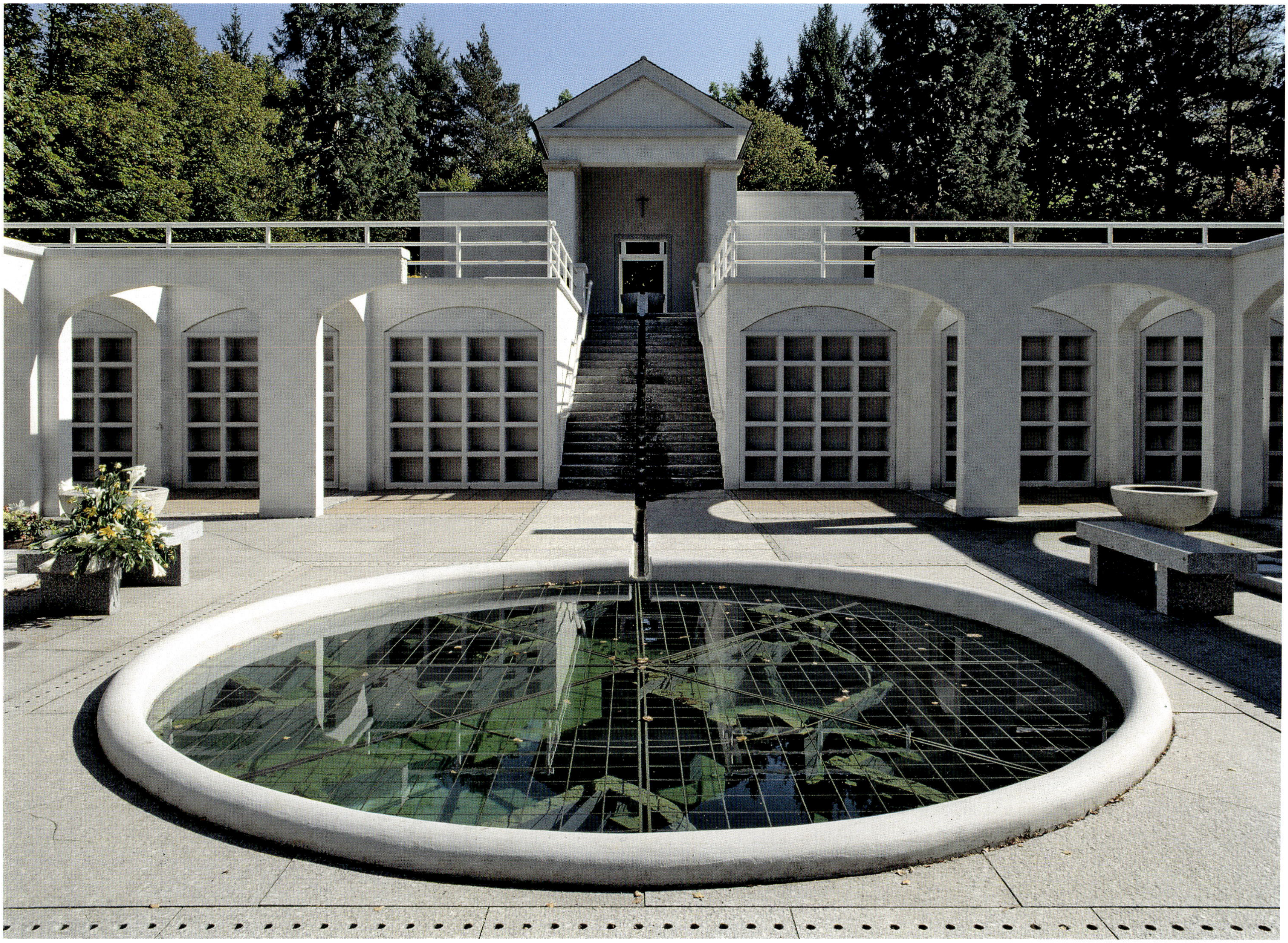

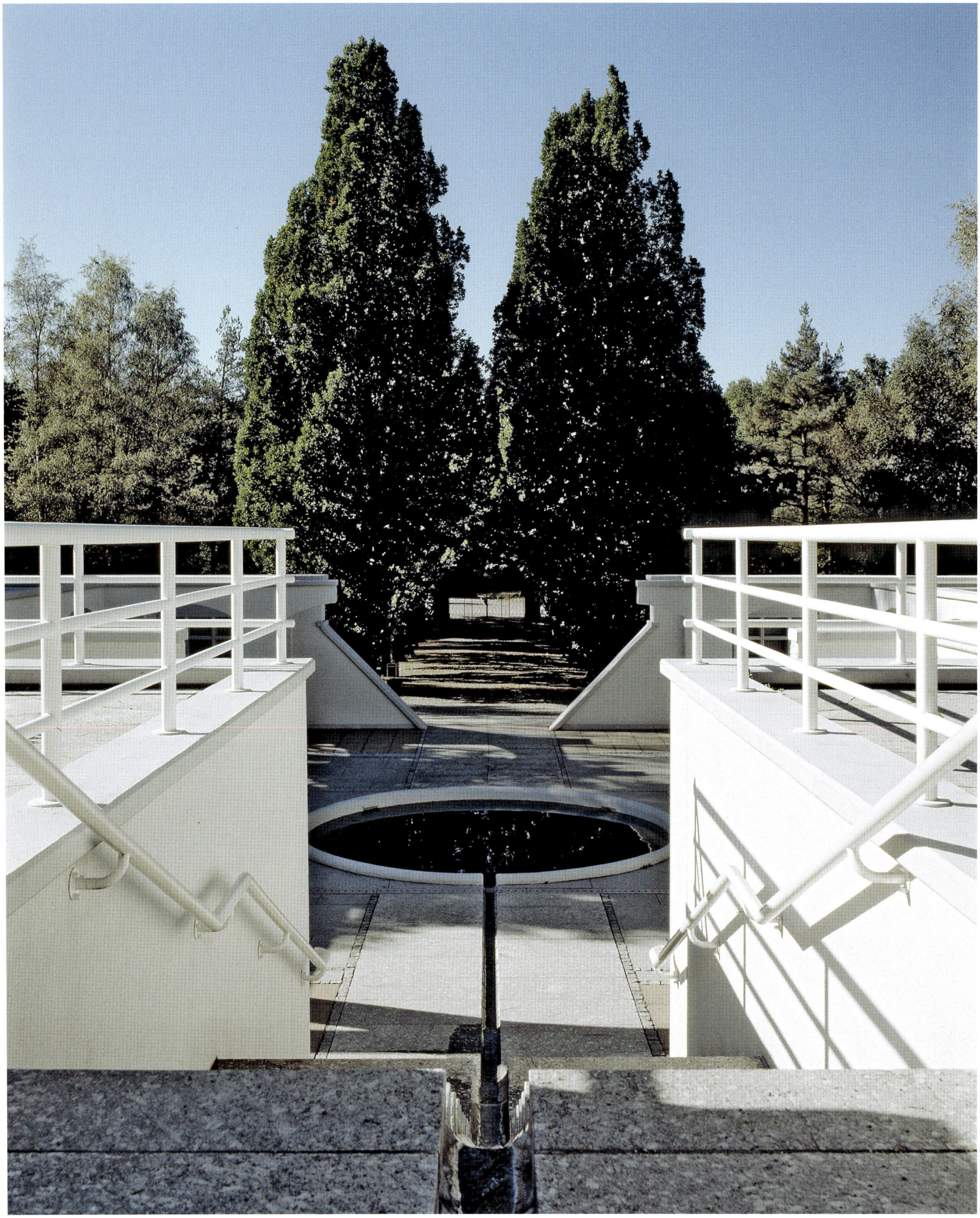

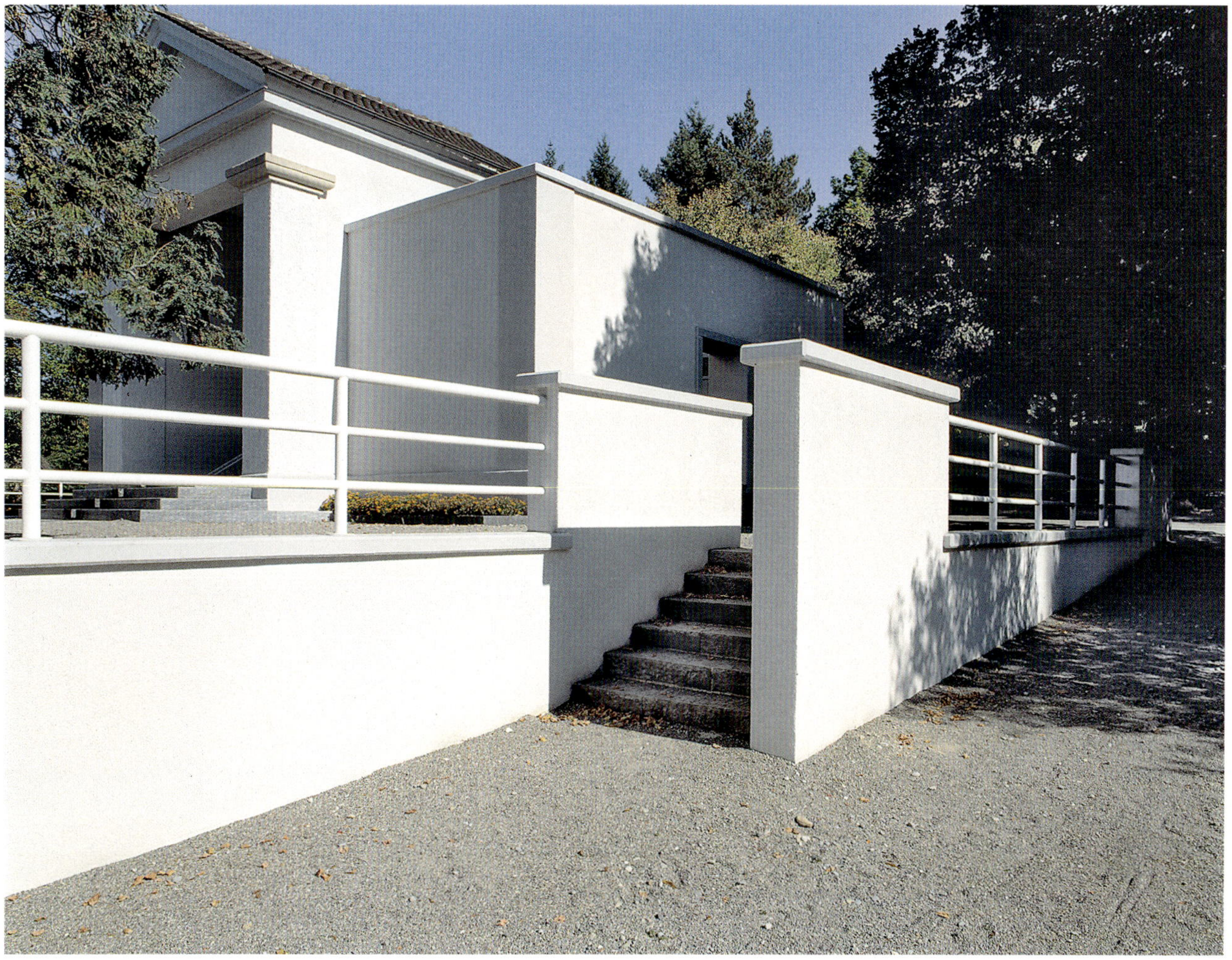

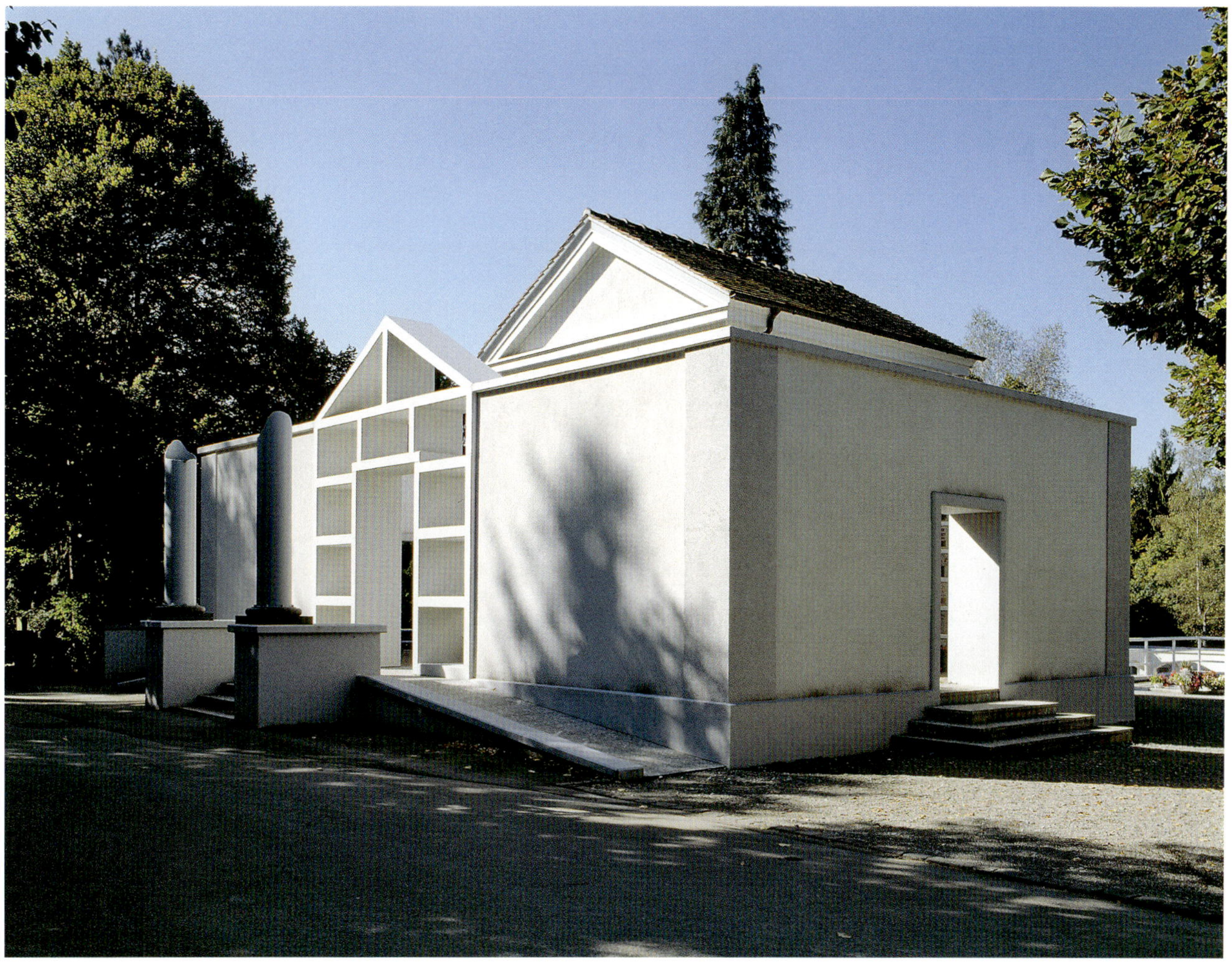

4. View of the central axis from above, with the fountain pool and the avenue of oaks.
5. A lateral ascending stair to the higher part of the urn complex.
6. Rear view of the converted old consecration hall with two stumps of broken steel pillars on both sides of the access stairs.

All photos were taken in the years following completion, between 1986 and 1988.

4. Blick von oben in die zentrale Achse mit dem Brunnenbecken und der Eichenallee.
5. Seitliche Aufgangstreppe zum höher gelegenen Teil der Anlage.
6. Rückansicht der umgebauten alten Aussegnungshalle mit zwei abgebrochenen Säulenstümpfen aus Stahl auf beiden Seiten der Zugangstreppe.

Alle Photos entstanden in den Jahren nach der Fertigstellung, zwischen 1986 und 1988.

Main entrance to Landesgartenschau Freiburg im Breisgau, 1986. Designed and implemented based on a commission for the Gartenschau GmbH Freiburg, and later bought by the city of Freiburg

Today, the former Landesgartenschau (regional garden show) site goes by the name Seepark Betzenhausen, and is very popular among residents of the neighbouring housing areas. In the 1980s, when the civic administration of Freiburg decided to close the former sand and gravel quarry belonging to the Flückinger firm and to turn it into a park with a lake, the site did not exactly look inviting. This, however, was a question of long-term thinking, and the development ultimately proved the planners to be right.

In 1985/86, my task was to design a main entrance for the Landesgartenschau, and thus also for the future Seepark Betzenhausen. The problem was that the place designated for this was situated a long way from the new park, on an exit road (the Sundgauallee) amid mundane and unassuming residential developments. This meant that my design had to stand out from suburban uniformity and act like a »green park advertisement building«. I chose timber as a building material, and proposed a kind of exaggeration of the accustomed building reception gestures. Not a gate, but a collection of gates with the ambience of different times – a mediaeval city gate, a house entrance, a garden gate, an arbour gate, an »autobahn gate« to trap visitors. At the time, I had not considered actually greening the wooden architectural elements. Instead, I planned regularly planted trees for the rear area, where the actual access path to the park begins.

The implemented solution was a success, and was well received by visitors. The gateway site had achieved its goal. As I had imagined that this would be a temporary structure, I was somewhat surprised that the Freiburg municipal council decided to purchase the ensemble at the end of the Landesgartenschau. Wooden buildings have a limited lifespan, and my enthusiasm for the proceedings was therefore limited. A few years later, the ensemble was showing clear traces of ageing. I therefore made a proposal to the head of the building department for the city of Freiburg, who called me at the beginning of the new millennium, that he should have the gates demolished. He was surprised by my request, and told me how accustomed the residents had grown to their Betzenhausener-Tor-Platz (Betzenhausen gate plaza). Some regarded the gates as a striking icon for the city, as objects with an identity-building function. They said that the demolition would create a deep wound in their residential area.

After a long silence, the city of Freiburg architecture official responsible contacted me several times in 2014 and 2015. The plaza is still being discussed, in the municipal council and publicly. The redesign is set to begin, at last, in 2017 – without the gates, and without me. So, at least, he informed me.

Haupteingang zur Landesgartenschau Freiburg im Breisgau, 1986. Entworfen und realisiert im Auftrag der Gartenschau GmbH Freiburg und später von der Stadt Freiburg angekauft

Heute nennt sich das ehemalige Landesgartenschaugelände Seepark Betzenhausen und ist sehr beliebt bei den Bewohnern der angrenzenden Wohngebiete. Als sich die Stadtverwaltung Freiburg zu Beginn der 1980er Jahre dazu entschloß, die bisherigen Sand- und Kiesabbaugruben der Firma Flückinger zu schließen und einen Park mit See daraus zu formen, sah das Gelände nicht gerade einladend aus. Aber man dachte langfristig und die Entwicklung gab den Planern recht.

Meine Aufgabe bestand 1985/86 darin, einen Haupteingang für die Landesgartenschau und damit für den zukünftigen Seepark Betzenhausen zu entwerfen. Das Problem bestand darin, daß der dafür vorgesehene Platz weit abseits vom neuen Park, an einer Ausfallstraße, der Sundgauallee, zwischen unauffällig-alltäglicher Wohnbebauung lag. Deswegen mußte sich mein Entwurf vom vorstädtischen Einerlei deutlich unterscheiden und wie ein »grüner Park-Reklamebau« wirken. Ich wählte als Baumaterial Holz und schlug eine Art Übertreibung gewohnter Bau-Empfangsgesten vor. Nicht ein Tor, sondern eine Torversammlung mit verschiedenen Zeitanklängen – von mittelalterlichem Stadttor über Hauseingang, Gartentür, Laubentor bis zum »Autobahntor« – sollte die Besucher »einfangen«. An eine tatsächliche Begrünung der hölzernen Architekturteile dachte ich damals nicht. Dafür plante ich im hinteren Bereich, dort wo der eigentliche Zugangsweg zum Park beginnt, regelmäßig gepflanzte Bäume.

Die realisierte Lösung war ein Erfolg und kam gut bei den Besuchern an. Der Torplatz hatte sein Ziel erreicht. Da es sich in meiner Vorstellung um eine temporäre Anlage handelte, war ich etwas überrascht darüber, daß sich der Freiburger Gemeinderat dazu entschloß, das Ensemble nach dem Ende der Landesgartenschau anzukaufen. Holzbauten haben eine begrenzte Lebensdauer. Deswegen war ich nur mäßig begeistert über die Vorgänge. Nach wenigen Jahren zeigte das Ensemble deutliche Alterungsspuren. Deswegen schlug ich dem Baubürgermeister der Stadt Freiburg, der mich zu Beginn des neuen Jahrtausends anrief, vor, die Tore abreißen zu lassen. Er wunderte sich über meinen Wunsch und teilte mir mit, wie sehr sich die Anwohner an ihren Betzenhausener-Tor-Platz gewöhnt hätten. Manche würden die Tore als markante Stadtzeichen und damit als Identifikationsobjekte wahrnehmen. Der Abriß würde eine tiefe Wunde in ihr Wohngebiet reißen, sagen sie.

Nach längerer Pause rief mich der verantwortliche Architektur-Beamte der Stadt Freiburg 2014 und 2015 mehrfach in dieser Sache an. Noch immer wird im Gemeinderat und in der Öffentlichkeit über den Platz diskutiert. Von 2017 an soll jetzt endgültig mit der Umgestaltung – ohne Tore und ohne mich – begonnen werden. So seine Aussage.

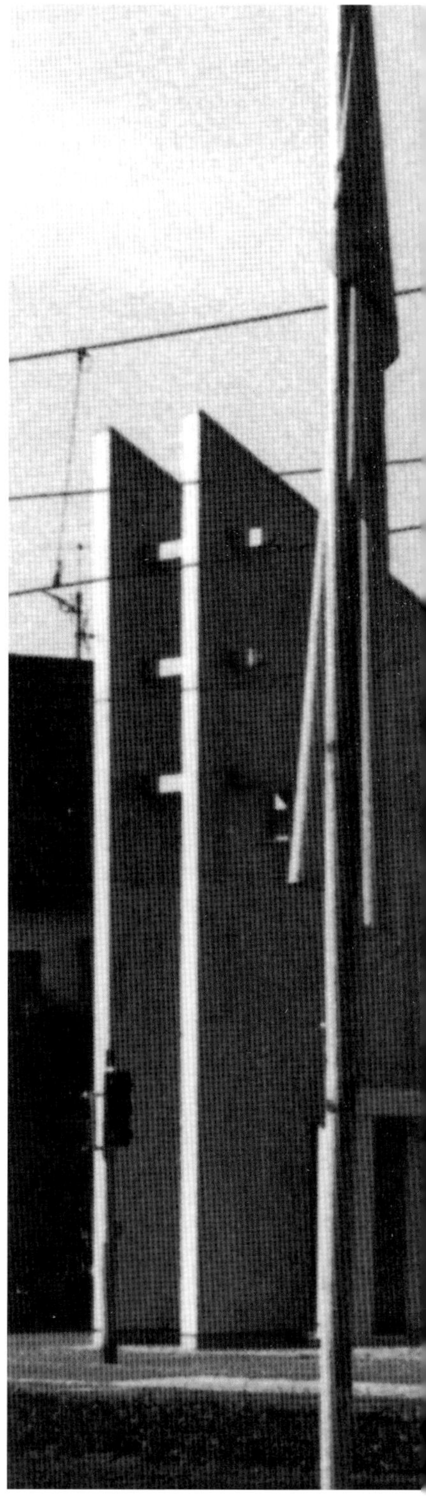

1. Day view of the Betzenhausener Torplatz. In the »regional garden show guidebook«, my gate plaza is described as follows: »The artistic design of the entrance area was carried out by Hans Dieter Schaal from Ulm. The artist himself sees the southern part of the plaza, toward the Sundgauallee, as a ›stage‹ with a backdrop of large trees. Upon it are arranged the basic forms for the entrance, together with a wedge-shaped wall element, in a varied ensemble of four gate elements in total. These beget curiosity, and invite people to explore the plaza and the lake park area beyond it.« (Photo: Hans Dieter Schaal, 1986.)

1. Tagansicht des Betzenhausener Torplatzes. Im »Landesgartenschau-Führer« wird mein Torplatz mit folgenden Worten beschrieben: »Die künstlerische Gestaltung des Eingangsbereichs wurde von Hans Dieter Schaal aus Ulm ausgeführt. Der Künstler selbst versteht den südlichen Teil des Platzes zur Sundgauallee als ›Bühne‹ vor einem Hintergrund aus großen Bäumen. Auf ihr werden die Grundformen für den Eingang zusammen mit einem keilförmigen Wandelement an einem spannungsvollen Ensemble von insgesamt vier Torelementen arrangiert, das neugierig macht, einlädt, den Platz und das dahinterliegende Seeparkgelände zu erkunden.« (Photo: Hans Dieter Schaal, 1986.)

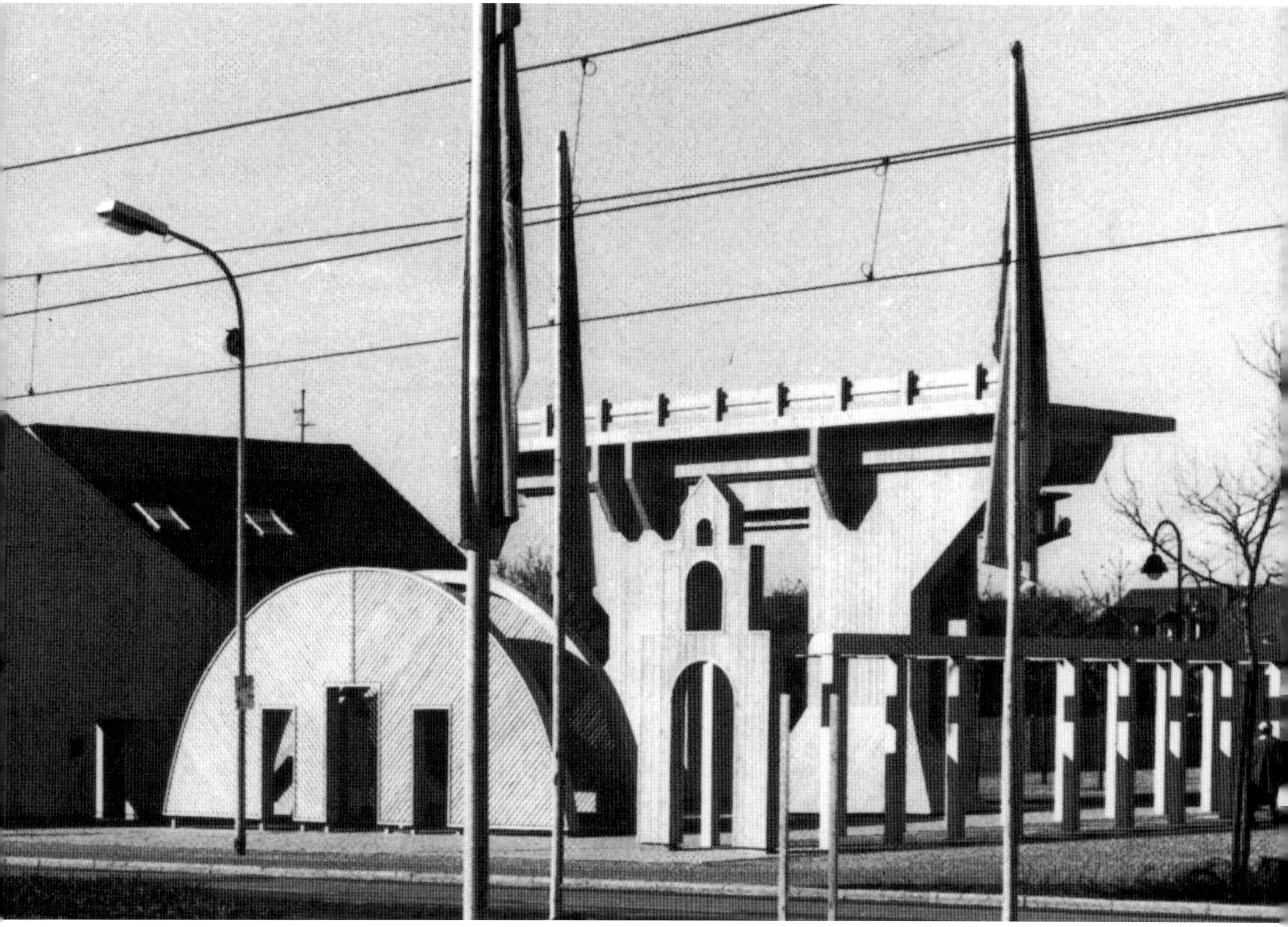

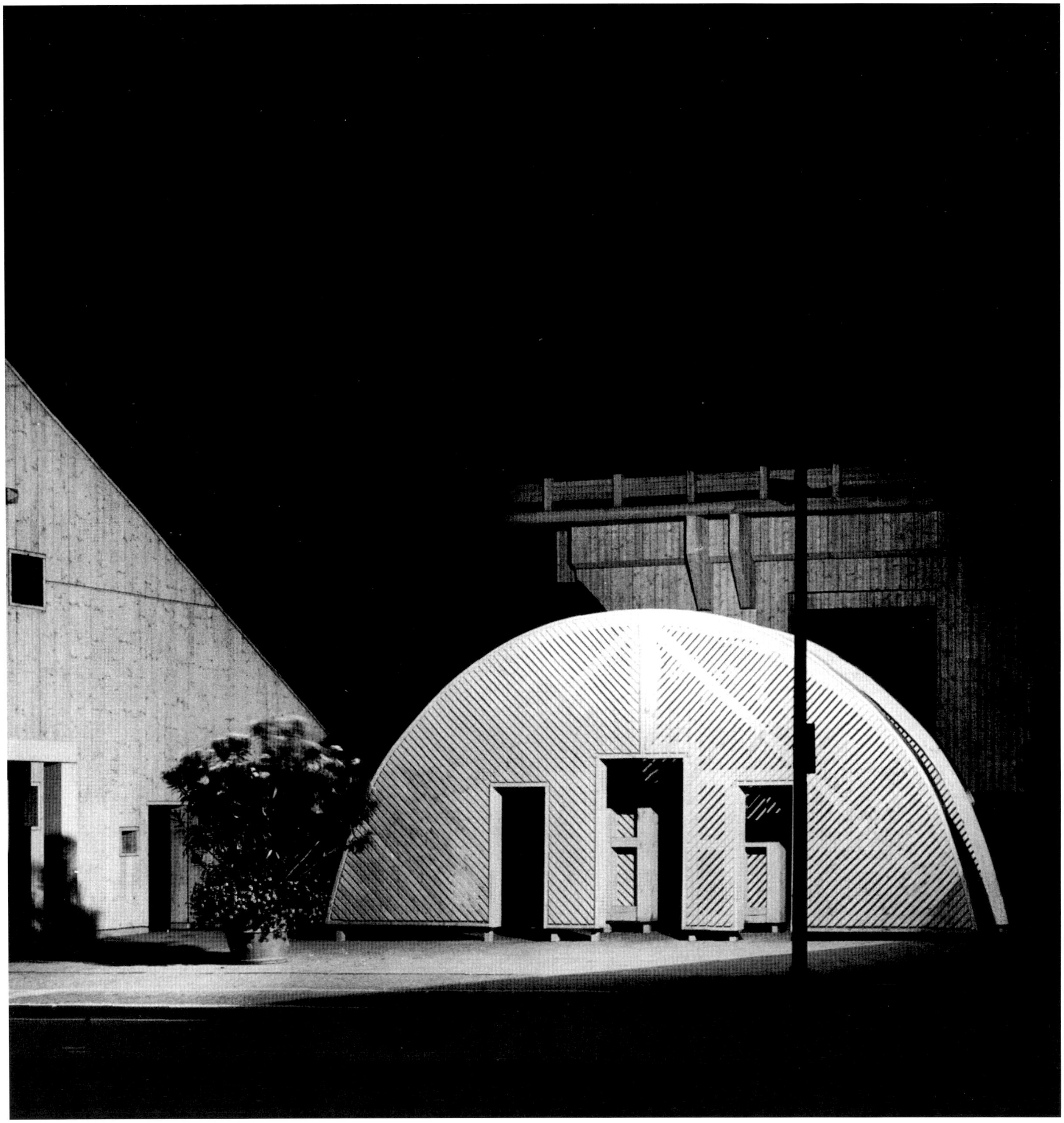

2. Night view of the Betzenhausener Torplatz. (Photo: Hans Dieter Schaal, 1986.)
3. Betzenhausener Torplatz. A detail view of the wooden gate structures. (Photo: Hans Dieter Schaal, 1986.)

2. Nachtansicht des Betzenhausener Torplatzes. (Photo: Hans Dieter Schaal, 1986.)
3. Betzenhausener Torplatz. Detailansicht der hölzernen Torbauten. (Photo: Hans Dieter Schaal, 1986.)

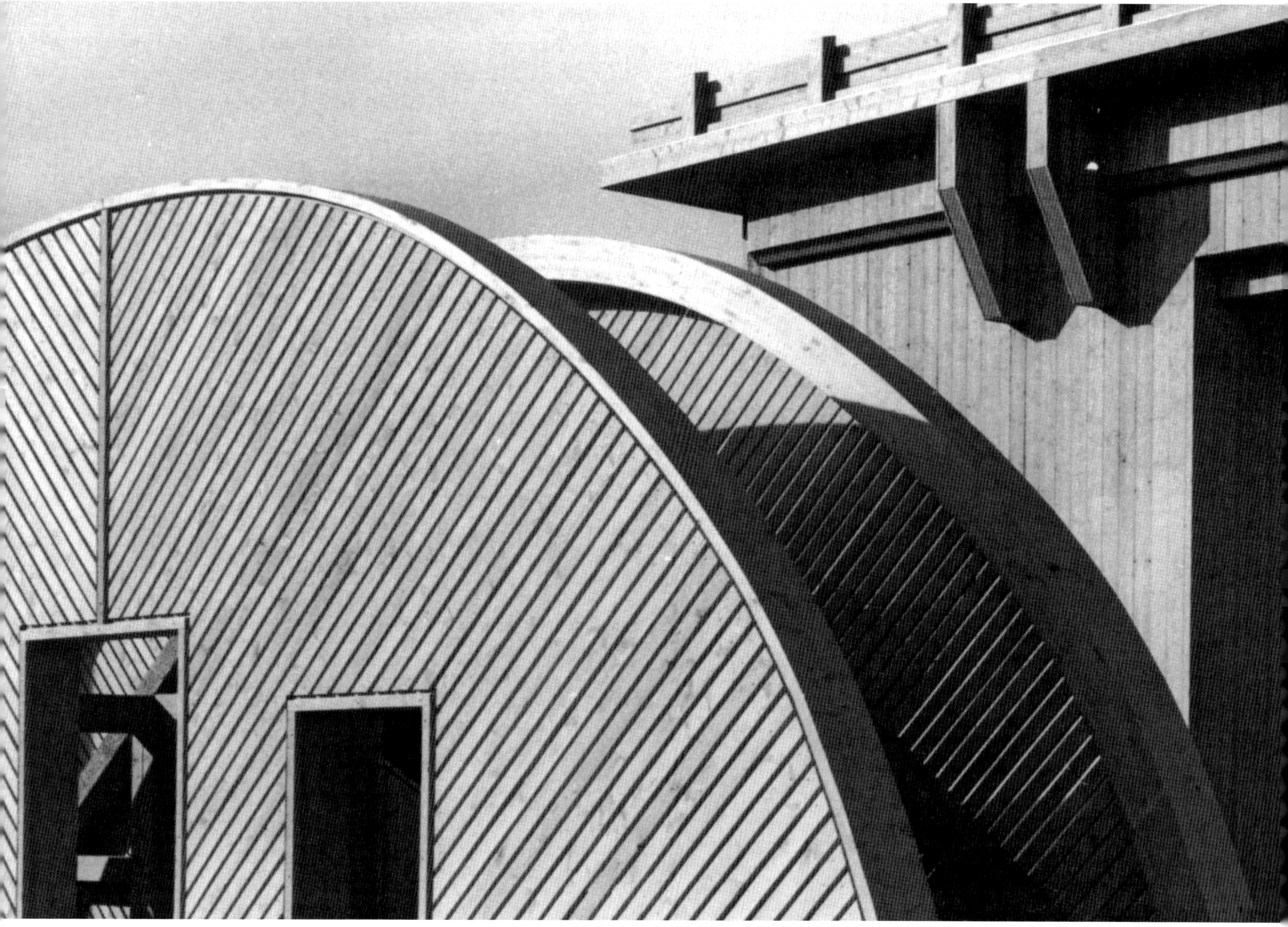

Bundesgartenschau 1995, Berlin, area of the Lehrter Bahnhof, 1987–1990. A preliminary design commissioned by the Buga-GmbH Berlin

The area to the south of today's new Berliner Hauptbahnhof (Berlin central station) has been lying neglected and overgrown since the end of the war. No one was interested in the fact that ruins and traces of the old Lehrter Bahnhof railway station and the former Ausstellungspalast (exhibition palace) of the Berlin Secession could be seen here.

As my thoughts and ideas for the Britzer Bundesgartenschau (Britz federal garden show) in Berlin had made a great impression on Buga managing director Hendrik Gottfriedsen, he invited me to submit proposals for the Bundesgartenschau Berlin 1995 (1995 Berlin federal garden show), for which this area was the selected site.

I investigated this wasteland landscape as a seeker after architectonic traces and a landscape archaeologist, and developed a concrete plan to give the impression of an interweaving of history, the present day, and the future. I wanted to present the existing vegetation, particularly the old trees at what was once the Secession entrance – and also the ruins – as messengers from the past. I therefore grouped many of my previously developed themes and motifs around a large round central meadow area with a ring of colourful flowers. On the periphery of the former Secession palace, I built glass walls with viewing terraces floating above. I reconstructed the foundation walls of the one-time exhibition halls at knee-height, and placed themed exhibitions on cereals, flowers, and routes within the open areas. I was particularly interested in the underworlds of plants and trees concealed in the earth.

To this was added my new theme: landscape spaces. As with my stage sets, I built rectangular living room space capsules whose front and rear walls existed only in fragmentary form or as windows, thus exposing clear views of artistically formed landscape and garden zones. They included painted images (e.g. views of oceans, mountains, and tropical jungles). The garden landscape merged into an exhibition of paintings (panoramas), and transformed into a framed nature/architecture composition with fictional long-distance views.

Unfortunately, the 1989 GDR peaceful revolution put a stop to this project. My publicly exhibited and much-discussed plans and models were quickly put aside after the reunification (they were later sent back to me at Attenweiler), and Herr Gottfriedsen looked for a suitable site in the new regions. In the end, the Bundesgartenschau 1995 took place without me in Cottbus.

Bundesgartenschau Berlin 1995, Gelände des Lehrter Bahnhofs, 1987–1990. Vorentwurf im Auftrag der Buga-GmbH Berlin

Seit Kriegsende lag das Gebiet südlich des heutigen, neuen Berliner Hauptbahnhofs brach und verwilderte still vor sich hin. Daß hier noch Ruinen und Spuren des alten Lehrter Bahnhofs und des ehemaligen Ausstellungspalastes der Berliner Sezession zu sehen waren, interessierte niemand.

Da meine Überlegungen und Ideen zur Britzer Bundesgartenschau in Berlin beim Buga-Geschäftsführer Hendrik Gottfriedsen großen Eindruck hinterlassen hatten, lud er mich ein, Vorschläge für die Bundesgartenschau Berlin 1995 auf diesem ausgewählten Gelände zu machen.

Als architektonischer Spurensucher und Landschaftsarchäologe untersuchte ich die verwilderte Landschaft und entwickelte einen konkreten Plan, der wie ein Geflecht aus Geschichte, Gegenwart und Zukunft wirken sollte. Die vorhandene Vegetation, vor allem die alten Bäume beim einstigen Sezessionseingang, wollte ich – neben den Ruinenresten – als Botschafter der Vergangenheit inszenieren. Dazu gruppierte ich viele meiner bisher entwickelten Themen und Motive um einen großen, runden Zentralwiesenbereich mit buntem Blumenring. Im Randbereich des ehemaligen Sezessionspalastes baute ich Glashallen mit darüberschwebenden Aussichtsterrassen. Die Grundmauern der einstigen Ausstellungssäle rekonstruierte ich kniehoch und fügte in die Freibereiche Themenausstellungen über Getreide, Blumen und Wurzeln ein. Die in der Erde versteckten Unterwelten der Pflanzen und Bäume interessierten mich dabei besonders.

Dazu kam mein neues Thema: Landschaftsräume. Ich baute – ähnlich wie in meinen Bühnenbildern – rechteckige Wohnzimmer-Raumkapseln, deren Vorder- und Rückwände nur fragmentarisch oder als Fenster vorhanden waren und damit den Durchblick auf künstlich geformte Landschafts- und Gartenzonen, einschließlich gemalter Bilder (z.B. Blicke auf Meere, Gebirge und tropische Urwälder), frei gaben. Die Gartenlandschaft ging über in eine Gemäldeausstellung (Panoramen) und verwandelte sich in eine gerahmte Natur-Architektur-Komposition mit fiktiven Fernblicken.

Leider machte die »friedliche Revolution 1989 in der DDR« das Projekt zunichte. Meine öffentlich ausgestellten und viel diskutierten Pläne und Modelle wurden nach der Wiedervereinigung schnell zur Seite gelegt (später an mich nach Attenweiler zurückgeschickt) und Herr Gottfriedsen hielt Ausschau nach einem passenden Gelände in den neuen Ländern. Am Ende fand die Bundesgartenschau 1995 ohne mich in Cottbus statt.

1. Model (Photo: Hans Dieter Schaal.)
2. A view through one of the central »landscape rooms«, with patio doors opening onto the site of the former Berlin Secession. At the top of the flower meadow, where the foundation walls of the one-time exhibition halls are made visible, the reconstruction of the old Secession entrance building, with its glass dome. 1988/1989.

pp. 48/49
3. Overall plan. Floor plan showing Spree (at the lower edge), Humboldt harbour (on the right-hand side) and a tram line, incorporating the new Berlin central station zone (on the upper right-hand side). 1988/1989.

1. Modell. (Photo: Hans Dieter Schaal.)
2. Blick durch eines der zentralen »Landschaftszimmer« mit geöffneten Terrassentüren hinaus auf das Gelände der ehemaligen Berliner Sezession. Am Kopfende des Blumenfeldes mit den angedeuteten Grundmauern der einstigen Ausstellungssäle: die Rekonstruktion des alten Sezessionseingangsgebäudes mit Glaskuppel. 1988/1989.

S. 48/49
3. Gesamtplan. Grundriß mit Spree (am unteren Rand), Humboldthafen (am rechten Rand) und S-Bahntrasse, einschließlich Zone des neuen Berliner Hauptbahnhofs (am rechten oberen Rand). 1988/1989.

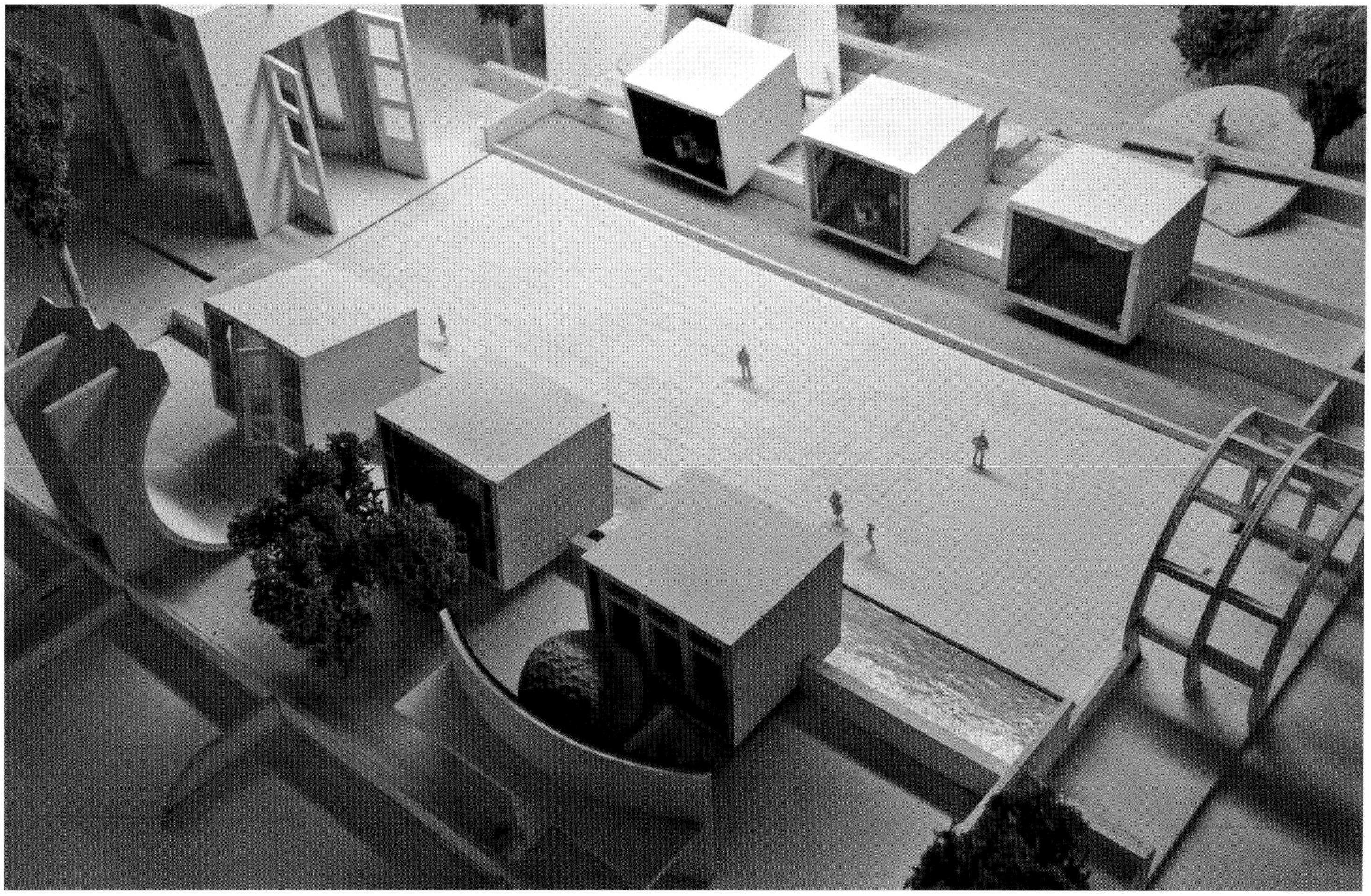

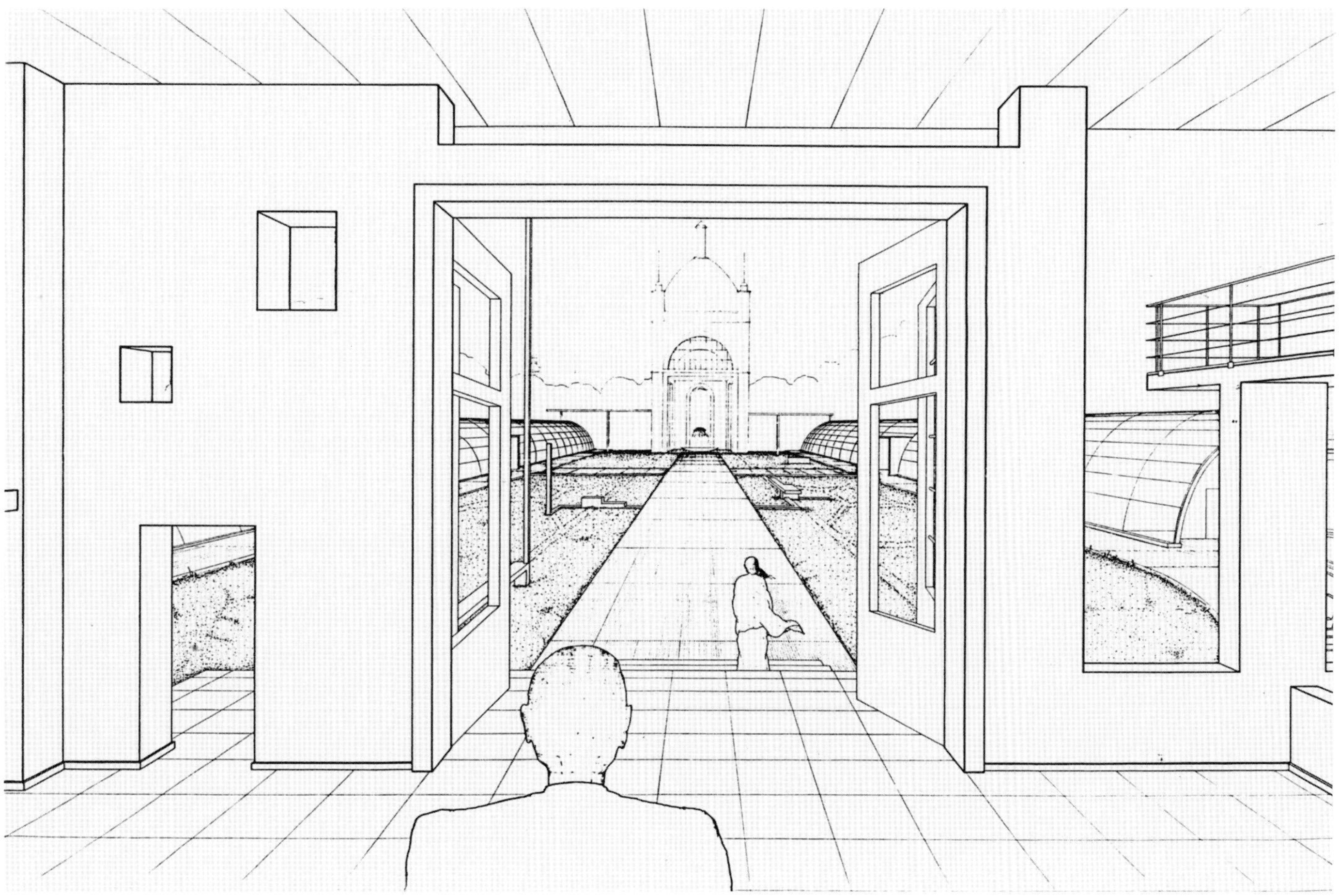

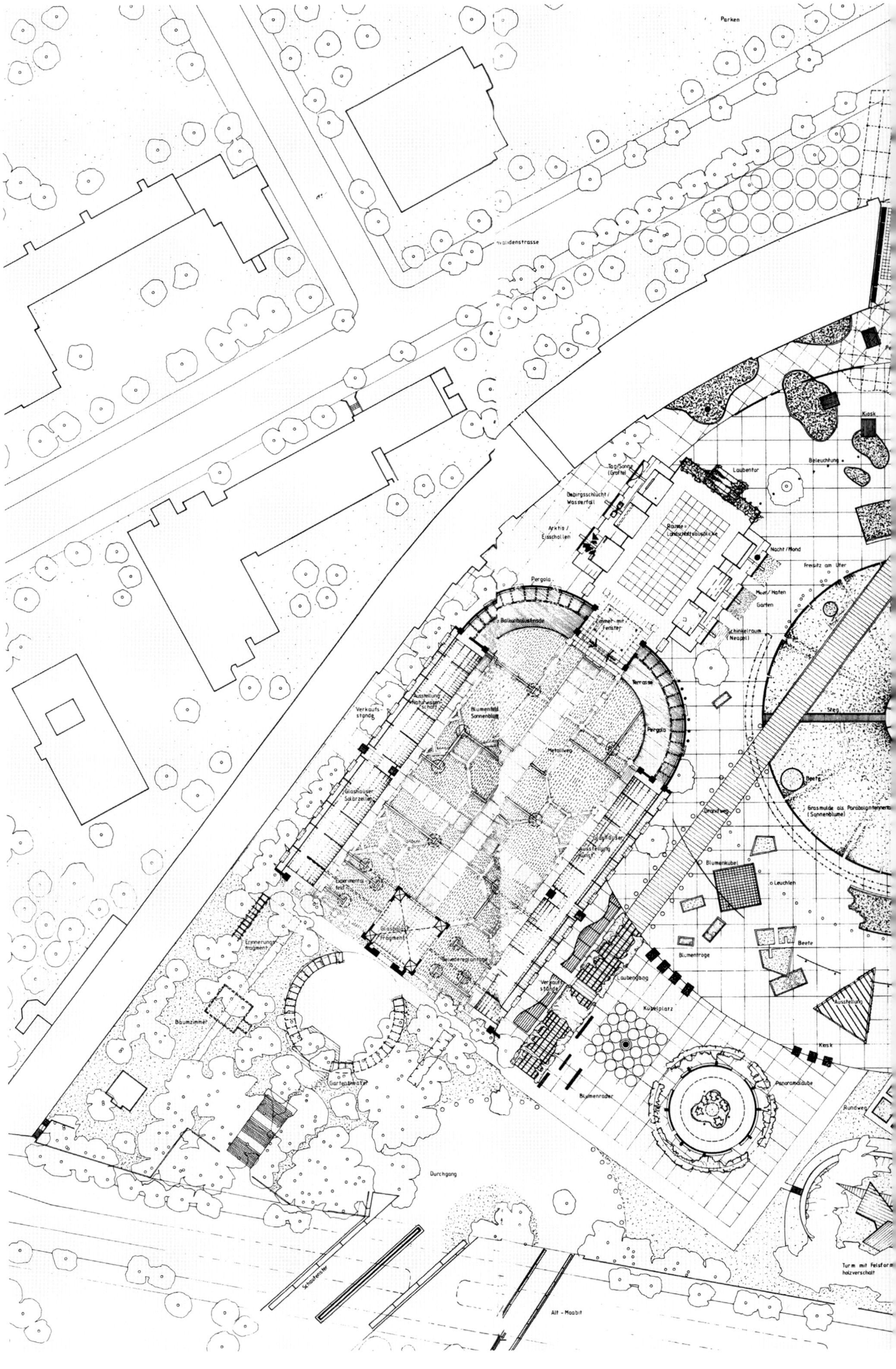
Parken
Tag/Sonne (Grotte)
Laubentor
Beleuchtung
Kiosk
Gebirgsschlucht / Wasserfall
Arktis / Eisschollen
Räume = Landschaftsausblicke
Nacht / Mond
Freisitz am Ufer
Meer / Hafen
Garten
Pergola
Zimmer mit Fenster
Schinkelraum (Neapel)
Terrasse
Steg
Metallweg
Beete
Granitweg
Verkaufsstände
Glashäuser Solarzellen
Glashäuser Ausstellung Kunst
Blumenkübel
Leuchten
Experimentalfeld
Glaspalast Fragment
Belvedereplantage
Blumentröge
Laubengang
Ausstellung
Erinnerungsfragment
Baumzimmer
Kübelplatz
Kiosk
Gartentheater
Panoramalaube
Blumenräder
Rundweg
Durchgang
Schaufenster
Alt - Moabit

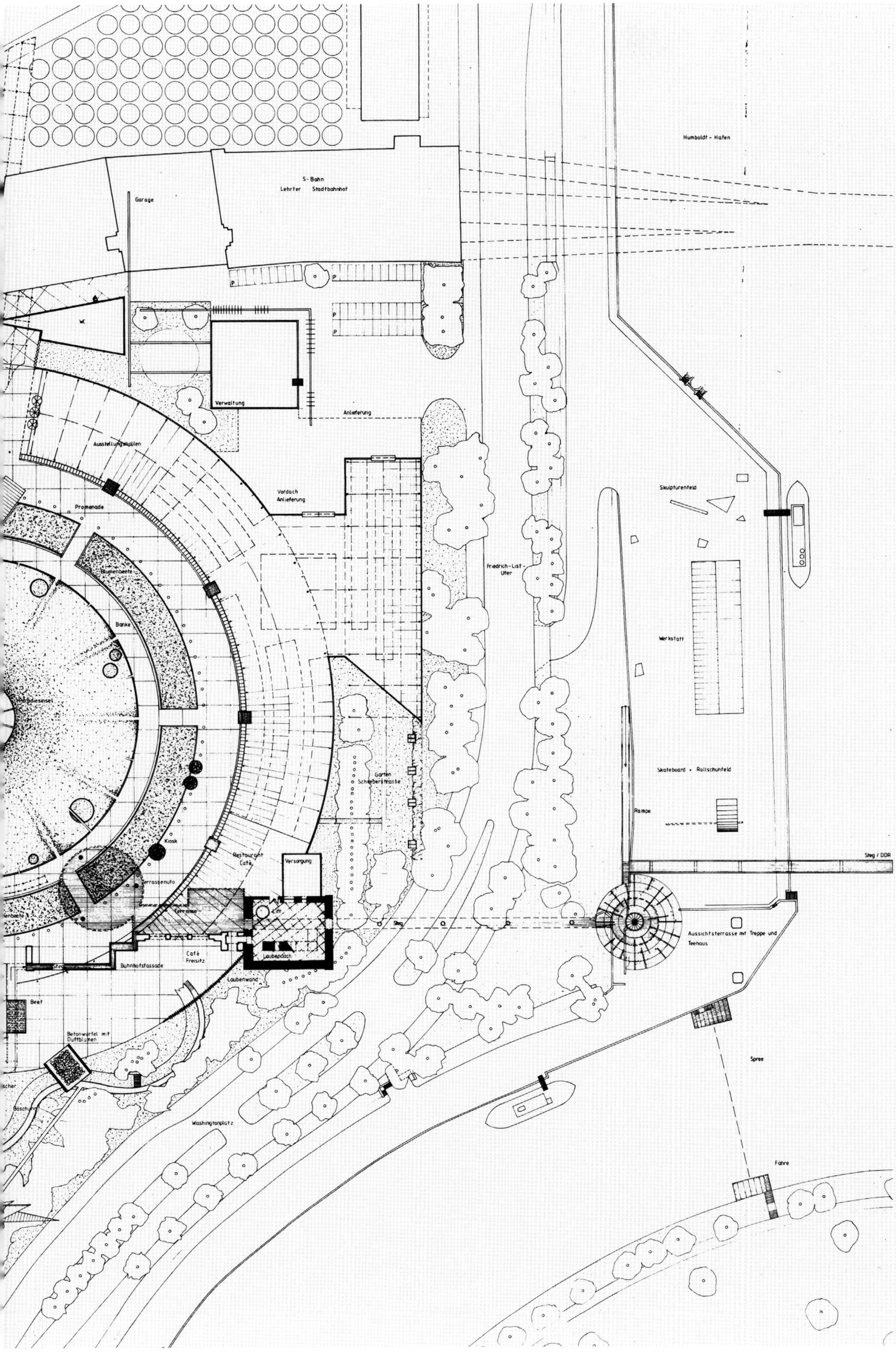

Humboldt - Hafen
S-Bahn
Lehrter Stadtbahnhof
Garage
WC
P
Verwaltung
Anlieferung
Ausstellungshallen
Vordach
Anlieferung
Promenade
Blumenbeete
Banke
Skulpturenfeld
Friedrich-List-Ufer
Werkstatt
Garten
Schreberstrasse
Skateboard + Rollschuhfeld
Rampe
Kiosk
Restaurant
Café
Versorgung
Steg / DDR
Terrassenufo
Terrasse
Lift
Steg
Aussichtsterrasse mit Treppe und
Teehaus
Café
Freisitz
Laubendach
Bahnhofsfassade
Laubenwand
Beet
Betonwürfel mit
Duftblumen
Böschung
Spree
Washingtonplatz
Fähre

»Hans Dieter Schaal – Architekturen 1970 to 1990«, exhibition at the Kunstgebäude Stuttgart, exhibition catalogue with contributions by Johann-Karl Schmidt, Frank R. Werner and Gerhard R. Koch

For this exhibition, I built 30 large (1 x 1 metre) park, garden, and plaza models, to represent my idea of a new landscape garden architecture. Although I do in fact love the colour green in all its shades (more than the varied colours of flowers), I produced these models in my usual grey (like the stage-set architectures and my pictures). With hindsight, I rather exaggerated this stylisation in the direction of the monochrome, in a way that was not appropriate to the theme.

Some of the models displayed proposals for poplar plantings. Avenues as we know them, but also avenues that dance freely out of their line, forming curves and waves, and thus forming entirely new tree spaces. In other models, quadratic, rectangular, and oval chestnut groves could be seen. There were also oak groves with central clearings. For these, I proposed arbours, pyramids, or a central bench where visitors could sit and consider who really occupied this central space in nature. I was always interested in the question of what could be made and formed through tree plantings – including suggestions of architecture – above and beyond our present-day notions and our conventional images? What kind of spaces, rooms, halls, paths, dramaturgies, content, and narratives could be created in this way, whilst referencing historical gardens?

The expressive language of trees is rich and varied: tall, proud poplars and cypresses, round, portly chestnut, birch, and walnut trees, venerable oaks, prickly pines and spruces, Gothic firs, cheerful, playful beeches, and melancholy weeping willows. All of these belong as they always have – in small, still-growing, and large versions – to my expressive repertoire (which is borrowed and taken from nature). Also, carefully integrated natural stone walls, wood, steel, and concrete constructions. Suggestions of houses, greened arcade walks, ruins, and doors.

The interweaving of natural, landscape, and architecture elements was important to me. Although I love exciting contrasts, I was primarily arguing for peaceful, supportive (hence the scaffolding aspect) and sometimes also stimulating and entertaining dialogues.

»Hans Dieter Schaal – Architekturen 1970–1990«, Ausstellung im Kunstgebäude Stuttgart, Ausstellungskatalog mit Beiträgen von Johann-Karl Schmidt, Frank R. Werner und Gerhard R. Koch

Für diese Ausstellung baute ich 30 große (1 x 1 Meter) Park-, Garten- und Platz-Modelle, in denen ich meine Vorstellung einer neuen Landschaftsgarten-Architektur darstellte. Obwohl ich eigentlich die Farbe Grün in allen Abstufungen sehr liebe (mehr als die Buntheit der Blumen), wählte ich für diese Modelle mein übliches Grau (wie bei den Bühnenarchitekturen und meinen Bildern). Im Rückblick eine etwas übertriebene Stilisierung in Richtung Monochrom, die dem Thema nicht gerade entsprach.

Einige Modelle zeigten Vorschläge für Pappelpflanzungen. Alleen, wie wir sie kennen, Alleen, die aus der Reihe tanzen, Bögen und Wellen formen, dabei vollkommen neue Baum-Räume bilden. In anderen Modellen waren quadratische, rechteckige und ovale Kastanien-Haine zu sehen. Auch Eichen-Haine mit Lichtungen in der Mitte. Hier schlug ich Lauben, Pyramiden oder eine zentrale Bank vor, auf der Besucher sitzend darüber nachdenken konnten, wer diese Natur-Mitte wirklich einnimmt. Mir ging es immer um die Frage: Was läßt sich mit Baumpflanzungen – einschließlich architektonischer Andeutungen – jenseits unserer heutigen Vorstellungen und gewohnten Bilder alles machen und formen? Welche Art Räume, Säle, Hallen, Wege, Dramaturgien, Inhalte und Erzählungen könnten – in Anknüpfung an historische Gärten – dabei entstehen?

Die Ausdruckssprache der Bäume ist reich und vielfältig: Es gibt die steilen, stolzen Pappeln und Zypressen, die runden, behäbigen Kastanien-, Buchen- und Nußbäume, die altehrwürdigen Eichen, die stachligen Pinien und Kiefern, die gotischen Tannen, die fröhlich-verspielten Birken und die melancholischen Trauerweiden. Sie alle gehörten und gehören – in kleinen, wachsenden und großen Versionen – zu meinem (geliehenen, aus der Natur übernommenen) Ausdrucksrepertoire. Dazu vorsichtig eingeflochtene Natursteinwände, Holz-, Stahl- und Beton-Konstruktionen. Angedeutete Häuser, eingegrünte Laubengänge, Ruinen und Türen.

Die Verflechtung von Natur-, Landschafts- und Architektur-Elementen war mir wichtig. Obwohl ich spannungsvolle Gegensätze liebe, plädierte ich primär für friedliche, unterstützende (Gerüstaspekt), manchmal auch geistreich-unterhaltende Dialoge.

1. Walled poplar grove. Model.
2. Poplar planting. Model.

1. Ummauerter Pappelhain. Modell.
2. Pappelpflanzungen. Modell.

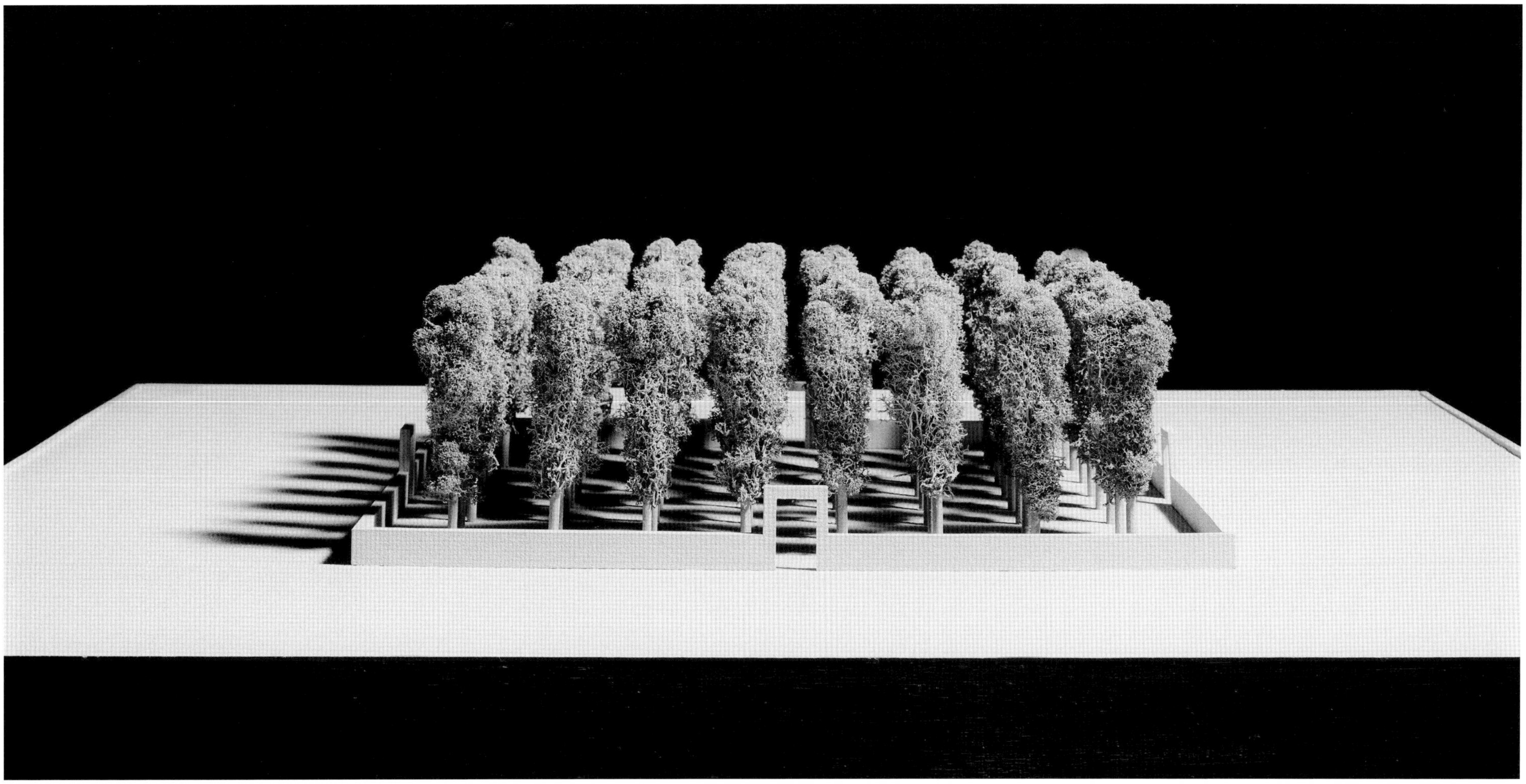

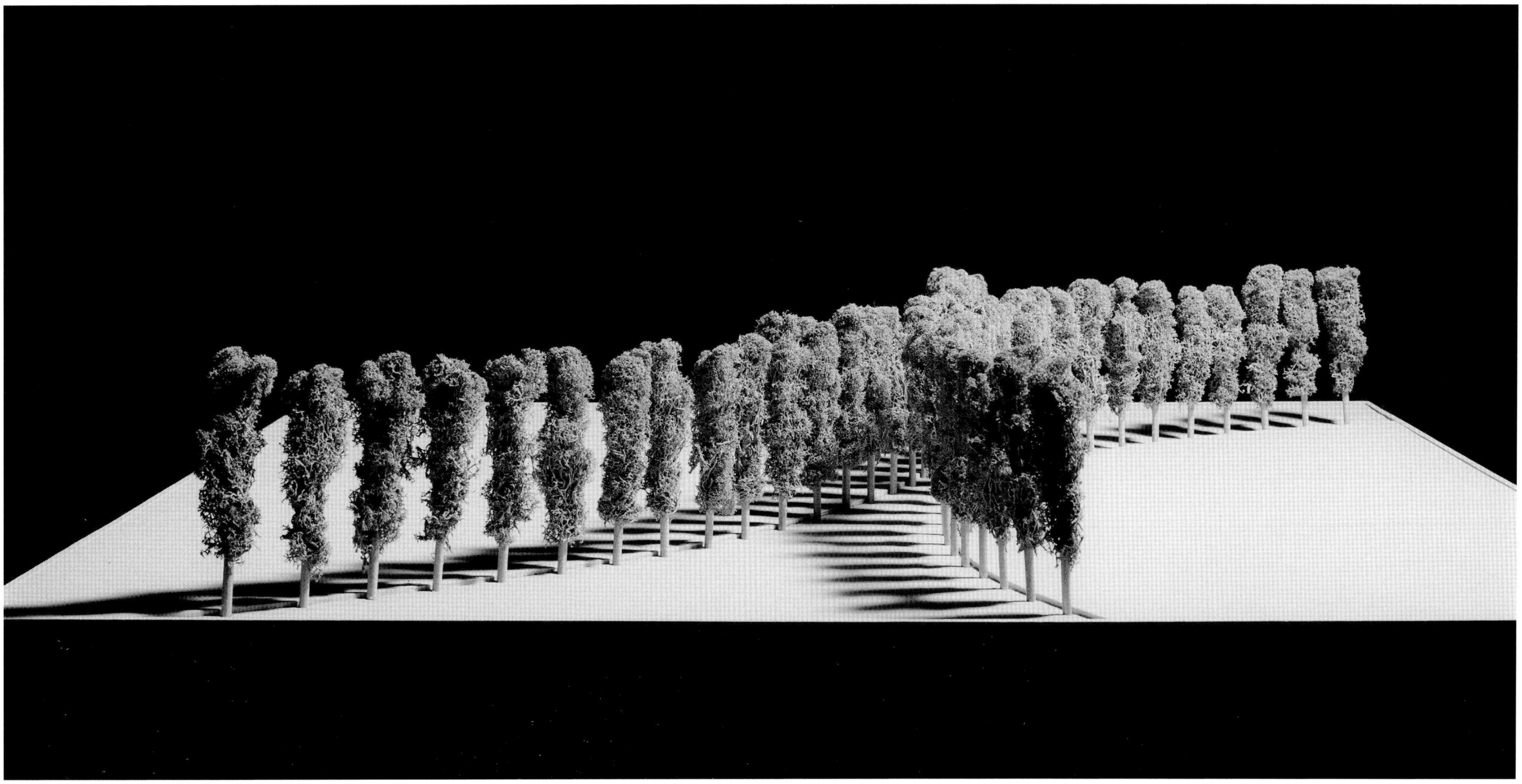

New Landscape Architecture, created between 1990 and 1994, published by Ernst & Sohn, Berlin, 1994

I spent four years working on this 380 page book. I wanted to bring together all of my thoughts, insights, and planning proposals on the subject of »landscape and garden design« and »new landscape architecture« up to that point. In doing so, I also looked back (without anger) at the garden motifs of ancient Rome, the Renaissance, the Baroque, the classical era, and romanticism. In all ages, trees and bodies of water have looked the same, and always will. It is only human garden and park compositions, their path systems and narrative content, that have changed, and continue to change.

In the 20th century, human beings were predominantly arrogant with regard to their natural environment. This led to garden and park language dwindling into something functional. The new Volkspark is open to almost all potential uses. However, some nature enthusiasts switched to allotment gardening and rambling movements, or joined esoteric nudist oases. Art now played barely any role. The Bauhaus doctrine neglected nature and landscape almost entirely. Unfortunately, the Nazis did pay excessive attention to nature, conflating it with »blood and soil«. It was only at the end of the 20th century that the pendulum swung back the other way in favour of natural landscapes, in reaction to industrial destruction of nature and threats to the environment.

In my book, I continued the path embarked on in Stuttgart and Rome. Above all, I was drawn to the combining of old garden motifs with new images from industrial and urban reality, but also from theatre and film, tourism, sport, children's games, and entertainment.

The book did not set out any new theory. Instead, it aimed to prompt the reader to expand their own notions and fantasies of garden and park designs. I was therefore particularly pleased about the moving foreword written by English landscape garden designer Geoffrey Jellicoe (renowned and conscious of tradition, and much admired by me) for the British/American edition of my book, in 1993 (shortly before his death). I quote its closing sentence:

»… Study these pages, dear reader, and you will initially be confused, but will later be charmed and finally – who knows – curiously inspired.«

Hence the book's English title: *Landscape as inspiration*.

***Neue Landschaftsarchitektur,* entstanden zwischen 1990 und 1994, erschienen bei Ernst & Sohn, Berlin, 1994**

An dem 380-seitigen Buch arbeitete ich vier Jahre lang. Mir ging es darum, alle meine bisherigen Überlegungen, Erkenntnisse und Planungsvorschläge zu den Themen »Landschafts- und Gartengestaltung« und »neue Landschaftsarchitektur« zusammenzufassen. Dabei warf ich auch einen Blick zurück (ohne Zorn) auf die Gartenmotive der römischen Antike, der Renaissance, des Barock, der klassischen Zeit und der Romantik. Bäume und Wasserflächen sahen und sehen zu allen Zeiten gleich aus. Nur die menschlichen Garten- und Park-Kompositionen, die Wegführungen und Erzählinhalte, veränderten und verändern sich.

Im 20. Jahrhundert überwog die Übermütigkeit der Menschen gegenüber ihrer natürlichen Umwelt. Dadurch verkümmerte auch die Garten- und Park-Sprache zu etwas Funktionalem. Die neuen Volksparks ließen fast alle Nutzungsmöglichkeiten offen. Manche naturbegeisterten Menschen allerdings wechselten zur Schrebergarten- und Wandervogelbewegung oder traten in esoterische FKK-Oasen ein. Der Kunstaspekt spielte kaum noch eine Rolle. In der Bauhauslehre wurden Natur und Landschaft fast ganz übersehen. Dafür warfen leider die Nazis einen überstarken Blut-und-Boden-Blick darauf. Erst gegen Ende des 20. Jahrhunderts schlug das Pendel, ausgelöst durch die industriellen Naturzerstörungen und Umweltbedrohungen, wieder zugunsten der Naturlandschaften um.

Ich verfolgte in meinem Buch weiter jenen Weg, den ich bereits in Stuttgart und Rom eingeschlagen hatte. Mich reizte vor allem die Verbindung von alten Gartenmotiven mit neuen Bildern aus der industriellen und städtischen Realität, aber auch aus dem Theater- und Film-Bereich, dem Tourismus, dem Sport, dem Kinderspiel und der Unterhaltung.

Das Buch stellte keine neue Theorie auf, sondern wollte die Leser zur Erweiterung der eigenen Garten- und Parkgestaltungsvorstellungen und -phantasien anregen. Deswegen freute ich mich besonders über das Vorwort des von mir bewunderten, berühmten und traditionsbewußten englischen Landschafts- und Gartengestalters Geoffrey Jellicoe, der für die englisch-amerikanische Ausgabe meines Buches 1993 (kurz vor seinem Tod) ein bewegendes Vorwort schrieb, dessen Schlußsatz ich hier zitiere:

»… Lieber Leser, erforsche diese Seiten, und Du wirst zunächst verwirrt sein, dann entzückt und schließlich – wer weiß! – auf unerklärliche Weise inspiriert.«

Deswegen lautete der englische Buchtitel: *Landscape as inspiration*.

1–3. Some sketches from the book. Scenes in a park, inspired by film set constructions in Cinecittá, Rome's film city. 1990/1993.

1–3. Einige Skizzen aus diesem Buch. Szenen im Park, angeregt durch Filmsetaufbauten in der römischen Filmstadt Cinecittá. 1990/1993.

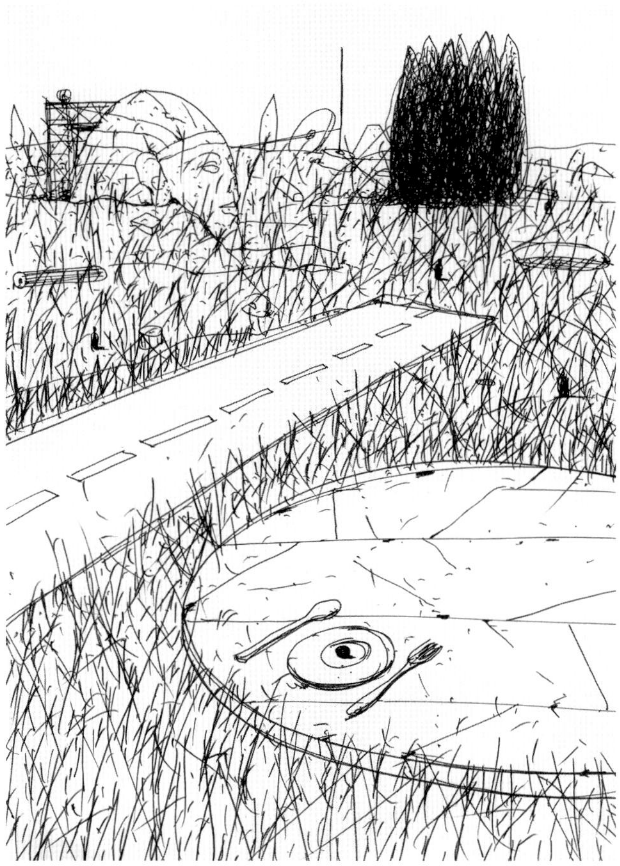

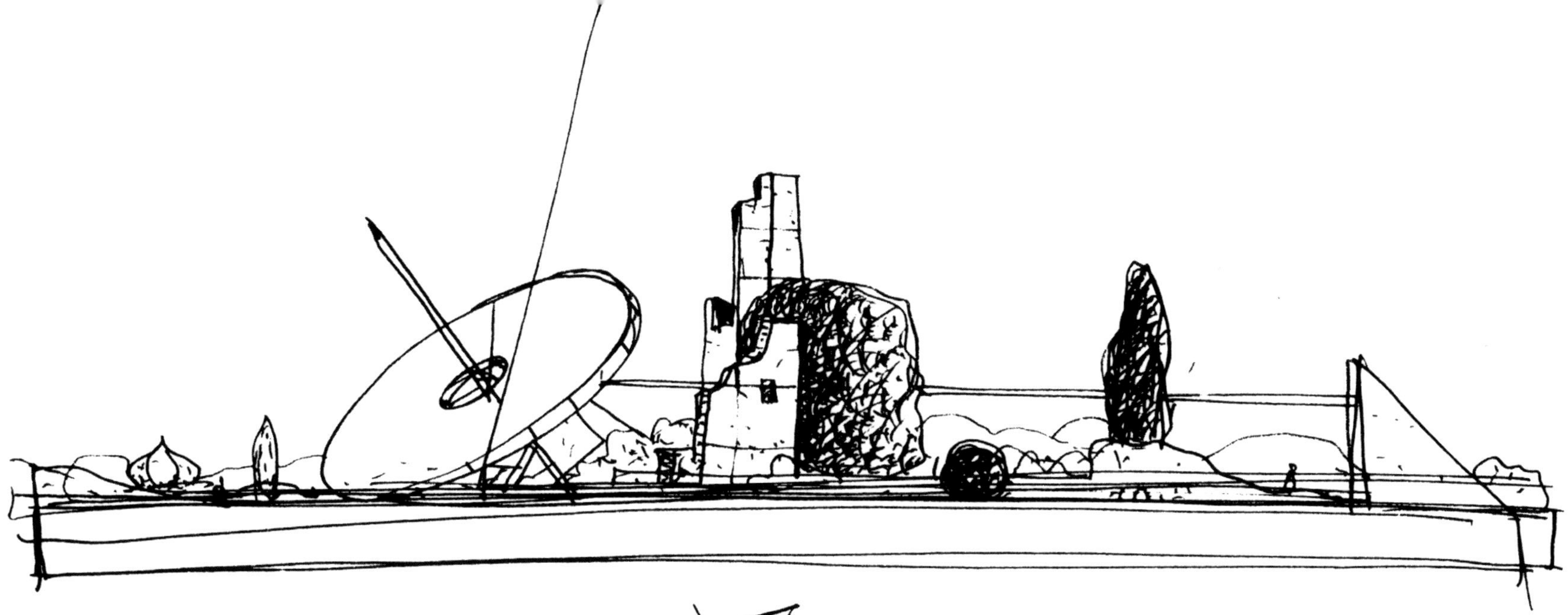

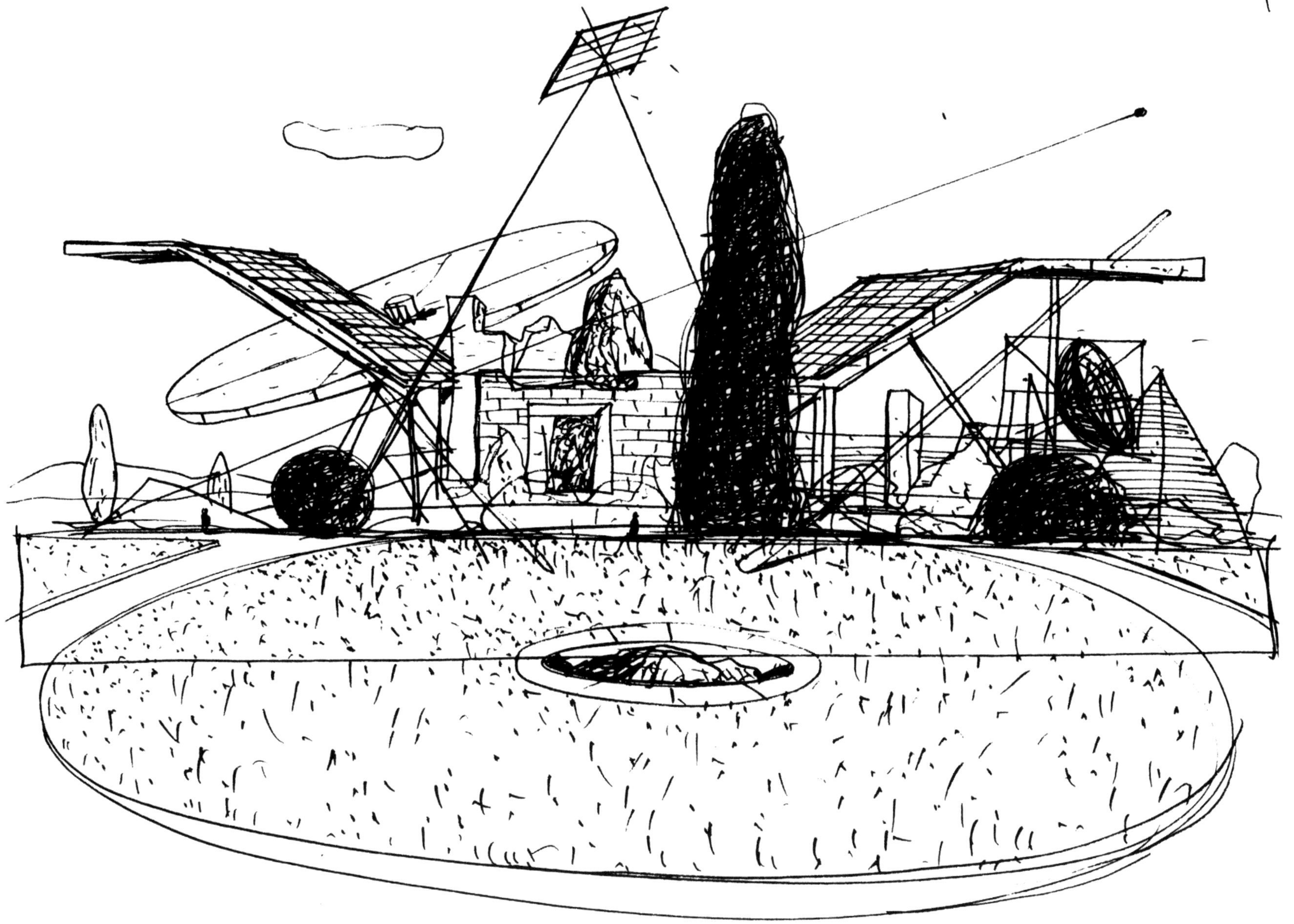

Villa Moser-Leibfried and »Stangenwald«, Stuttgart, 1993. Two art installations erected in connection with the Internationale Gartenbauausstellung – IGA and still standing in the same location today

With the Internationale Gartenbauausstellung 1993 (the 1993 international garden exhibition), Hans Luz succeeded in closing the »Green U« that he had initiated, and in thereby completing it. Thus, a very extensive, park-like green corridor had been created between the Stuttgarter Hauptbahnhof (Stuttgart central station), the upper and lower Schloßgarten, the Berger Sprudler (mineral baths), the Rosensteinpark, the Leibfried garden at Pragsattel, and the Killesberg. An enormous inner-city landscape undertaking, into which, during the IGA-1993, ten art installations were integrated, in addition to the »Gardens of the World« and numerous flower exhibitions. The project was headed by Frank R. Werner. He selected eight globally active garden and landscape artists, and invited them to develop projects for Stuttgart. I developed two projects: Villa Moser-Leibfried and »Stangenwald«.

Villa Moser-Leibfried

Circa 1875, Stuttgart's Eduard Otto Moser, wealthy owing to his confectionery and chocolate-producing business, had a fine villa built for himself in the neo-Renaissance style on the Pragsattel. He modelled it on the Villa Berg (close by but lower-lying) which belonged to the crown prince (subsequently king) Karl I. Following the death of the villa's bourgeois founder and his wife, the private gentleman Karl Ernst Leibfried bought the villa property – along with its regularly laid-out garden, which included a fountain grotto, a cascade, and a sequoia. In 1944, the villa and park were destroyed in a bombing raid. Only the sequoia and remnants of the cellar, the drive, and the terraces survived this catastrophe. The ruined site was subsequently neglected, and was taken over by a positive jungle of vegetation. In 1955, the city of Stuttgart purchased the site, but let it continue to lie unused and running wild.

The Villa Moser-Leibfried did not emerge again into the public consciousness until circa 1990 and the Internationale Gartenbauausstellung and the aforementioned »Green U initiatives«. Initially, Herman de Vries, one of the participating landscape artists, proposed erecting a fence around the ruined site and leaving this wasteground to nature and its opportunist vegetation. However, the garden show planners wanted visitors to be able to view the site, without actually setting foot on it. And so I became involved and designed a walkway and step system that adversely affected the site's Romantic ruined condition as little as possible. I did not pretend to reconstruct the villa. My aim was a path of discovery through the wilderness, with only a few suggestions of architecture: drive, entrance steps, an arbour-like entrance gate, birdhouses, walkways with viewing pavilions, and steps down to the former garden area.

During the Internationale Gartenbauausstellung, the whole site was fenced off on a large scale. One had to pay entrance money in order to get in. Shortly after the end of the exhibition, the fence was removed, allowing visitors to wander over the walkways of my art installation night or day. As a result, vandals and individuals with spray cans held their destructive parties here, throwing rubbish and bottles into the open cellar areas. Not one plank was safe from them. After a short time, ruin was added to ruin. No one put a stop to these unwelcome activities, and no one turned up to do repairs. Apparently, the Stuttgart garden authorities did not have sufficient money or staff. The site was no longer cared for at all. Eventually, fur actuarial reasons, the Moser-Leibfried site was closed off with fences and boards. It appears that Herman de Vries's concept ultimately triumphed – that is, if it is to remain this way?

»Stangenwald«

Although I have no objection to the slow greening of my Villa Moser-Leibfried art installation, this 25-meter-wide and 36-meter-long site was initially intended as an artistic, stylised woodland architecture zone with a bare, white steel pergola and no overgrowth. The 67 white concrete pillars, each with a diameter of 36 centimetres, grow out of the intersection points of the quadratic panel structure. On the plaza's periphery, five pillars lie unprocessed and not erected. A fictional permanent building site?

Frank R. Werner described this plaza in a series of very poetic sentences:

»… A petrified forest.

Suggestions of a space, half nature, half pillared hall, between the worlds. ... Unclear as regards function. Entrance hall, gates form themselves and dissolve into interstitial spaces, sundial. Light rake, time trap, labyrinth. As yet not architecture, and no longer so. Building site of the forest, and building site for a house.

The roof is absent, is dissolved into a grid, arcades, arbour hall, geometry, steps.
Going, staying.
Artificial nature, natural nature …
Going in lines.
Going in serpentine lines.
Circles of going.
Vortexes, rhythms,
Melodies …
Rising and falling.
Geometry.«

Villa Moser-Leibfried und »Stangenwald«, Stuttgart, 1993. Zwei Kunstinstallationen, die im Rahmen der Internationalen Gartenbauausstellung – IGA errichtet wurden und heute noch an Ort und Stelle stehen

Mit der Internationalen Gartenbauausstellung 1993 gelang es Hans Luz, das von ihm initiierte »Grüne U« zu schließen und damit zu vollenden. Es bedeutet, daß zwischen Stuttgarter Hauptbahnhof, dem oberen und unteren Schloßgarten, den Berger Sprudlern (Mineralbäder), dem Rosensteinpark, dem Leibfriedschen Garten am Pragsattel und dem Killesberg eine sehr weitläufige, parkartige Grünverbindung geschaffen wurde. Ein riesiges, innerstädtisches Landschaftsunternehmen, in das während der IGA-1993 – neben den »Gärten der Welt« und zahlreichen Blumenausstellungen – auch zehn Kunstinstallationen integriert waren. Dieses Projekt leitete Frank R. Werner. Er suchte acht weltweit tätige Garten- und Landschaftskünstler aus und lud sie ein, Projekte für Stuttgart zu entwickeln. Zwei davon stammen von mir: Villa Moser-Leibfried und »Stangenwald«.

Villa Moser-Leibfried, Stuttgart, 1993

Um 1875 ließ sich der zu Reichtum gekommene Stuttgarter Konditor und Schokoladenfabrikant Eduard Otto Moser eine stattliche Villa im Neorenaissance-Stil auf dem Pragsattel errichten. Sein Vorbild war die nicht weit entfernte, aber tiefer gelegene Villa Berg des württembergischen Kronprinzen und späteren Königs Karl I. Nach dem Tod des bürgerlichen Erbauers und seiner Ehefrau kaufte der Privatier Karl Ernst Leibfried das Villenanwesen mit streng angelegtem Garten, einschließlich Brunnengrotte, Kaskade und einem Mammutbaum. 1944 wurden Villa und Park bei einem Bombenangriff zerstört. Nur der Mammutbaum und Reste des Kellers, der Vorfahrt und der Terrassen überstanden die Katastrophe. Danach blieb das Ruinengelände unbeachtet und urwaldartige Vegetation nahm davon Besitz. 1955 erwarb die Stadt Stuttgart das Grundstück, ließ es jedoch weiterhin ungenutzt verwildern.

Erst mit der Internationalen Gartenbauausstellung und den besagten »Grünen-U-Bestrebungen« trat die Villa Moser-Leibfried um 1990 wieder ins öffentliche Bewußtsein. Zunächst schlug Herman de Vries, einer der mitbeteiligten Landschaftskünstler, vor, einen Zaun um das Ruinengelände zu errichten und die verwilderte Zone endgültig der Natur und ihrer Zufallsvegetation zu überlassen. Die Gartenschauplaner jedoch wollten, daß die Besucher das Gelände besichtigen können, ohne es allerdings zu betreten. So kam ich ins Spiel und entwarf ein Steg- und Treppensystem, das so wenig wie möglich verletzend in den romantischen Ruinenzustand eingreift und außerdem nicht vorgibt, die Villa zu rekonstruieren. Mein Ziel war ein Entdeckerweg durch die Wildnis mit wenigen Architekturandeutungen: Vorfahrt, Eingangstreppe, Eingangstor als Laube, Vogelhäuser, Stege mit Aussichtspavillons und Treppen in den früheren Gartenbereich hinunter.

Während der Internationalen Gartenbauausstellung war das Gesamtgelände weiträumig umzäunt. Man mußte Eintritt bezahlen, um hineinzukommen. Kurz nach Ende der Ausstellung wurde der Zaun entfernt und Besucher konnten Tag und Nacht auch über die Stege meiner Kunstinstallation wandern. Die Folge: Vandalen und Sprayer feierten hier abends und nachts ihre Zerstörungsparties, warfen Müll und Flaschen in die offenen Kellerbereiche. Kein Brett war mehr sicher vor ihnen. Nach kurzer Zeit fügte sich Ruine in Ruine. Niemand bremste die unerfreulichen Aktivitäten, niemand tauchte auf und reparierte. Das Stuttgarter Gartenbauamt hatte weder Geld noch Personal dafür, wie man sagte. Es fand überhaupt keine Pflege mehr statt. Irgendwann wurde aus versicherungstechnischen Gründen das Moser-Leibfried-Gelände mit Zaun und Brettern abgesperrt, so daß das Konzept von Herman de Vries letztlich zu siegen scheint. Ob es dabei bleiben wird?

»Stangenwald«, Stuttgart, 1993

Während ich gegen die langsame Eingrünung meiner Villa Moser-Leibfried-Kunst-Installation nichts einzuwenden habe, ist dieser 25 Meter breite und 36 Meter lange Platz von Anfang an als künstlich-stilisierte, unbewachsene Wald-Architektur-Zone mit kahler, weißer Stahl-Pergola gedacht gewesen. Die 67 weißen Betonsäulen mit einem Durchmesser von 35 Zentimeter wachsen aus den Schnittpunkten der quadratischen Plattenstruktur. Fünf Säulen liegen unverarbeitet und nicht aufgestellt am Rand des Platzes. Eine fiktive Dauerbaustelle?

Frank R. Werner beschrieb den Platz im offiziellen IGA-Kunstkatalog mit sehr poetischen Sätzen:

»… Ein versteinerter Wald.
Ein angedeuteter Raum, halb Natur, halb Säulenhalle, zwischen den Welten. … Unklar in der Funktion. Eingangshalle, Tore bilden sich, lösen sich auf in Zwischenräume, Sonnenuhr. Lichtrechen, Zeitfalle, Labyrinth.

Noch keine Architektur und keine mehr. Baustelle des Waldes und Baustelle zum Haus.

Das Dach fehlt, ist aufgelöst in ein Raster, Laubengänge, Laubenhalle, Geometrie, Schritte.
Gehen, bleiben.
Künstliche Natur, natürliche Natur …
Gehen in Linien.
Gehen in Serpentinen.
Kreisen des Gehens.
Verwirbelungen, Rhythmen,
Melodien …
Aufsteigend und fallend.
Geometrie.«

1. Villa Moser-Leibfried. A view of the former drive and the villa entrance between two giant chestnut trees. The entrance gate has been transformed into a semicircular arbour gate, with birdhouses on a system of poles. Anyone entering this gate did not get far. The path ended in a cul-de-sac, at a railing. From here, visitors could see only the ruined remains of the cellar area, with lush opportunistic vegetation. All of the photos that follow show the state of the site shortly before the IGA's opening in 1993.
2. Isometrtic view of the whole complex.

1. Villa Moser-Leibfried. Blick auf die ehemalige Vorfahrt und den Villeneingang zwischen zwei riesigen Kastanienbäumen. Das Eingangstor hat sich in ein halbrundes Laubentor mit Vogelhäusern auf einem Stangensystem verwandelt. Wer eintrat, kam nicht weit. Der Weg endete sackgassenartig an einem Geländer. Besucher sahen von hier aus nur auf die Ruinenreste der Kellerzone, dazu die üppige Zufallsvegetation. Alle nachfolgenden Photos zeigen den Zustand kurz vor der IGA-Eröffnung 1993.
2. Isometrie der Gesamtanlage.

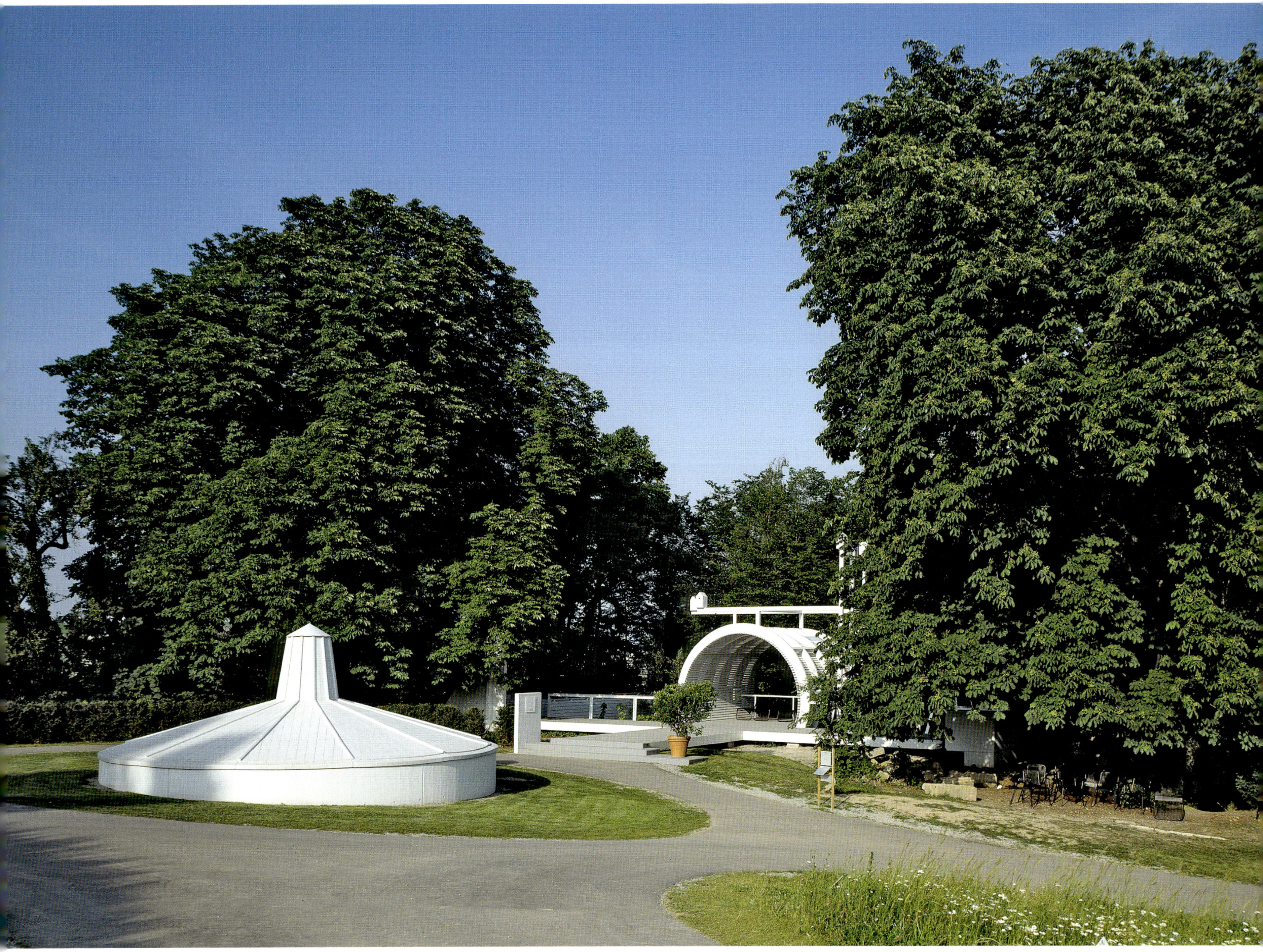

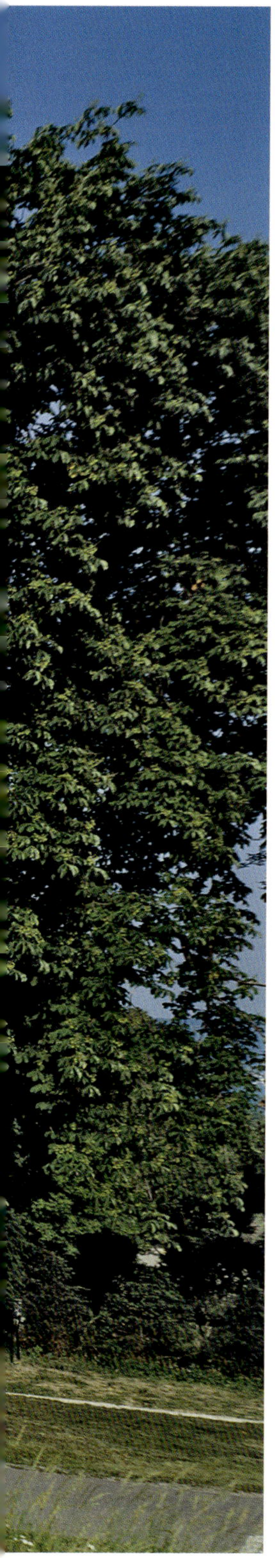

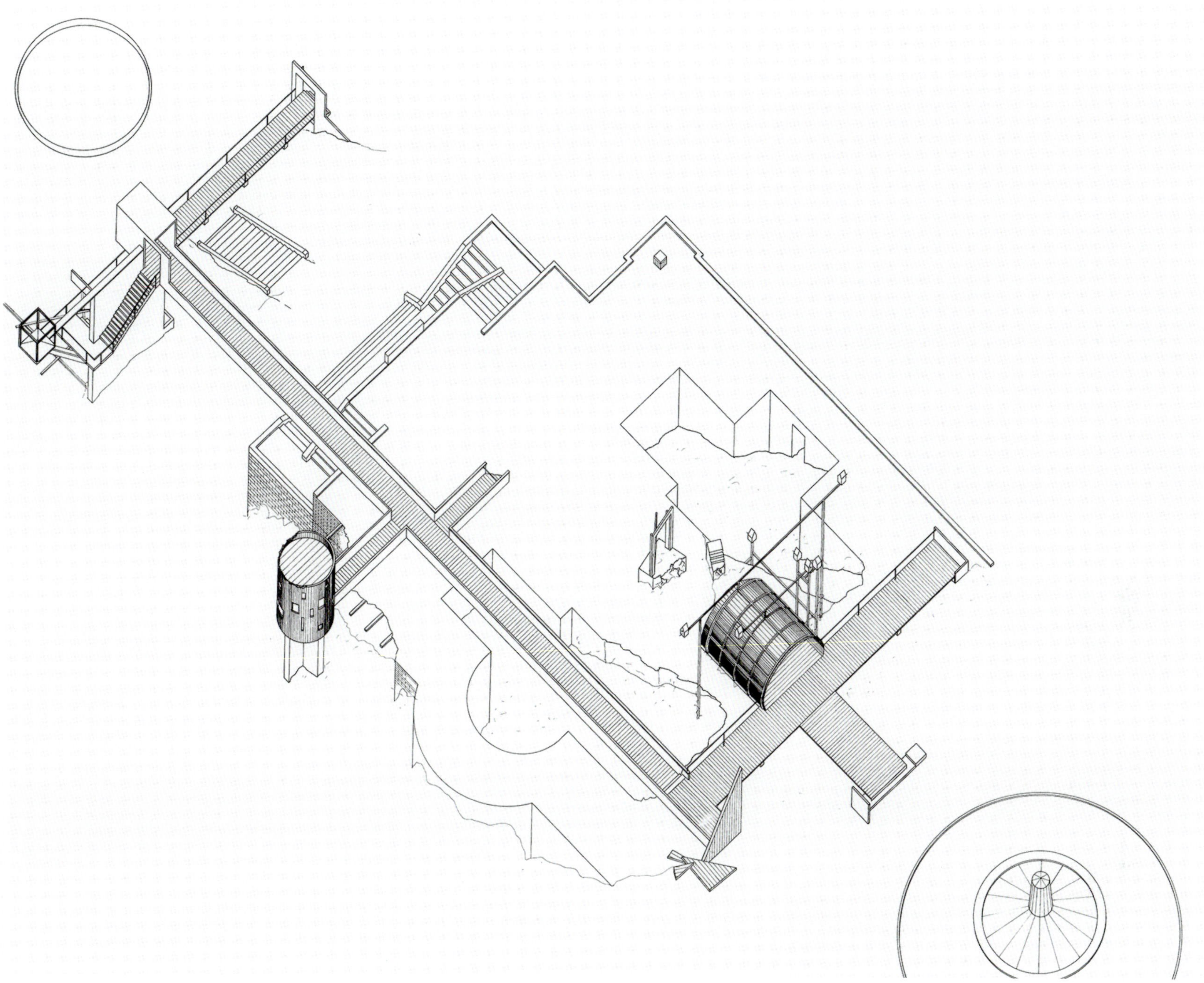

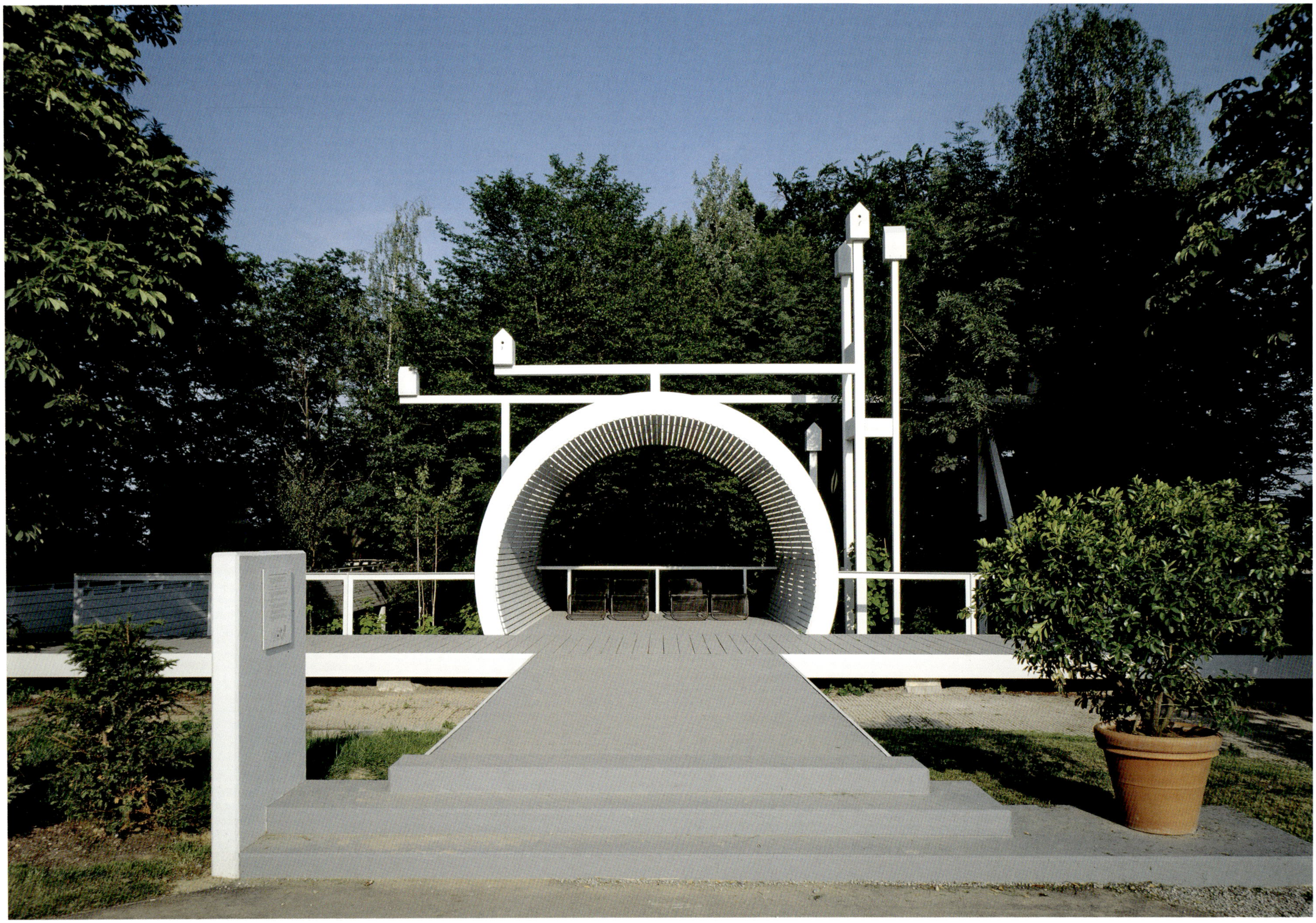

3. Villa Moser-Leibfried. Entrance gate with birdhouse construction.
4, 5. Villa Moser-Leibfried. The entrance gate, seen from the side.

3. Villa Moser-Leibfried. Eingangstor mit Vogelhaus-Konstruktion.
4, 5. Villa Moser-Leibfried. Das Eingangstor von der Seite gesehen.

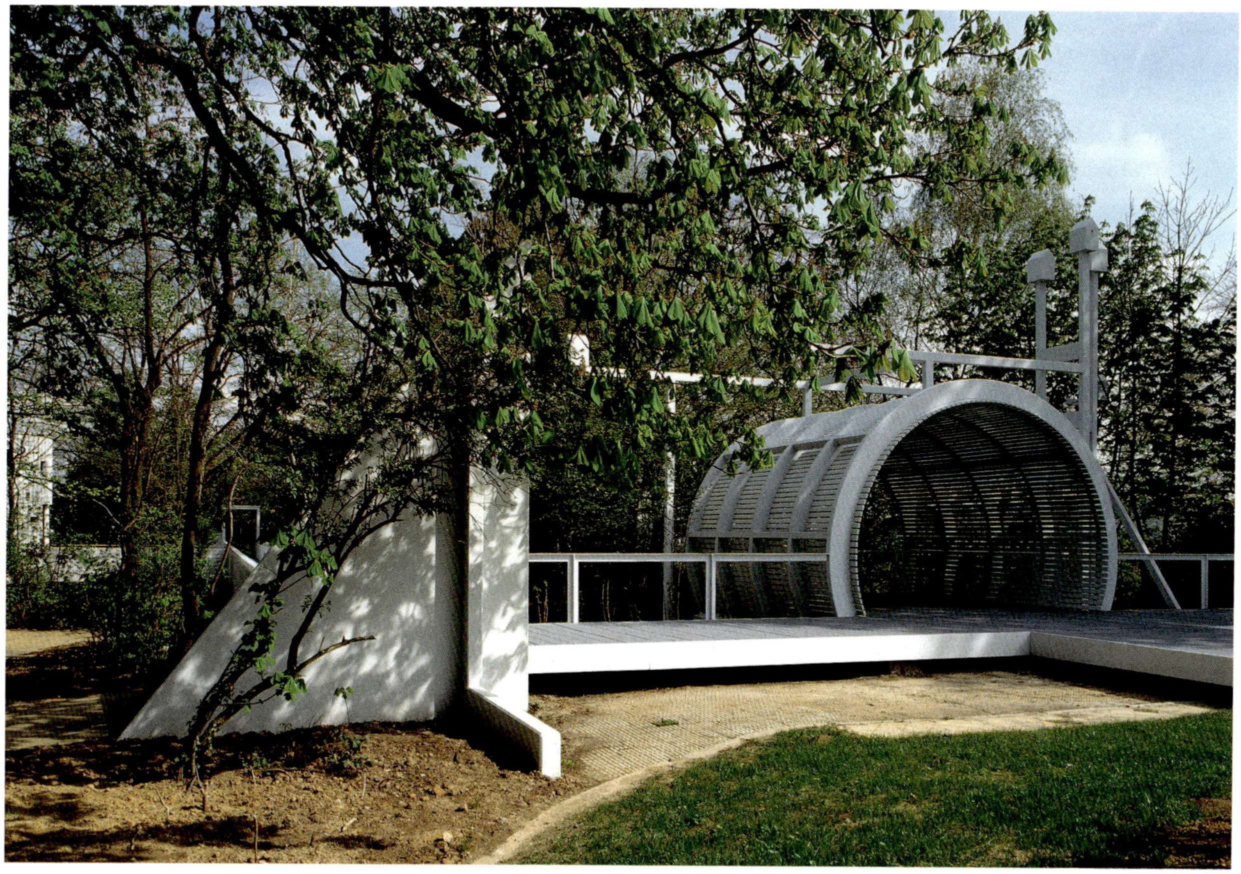

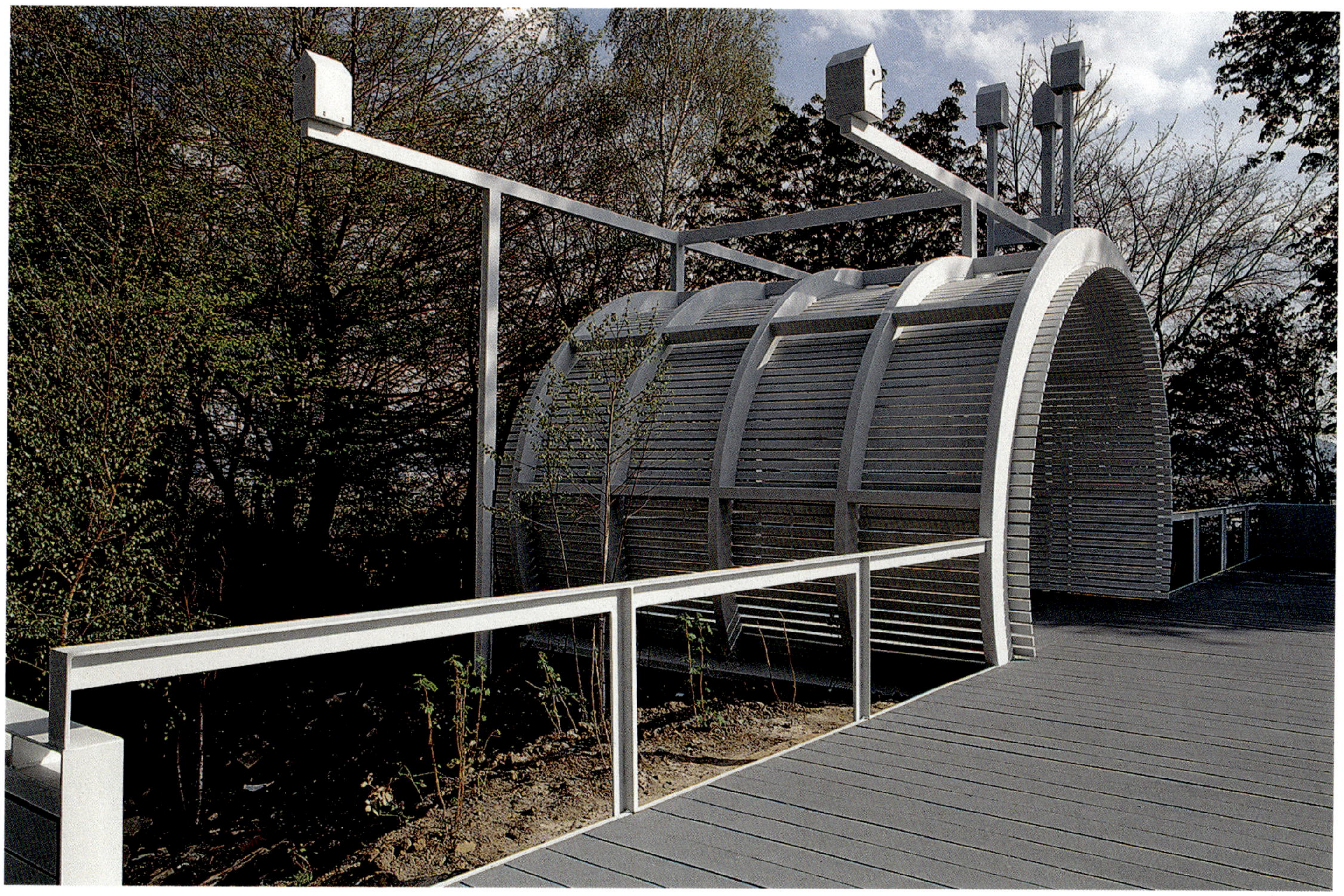

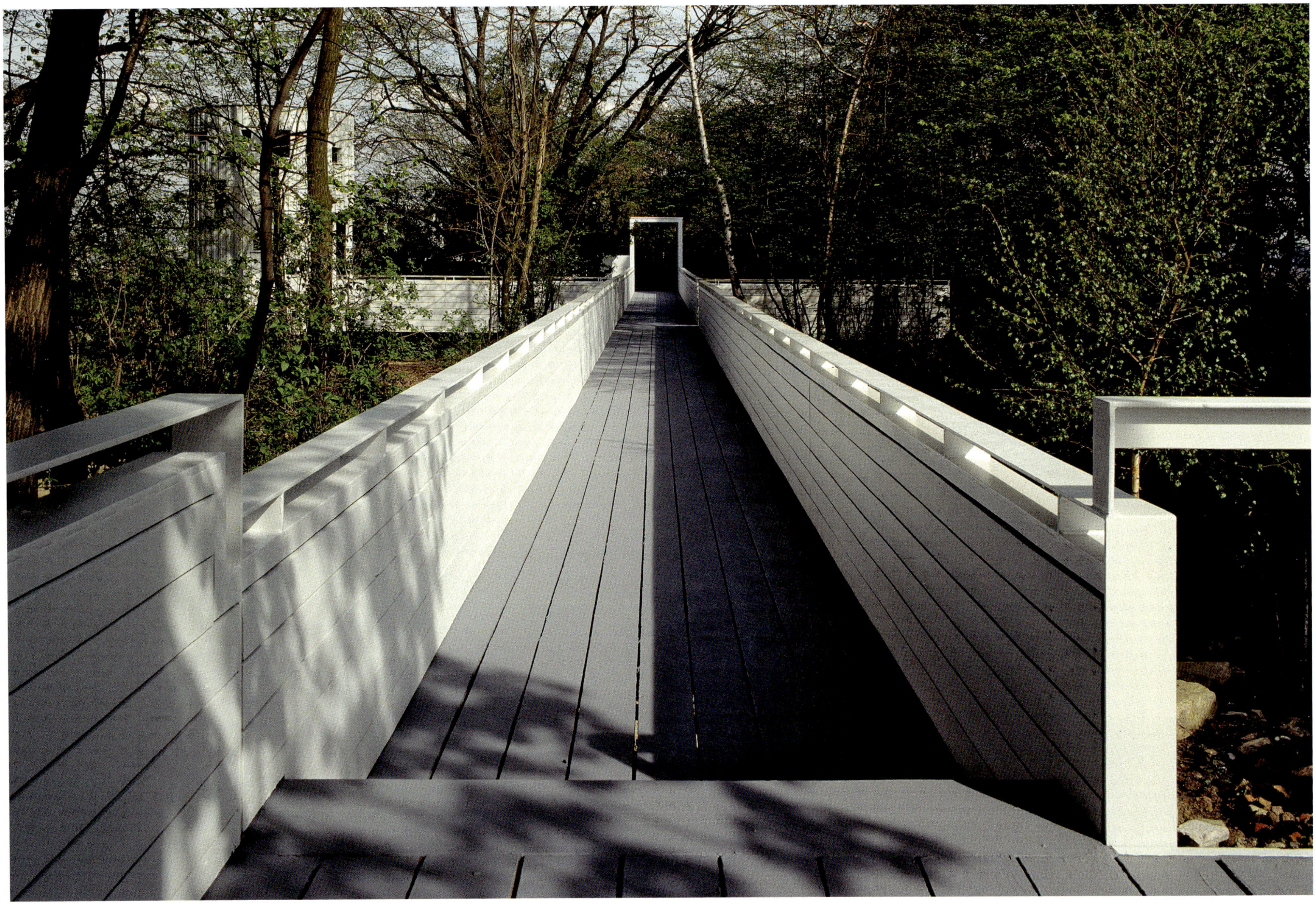

6. Villa Moser-Leibfried. Beyond the central axis, the walkway for the through route leads over the ruined cellar, with lush opportunistic vegetation.
7, 8. Villa Moser-Leibfried. The walkway branches off to a round »belvedere«, which was never a real belvedere. Inside, one finds only small windows to permit a view of the trees all around. The main sound to be heard was not so much the rustle of leaves and the twittering of birds as the near-constant traffic noise from the low-lying and much-used Pragstraße road.

6. Villa Moser-Leibfried. Der Durchgangssteg führt, außerhalb der Mittelachse, über die Kellerruinen mit üppiger Zufallsvegetation.
7, 8. Villa Moser-Leibfried. Steg-Abzweigung zu einem runden Belvedere, das nie ein wirkliches Belvedere war. Im Innenraum lassen nur kleine Fenster den Blick in die Bäume ringsum zu. Als Grundgeräusch war weniger Blätterrauschen und Vogelgezwitscher zu hören, als vielmehr permanenter Verkehrslärm von der tiefer gelegenen, stark befahrenen Pragstraße.

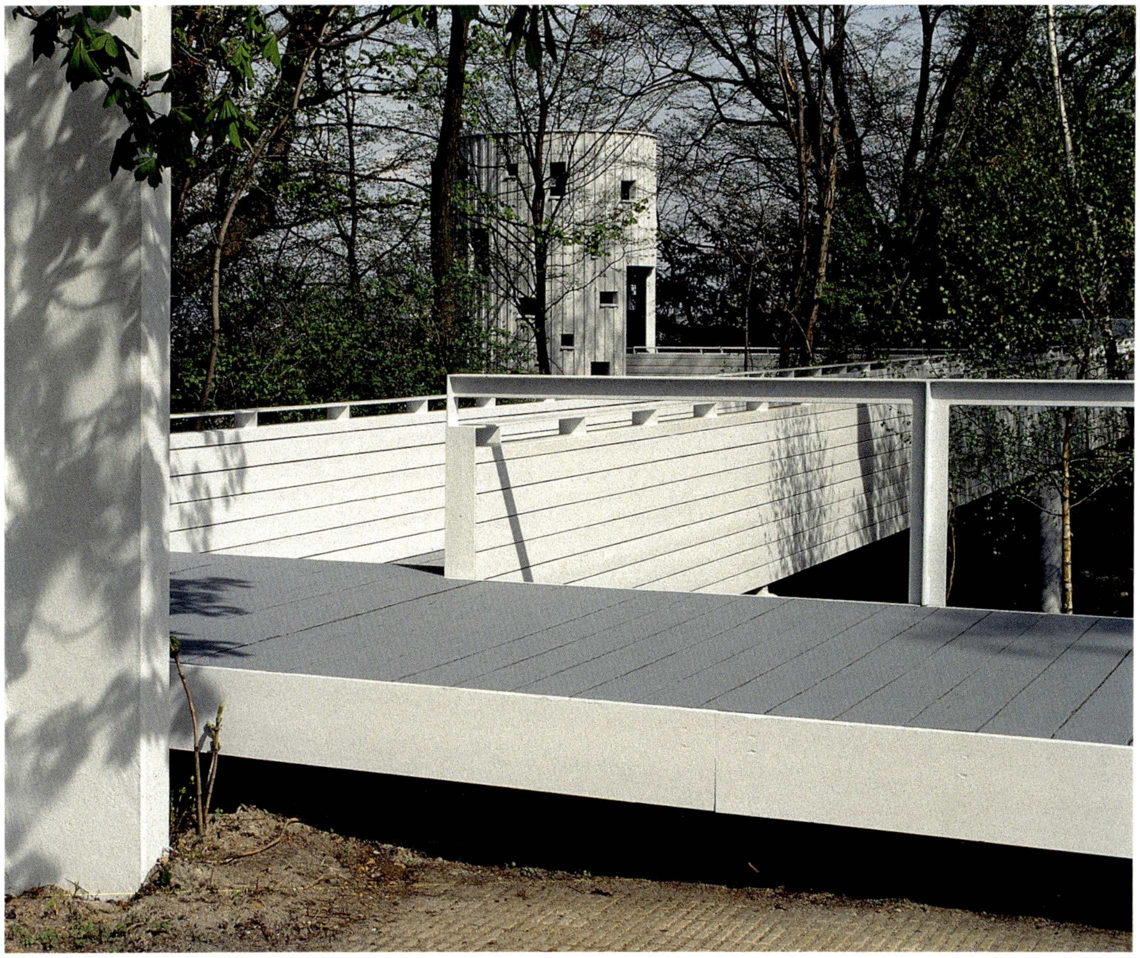

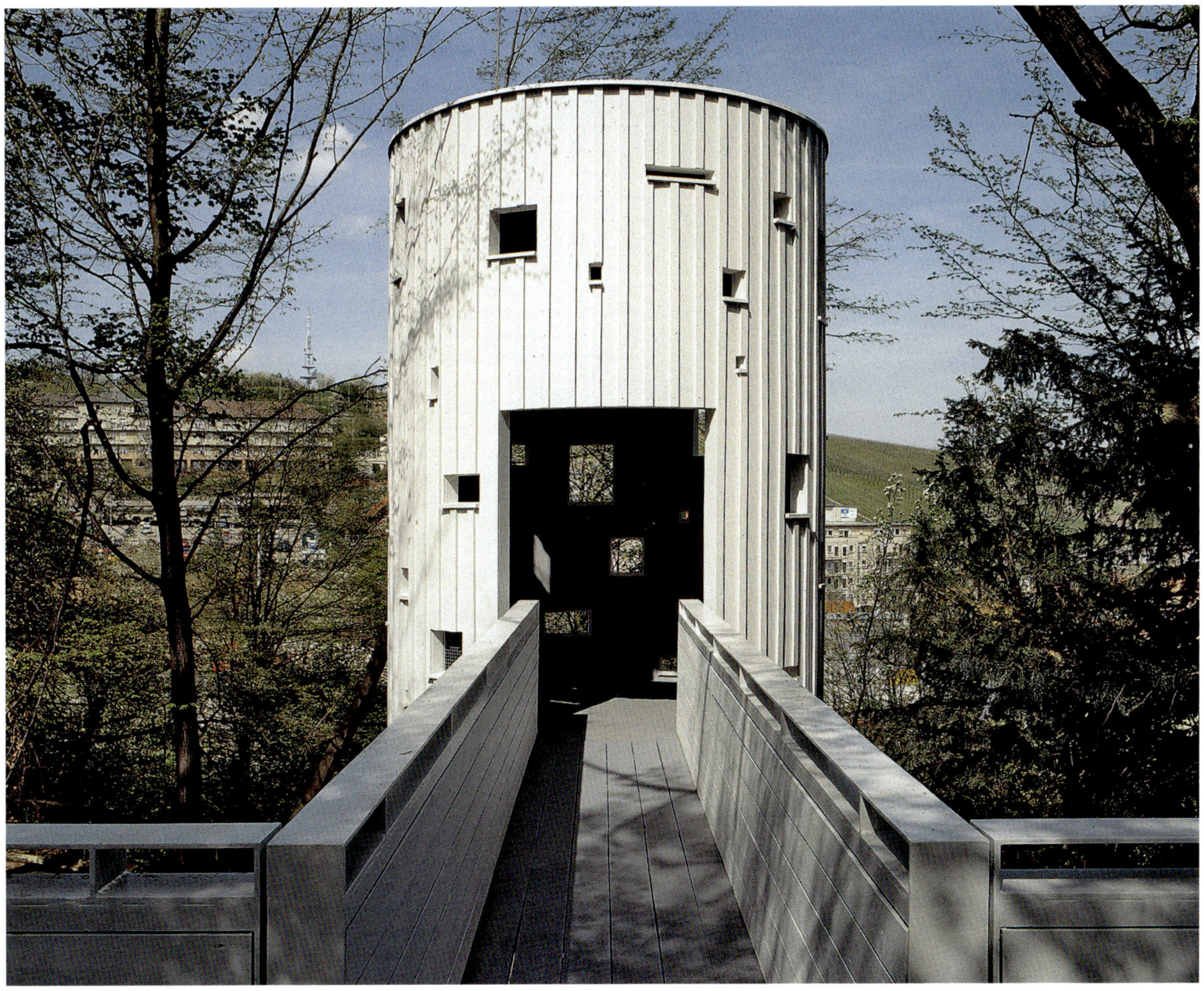

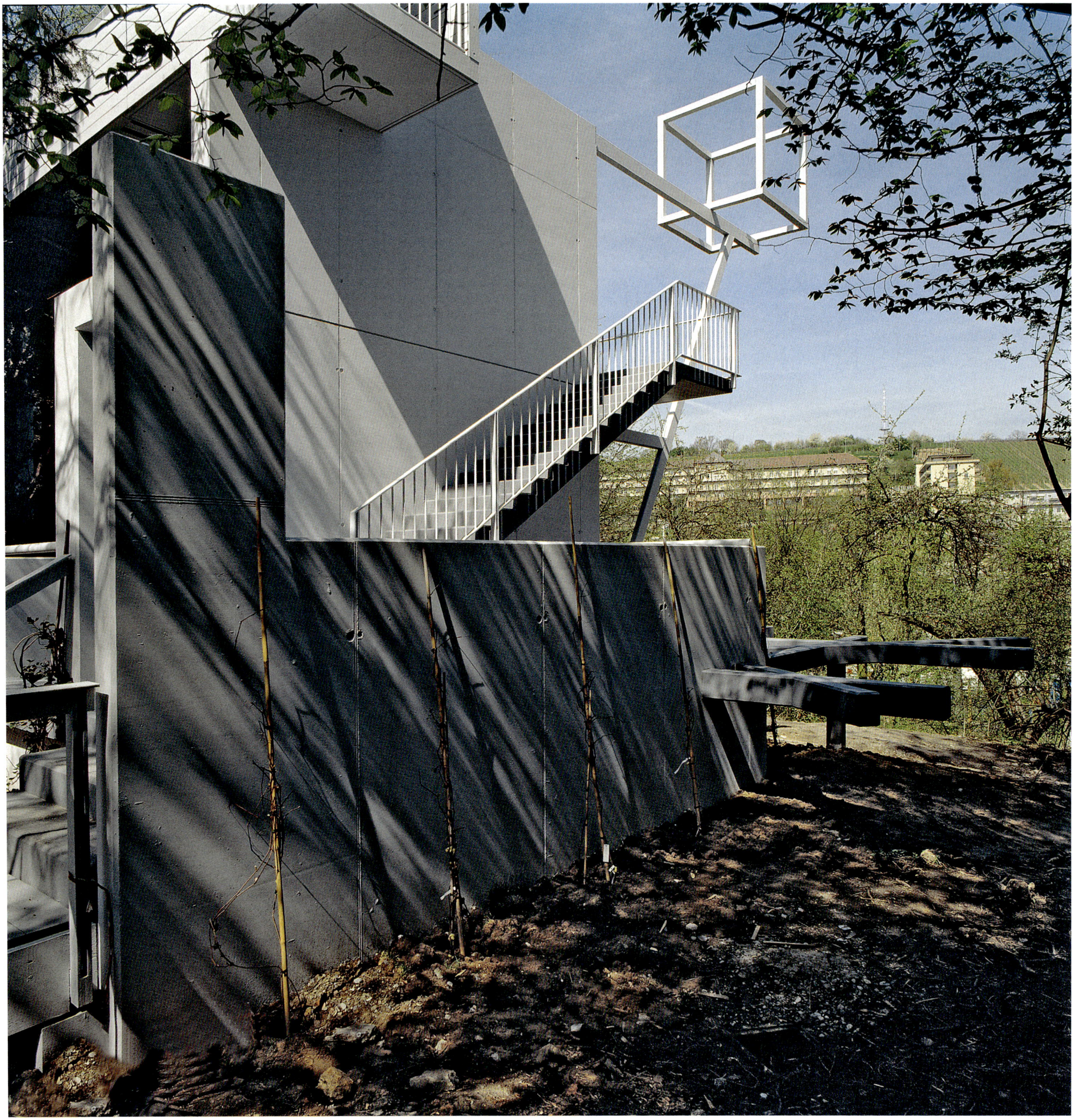

9. Villa Moser-Leibfried. Stair leading down into the lower-lying, former garden area of the villa.
10, 11. Villa Moser-Leibfried. Views through thick wild vegetation that has spread over what was originally a garden laid out in an Italian Renaissance style.

9. Villa Moser-Leibfried. Treppe hinunter in den tiefer gelegenen, einstigen Gartenbereich der Villa.
10, 11. Villa Moser-Leibfried. Blicke durch dichte, wilde Vegetation, die sich im Bereich des ursprünglich im italienischen Renaissancestil angelegten Gartenbereichs ausgebreitet hat.

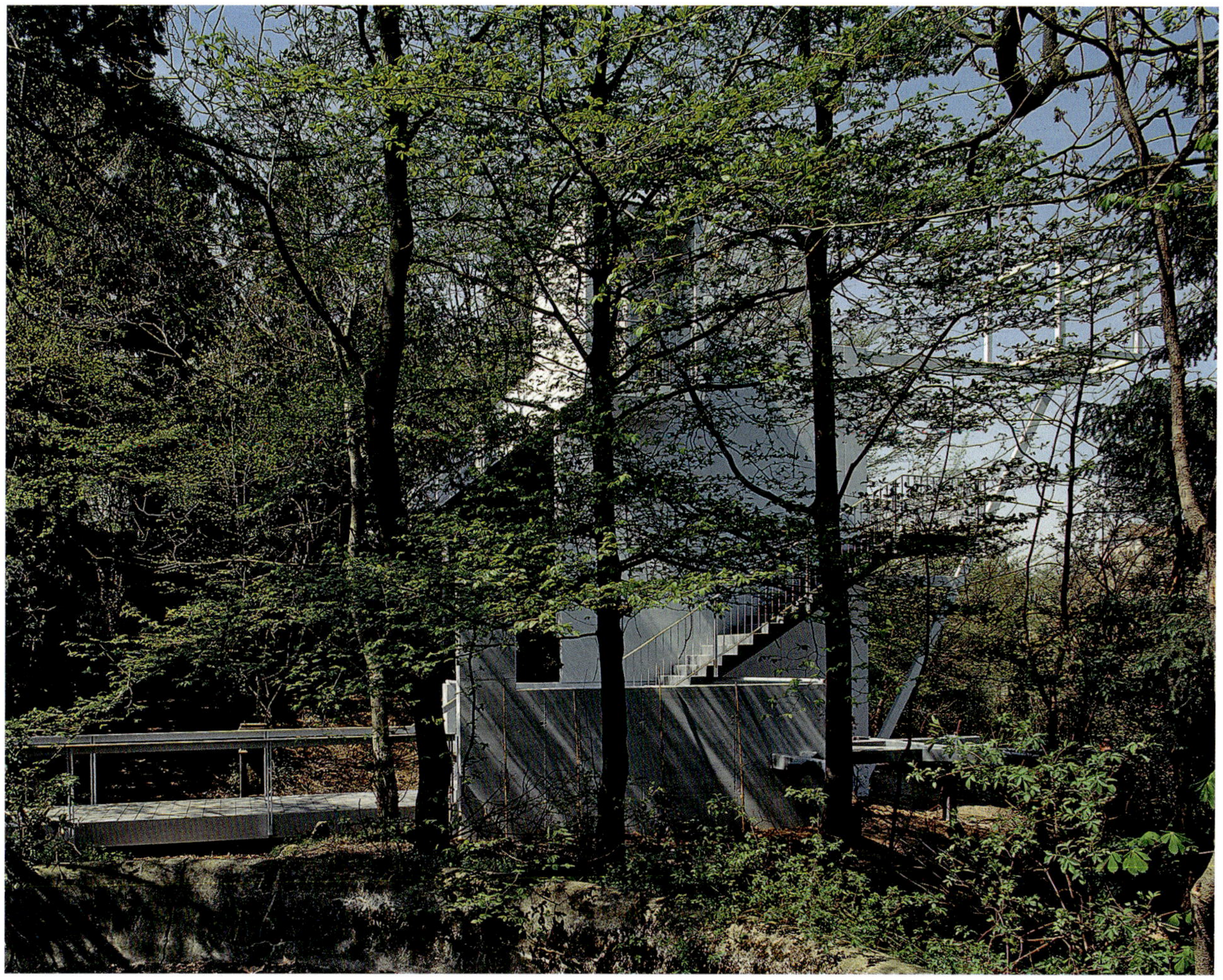

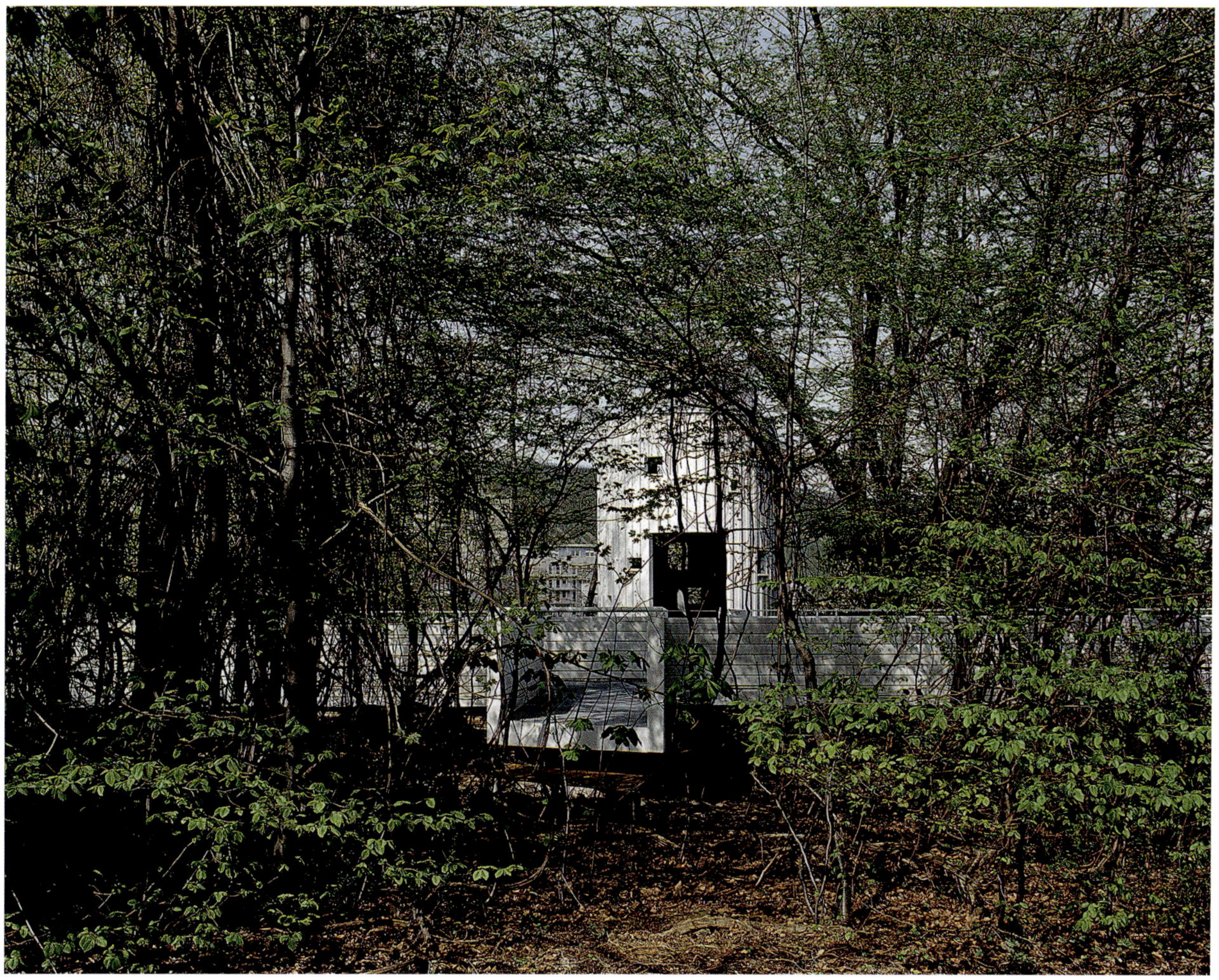

12. »Stangenwald«. A view from the west.
13. »Stangenwald«. Site plan.

12. »Stangenwald«. Blick von Westen.
13. »Stangenwald«. Lageplan.

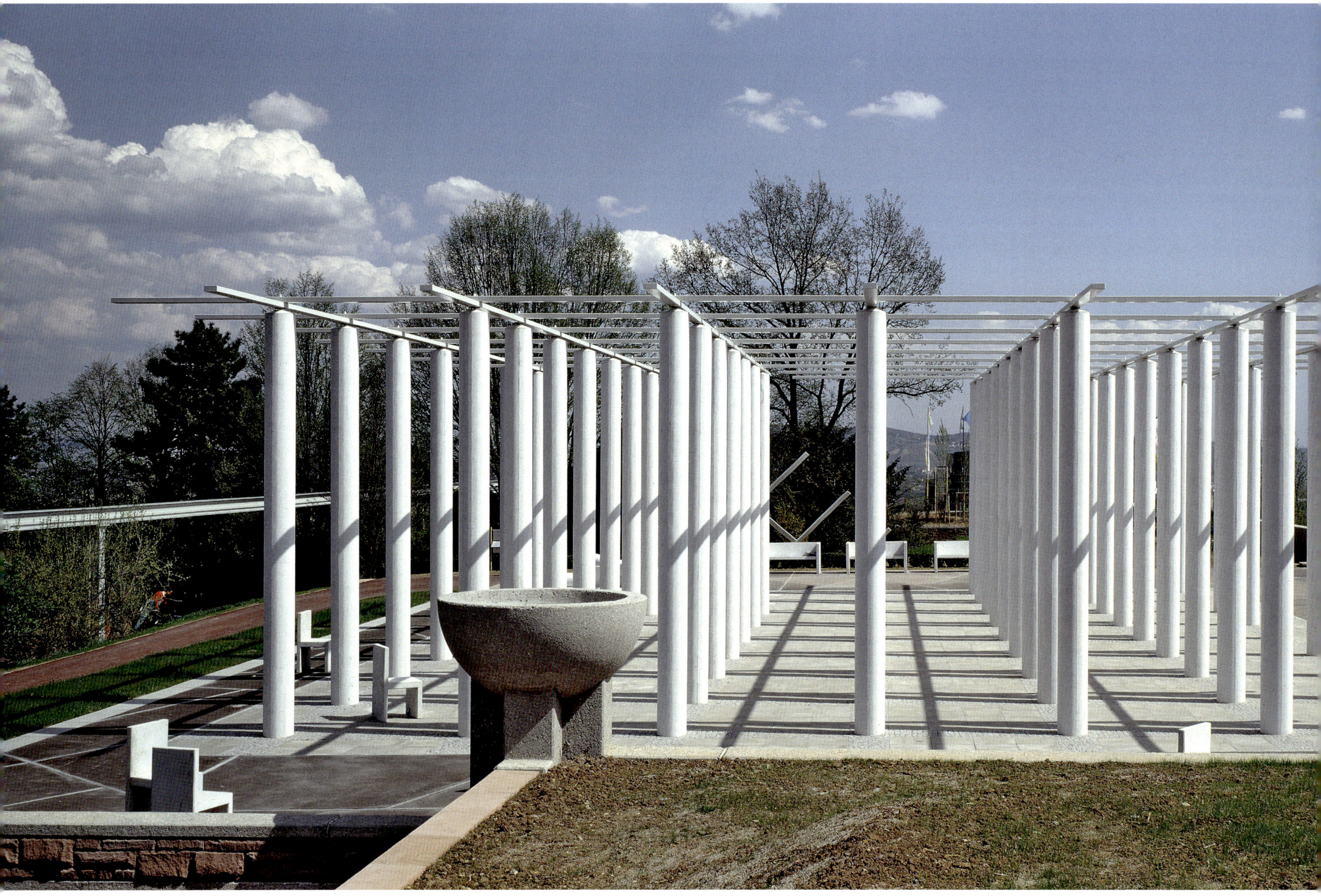

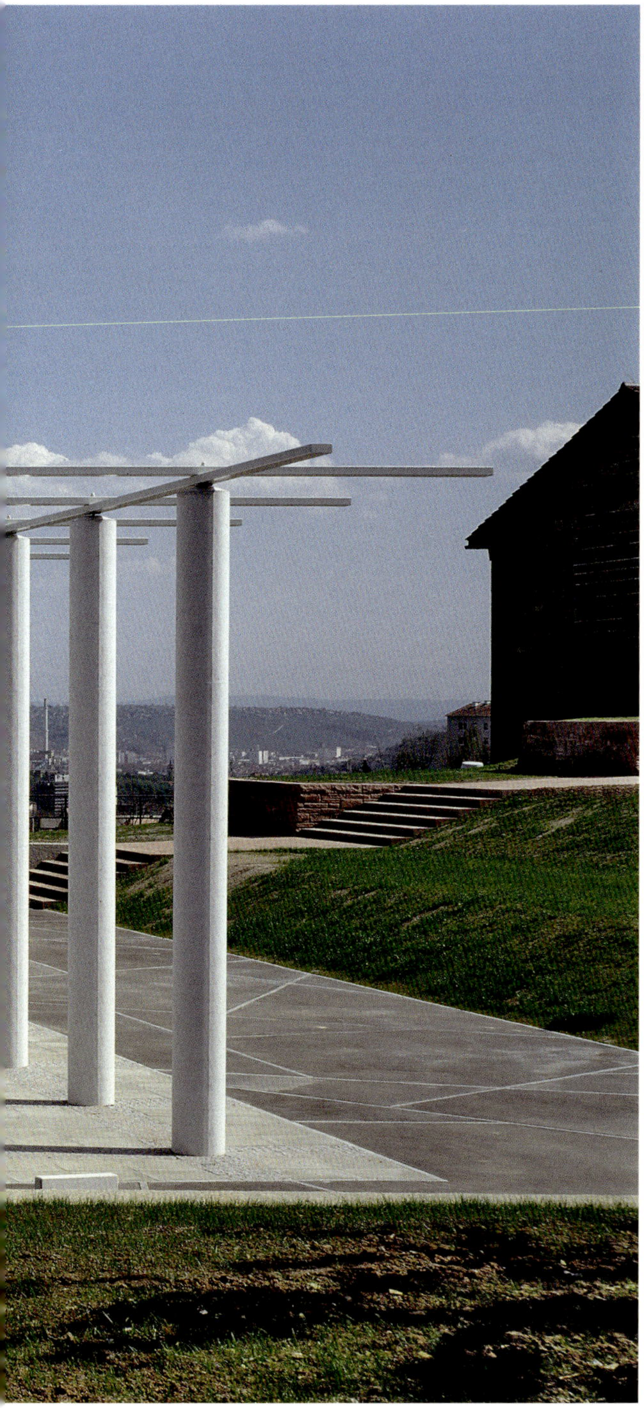

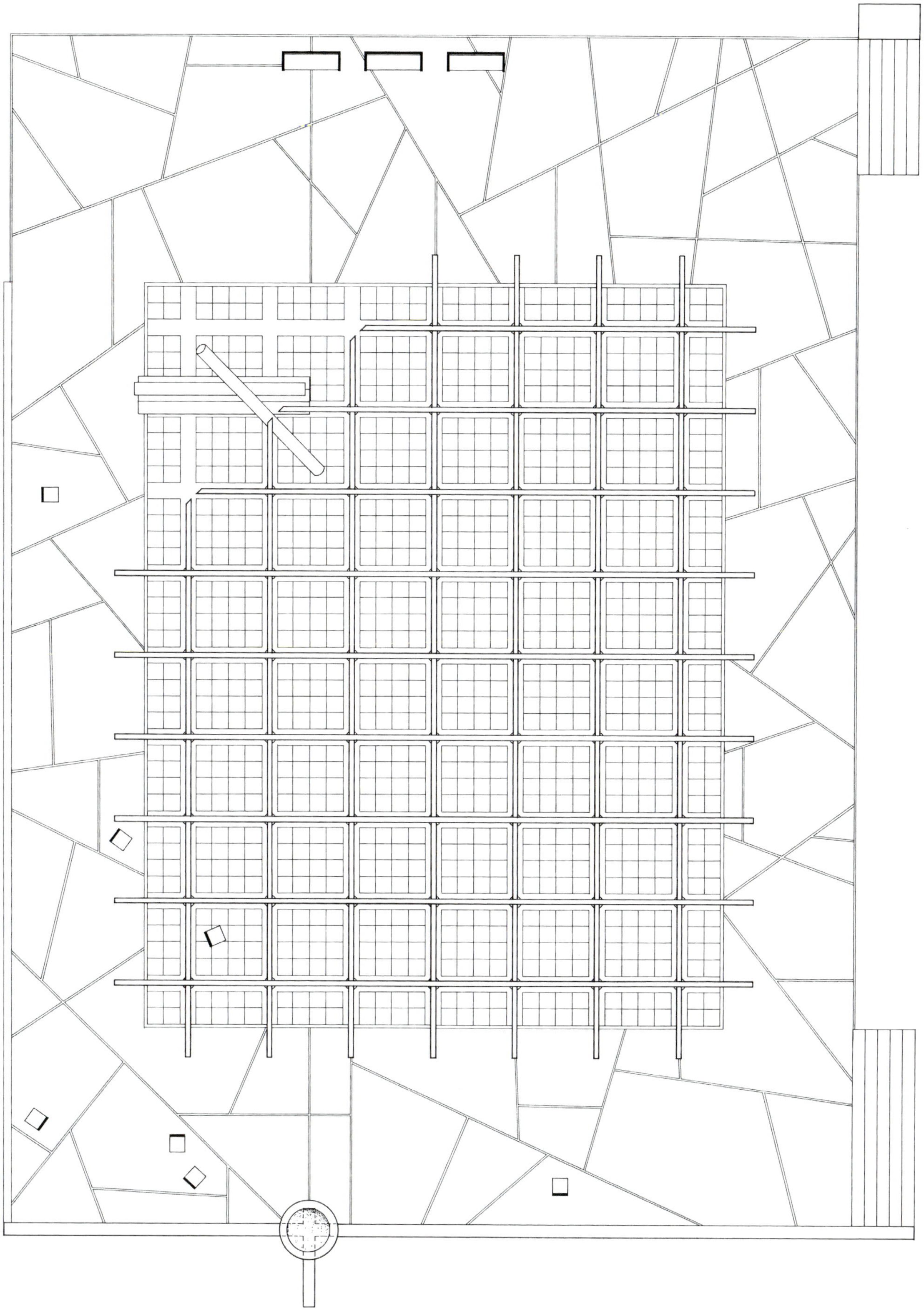

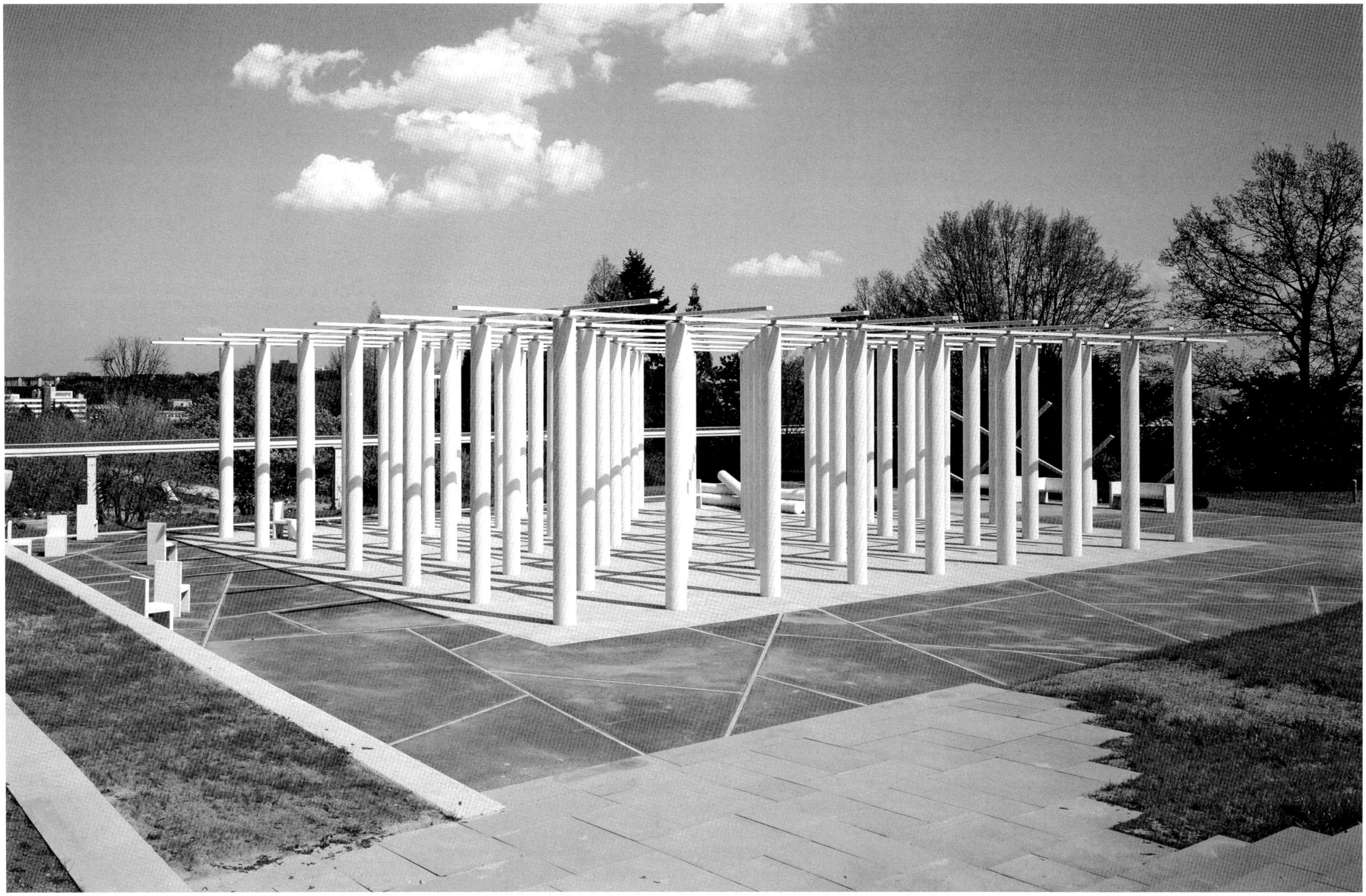

14. »Stangenwald«. View from the south-west.
15. »Stangenwald«. View from the north-east. In the foreground are the five horizontal, non-erected pillars.

14. »Stangenwald«. Blick von Südwesten.
15. »Stangenwald«. Blick von Nordosten. Im Vordergrund die fünf liegenden, nicht aufgestellten Säulen.

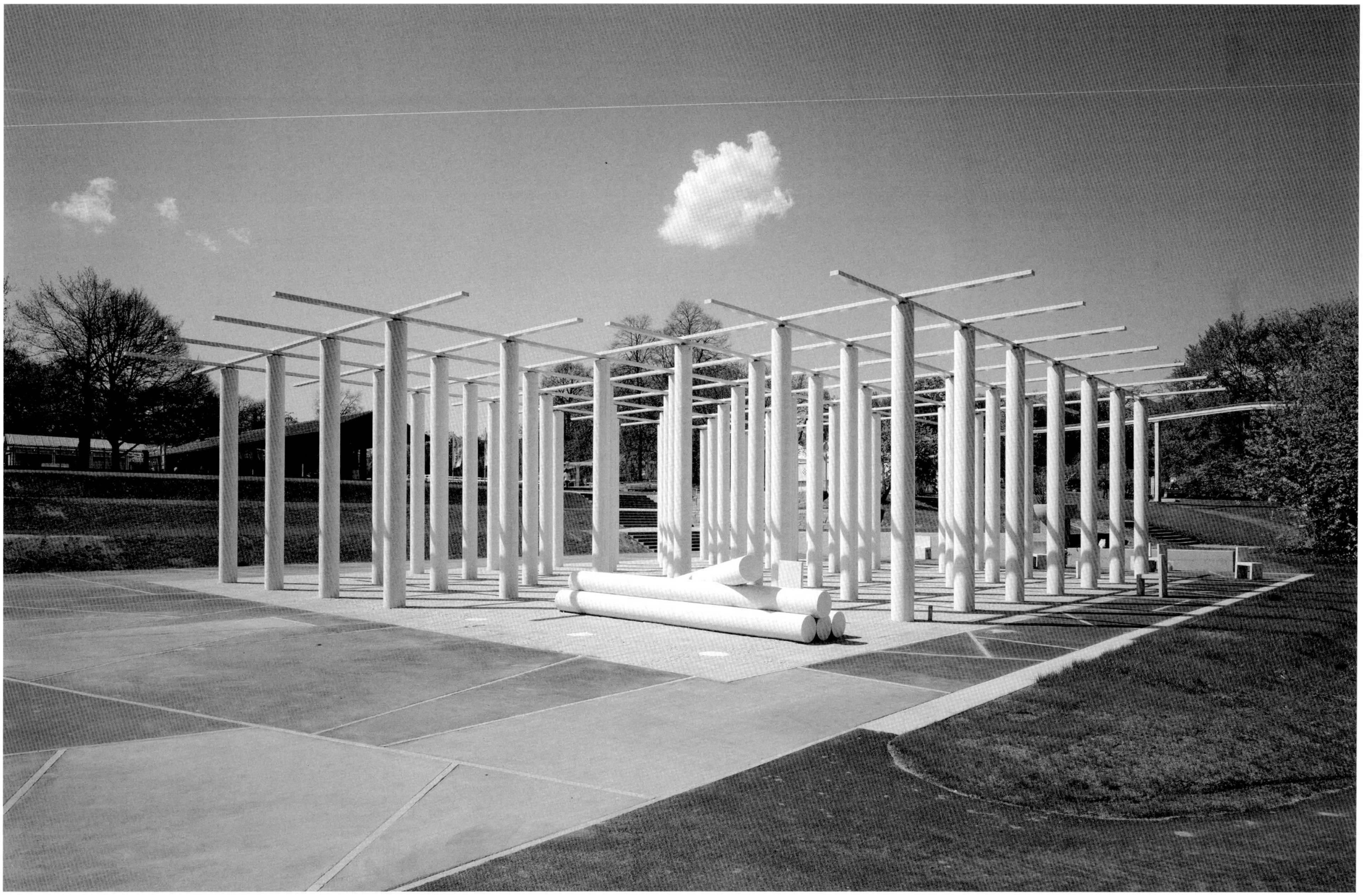

Memorial for the Murdered Jews of Europe, Berlin, 1995

This competition marked my second entrance into the field of memorial sites, which was to be highly characteristic of my work in the first decade of the new millennium.

In 1995, following lengthy discussions partially conducted in public, an »anonymous, Germany-wide artistic competition« was declared for the planned Memorial for the Murdered Jews of Europe. All artists, landscape designers, and architects who had been living in Germany for at least six months were eligible to take part. Additionally, twelve prominent international figures were invited. Almost 1000 interested parties requested the documents. 528 ultimately submitted proposals, myself among them.

The jury was faced with a mammoth task. However, two first-prize-winning designs did emerge: the painter Christine Jackob-Marks and architect Hella Rolfes' giant, inclined gravestone with hundreds of thousands of victims' names, and Simon Ungers' transversely positioned steel square with the engraved name of the concentration camps, raised so that it could be walked under. Ultimately, no design received the approval of Helmut Kohl and the other relevant political figures.

There was therefore a new by-invitation (and therefore remunerated) international competition, from which Peter Eisenman (initially jointly with the sculptor Richard Serra) emerged as the victor. Today, his fictional cemetery without a name is among the chief sights in Berlin.

My proposal was quickly rejected.

I had proposed a severely framed, rectangular black lake with a narrow transverse path, which was to lie in a walled garden park. The diagonal main path led through a dark tunnel of sadness. »A tunnel of night, of darkening, and error. Time stands still, all thoughts concentrate themselves on what has happened. Urns with earth from the concentration camps are sunken into the side walls.« (From my explanatory text). Two 35-meter-high black wings (concrete with granite facing) grow out of the two sides of the tunnel of sadness. In my explanatory text, I talked about a »black angel of death« and »monumental sadness«.

Denkmal für die ermordeten Juden Europas, Berlin, 1995

Mit diesem Wettbewerb betrat ich zum ersten Mal den Gedenkstättenbereich, der im ersten Jahrzehnt des neuen Jahrtausends bei mir werkbestimmend werden sollte.

Nach langen, teilweise öffentlich geführten Diskussionen wurde 1995 ein »anonymer, bundesoffener künstlerischer Wettbewerb« für das geplante Denkmal für die ermordeten Juden Europas ausgeschrieben. Künstler, Landschaftsgestalter und Architekten, die seit mindestens sechs Monaten in Deutschland wohnten, konnten daran teilnehmen. Zwölf internationale Berühmtheiten wurden dazu eingeladen. Fast 1000 Interessierte ließen sich die Unterlagen schicken. 528 von ihnen gaben am Ende ab. Ich war einer von ihnen.

Eine Mammutaufgabe für die Jury. Zwei erste Preise kristallisierten sich trotzdem heraus: für die Malerin Christine Jackob-Marks und die Architektin Hella Rolfes (eine riesige, schräg geneigte Grabplatte mit Hunderttausenden von Opfernamen) und Simon Ungers (ein quergestelltes, hochgebocktes und damit untergehbares Stahlquadrat mit den eingravierten Namen der Konzentrationslager). Letztlich fand kein Entwurf die Zustimmung von Helmut Kohl und den anderen politisch Verantwortlichen.

Deswegen gab es einen erneuten, eingeladenen (und damit honorierten), internationalen Wettbewerb, aus dem Peter Eisenman (zunächst gemeinsam mit dem Bildhauer Richard Serra) als Sieger hervorging. Sein fiktiver Friedhof ohne Namen gehört heute zu den Hauptsehenswürdigkeiten Berlins.

Mein Vorschlag wurde schnell aussortiert.

Ich hatte einen streng gefaßten, rechteckigen schwarzen See mit einem schmalen Querweg vorgeschlagen, der in einem ummauerten Gartenpark liegen sollte. Der diagonale Hauptweg führte durch einen dunklen Trauer-Tunnel. »Ein Tunnel der Nacht, der Verfinsterung und Verirrung. Die Zeit bleibt stehen, alle Gedanken konzentrieren sich auf das Geschehene. In die Seitenwände sind Urnen mit Erde aus den verschiedenen Konzentrationslagern versenkt.« (Aus meinem Erläuterungstext). Zwei 35 Meter hohe, schräg geneigte schwarze Flügel (Beton mit schwarzem Granitvorsatz) wachsen aus den beiden Seiten des Trauer-Tunnels. Ich sprach in meinem Erläuterungstext von einem »schwarzen Todesengel« und »monumentaler Trauer«.

1, 2. Model for the competition entry.

1, 2. Modell des Wettbewerbsbeitrags.

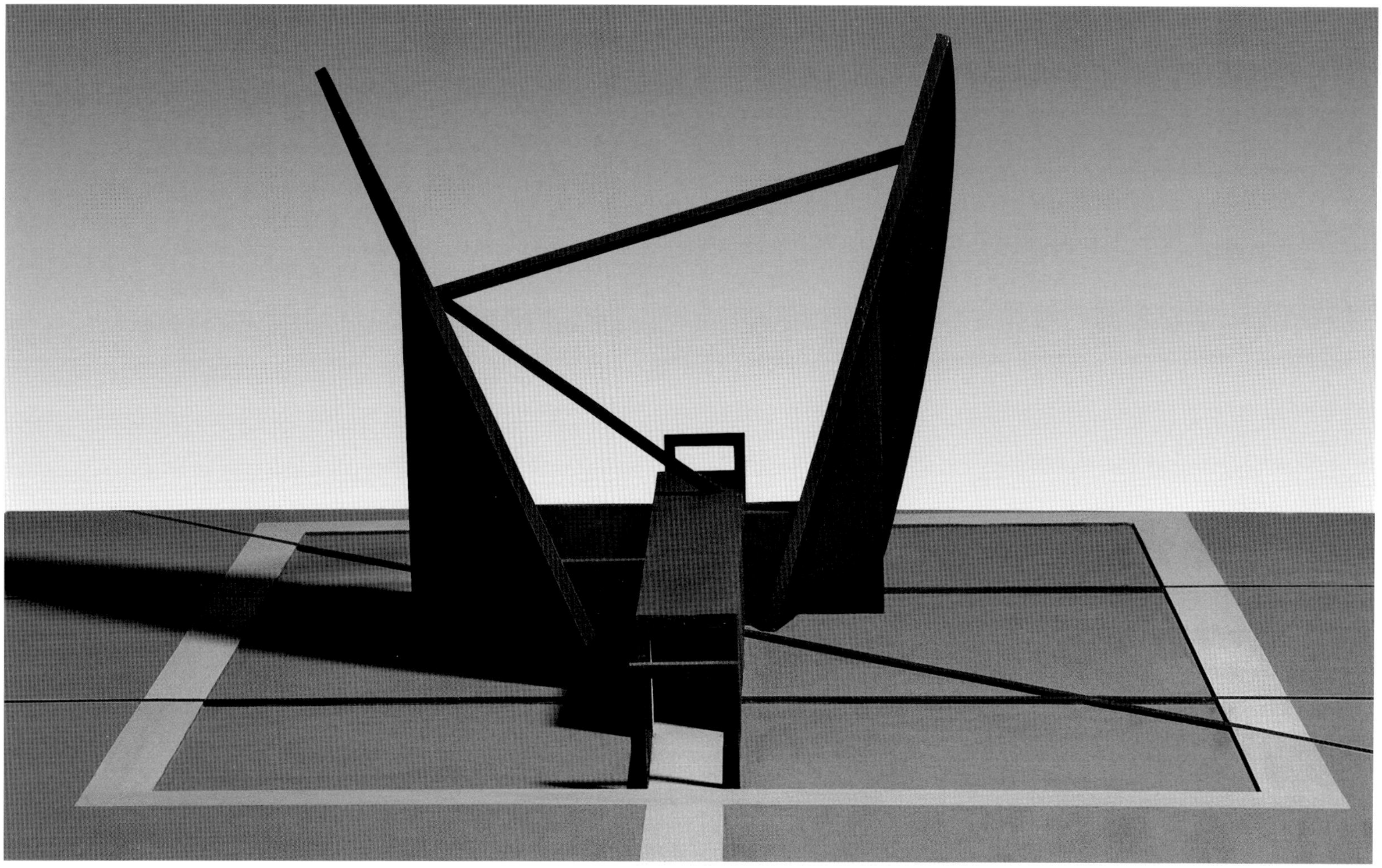

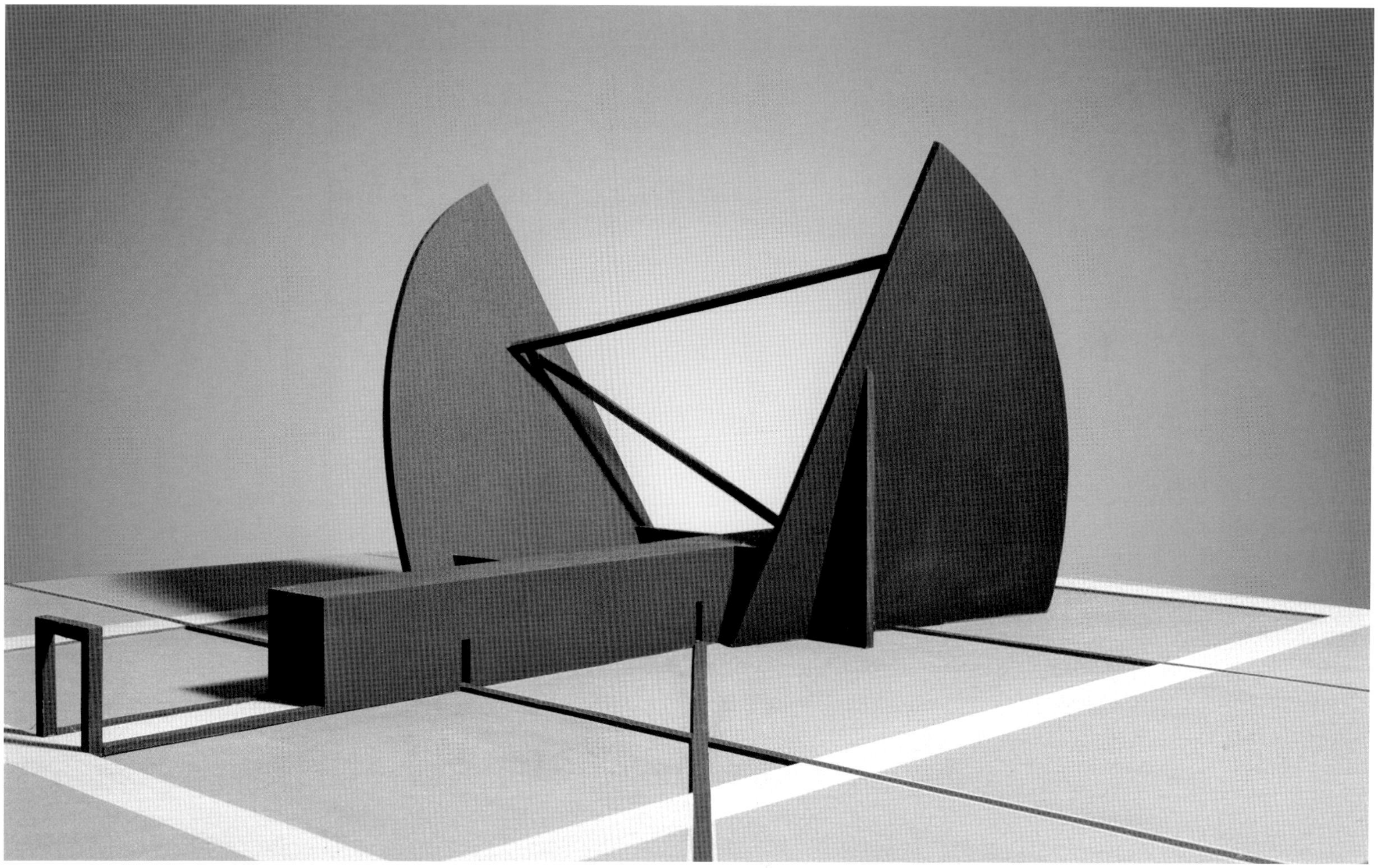

Exhibition in the German pavilion for the Venice Architecture Biennale 1996

This project did not take place in the open air, but was concerned with what was at the time Germany's largest and most extensive renaturation project: the IBA-Emscher-Park, under the leadership of Karl Ganser. The official title for the exhibition was: »Change without Growth – Urban Construction Culture in the 21st-Century. The IBA Emscher Park as an Example«.

The project was curated by Kunibert Wachten, with the American Colleen Schmitz as project head. Together, we chose the most interesting architecture and landscape design projects. They were presented in the four side rooms of the German pavilion in Venice, with photos and models.

I was to develop and construct a symbolically combined landscape image for the main hall. After my design ideas with coal briquettes or a coke field, I proposed the white landscape wave that later irritated some visitors, architects, and critics. I was thinking of the gentle swing back into a harmonious landscape, away from exploitation, overexploitation, undermining, and destruction. The Ruhrgebiet was once famous for its rich coal deposits. As a result, numerous mines and steelworks were built there. Following the closure of most of the coal pits and mines, the whole of the Ruhrgebiet landscape is today undermined by a labyrinthine tunnel system, which has now been partially flooded – owing to fear of collapses of landscapes and cities.

Beneath the wave, I documented the coal-dust underworlds of pits and mines. Only a few remnants of the tunnels project from the wave's surface, like white plaster casts of black shafts. In their cavities, photos of the former industrial landscape can be seen. Flickering memories, but here they are without smoke, smell and noise.

Ausstellung im deutschen Pavillon für die Architektur-Biennale Venedig 1996

Dieses Projekt fand zwar nicht im Freien statt, beschäftigte sich jedoch mit dem damals größten und umfangreichsten Renaturierungsprojekt Deutschlands: der IBA-Emscherpark, die unter der Leitung von Karl Ganser stand. Der offizielle Titel der Ausstellung lautete: »Wandel ohne Wachstum – Stadt-Bau-Kultur im 21. Jahrhundert. Am Beispiel der IBA Emscher Park«.

Kurator des Projekts war Kunibert Wachten. Projektleiterin: die Amerikanerin Colleen Schmitz. Gemeinsam wählten wir die interessantesten Architekturen und Landschaftsgestaltungsprojekte aus. Sie wurden in den vier Seitenräumen des deutschen Pavillons in Venedig mit Photos und Modellen präsentiert.

Ich sollte für die Haupthalle ein symbolisch zusammenfassendes Landschaftsbild entwickeln und bauen. Nachdem meine Gestaltungsideen mit Kohlebriketts oder einem Koksfeld von den verantwortlichen Herren abgelehnt worden waren, schlug ich jene weiße Landschaftswelle vor, die später manchen Besucher, Architekten und Kritiker irritierte. Ich dachte dabei an die sanfte Zurückschwingung in eine harmonische Landschaft, weit entfernt von Ausbeutung, Raubbau, Untergrabung und Zerstörung. Das Ruhrgebiet war einst berühmt für seine reichen Kohlevorkommen. Deswegen siedelten sich hier zahlreiche Zechen und Stahlwerke an. Nach Schließung der meisten Kohlegruben, Zechen und Stahlwerke ist die gesamte Ruhrgebietslandschaft heute untergraben von einem labyrinthischen Stollensystem, das inzwischen teilweise geflutet wurde – aus Angst vor dem Einbrechen der Landschaften und Städte.

Unter der Welle dokumentierte ich die kohlestaubigen Unterwelten der Gruben und Zechen. Aus der Wellenoberfläche ragten nur wenige Stollen-Reste wie weiße Gipsabgüsse von schwarzen Schächten. In deren Hohlräumen waren Photos der einstigen Industrielandschaft zu sehen. Nachflackernde Erinnerungen, hier ohne Rauch, Gestank und Lärm.

1. Model of main hall in Venice. (Photo: Hans Dieter Schaal.)
2, 3. The overall theme of the Venice Architecture-Biennale 1996, headed by Hans Hollein, was: »The Architect as Seismograph«. Draft sketches.

.

1. Modell der Haupthalle in Venedig. (Photo: Hans Dieter Schaal.)
2, 3. Das Gesamtthema der Architektur-Biennale Venedig 1996, die von Hans Hollein geleitet wurde, lautete: »Der Architekt als Seismograph«. Entwurfsskizzen.

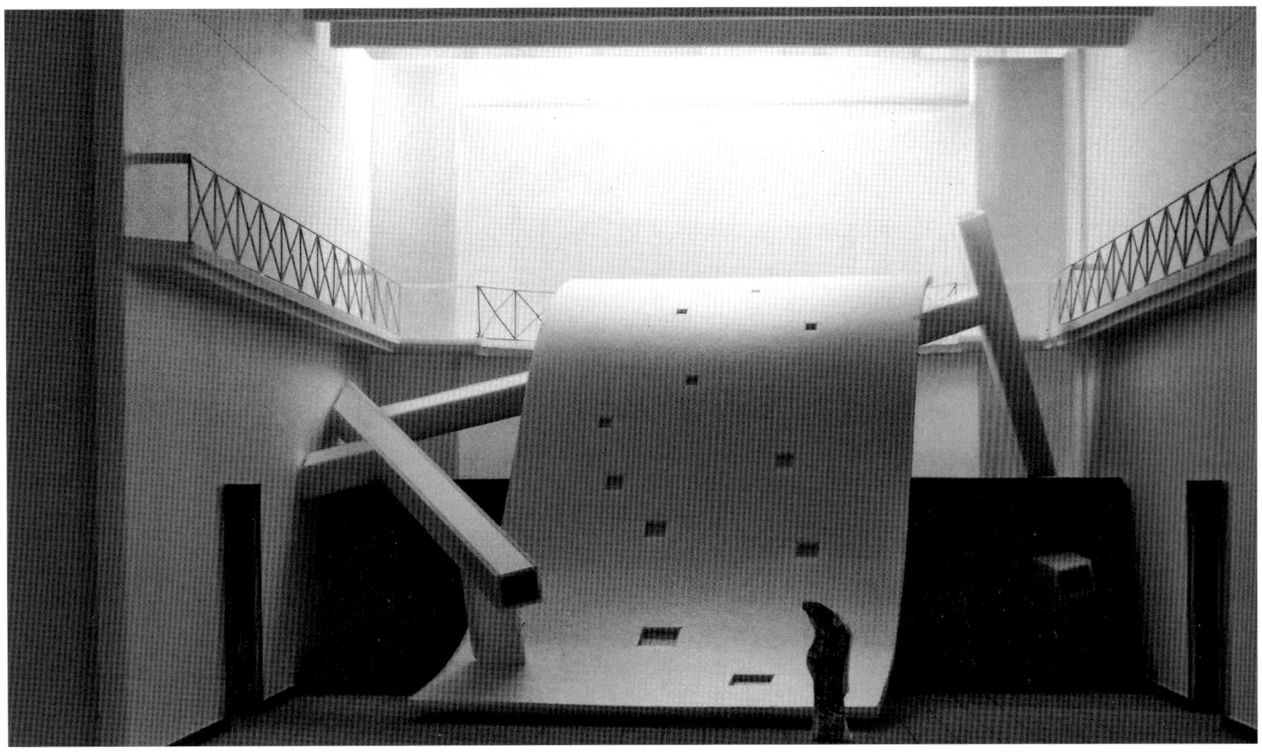

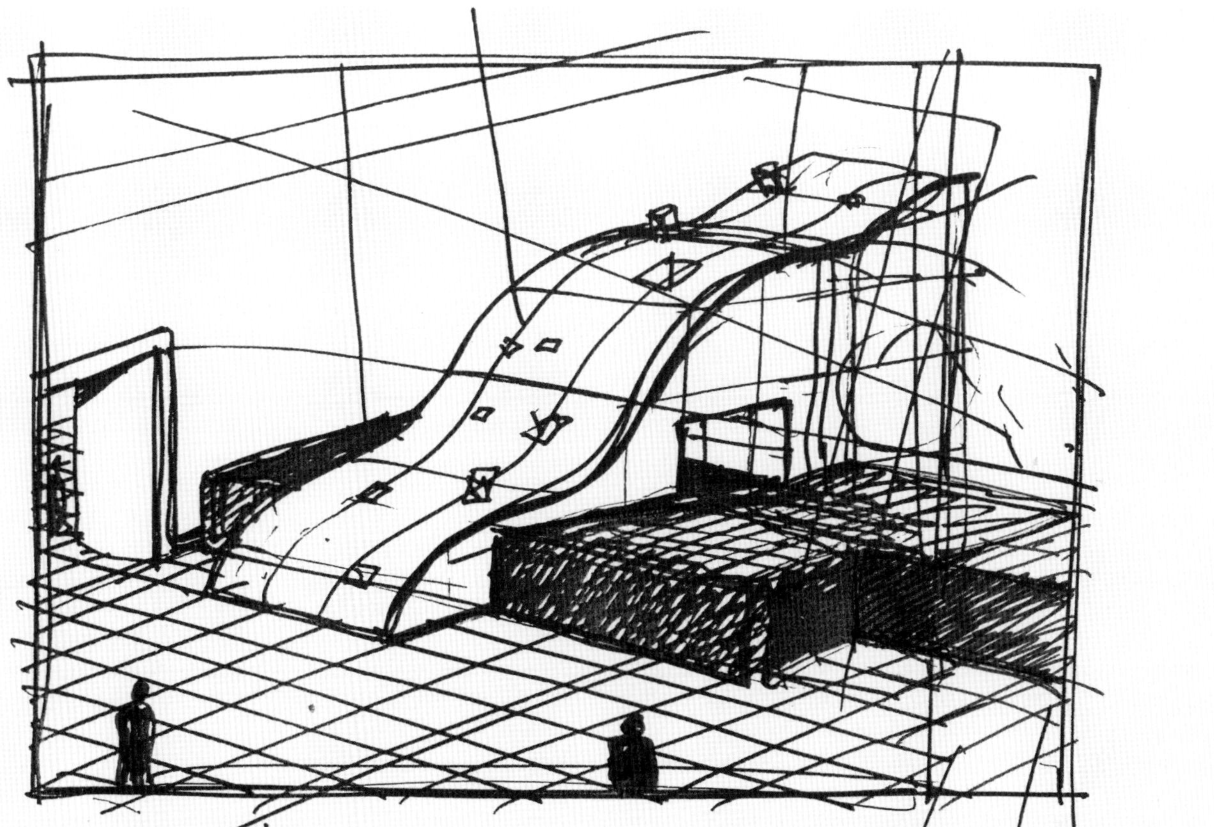

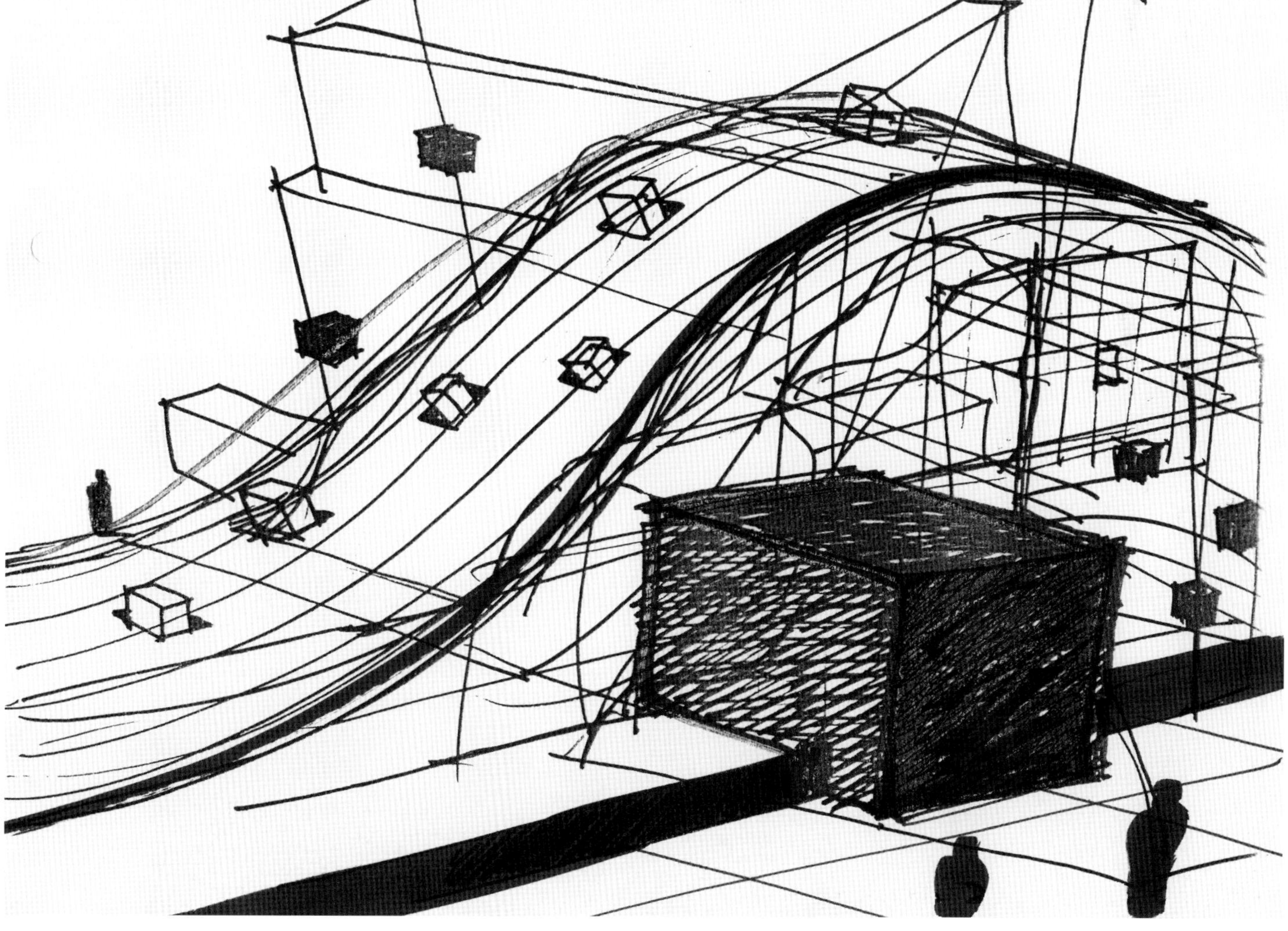

»Reisigstadt« (brushwood city), Landesgartenschau Böblingen, 1996

In 1996, the working group Janson-Wolfrum (architects and urban planners) and Schmelzer-Bezzenberger (landscape architects) won a competition to handle the overall planning for the Landesgartenschau Böblingen. Individual exhibition areas were allotted to other firms in the region. One temporary aspect was the responsibility of the Stuttgart landscape architecture firm Christof Luz, the son of Hans Luz.

He invited me to design the »Wandelgarten der Fachverbände« (promenade garden of the professional associations). Rather provocatively, I proposed that the whole designated area for the garden should be covered to a depth of three to four meters in brushwood, with a large, round space left clear in the middle. Into the remaining mass of deadwood, I planned to cut various living and spending-time rooms with doors, hallways, furniture, wall fragments, and windows. This would produce novel »nature rooms« of a kind never seen before, without a roof.

There were other natural materials that might have been used: stone, straw, bark, thicker branches, or timber logs. Hitherto, brushwood had never been used for home-making purposes – except by animals and birds. Its suitability is limited, and it burns easily.

At first, the idea met with somewhat grudging approval. Construction duly began. However, when deliveries of brushwood from all across Baden-Württemberg became ever more scanty and ultimately stopped entirely, those responsible began to fear that the piece would be unfinished when the garden show opened. This agitation led them to break off and to finish the rooms by cobbling together lousy reed mats on construction scaffolding. Christof Luz and myself distanced ourselves from the project, which should have been original, witty, and very romantic.

»Reisigstadt«, Landesgartenschau Böblingen, 1996

Die Gesamtplanung der Landesgartenschau Böblingen hatte 1996 die Arbeitsgemeinschaft Janson-Wolfrum (Architekten und Stadtplaner) und Schmelzer-Bezzenberger (Landschaftsarchitekten) über einen Wettbewerb gewonnen. Einzelne Ausstellungsbereiche wurden an andere Büros aus der Region vergeben. Einen temporären Teil betreute das Stuttgarter Landschaftsarchitekturbüro Christof Luz, der Sohn von Hans Luz.

Er war es, der mich dazu einlud, den »Wandelgarten der Fachverbände« zu gestalten. Ich schlug etwas provozierend vor, die gesamte, dafür vorgesehene Fläche drei bis vier Meter hoch mit Reisig zu bedecken und in der Mitte einen großen, runden Platz auszusparen. In die restliche Totholzmasse wollte ich diverse Wohn- und Aufenthaltsräume mit Türen, Fluren, Möbeln, Wandfragmenten und Fenstern schneiden. Auf diese Weise sollten neuartige, bisher so noch nie gesehene »Naturzimmer« ohne Dach entstehen.

Auch andere Natur-Materialien wären in Frage gekommen: Steine, Stroh, Rinde, dickere Äste oder Holzstämme. Reisig wurde bisher – außer von Tieren und Vögeln – noch nie für Wohnzwecke benutzt. Es ist nur bedingt geeignet und leicht brennbar.

Zunächst fand die Idee eine etwas widerwillige Zustimmung. Es wurde auch mit dem Bau begonnen. Nachdem allerdings die Zulieferung von Reisig aus ganz Baden-Württemberg immer spärlicher ausfiel und zuletzt ganz stoppte, wurden die Verantwortlichen von der Angst überfallen, zur Eröffnung mit einem halbfertigen Werk dazustehen. Man brach aufgeregt ab und pfuschte die Räume nur noch mit lausigen Schilfmatten an Baugerüsten zu Ende. Christof Luz und ich distanzierten uns von dem Projekt, das eigentlich originell, witzig und sehr romantisch hätte werden können.

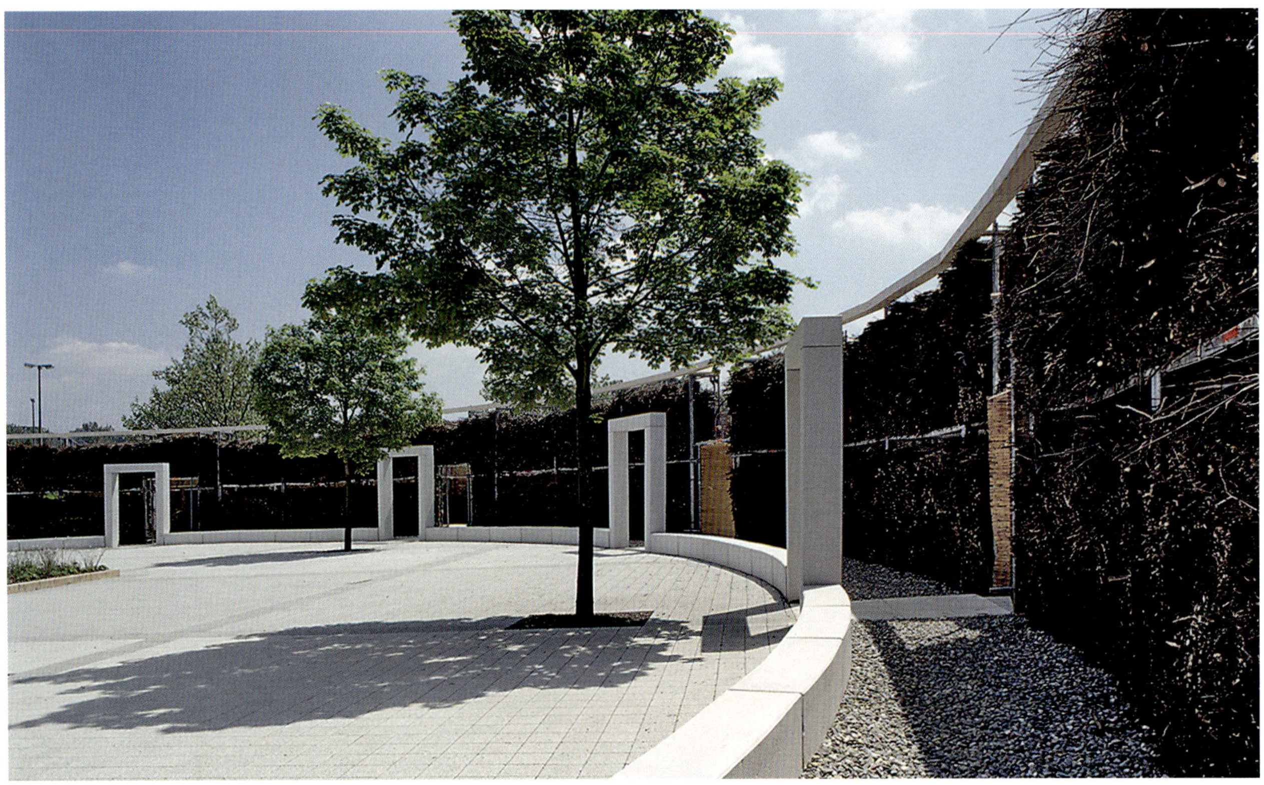

1. The central plaza, with its circular stone bench and doors made of white concrete in front of the brushwood wall. The photo shows it as it was shortly before the Gartenschau opened.
2. Sketch of the planned plaza brushwood complex.

1. Der zentrale Platz mit ringförmiger Steinbank und Toren aus weißem Beton vor der Reisigwand. Das Photo zeigt den Zustand kurz vor Eröffnung der Gartenschau.
2. Skizze der geplanten Platzanlage aus Reisig.

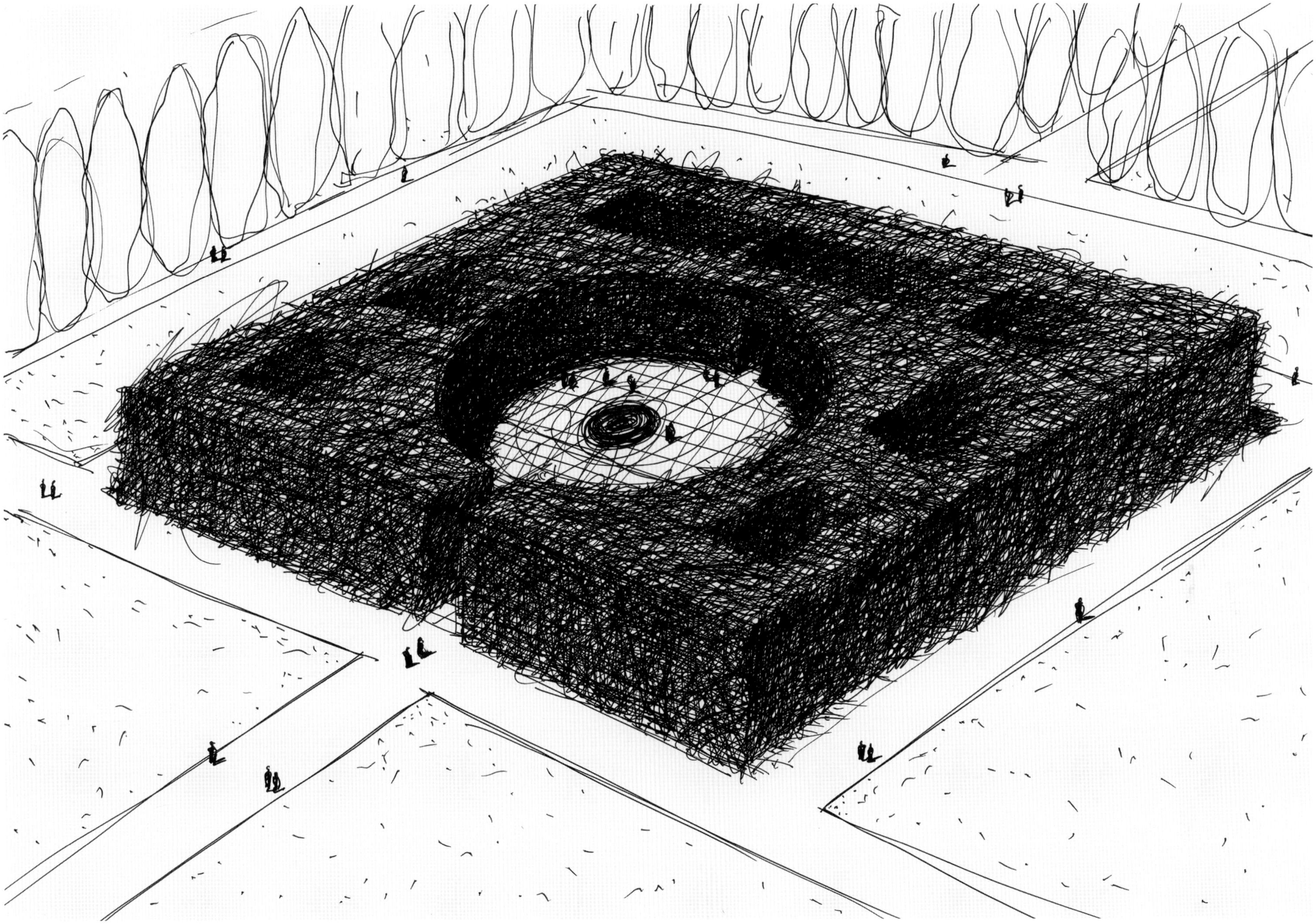

3, 4. View of individual space zones, which comes close to my ideas of garden spaces. Photos 1996. The incomplete and thus unsuccessful areas are not represented here.

3, 4. Blick in einzelne Raumzonen, die meinen Ideen von Gartenräumen nahe kamen. Photos 1996. Die unfertigen und damit mißglückten Bereiche werden hier nicht abgebildet.

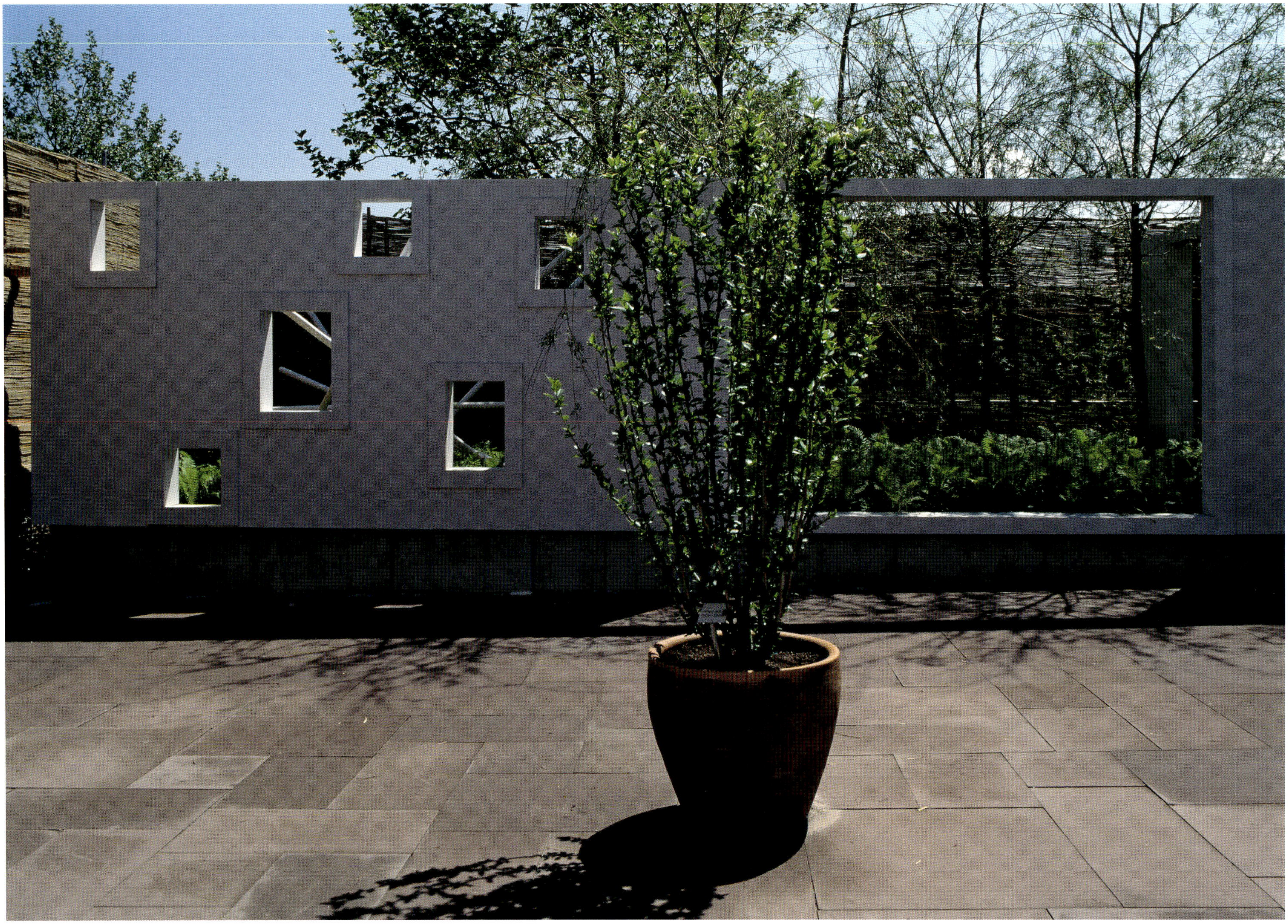

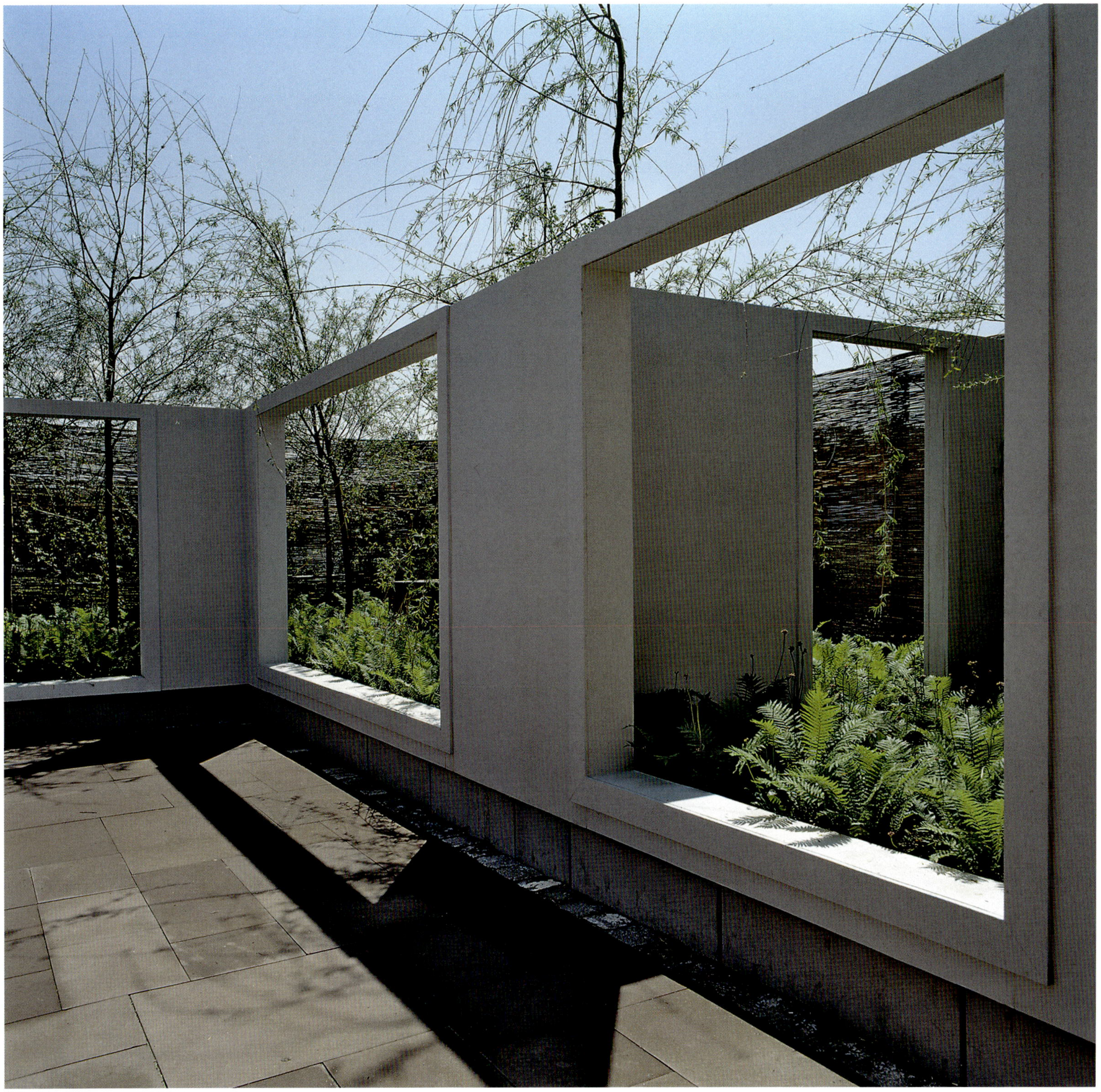

Monopteros, Hohenheimer Gärten, Stuttgart 1998

The historic Hohenheimer Gärten (gardens), laid out under the Württemberg duke Karl Eugen between 1776 and 1793, were extended between 1990 and 2000 by Hans Luz as an »English park« with freely curved paths and few trees. In 1997, he invited me to create a Monopteros to top the viewing hill he had created by piling up earth. I designed a double ring structure with eight white concrete pillars in each ring, beneath a round architrave.

Hans Luz planted his beloved circle of trees, composed of six pillar hornbeams, around my Monopteros. As a consequence, the white pillars can only be seen in winter; in summer, they are concealed by the low-set crowns of the trees. This is an exciting dialogue between architecture and nature, relating to my old theme of »artificial – natural«.

At the same time, there are also certain cosmic aspects. Anyone standing in the centre of the constructed circle and looking upwards through the two architrave rings can observe (and measure) – apart from the sky and clouds – the sun, the moon, and the stars. Thus, it is like an old observatory (without a telescope).

Adolf Martin Steiner composed a text on the Monopteros, which was printed in his book on the »Hohenheimer Gärten«, 2008. It reads as follows:

»Visitors often ask: what is a monopteros? Some, however, say: it's not a monopteros. So, how does this name relate to the structure on the hill in the landscape garden?

The composite word »mono-pteros« derives from the Greek, and means »single wing«. In architecture, it describes a round temple possessing a simple ring of pillars supporting an entablature upon which a domeshaped roof rests, with an open inner space …

When one looks at the modern Monopteros in the Hohenheimer landscape garden, it has little in common with the classical Monopteros. It has two circles rather than one circle, each composed of eight pillars of concrete marble, each connected by an architrave, a ringform beam like a crown, whilst the entablature and domed roof are absent …

The Monopteros makes the hill into a predominating garden element, a viewing point with a fantastic panorama …«

Monopteros, Hohenheimer Gärten, Stuttgart, 1998

Die historischen Hohenheimer Gärten, angelegt unter dem württembergischen Herzog Karl Eugen zwischen 1776 und 1793, wurden in den Jahren 1990 bis 2000 von Hans Luz als »englischer Park« mit frei schwingenden Wegen und wenigen Bäumen erweitert. Er lud mich 1997 dazu ein, seinen inzwischen aufgeschütteten Aussichtshügel mit einem Monopteros zu krönen. Ich entwarf einen Doppelring aus jeweils acht weißen Betonsäulen, die von einem runden Architrav überdeckt werden.

Hans Luz pflanzte seinen geliebten Baumkreis aus sechs Säulen-Hainbuchen um meinen Monopteros. Folge: Die weißen Säulen sind nur im Winter zu sehen, da sie im Sommer von den tiefansetzenden Baumkronen verdeckt werden. Ein spannender Dialog zwischen Architektur und Natur über mein altes Thema »künstlich – natürlich«.

Gleichzeitig klingen hier auch kosmische Aspekte an. Denn wer im Zentrum des gebauten Kreises steht und nach oben schaut, kann durch die beiden Architrav-Ringe – neben Himmel und Wolken – Sonne, Mond und Sterne beobachten (oder vermessen) wie in einem alten Observatorium (ohne Fernrohr).

Adolf Martin Steiner verfaßte einen Text über den Monopteros, der in seinem Buch über die »Hohenheimer Gärten« 2008 abgedruckt wurde. Darin heißt es:

»Oftmals fragten schon Besucher: Was ist ein Monopteros? Mancher sagte aber gleich: Das ist kein Monopteros. Welche Bewandtnis hat es nun mit dem Bauwerk auf dem Hügel im Landschaftsgarten und mit diesem Namen?

Das zusammengesetzte Wort »monopteros« stammt aus dem Griechischen und bedeutet »Ein-Flügler«. In der Baukunst bezeichnet es einen Rundtempel, der einen einfachen Ring von Säulen besitzt, die ein Gebälk tragen, auf dem ein kuppelförmiges Dach ruht, und dessen Innenraum frei ist …

Betrachtet man den modernen Monopteros im Hohenheimer Landschaftsgarten, so hat er mit dem klassischen Monopteros wenig gemein. Denn nicht nur ein Kreis, sondern gleich zwei Kreise von je acht Säulen aus Betonmarmor sind jeweils mit einem Architrav, einem ringförmigen Balken, wie mit einer Krone verbunden, und ein Gebälk und ein Kuppeldach fehlen …

Mit dem Monopteros wurde der Hügel zum beherrschenden Gartenelement, zum Aussichtspunkt mit einem phantastischen Panorama …«

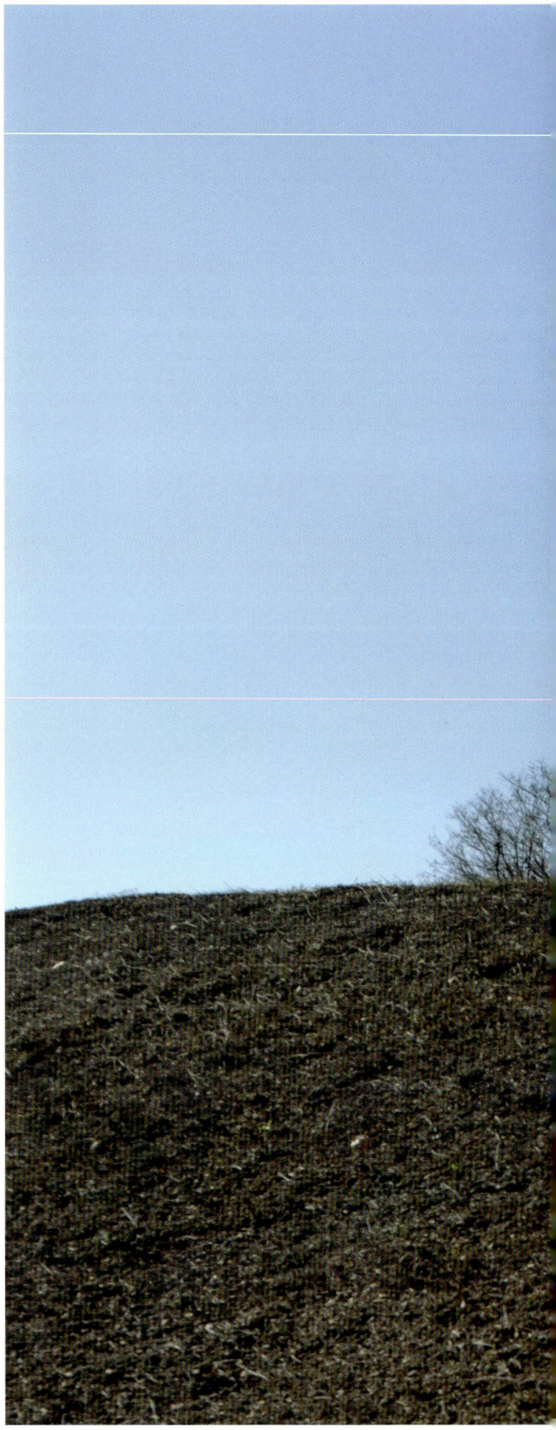

1. View of the Monopteros hill with bare winter pillar hornbeams. Photo 2015.

1. Ansicht des Monopteros-Hügels mit winterlich kahlen Säulen-Hainbuchen. Photo 2015.

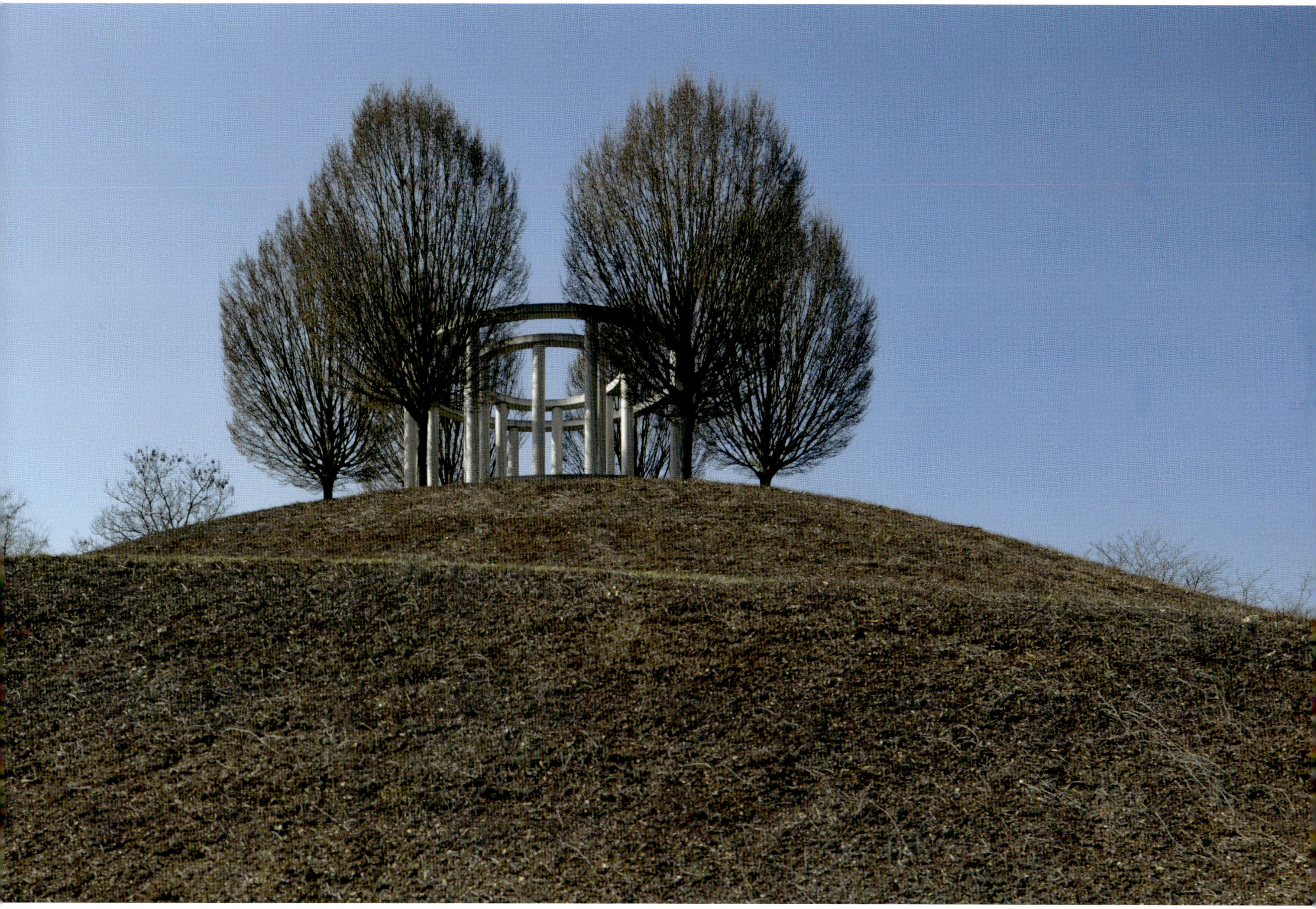

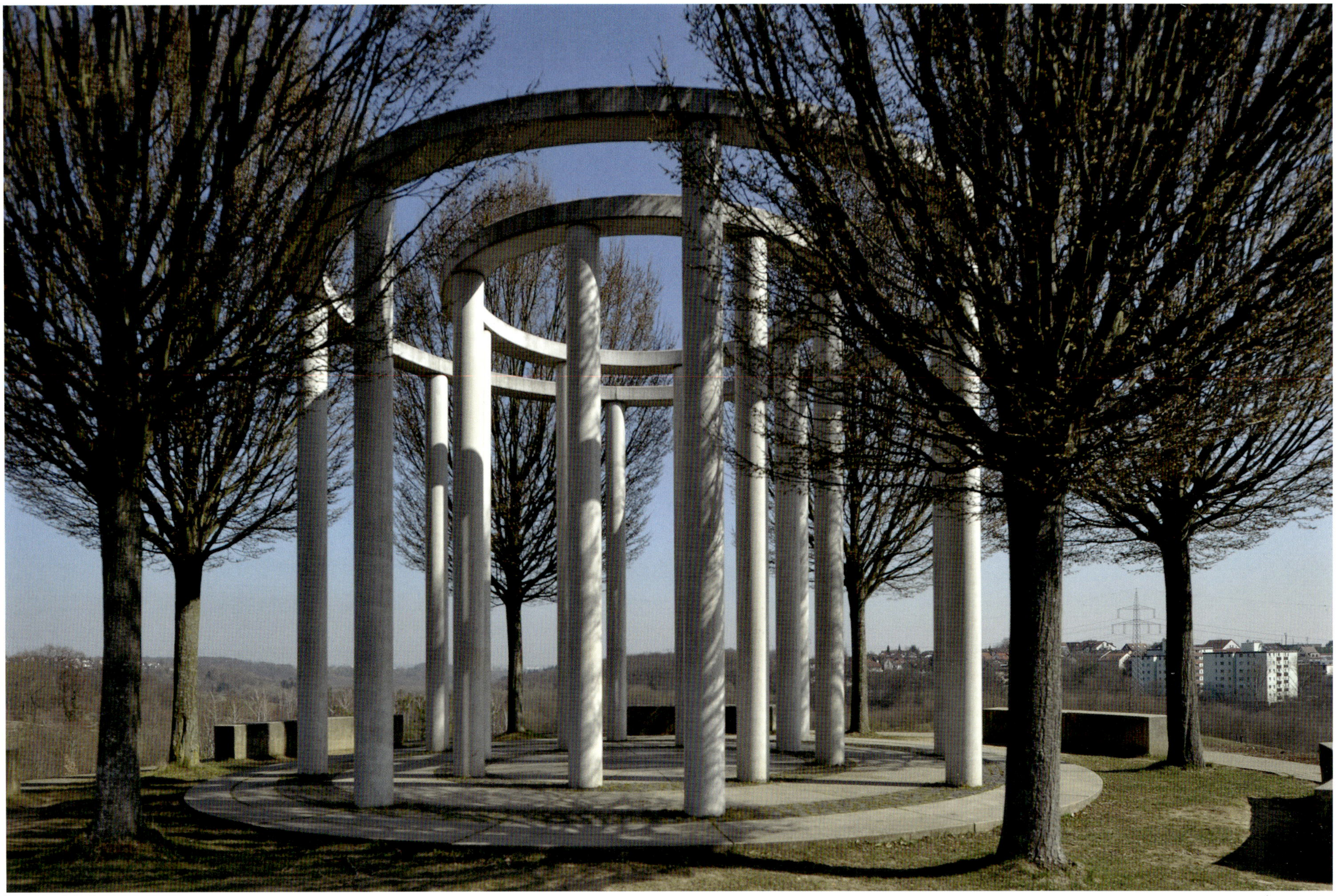

2. Viewing plateau with benches in the winter. Photo 2015.
3. The Monopteros in the summer.

pp. 80, 81
4. Viewing plateau. Trees with summer foliage. Photo 2016.
5. View looking upward, showing the two architrave rings. Surrounded by late-summer trees. Photo 2016.

2. Aussichtsplateau mit Bänken im Winter. Photo 2015.
3. Der Monopteros im Sommer.

S. 80, 81
4. Aussichtsplateau. Bäume mit Sommerbegrünung. Photo 2016.
5. Blick nach oben zu den beiden Architrav-Ringen. Mit spätsommerlichen Bäumen ringsum. Photo 2016.

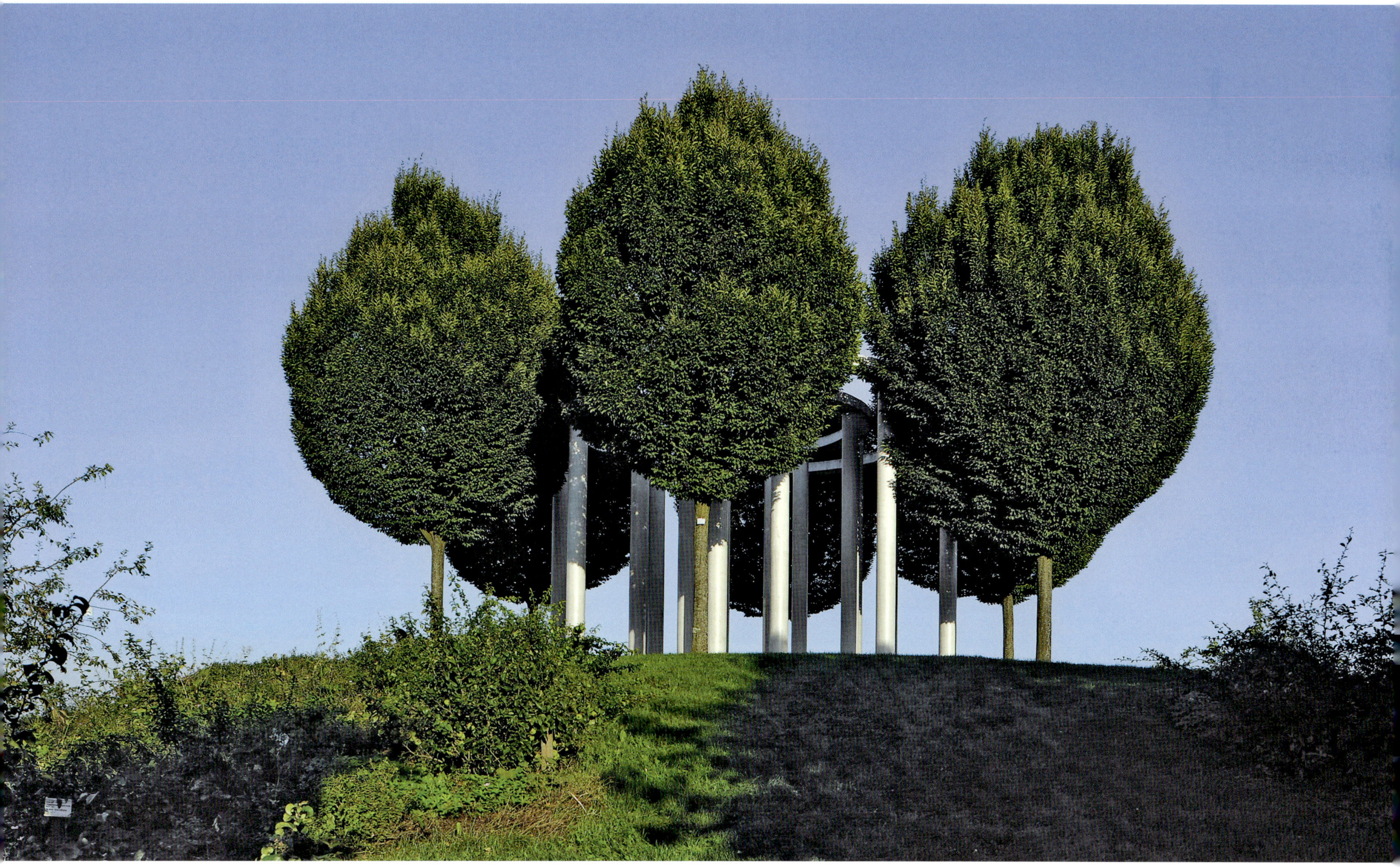

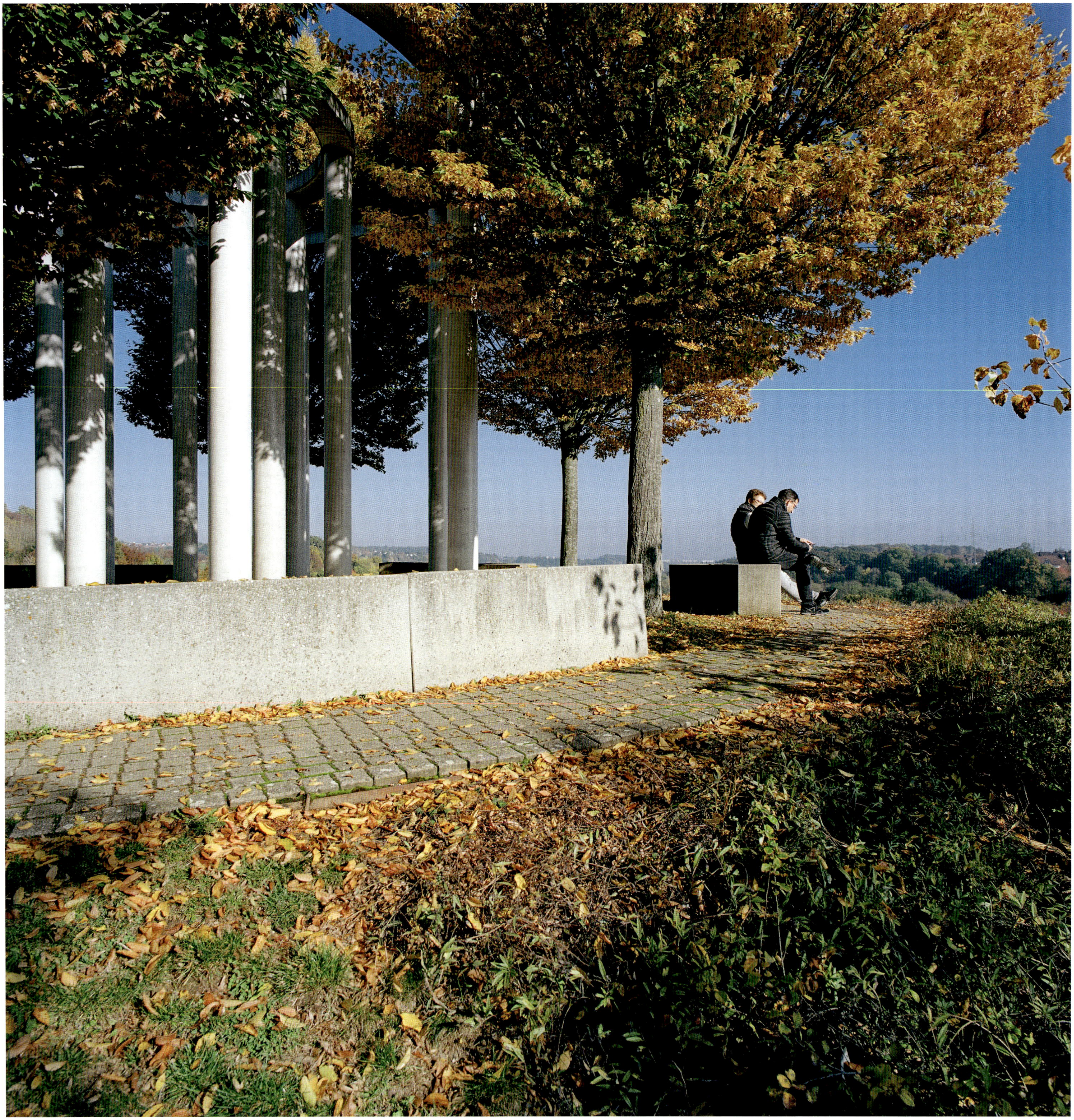

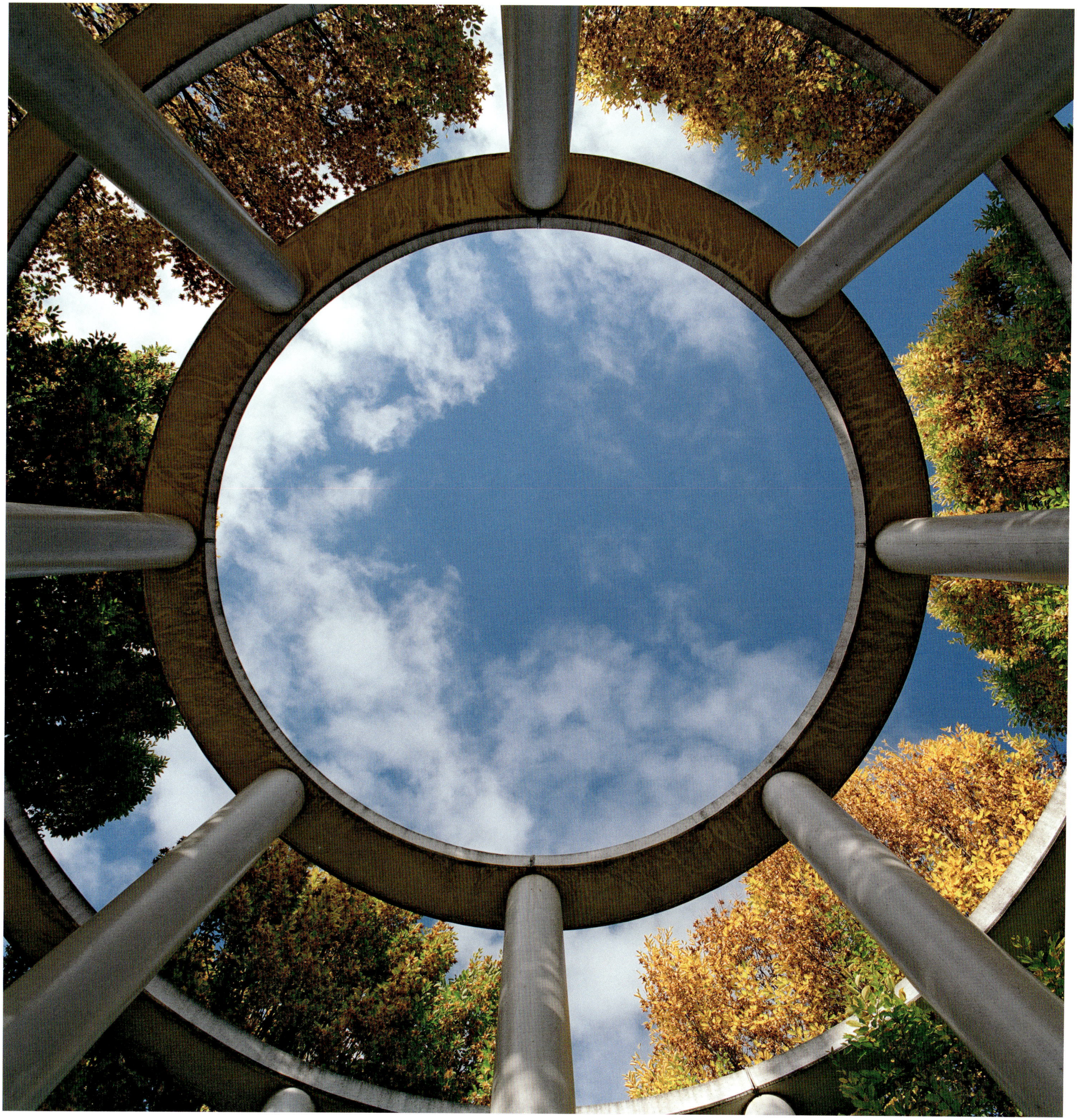

Wielandpark, Biberach an der Riß, 1998 to 2000, extended in 2003, reworked and renovated 2010–2014. Client: the city of Biberach an der Riß. Construction management: Biberach civil construction authority and the architecture firm of Günter Schmitt, Biberach (with garden architect Elisabeth Kimmich)

The Wielandpark, which originally bore the unpoetic and pragmatic name Bürger-Park (citizens' park) represented the first time I was able to realise my garden and park ideas in a somewhat more extensive and differentiated way. In contrast to most of the previously described works, this project actually involved the movement of earth, the excavation of a lake, the piling of a hill rampart, and the planting of numerous trees (with a number of trees having been previously cut down). Unfortunately, as with many of my projects, there was also a certain amount of resistance from residents and from the civic administration.

In addition to architectonic peripheral construction banalities and a somewhat obscured backyard position, the designated site offered (and continues to offer) an unusual highlight: the Gartenhäuschen (little garden house) in whose upper storey, from 1766 to 1769, the Swabian poet Christoph Martin Wieland spent afternoons working on his texts. He would have looked out on meadows, gardens, farmed land, trees, and the little river Riß, which meandered by beneath his window.

As I was no great lover or connoisseur of this classicist, ironic, sensual rococo Enlightenment poet, I contemplated an unconventional garden programme: what if Jean-Jacques Rousseau (1712–1778) and Christoph Martin Wieland (1733–1813) had met here? What kind of conversation and discussion might have taken place? This is admittedly pure fiction. In reality, the two never met. Nor do I know what they thought of each other. I simply imagined that it would be a meeting of two fundamentally different worldviews. Perhaps, where it came to gardens and nature, they were not so far apart? Even though our early classicist, who was praised by Johann Wolfgang von Goethe and even by Heinrich von Kleist, surely had no thoughts of revolution. I did not work with real figures, but instead used quotations from buildings and parks from the era known as the Enlightenment. I juxtaposed the little Wieland house with Rousseau's poplar island in Ermenonville, setting it in a large, round lake and building an additional artificial ruin, which might be understood as representing the Romantic's criticism of Wieland. On the paths and on the island, I also placed a number of stones with chiselled text quotations from the texts of both poets and thinkers.

One of these men looked for happiness in lovely gardens with an ambience of classical antiquity, and ultimately failed as a farmer in Ossmannstedt near Weimar. The other was in a constant state of flight, and never experienced the »liberating result« of his daring theses such as »All harm begins with the invention of private property« and »Back to nature« in the French Revolution.

In a tourists' guide to architecture, the Wielandpark is described as follows:

»A new park was fitted into the existing development. With the historic garden house of the poet Christoph Martin Wieland (on the edge of the park) as a starting point, a fictional dialogue develops between Wieland and the French philosopher Rousseau – both Enlightenment figures. The path system, space design and stage-set-like architecture motifs juxtapose severely regular garden architecture and free-growing nature. The theme is the conflict between social order and free human development. Other motifs incorporate a modern, media-based artistic aspect. The visitor passes through a skein of associations, like the viewer of a film. A rotunda planted with poplars is reminiscent of Rousseau's island place of burial.

Notwithstanding this, the park is an inviting and restorative place for contemplation, for movement and for communication, and does not exclude those who do not know how to interpret its messages.

This is a successful composition, ambitious both intellectually and in terms of garden art, competently implemented and a restorative place to spend time.«

This park also experienced casual vandalism: in the very first night after completion, the spheres were cut off the pinnacles of the little onion domes that I had set up as a regularly ranked »army« in the meadow in front of the viewing arbour (as successors to my Stuttgart garden gnomes). Later, people with spray cans came and defaced the entrance gates, the representations of fences, the semicircular arbour, and the ruin. Every morning saw the whole park strewn with rubbish. A certain group of young people liked to have parties near the lake, behind the ruin. The city had a sign placed at the park entrances forbidding use of the park at night (also, of course, due to the complaints of residents).

Wielandpark, Biberach an der Riß, 1998–2000, ergänzt 2003, überarbeitet und renoviert 2010 bis 2014. Auftraggeber: Stadt Biberach an der Riß. Bauleitung: Tiefbauamt Biberach und Architekturbüro Günter Schmitt, Biberach (mit Gartenarchitektin Elisabeth Kimmich)

Mit dem Wielandpark, der ursprünglich ganz unpoetisch und pragmatisch Bürger-Park hieß, konnte ich zum ersten Mal meine Garten- und Park-Ideen etwas umfangreicher und ausdifferenzierter realisieren. Im Gegensatz zu den meisten bisher beschriebenen Arbeiten, wurde hier tatsächlich Erde bewegt, ein See ausgehoben, ein Hügelwall aufgeschüttet und zahlreiche Bäume gepflanzt (vorher auch einige abgesägt). Leider gab es wie bei vielen anderen meiner Projekte auch manchen Widerstand von Anwohnern und Stadtverwaltung.

Der vorgesehene Ort bot und bietet, neben architektonischen Randbau-Banalitäten und der etwas versteckten Hinterhoflage, einen ungewöhnlichen Schwerpunkt: das Gartenhäuschen, in dessen Obergeschoß der schwäbische Dichter Christoph Martin Wieland von 1766 bis 1769 nachmittags an seinen Texten arbeitete. Sein Blick fiel damals auf Wiesen, Gärten, landwirtschaftlich genutzte Flächen, Bäume und das kleine Flüßchen Riß, das unter seinem Fenster vorbeimäanderte.

Da ich kein großer Freund und Kenner dieses antikisch-ironisch-sinnlichen Rokoko-Aufklärers war, überlegte ich mir ein ungewöhnliches Gartenprogramm: Was wäre, wenn sich hier Jean-Jacques Rousseau (1712 bis 1778) und Christoph Martin Wieland (1733–1813) begegnet wären? Welche Gespräche und Diskussionen hätten möglicherweise stattgefunden? Zugegeben: reine Fiktion. In Wirklichkeit sahen sich die beiden nie. Und was der eine über den anderen dachte, weiß ich auch nicht. Ich kann mir nur vorstellen, daß sich zwei grundsätzlich verschiedene Weltsichten begegnet wären. Oder doch nicht? Waren sie in Bezug auf Gärten und Natur nicht so weit voneinander entfernt? An Revolution freilich dachte unser Frühklassiker, den Johann Wolfgang von Goethe und sogar Heinrich von Kleist schätzten, bestimmt nicht.

Ich arbeitete nicht mit realen Figuren, sondern mit Bau- und Parkzitaten aus jener Zeit, die Aufklärung genannt wird. Das kleine Wieland-Häuschen konfrontierte ich mit Rousseaus Pappelinsel in Ermenonville, ließ sie in einem großen, runden See treiben, baute dazu eine künstliche Ruine, die als Kritik der Romantiker an Wieland verstanden werden könnte. Dazu legte ich einige Steine mit eingemeißelten Textzitaten aus den Schriften beider Dichter und Denker an die Wege und auf die Insel.

Der eine suchte sein Glück in lieblichen, antikisch-klassisch angehauchten Gärten und scheiterte am Ende als Landwirt in Oßmannstedt bei Weimar, der andere war ständig auf der Flucht und konnte das »befreiende Ergebnis« seiner gewagten Thesen wie »Alles Unheil beginnt mit der Erfindung des Privatbesitzes« und »Zurück zur Natur« in der Französischen Revolution nicht mehr erleben.

In einem touristischen Architekturführer wird der Wielandpark mit folgenden Worten beschrieben:

»Ein neuer Park wurde in die vorhandene Bebauung eingefügt. Ausgehend vom historischen Gartenhaus des Dichters Christoph Martin Wieland am Rande des Parks entwickelt sich ein fiktiver Dialog zwischen Wieland und dem französischen Philosophen Rousseau – beides Protagonisten der Aufklärung. In der Wegführung, Flächengestaltung und in den kulissenhaften Architekturmotiven stehen sich strenge Gartenarchitektur und frei wachsende Natur gegenüber. Sie thematisieren den Konflikt zwischen gesellschaftlicher Ordnung und freier Entfaltung des Menschen. Andere Motive beziehen einen modernen, medialen Kunstaspekt ein. Der Besucher geht durch ein Assoziationsgeflecht wie beim Betrachten eines Films. Ein Rondell mit Pappeln erinnert an Rousseaus Grabinsel.

Gleichwohl lädt der Park zum erholsamen, kontemplativen Aufenthalt, zu Bewegung und Kommunikation ein, ohne jemanden abzuweisen, der die Inhalte nicht zu deuten weiß.

Eine gelungene Anlage mit hohem intellektuellen und garten-künstlerischem Anspruch, fachgerechter Ausführung und erholsamem Aufenthaltsangebot.«

Alltäglicher Vandalismus auch hier: Gleich in der ersten Nacht nach Fertigstellung wurden die Gipfel-Kugeln der kleinen Zwiebeltürme, die ich als strenge »Armee« (Nachfolger meiner Stuttgarter Gartenzwerge) in der Wiese vor der Sichtlaube aufstellen ließ, abgeschlagen. Später kamen Sprayer und beschmierten die Eingangstore, die angedeuteten Zäune, die halbrunde Laube und die Ruine. Müll lag jeden Morgen im gesamten Park verstreut. Eine gewisse Gruppe von Jugendlichen liebte es, am See und hinter der Ruine Parties zu feiern. Daraufhin ließ die Stadt ein nächtliches Aufenthaltsverbotsschild an den Parkeingängen aufstellen. Natürlich auch, weil sich die Anwohner beschwert hatten.

1. Site plan of the whole area. 1998.

1. Lageplan der gesamten Anlage. 1998.

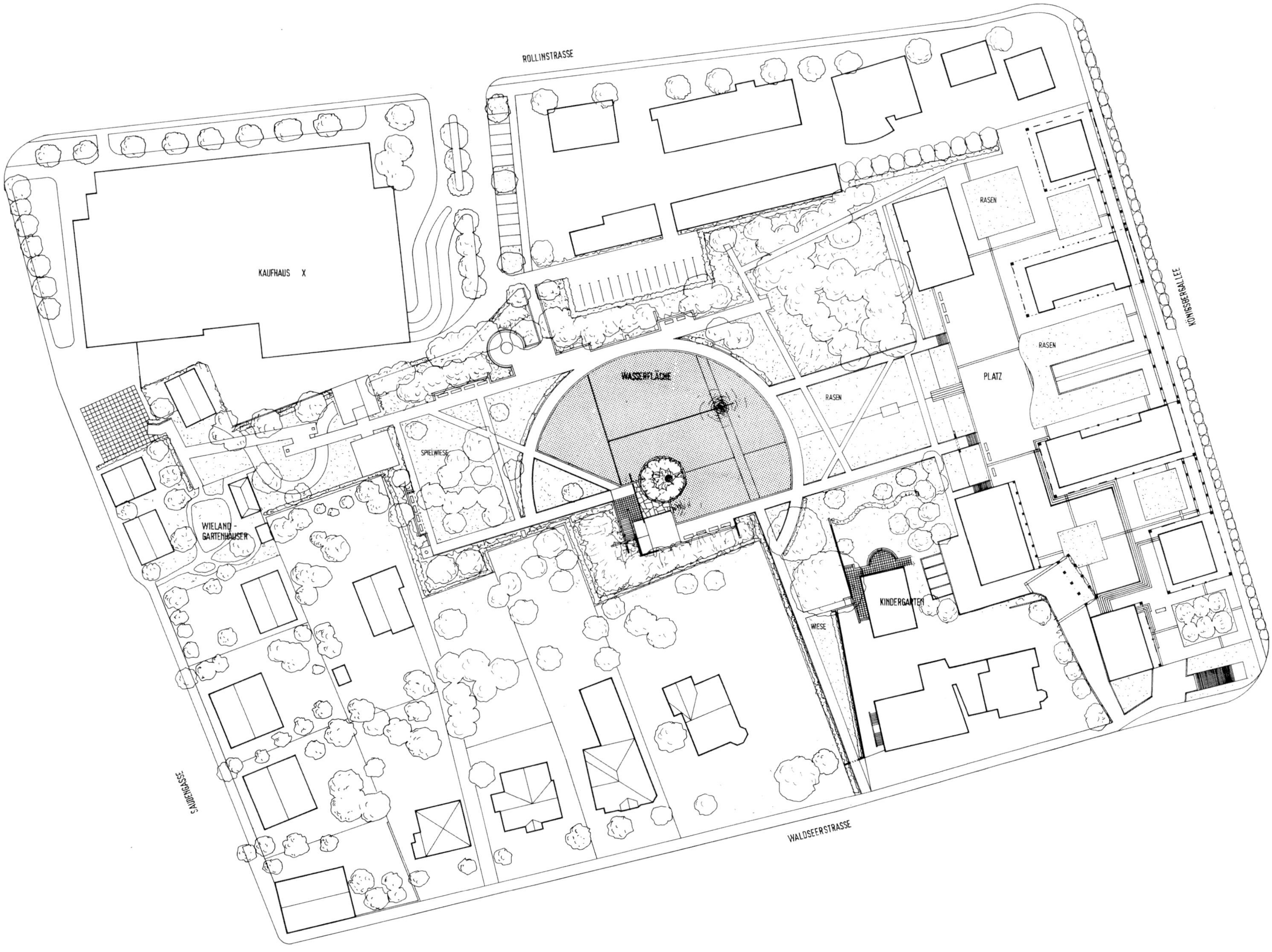

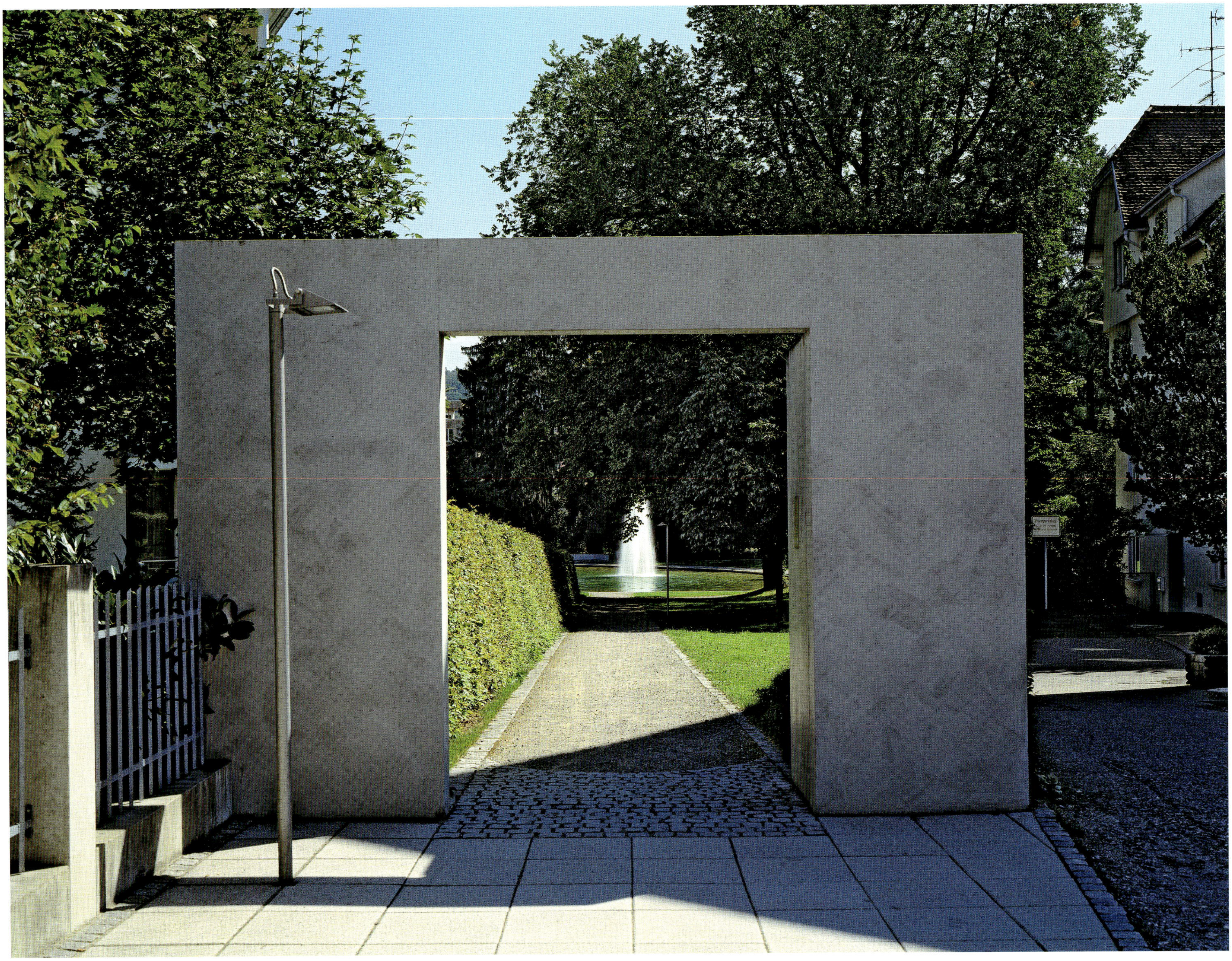

2. One of the concrete entrance gates. Photo 2003.
3. Open entrance area looking towards the inner city of Biberach. Photo 2003.

2. Eines der Eingangstore aus Beton. Photo 2003.
2. Offener Eingangsbereich in Richtung Biberacher Innenstadt. Photo 2003.

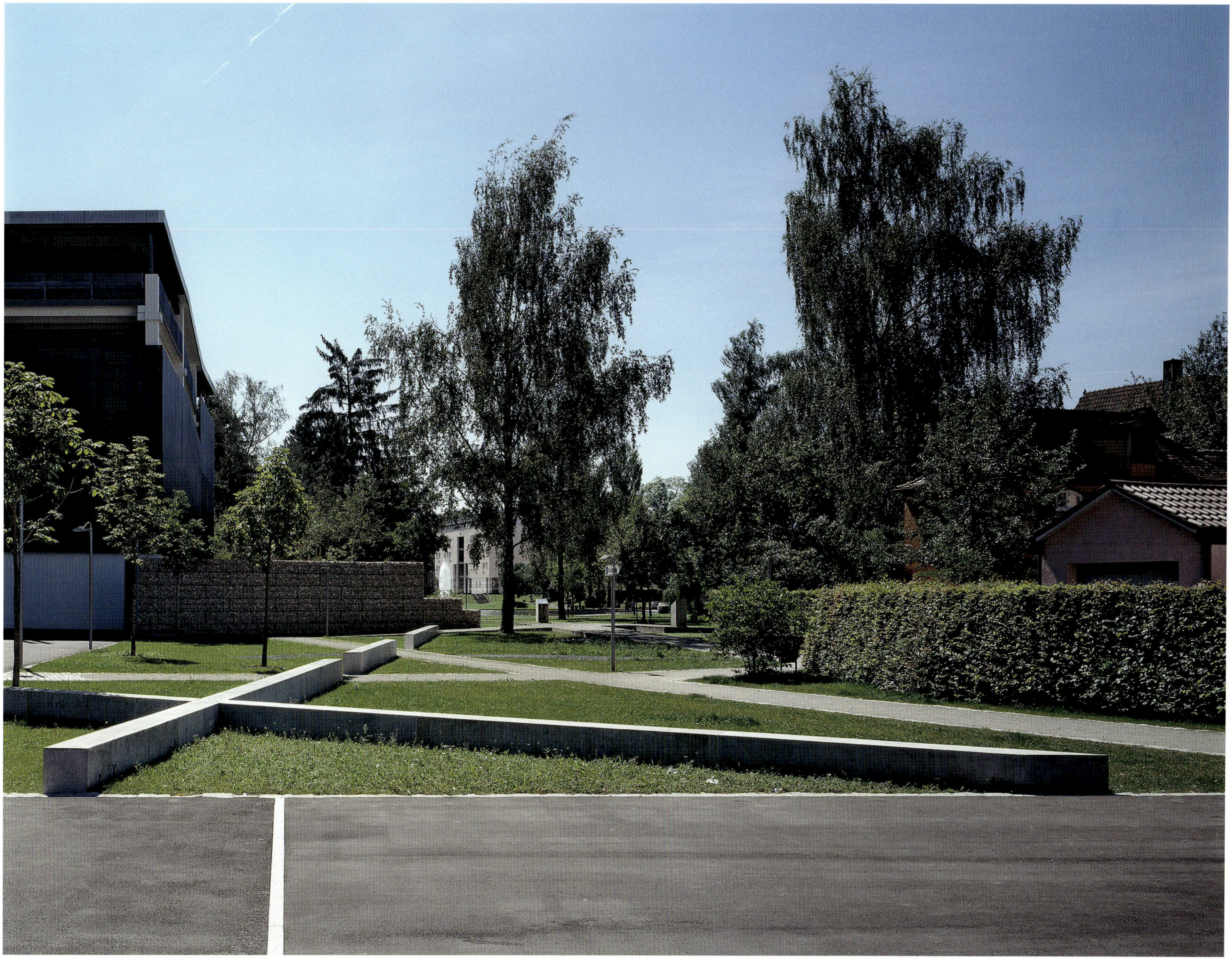

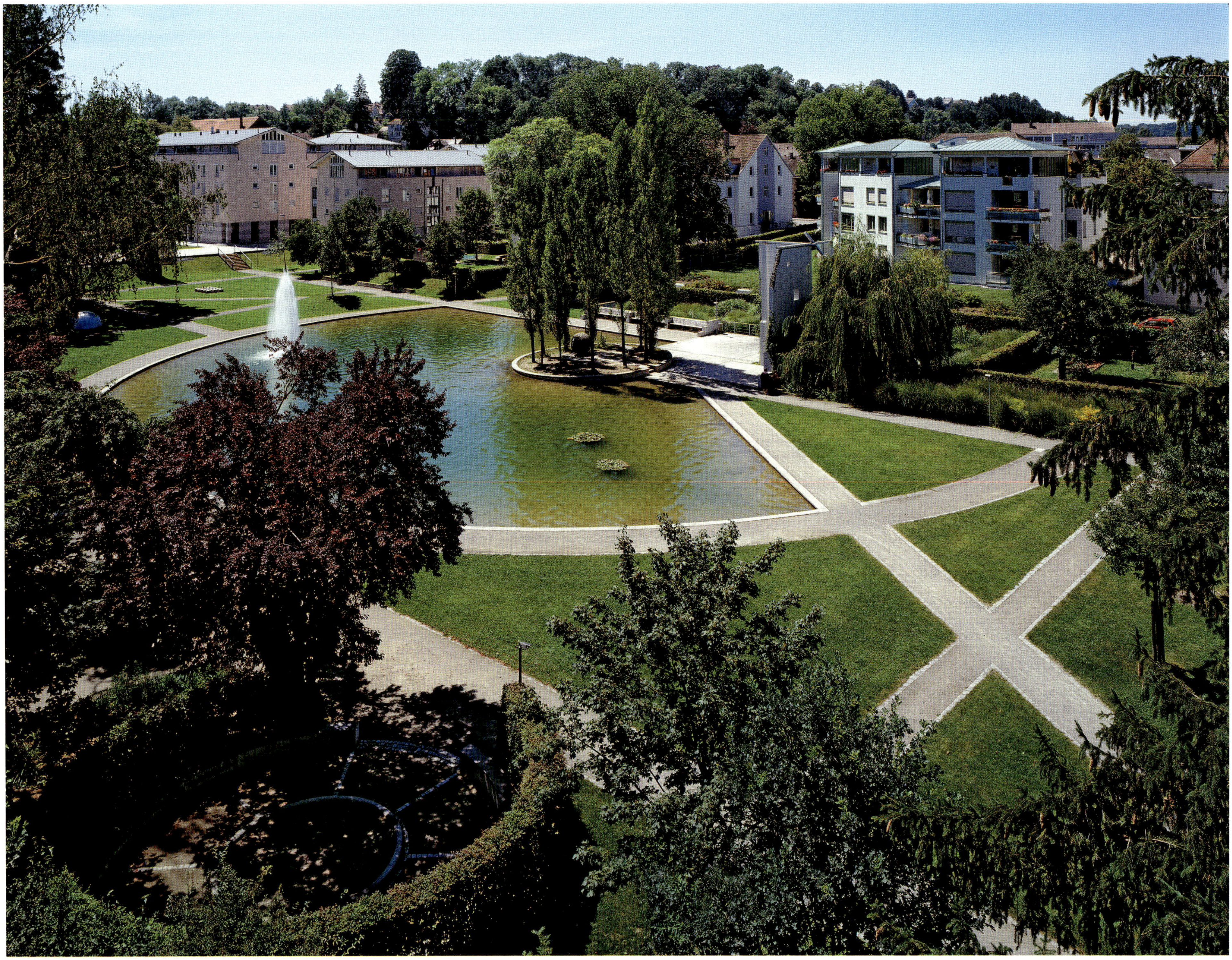

4. View of the small park landscape with its round lake, poplar island, and artificial ruins, from the top of the neighbouring parking garage of a former department store, which was converted some years ago into the district administration office. Photo 2003.
5. Another view from the neighbouring parking garage, in the direction of the town entrance and of Christoph Martin Wieland's garden house. Photo 2003.

4. Blick vom benachbarten Parkhaus-Oberdeck eines ehemaligen Kaufhauses, das vor einigen Jahren zum Landratsamt umgebaut wurde, über die kleine Parklandschaft mit rundem See, Pappelinsel und künstlicher Ruine. Photo 2003.
5. Noch einmal ein Blick vom benachbarten Parkhaus, Richtung Stadteingang und dem Gartenhaus von Christoph Martin Wieland. Photo 2003.

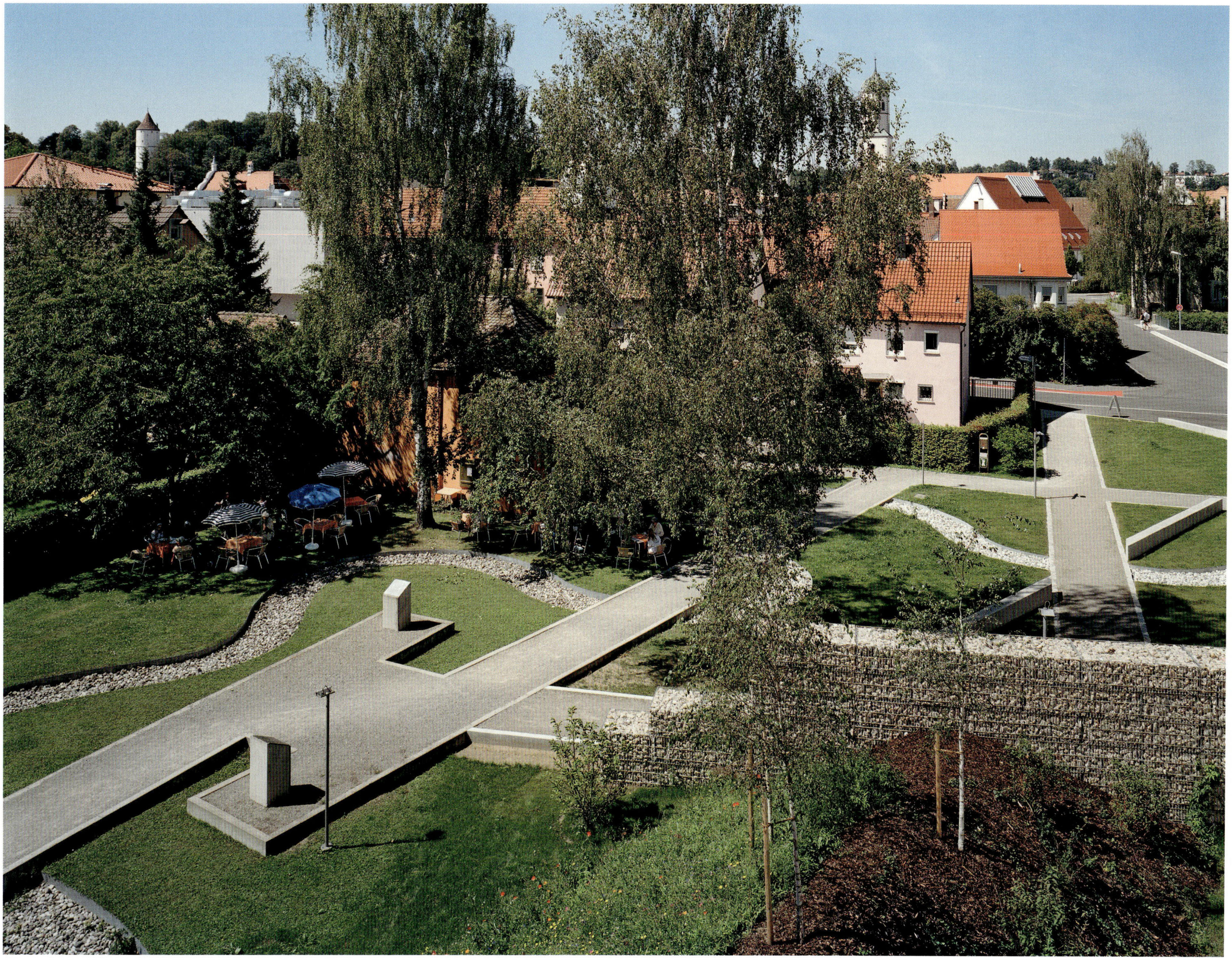

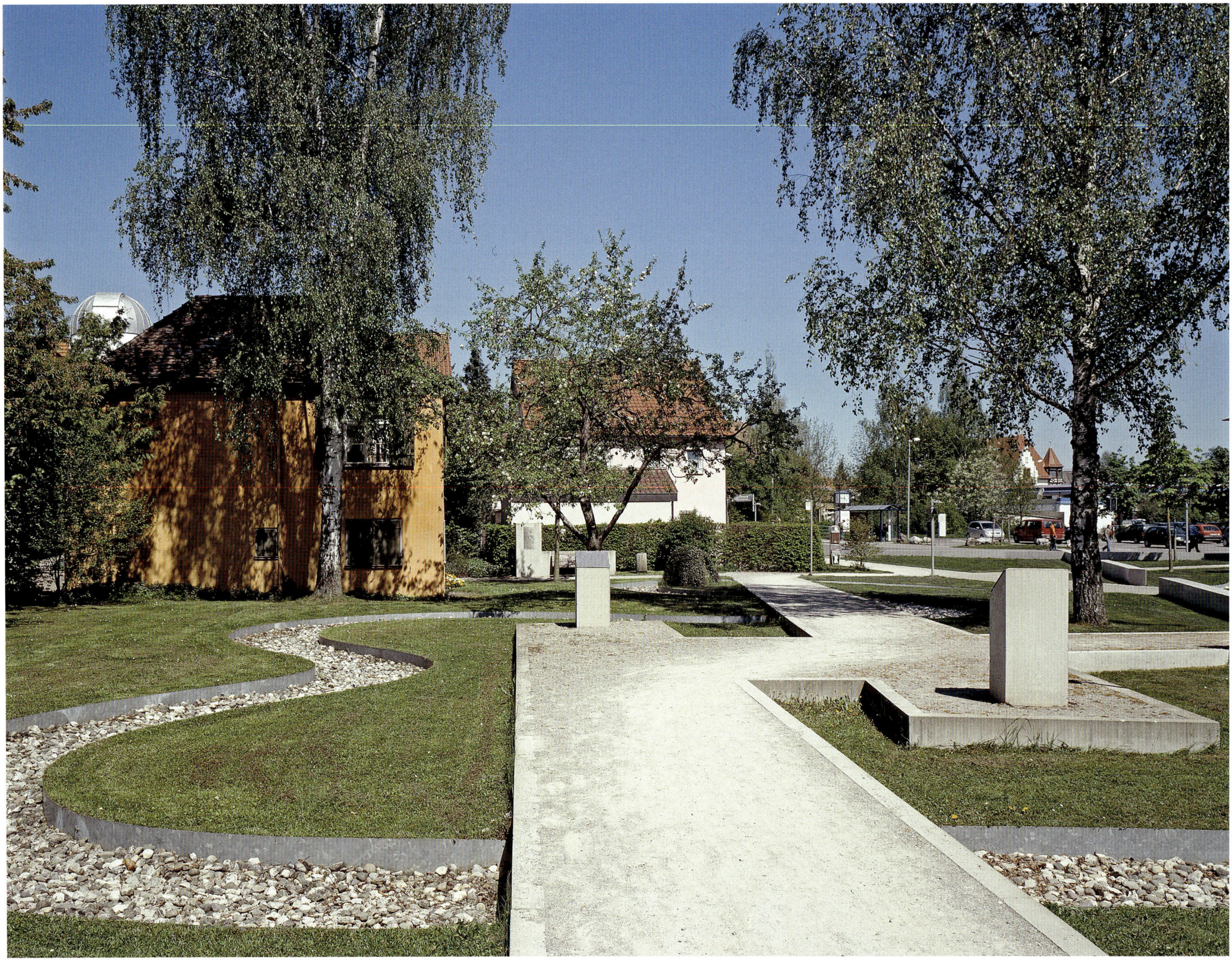

6. In the background is the Wieland-Gartenhaus, seen from the park side. In the foreground is an artificial path crossroads (annoying for cyclists!) featuring two stones with poems by Christoph-Martin-Wieland. Additionally, a suggestion of the course of the Riß. Photo 2003.
7. Christoph Martin Wieland's garden house, in which the town has created a small Wieland-Museum. In the foreground is an old memorial stone overgrown with ivy, on which is inscribed a poem. There is also a fictional suggestion of the former course of the Riß, with curved steel lines and granite gravel in various different sizes. Photo 2003.

6. Im Hintergrund das Wieland-Gartenhaus von der Parkseite. Im Vordergrund eine künstliche Wegkreuzung (zum Ärger der Radfahrer!) mit zwei Christoph-Martin-Wieland-Gedichtssteinen. Dazu der angedeutete Verlauf der Riß. Photo 2003.
7. Gartenhaus von Christoph Martin Wieland, in dem die Stadt ein kleines Wieland-Museum eingerichtet hat. Im Vordergrund ein alter, efeubewachsener Gedenkstein mit einem Gedicht. Dazu die fiktive Andeutung des ehemaligen Riß-Verlaufs: geschwungene Stahlränder und Granitkiesel in verschiedenen Größen. Photo 2003.

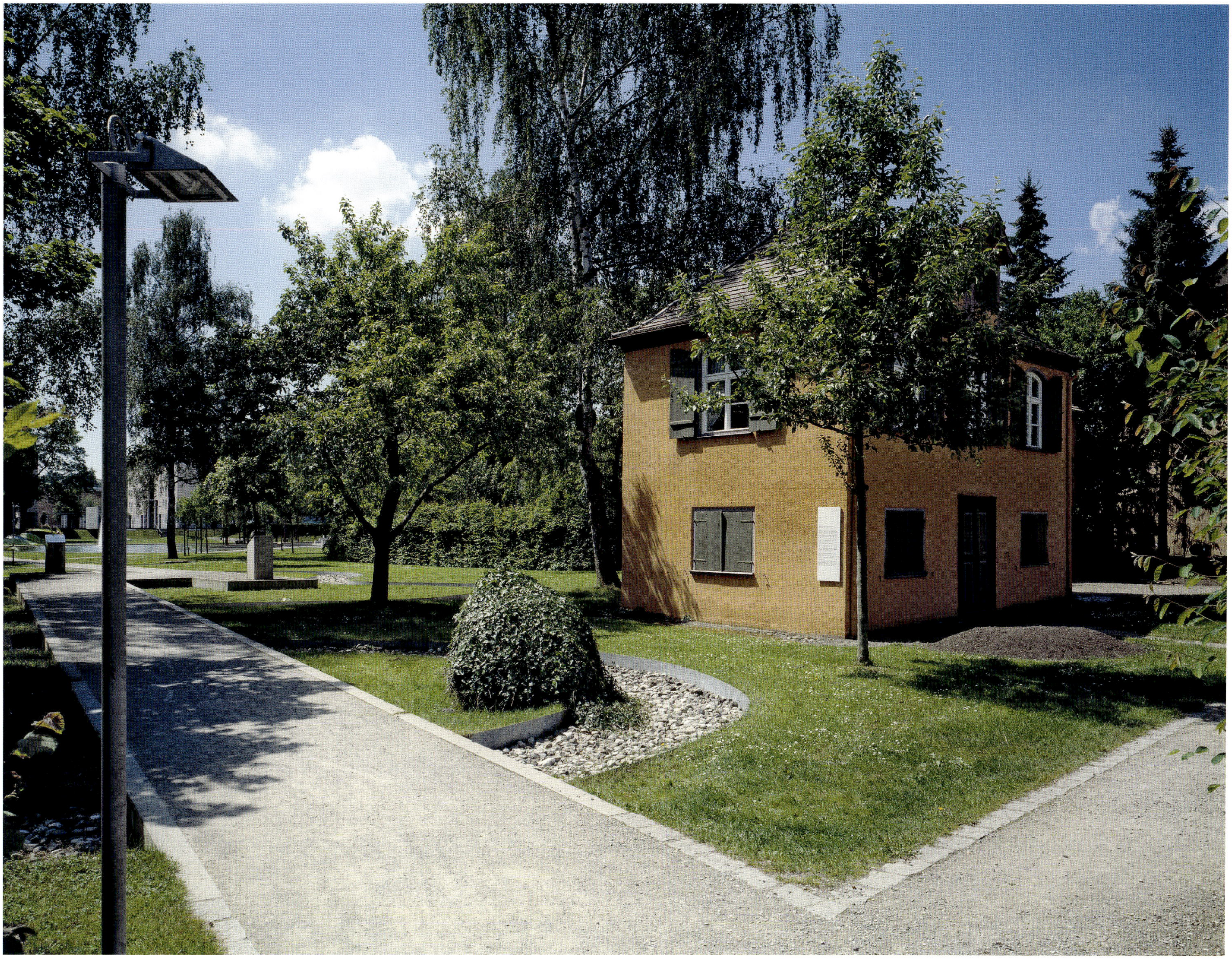

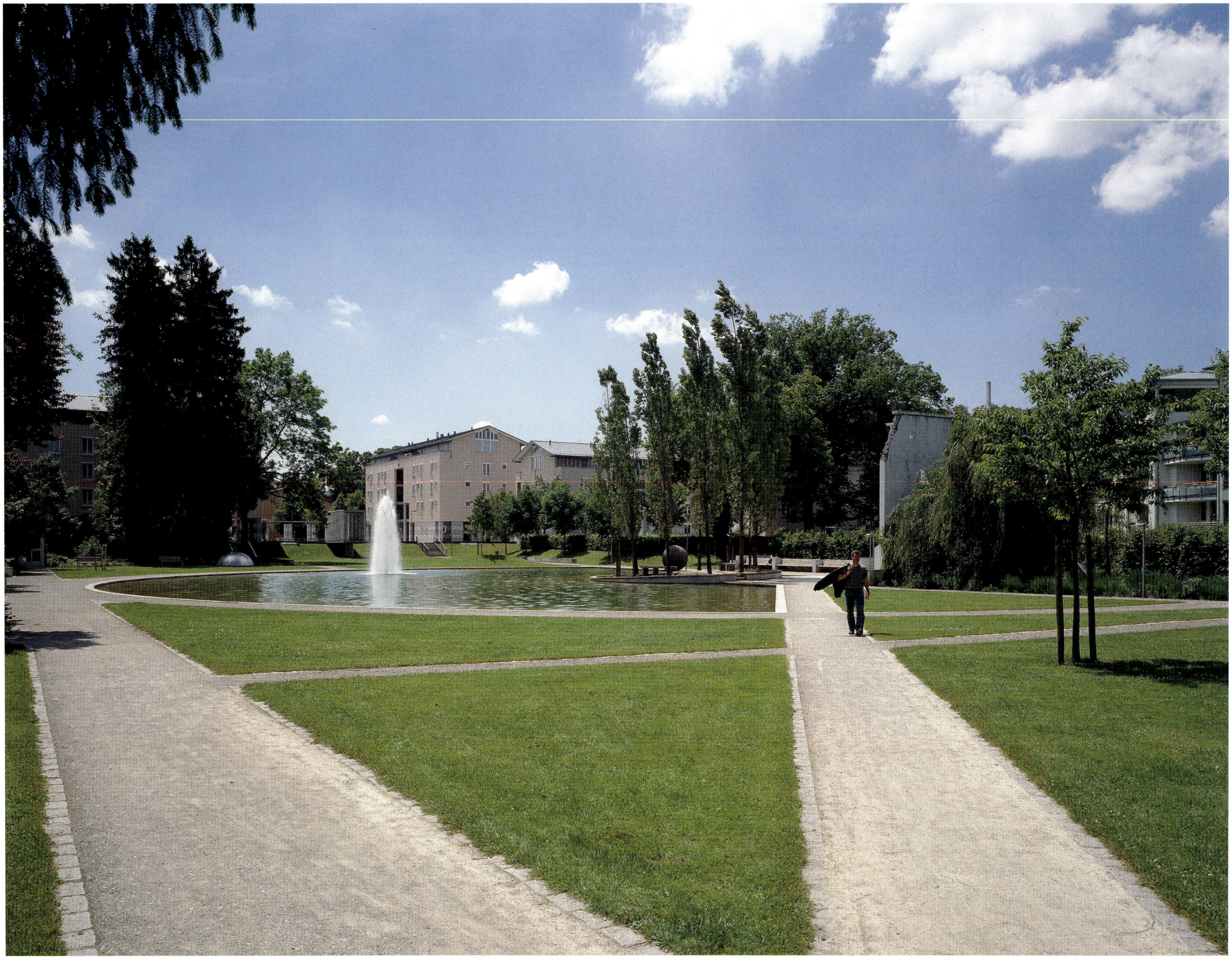

8. Park paths, in the direction of the lake, fountain, ruin and poplar island. Photo 2003.
9. Bench seating in the lake area. Photo 2003.

8. Parkwege, Richtung See, Fontäne, Ruine und Pappelinsel. Photo 2003.
9. Sitzbänke im Seebereich. Photo 2003.

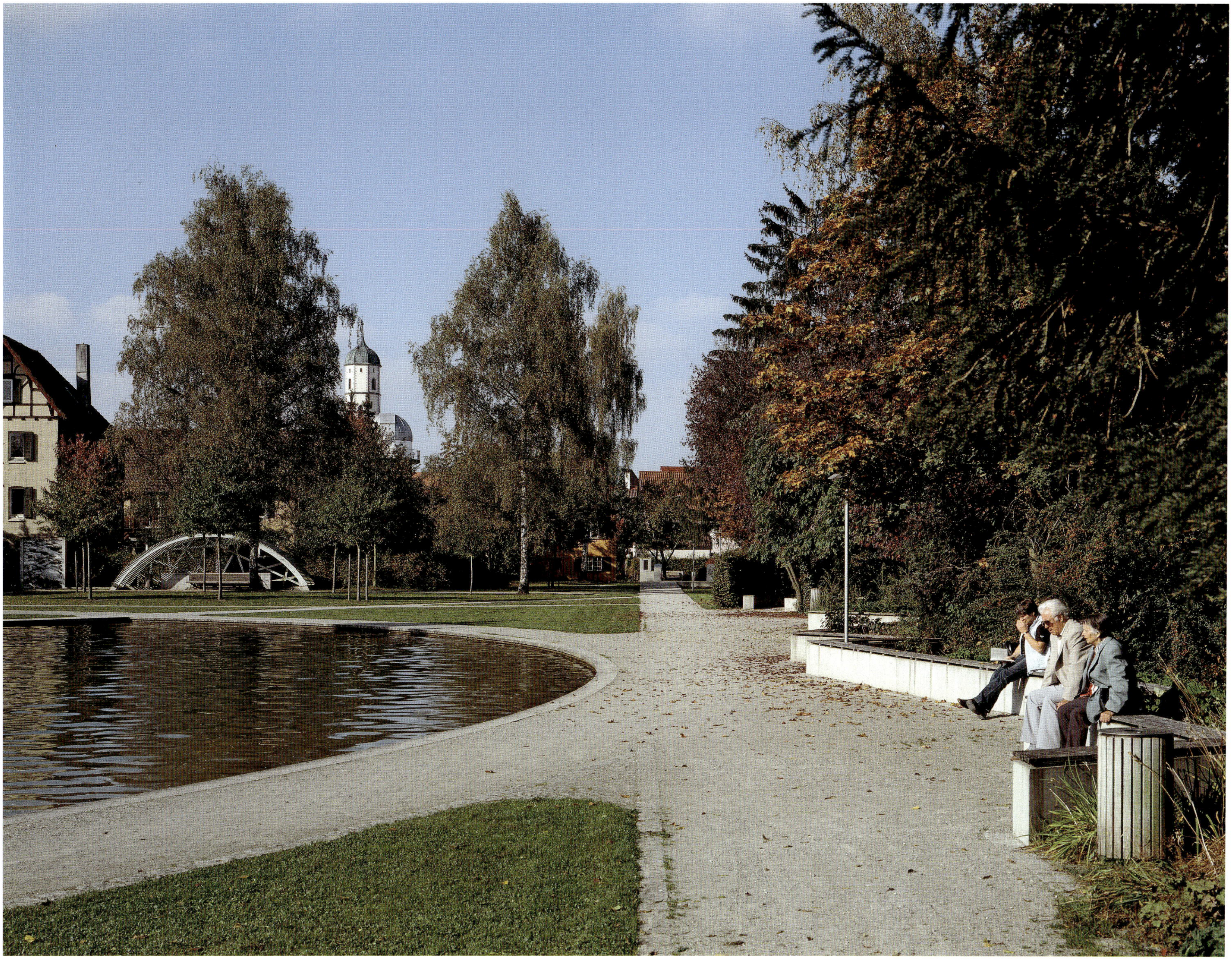

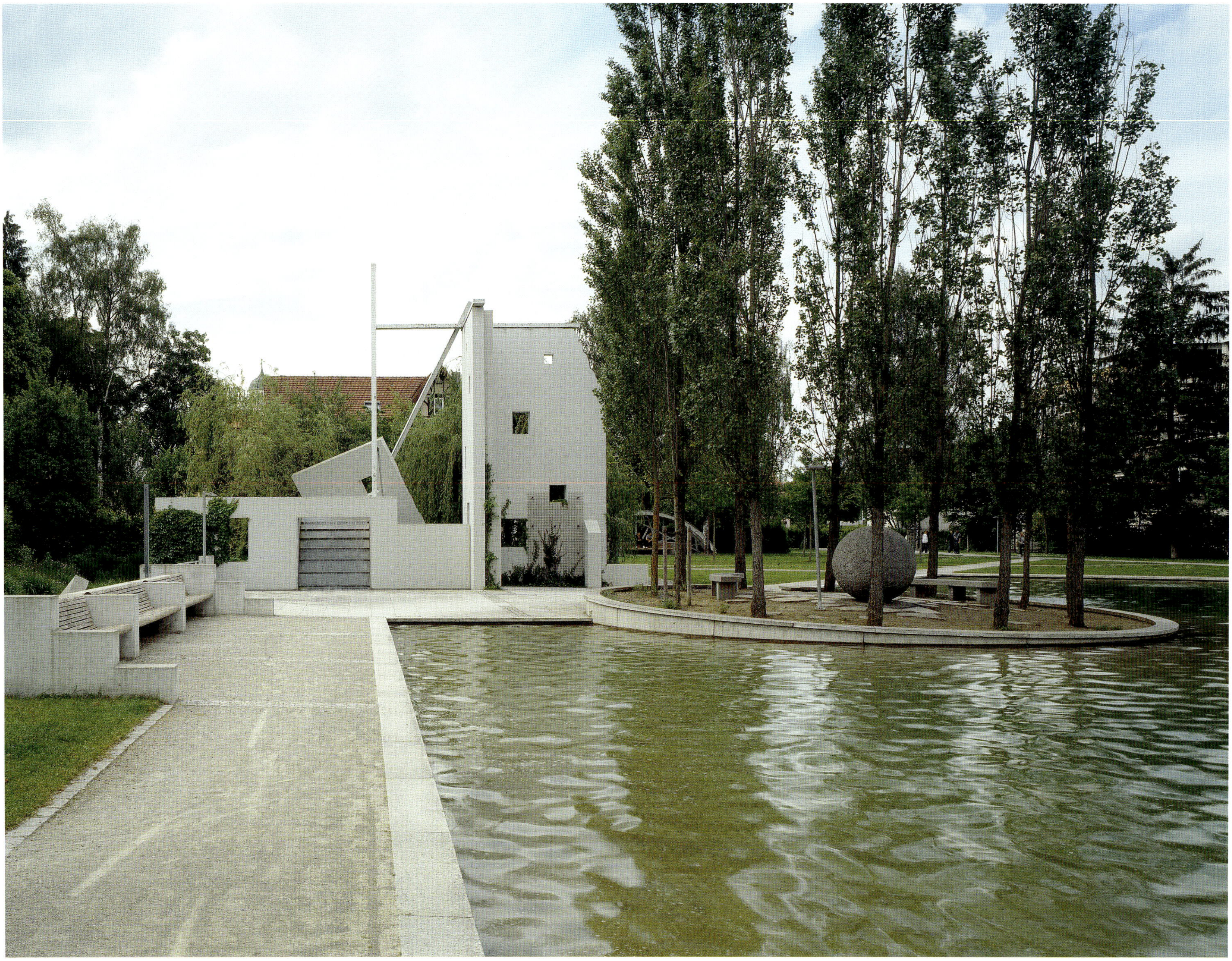

10. Lake, poplar island, and artificial ruin with water cascade. Today, the ruin is almost completely covered in ivy and wild vines. Photo 2003.
11. Ruin, lake, and poplar island. In the foreground is the back wall of a long bench. Photo 2003.

10. See, Pappelinsel und künstliche Ruine mit Wasserkaskade. Heute ist die Ruine fast vollständig mit Efeu und wildem Wein eingewachsen. Photo 2003.
11. Ruine, See und Pappelinsel. Im Vordergrund die Rückwand einer langen Sitzbank. Photo 2003.

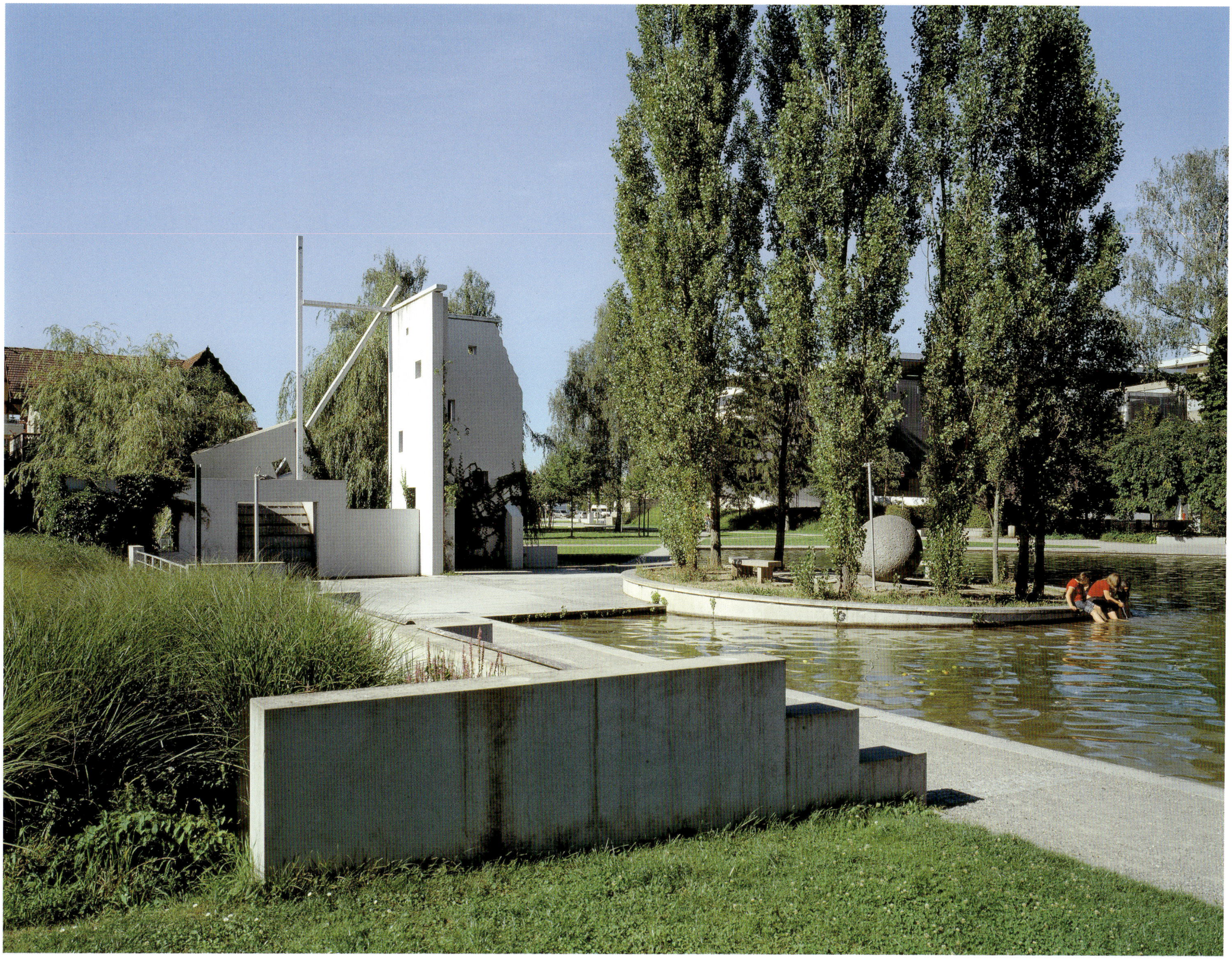

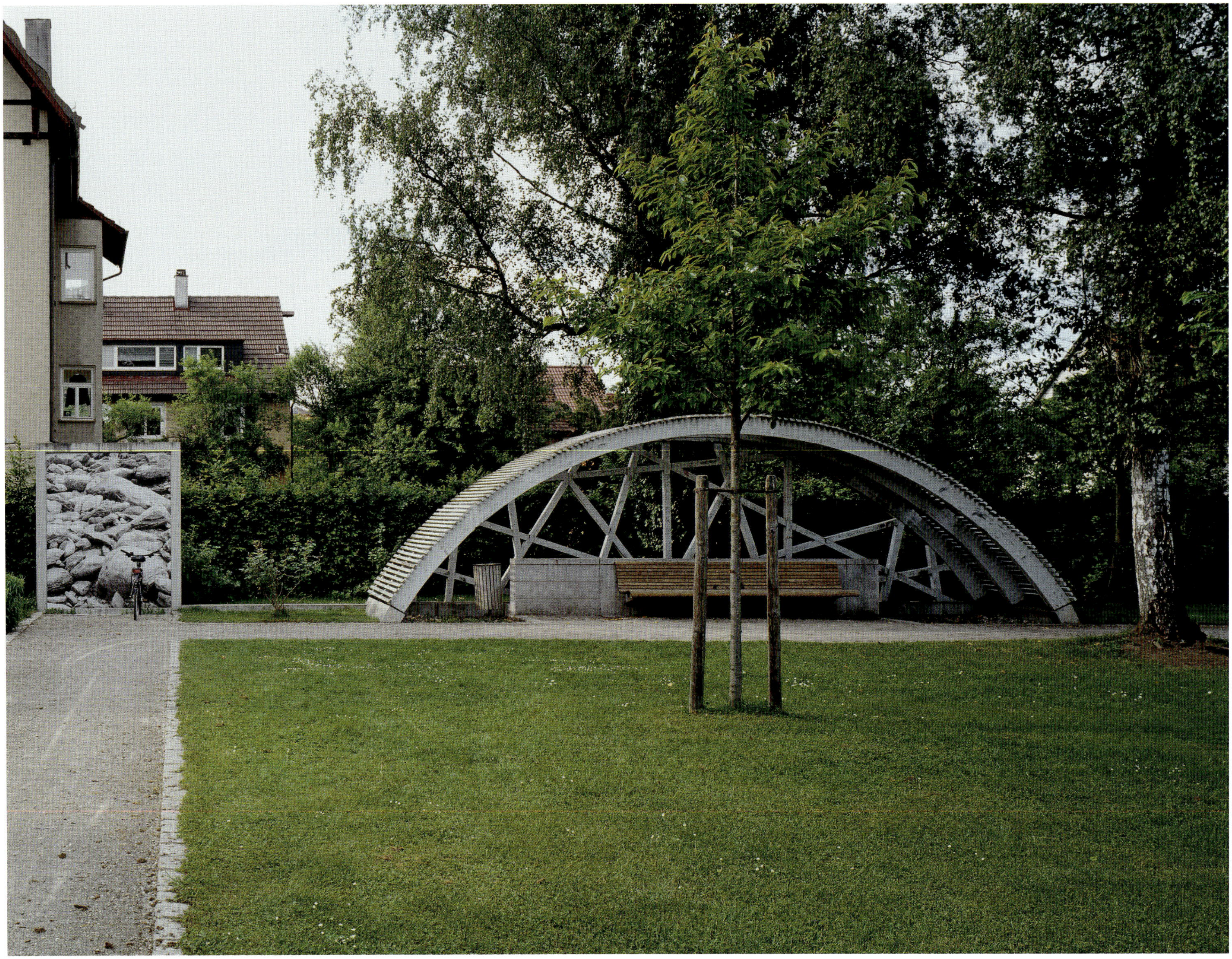

12. Semicircular arbour with bench. Initially erected in timber. Following damage by vandals, it was replaced in white-painted steel, for permanence. This is the old, slightly battered version. At the path's end, a photo with large gravel and rock fragments. This is a reference to the region's geological prehistory. At the time, this region was covered by a huge glacier, which buried rocks beneath it and crushed them to gravel. Photo 2003.
13, 14. »Rock house«. White-painted steel construction (suggestions of windows) with a block of natural stone. Photo 2003.

12. Halbrunde Laube mit Sitzbank. Zunächst in Holz errichtet. Nach Vandalenzerstörung in weiß lackiertem Stahl erneuert und so auf Dauer angelegt. Hier noch die alte, leicht ramponierte Fassung. Am Wegende ein Photo mit großen Kieseln und Felsbrocken. Es spielt auf die geologische Urzeit der Region an. Damals war das Land bedeckt von einem riesigen Gletscher, der Felsen unter sich begrub und zu Kieseln zermalmte. Photo 2003.
13, 14. »Felshaus«. Weiß lackierte Stahlkonstruktion (Fensterandeutungen) mit einem Block aus Naturstein. Photo 2003.

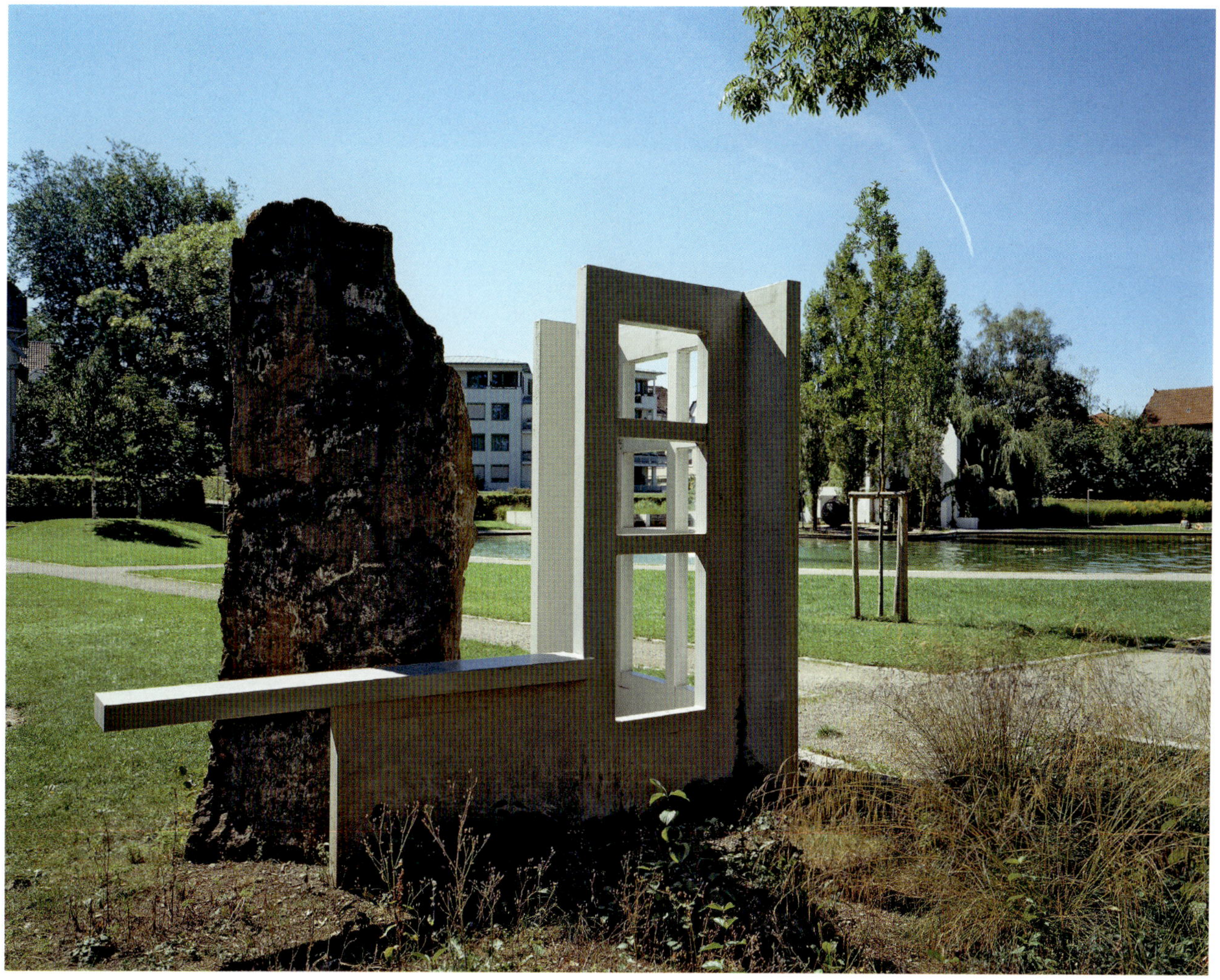

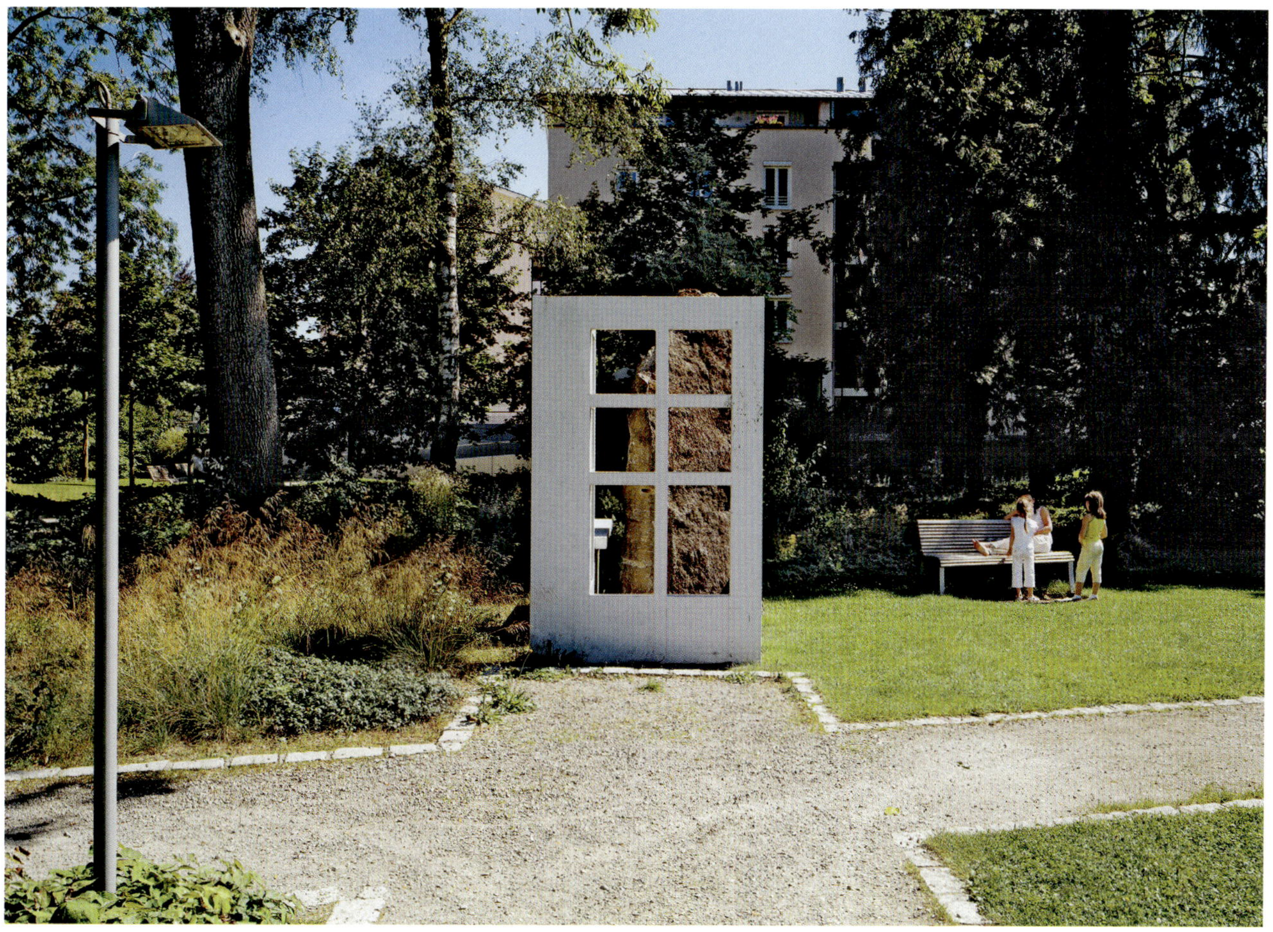

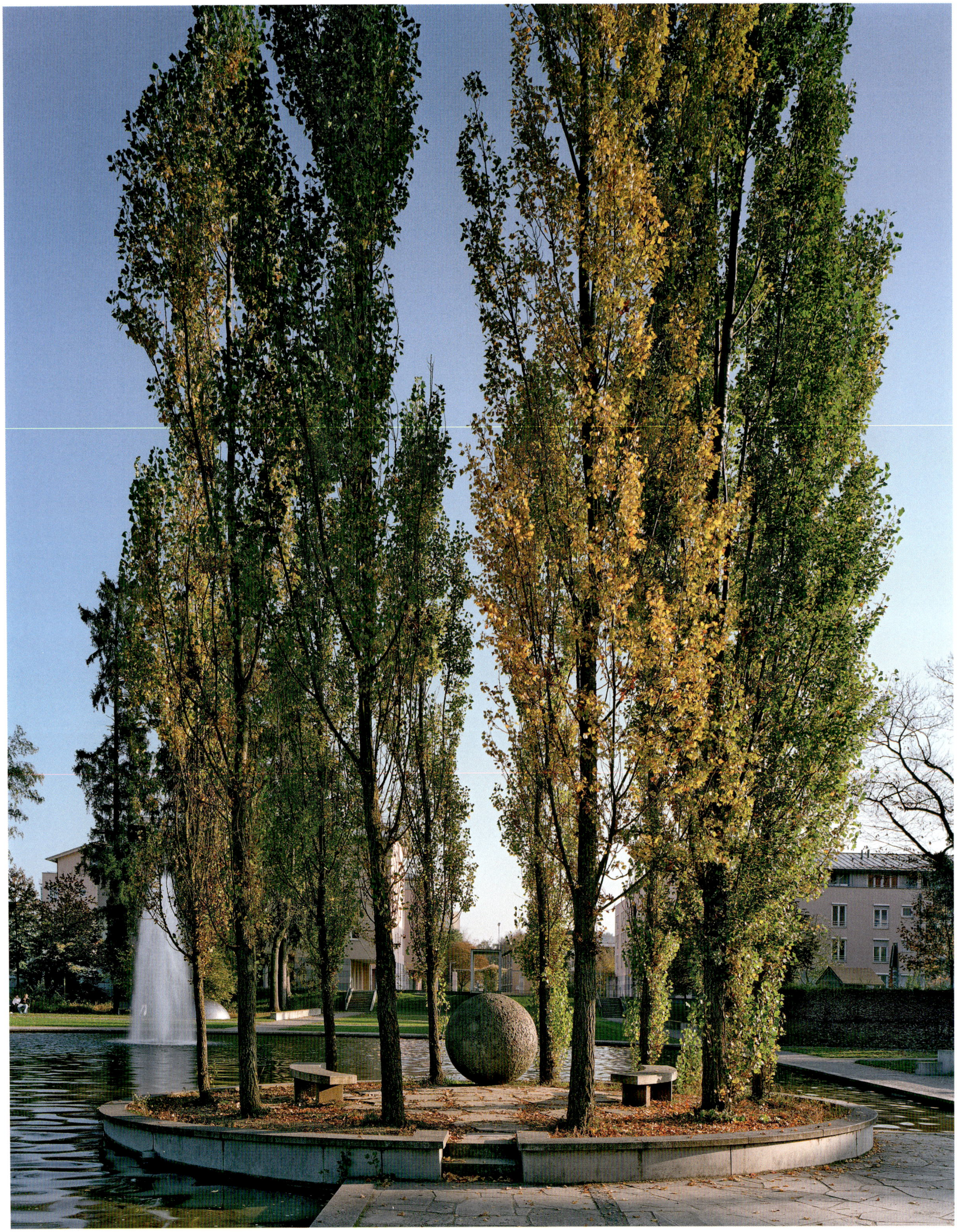

15. Poplar island with granite moon sculpture and semi-circular benches. Photo 2003.
16. Texts by Jean-Jacques Rousseau are chiselled into some of the paving stones. Photo 2003.

15. Pappelinsel mit Mond-Skulptur aus Granit und halbrunden Sitzbänken. Photo 2003.
16. In einzelne Bodenplatten wurden Texte von Jean-Jacques Rousseau eingemeißelt. Photo 2003.

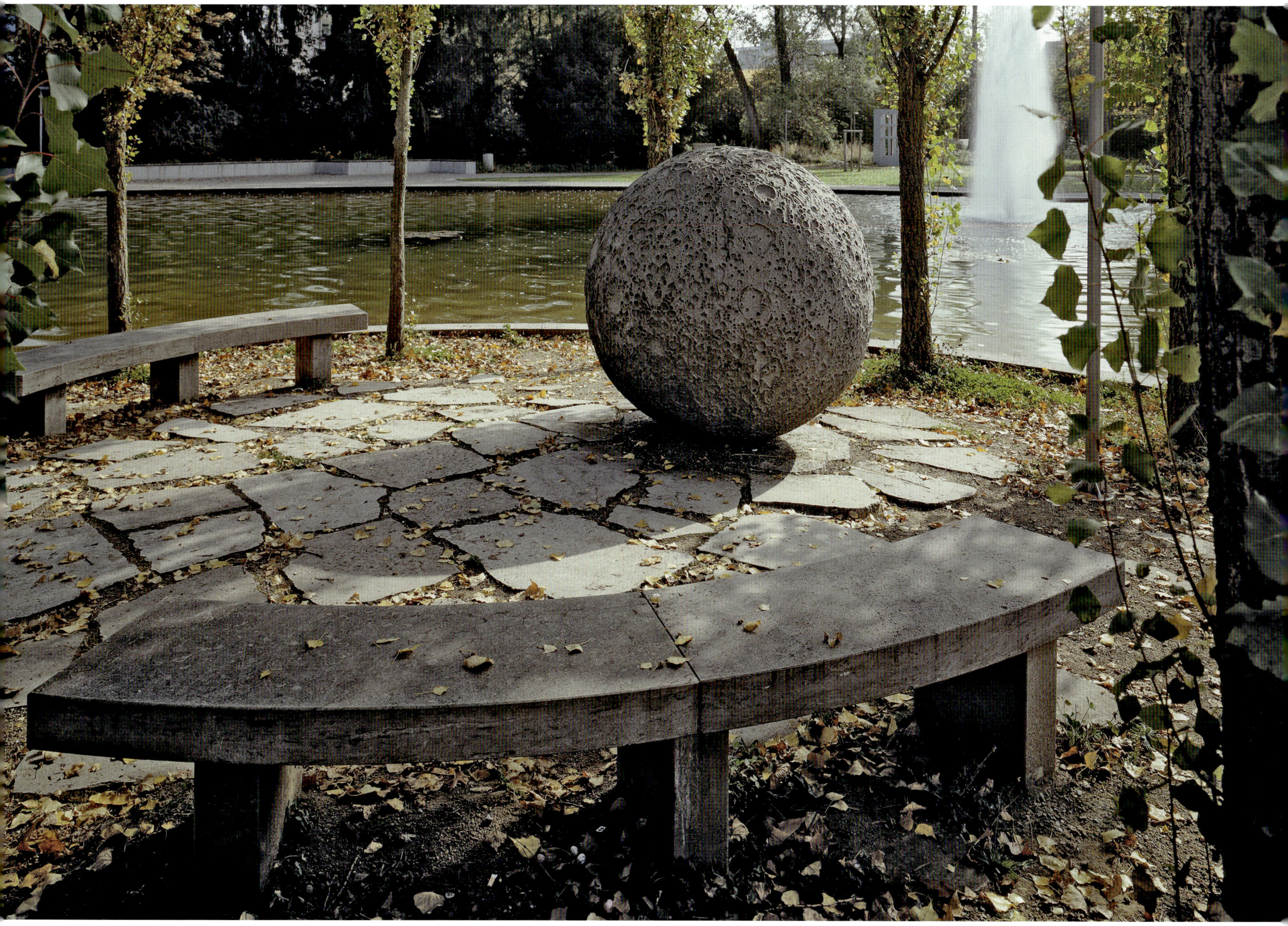

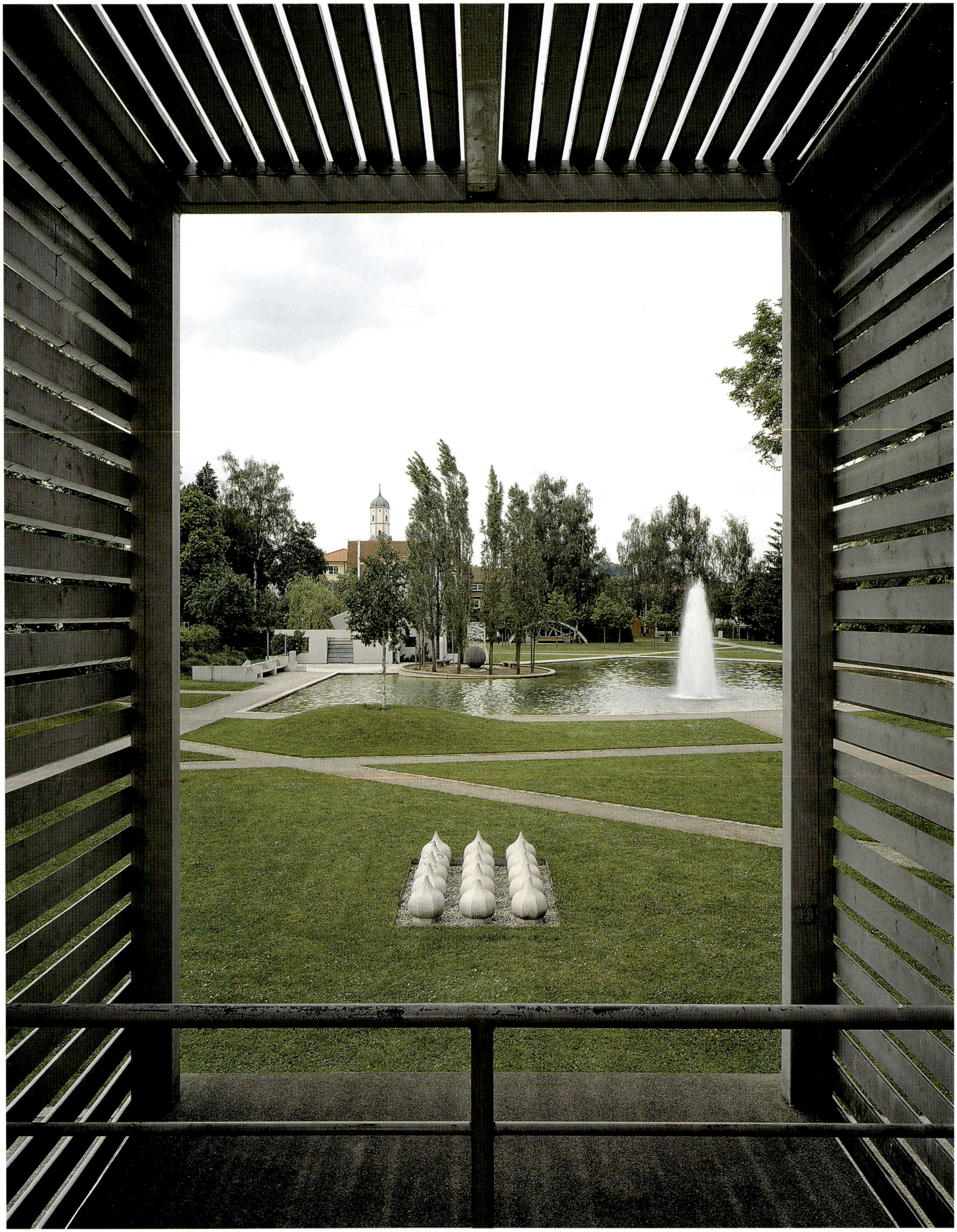

17. Viewing arbour with framed continuous view. Photo 2003.
18. The Viewing arbour is situated at the edge of a grassy escarpment in the south part of the park. Under the terrace is a parking garage). Photo 2003.

17. Sichtlaube mit gerahmtem Durchblick. Photo 2003.
18. Die Sichtlaube liegt am Rand einer Grasböschung im südlichen Parkbereich. Unter der Terrasse befindet sich ein Parkhaus). Photo 2003.

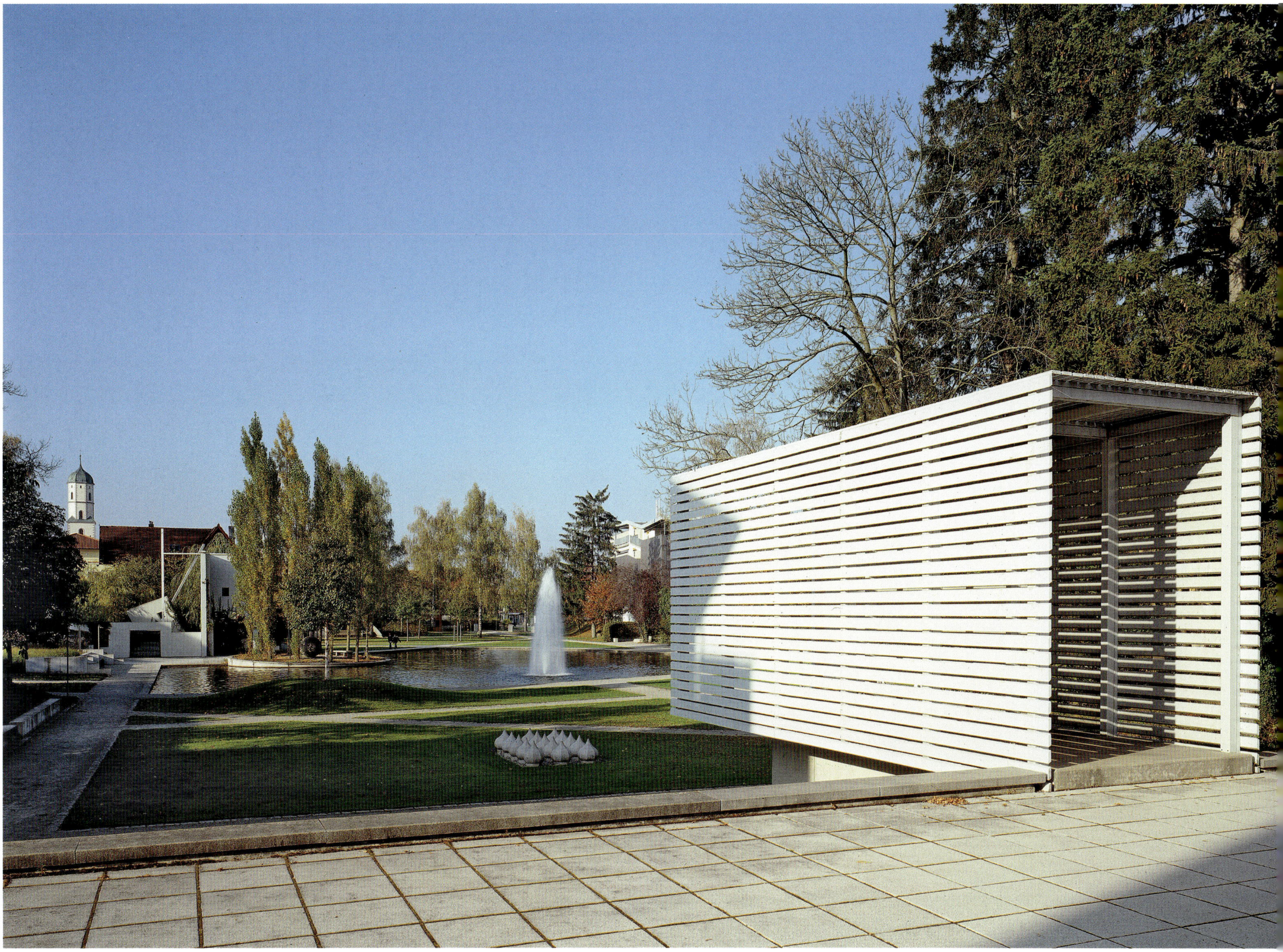

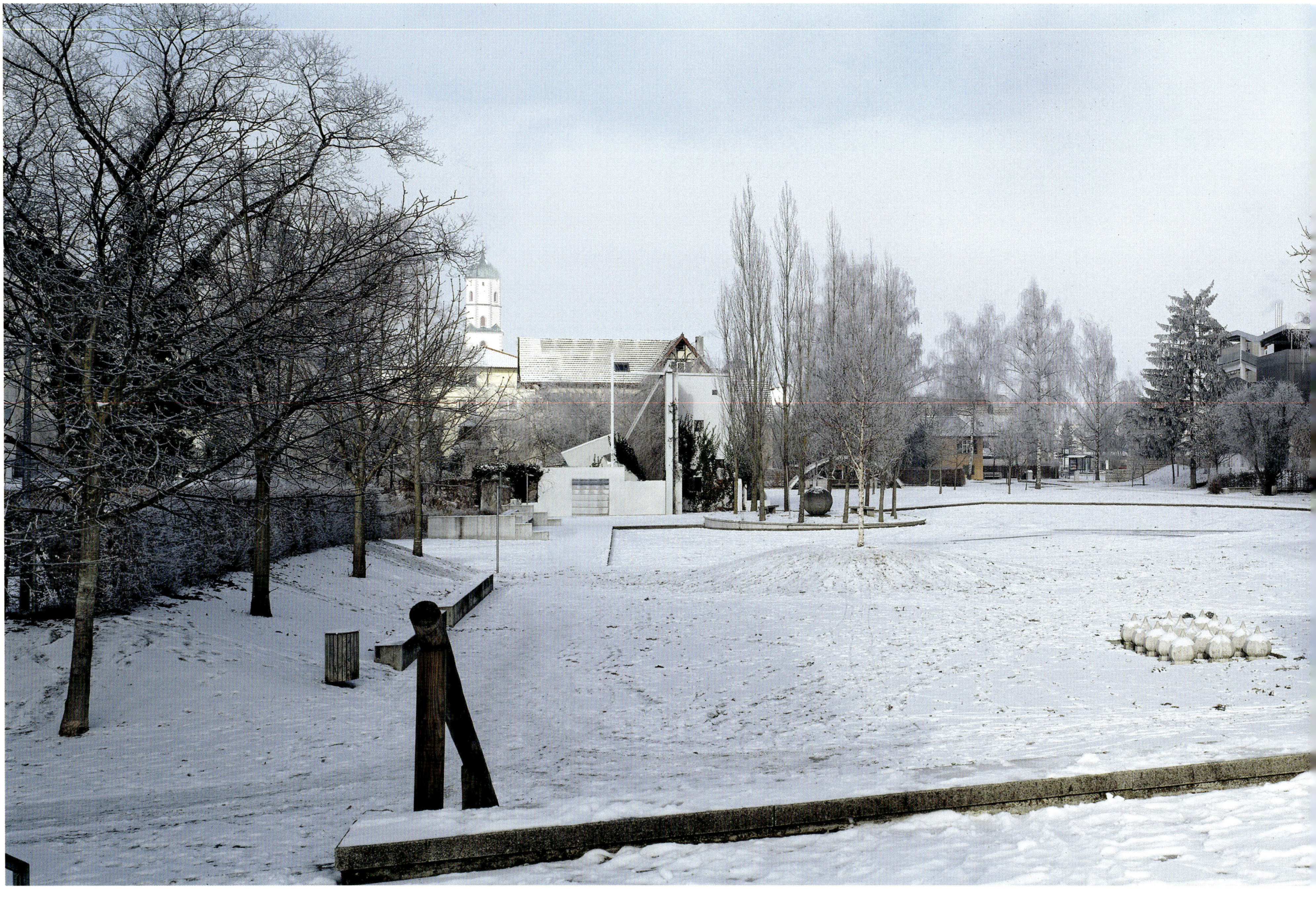

19. Winter image with viewing arbour. Photo 2009.

19. Winterbild mit Sichtlaube. Photo 2009.

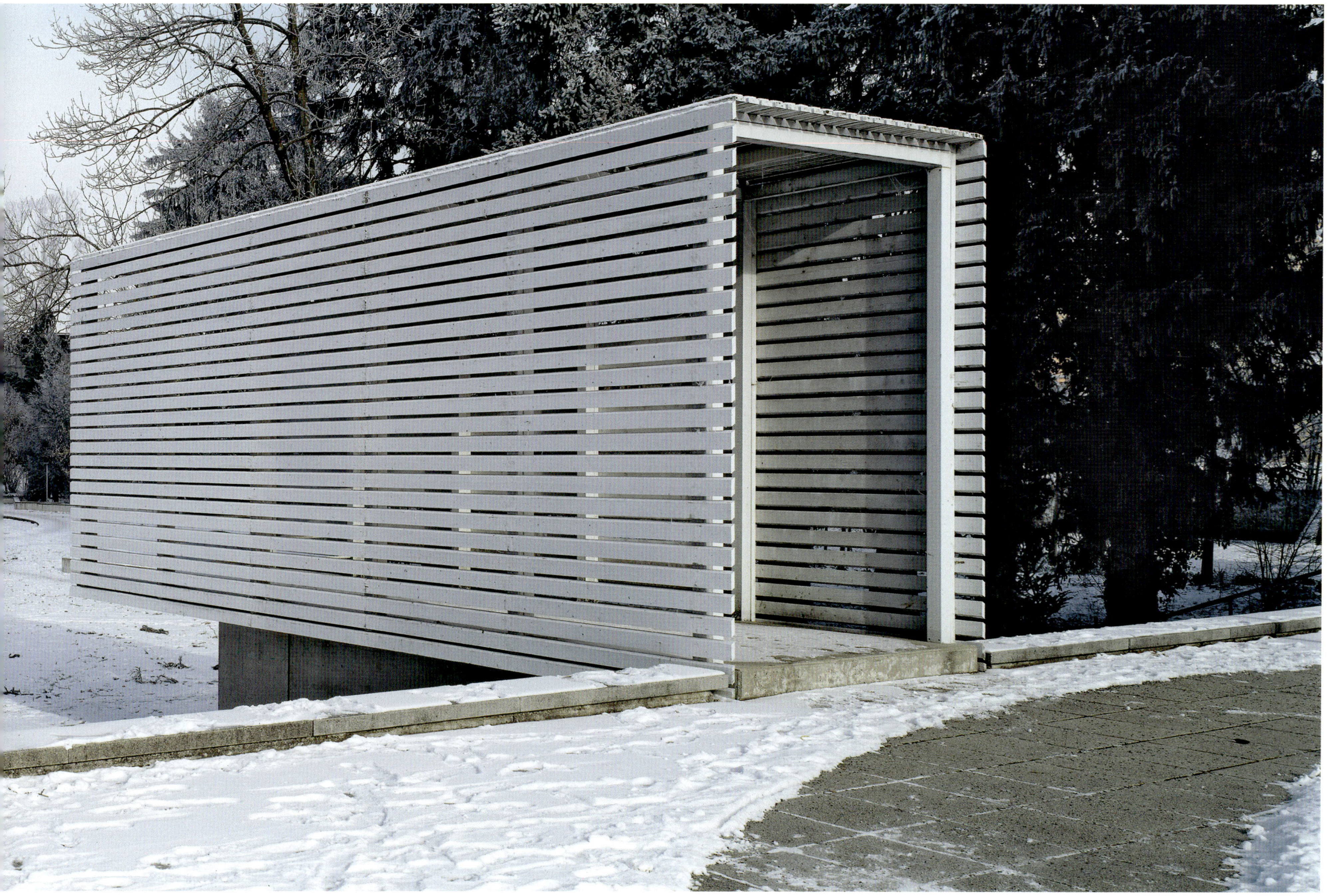

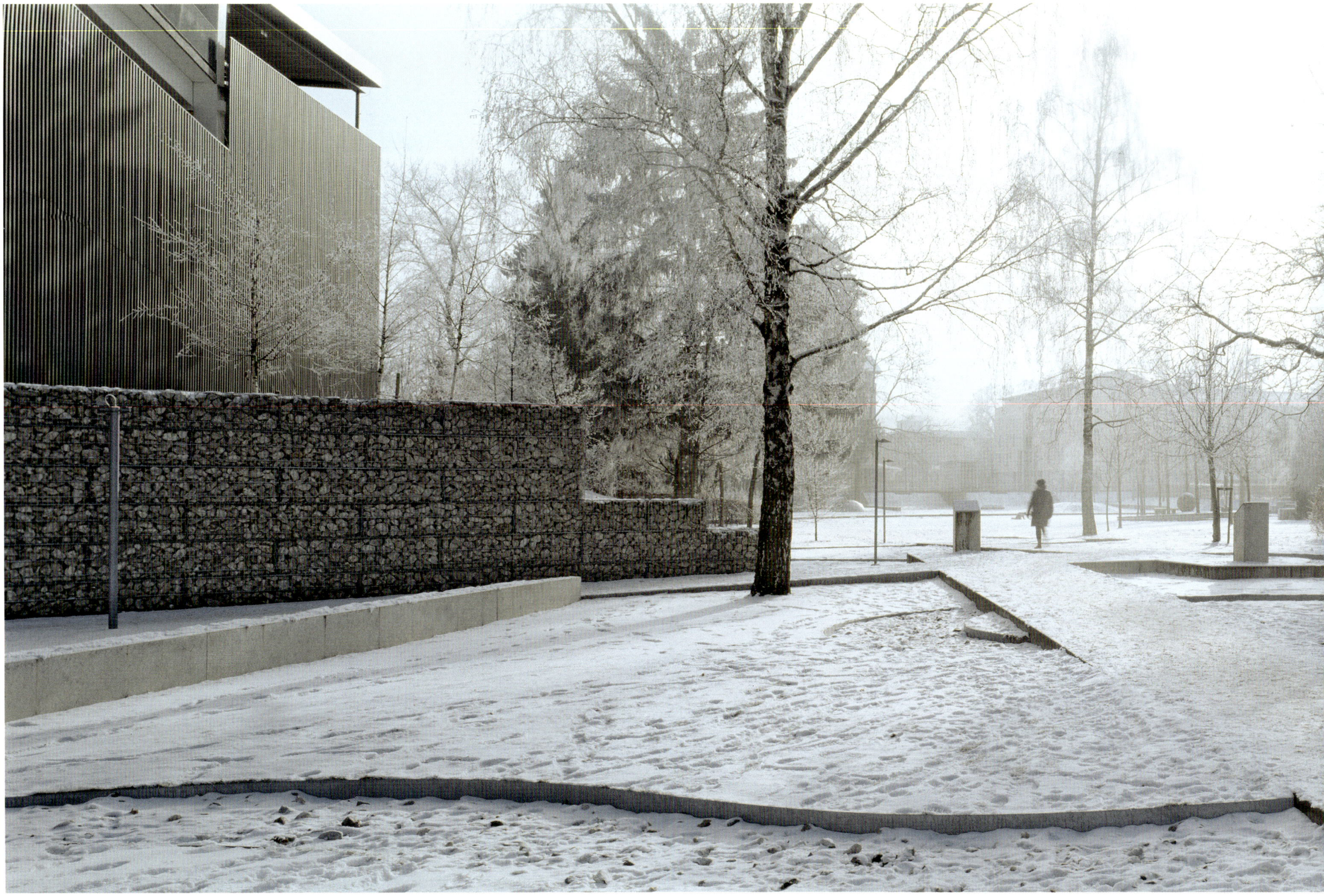

20. Winter image with Christoph Martin Wieland's garden house. Photo 2009.

20. Winterbild mit dem Gartenhaus von Christoph Martin Wieland. Photo 2009.

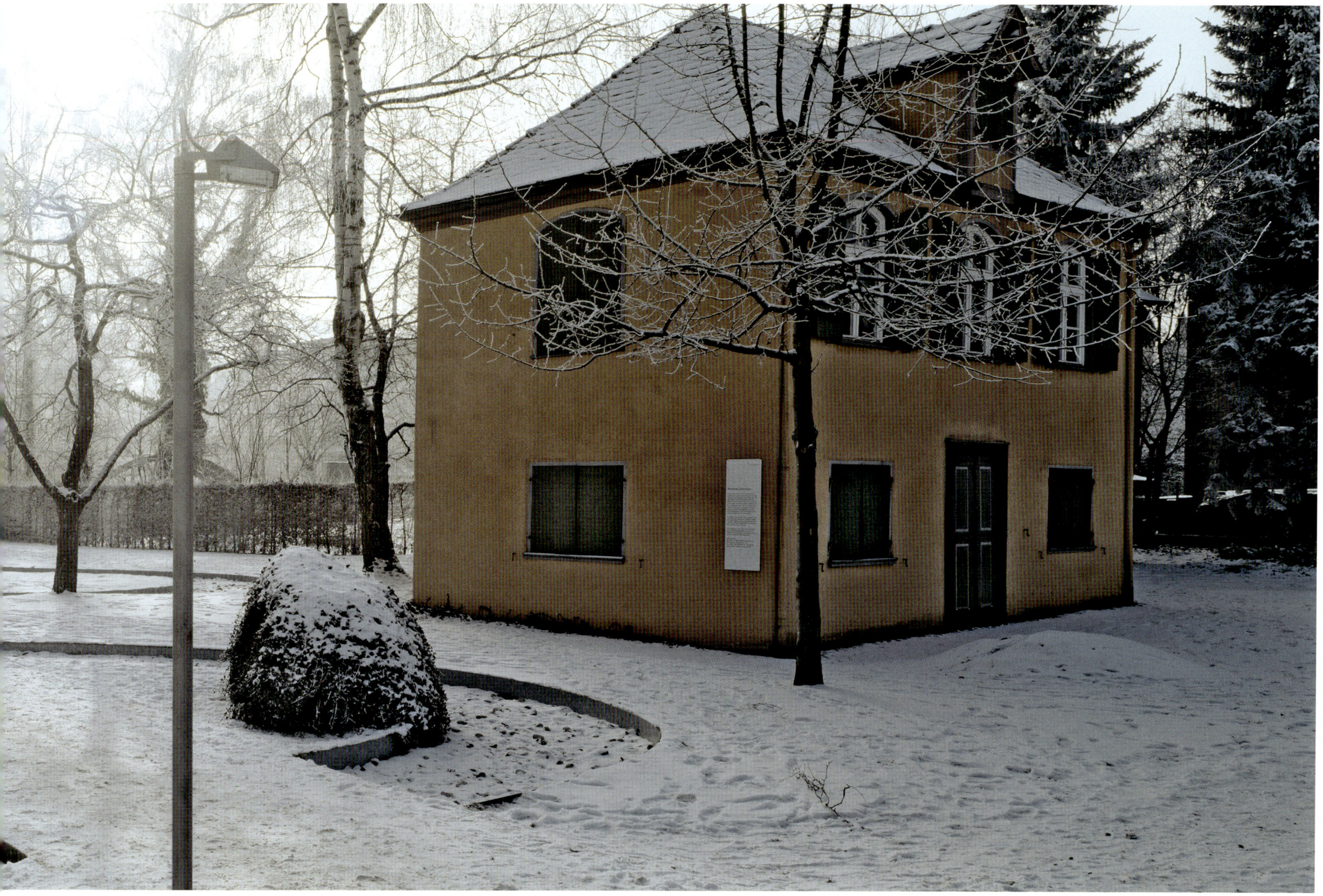

Adlershof, design proposals for the outside spaces of the Berliner Wissenschaftsstadt (Berlin science city), 2003

The Adlershof district in the east part of Berlin has been an important science and media location since GDR times. The first GDR television studios were set up here.

Following reunification, the city's politicians considered establishing a new, highly modern science city in Adlershof with high-tech businesses and university institutes. They envisaged a mixture of a British/American-type campus and Silicon Valley. The eventual reality was a disparate industrial area, with no real unity in its urban plan, and a struggle on its hands regarding its image.

This was why Gerald Blomeyer, head of an architecture and advice bureau in Berlin, was commissioned to come up with an overarching design idea. He invited me to take part as a provider of creative ideas. Together, we worked out a concept largely concerned with Adlershof's road and plaza spaces, but also with its open landscape spaces. Inspired by the most striking existing features such as the two spheres of the isothermic laboratories, (nicknamed the »Akademiebusen« academy bossom), I designed elements intended to combine science, the city, landscape and art. Many research laboratories and institutes in Adlershof, however, are concerned with invisible elementary particles from the nanorealm, with radiation and computer matters, which do not lend themselves to visible public representation. Solar and laser technology offer simpler possibilities.

Unfortunately, none of our ideas or proposals were well-received. None of them were adopted or made into a reality.

Adlershof, Gestaltungsvorschläge für die Außenräume der Berliner Wissenschaftsstadt, 2003

Der im Osten Berlins liegende Stadtteil Adlershof war schon zu DDR-Zeiten ein wichtiger Wissenschafts- und Medienstandort. Hier wurden die ersten Studios des DDR-Fernsehens eingerichtet.

Nach der Wende dachten die Stadtpolitiker darüber nach, in Adlershof eine neue, hochmoderne Wissenschaftsstadt mit High-Tech-Unternehmen und Universitätsinstituten zu etablieren. Ihnen schwebte eine Mischung aus englisch-amerikanischem Campus und Silicon Valley vor. In Wirklichkeit entstand ein disparates Industriegebiet, das sich städtebaulich zu keiner wirklichen Einheit schließt und seither um sein Image kämpft.

Darin lag der Grund, daß Gerald Blomeyer, der in Berlin ein Architektur- und Beratungsbüro betrieb, beauftragt wurde, eine übergeordnete Gestaltungsidee zu finden. Er lud mich als kreativen Ideenspender ein, daran teilzunehmen. Gemeinsam erarbeiteten wir ein Konzept, das sich vor allem mit den Straßen- und Platzräumen, aber auch mit den landschaftlichen Freizonen von Adlershof befaßte. Ich entwarf, angeregt von den bisher markantesten Zeichen wie etwa den beiden Kugeln der isothermischen Labore, die im Volksmund »Akademiebusen« genannt werden, Elemente, die Wissenschaft, Stadt, Landschaft und Kunst miteinander verbinden sollten. Viele Forschungslabors und Institute in Adlershof haben allerdings mit unsichtbaren Elementarteilchen aus dem Nanobereich, mit Strahlen und Computer-Kräften zu tun, die sich der öffentlich-sichtbaren Darstellung entziehen. Solar- und Lasertechnik bieten dafür einfachere Möglichkeiten.

Leider stießen alle unsere Ideen und Vorschläge auf wenig Gegenliebe. Nichts davon wurde aufgegriffen oder gar in die Realität umgesetzt.

1. A solar sculpture on an open meadow between the institute buildings.
2, 3. Two pages with sketches for proposals that I made at the time: science arbours with enlarged laboratory buildings, lit up at night by laser beams. Solar fields amid farmed land.

1. Solar-Skulptur auf einer freien Wiese zwischen den Institutsgebäuden.
2, 3. Zwei Skizzenblätter meiner damaligen Vorschläge: Wissenschaftslauben mit vergrößerten Laboreinbauten, nachts von Laserstrahlen beleuchtet. Solarfelder zwischen landwirtschaftlich genutzten Flächen.

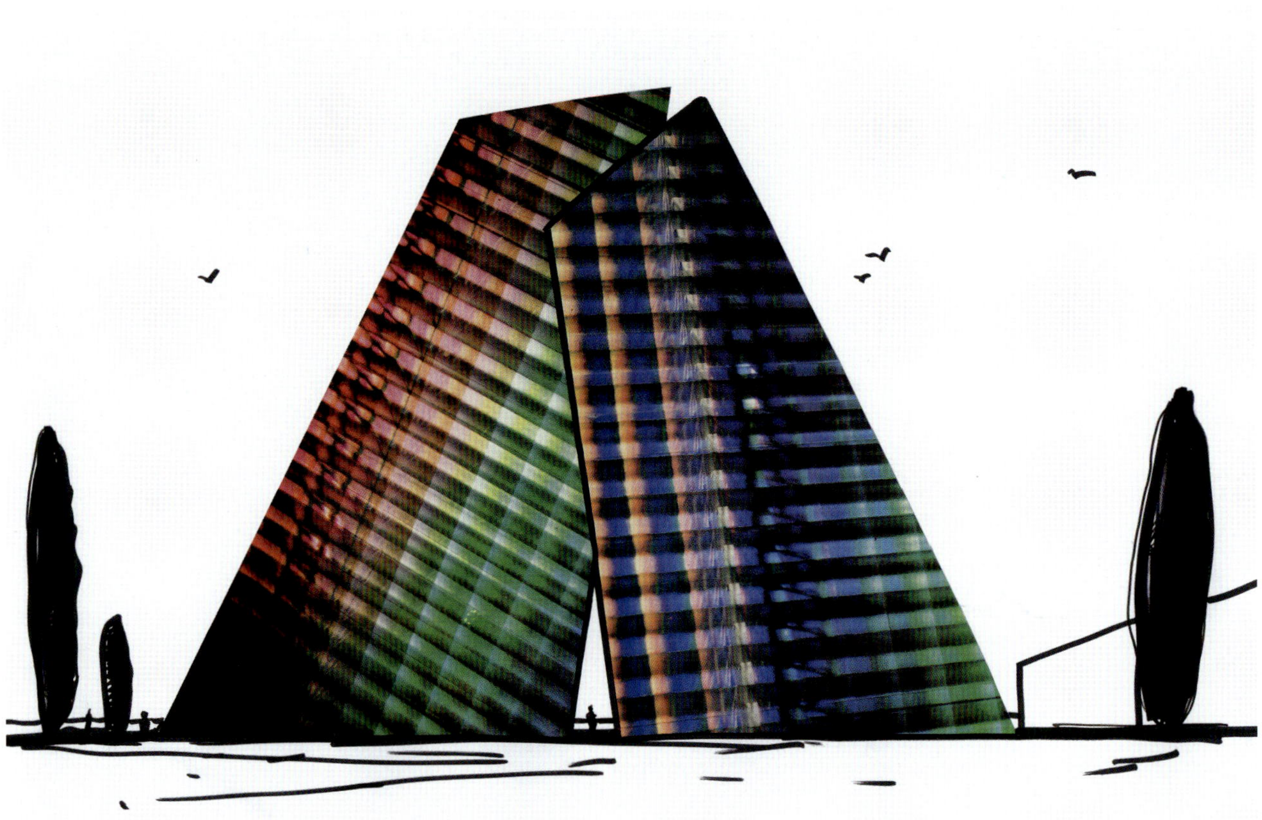

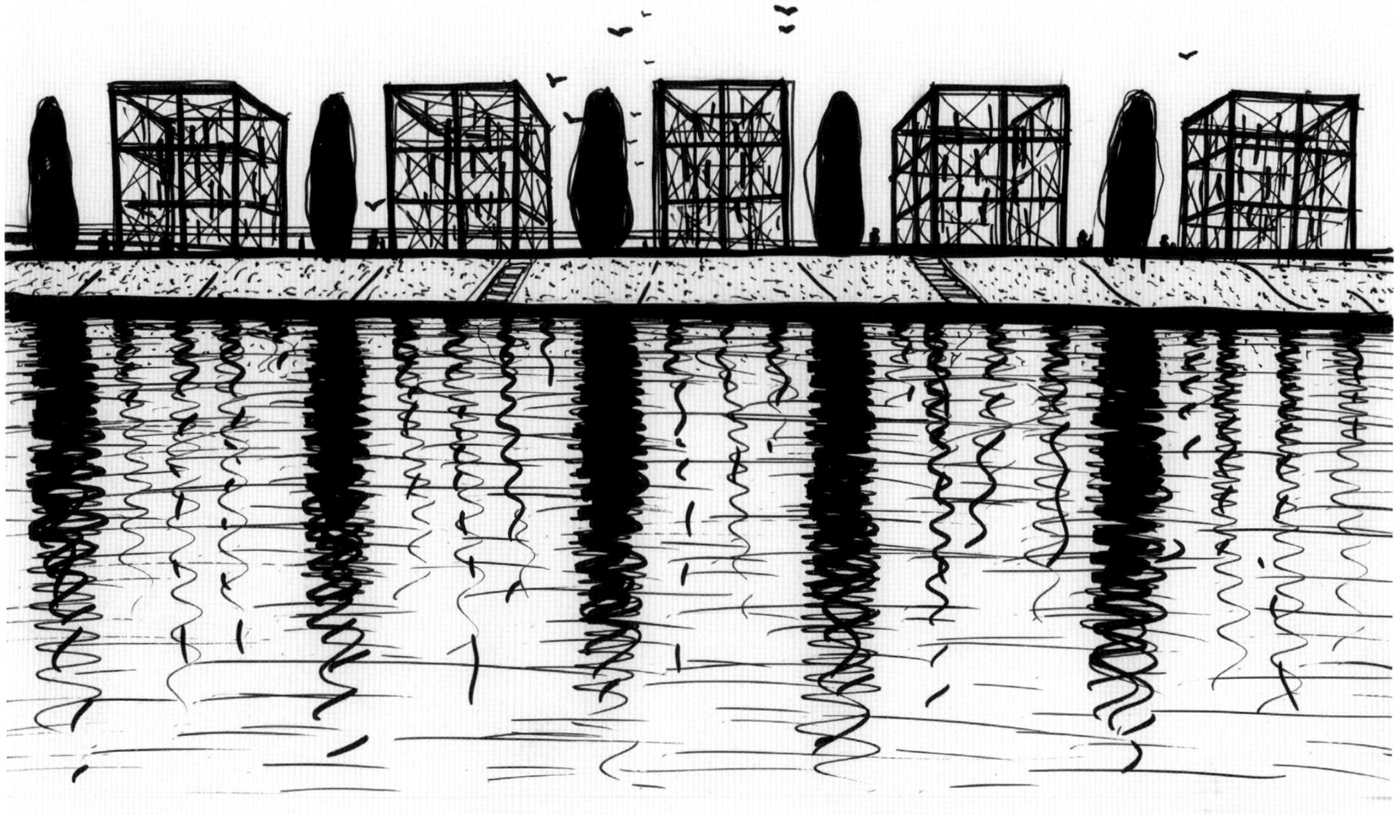

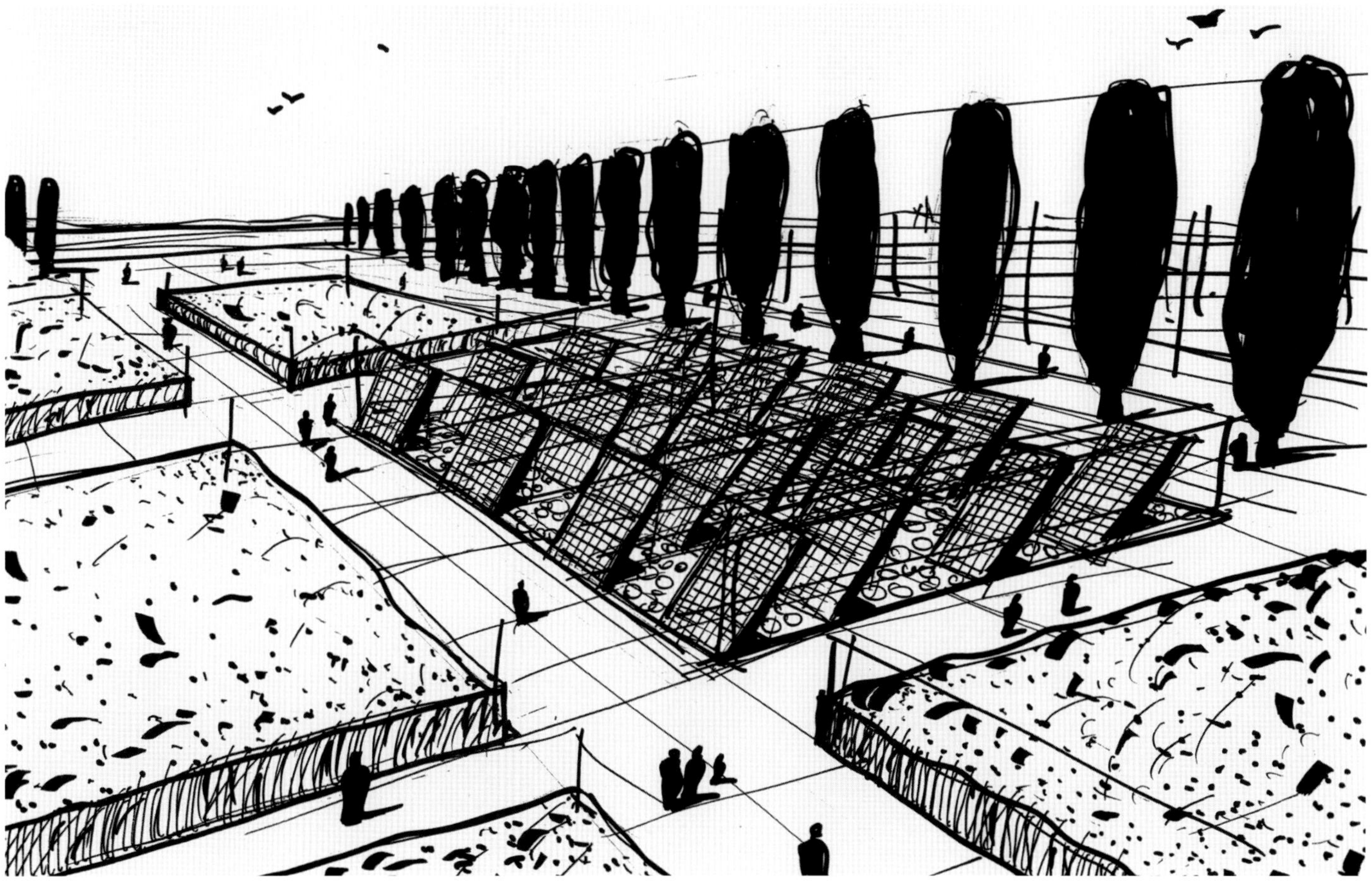

Art installations for the Landesgartenschau Kehl, 2004

The main area of the Landesgartenschau in Kehl was designed by the firm of Anne and Rüdiger Brosk from Essen. Christof Luz had responsibility for the entrance area on the German side of the Rhine. He invited me to develop art installations on the theme of »nature/landscape/gardens«. By then, my repertoire in this field was extensive. I therefore proposed numerous objects (too many?), including undulating hill zones, rock and stone compositions, massive wooden towers composed of enlarged wood stacks with steel cores, a giant arbour, and two green tall houses: a »skyscraper built from straw« and a »skyscraper built from corn cobs«. I was inspired by the land husbandry and forestry of the Black Forest, and also by the traditional maize and tobacco leaf drying houses of the Rhine region.

Unfortunately, none of my proposals appealed to those responsible for the Gartenschau.

Kunstinstallationen für die Landesgartenschau Kehl, 2004

Den Hauptbereich der Landesgartenschau in Kehl entwarf das Büro von Anne und Rüdiger Brosk aus Essen. Christof Luz war für den Eingangsbereich auf der deutschen Seite des Rheins zuständig. Er lud mich dazu ein, Kunstinstallationen zu entwickeln, die sich mit den Themen »Natur/Landschaft/Garten« befassen. Mein Repertoire auf diesem Gebiet war inzwischen umfangreich. Deswegen schlug ich zahlreiche Objekte (zu viele?) vor: darunter gewellte Hügelzonen, Fels- und Steinkompositionen, massive Holztürme aus vergrößerten Holzstapelv mit Stahlkernen, eine Riesenlaube und zwei grüne Hochhäuser: ein »Hochhaus aus Stroh« und ein »Hochhaus aus Maiskolben«. Angeregt dazu hatten mich die Land- und Forstwirtschaftsgebäude des Schwarzwalds, au-ßerdem die traditionellen Mais- und Tabakblätter-Trocknungshäuser der Rheinregion.

Leider fand keiner meiner Vorschläge Anklang bei den Gartenschauverantwortlichen.

1. Wooden towers – enlarged wood stacks with steel cores.
2. »Strohhochhaus«.

1. »Holztürme« – vergrößerte Holzstapel mit Stahlkernen.
2. »Strohhochhaus«.

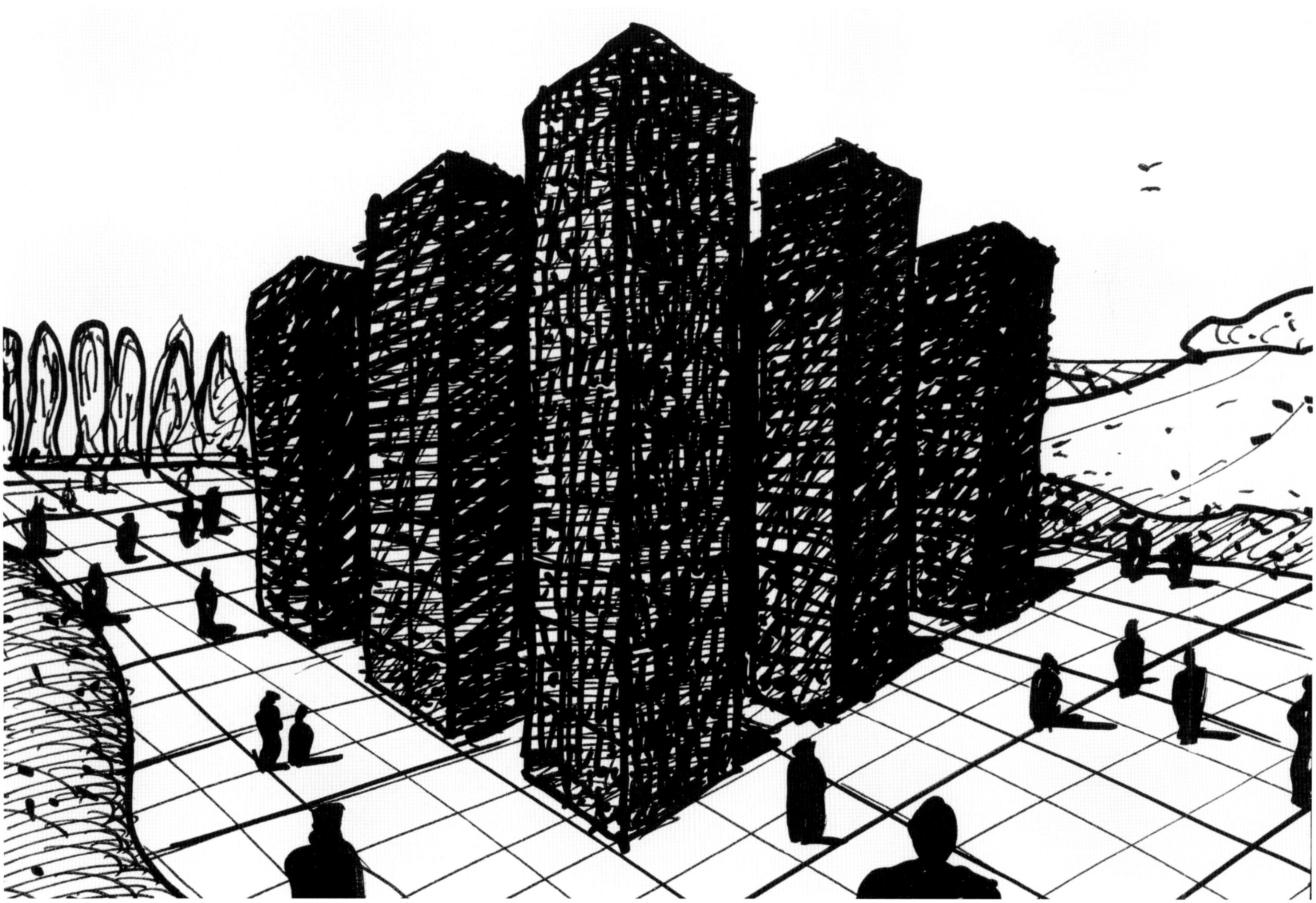

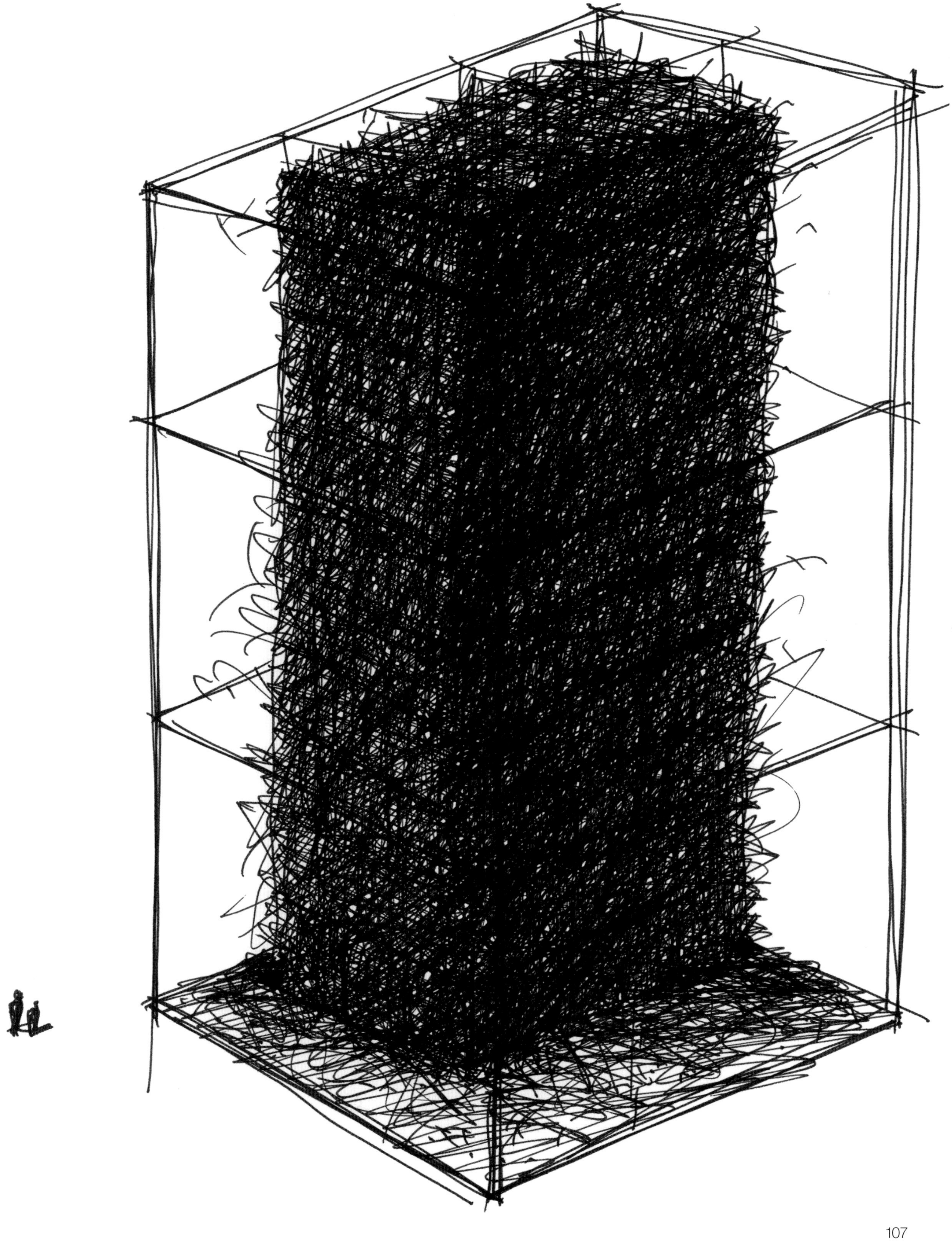

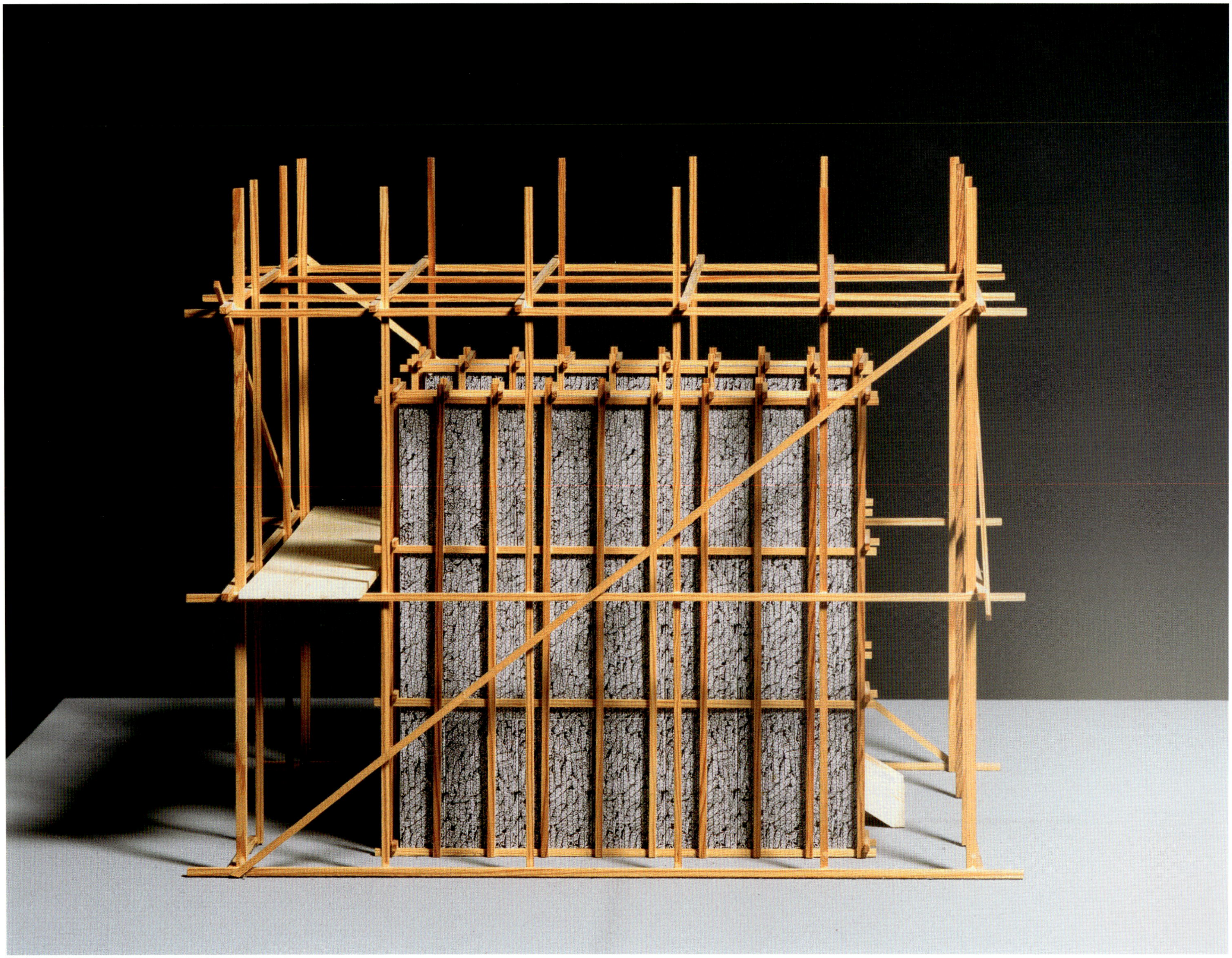

3. »Maishochhaus«, encased in a wooden framework construction. A vertical version around twelve meters tall, with a stair and integrated viewing terrace. Model.
4. »Maishochhaus«. Tipped version. Model.

3. »Maishochhaus«, gefangen in einer Holzfachwerkkonstruktion. Senkrechte, etwa zwölf Meter hohe Version, mit Treppenanlage und eingebauter Aussichtsterrasse. Modell.
4. »Maishochhaus«. Gekippte Version. Modell.

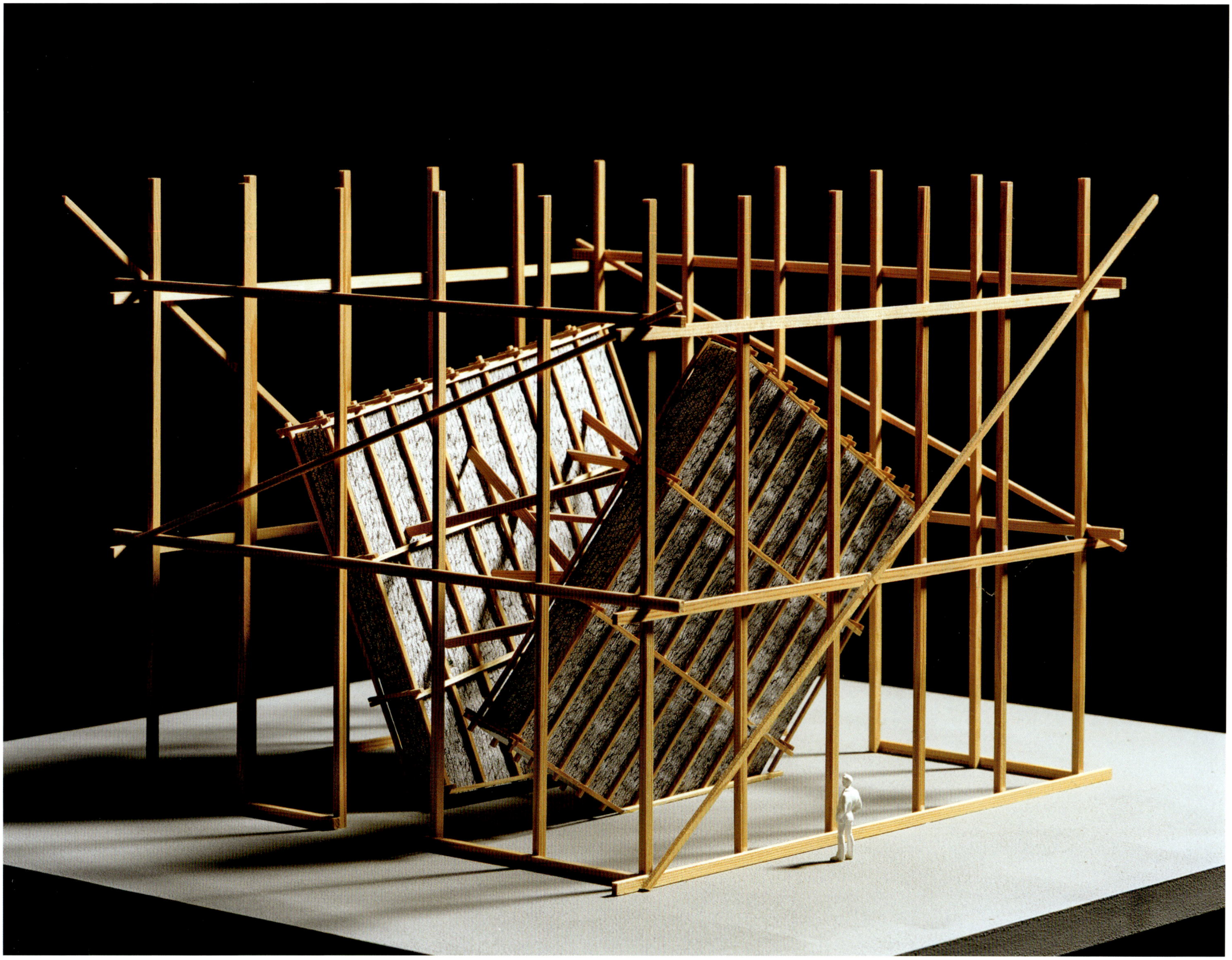

T4-Gedenkplatz (T4 memorial site), Berlin, competition entry, 2012. Invitation to tender and commission from: the city of Berlin

This previously little-regarded Berlin memorial site lies to the north of the Philharmonic on the Tiergartenstraße road. This was once the site of a building where, during the Nazi period, the »euthanasia« murders of physically and mentally handicapped persons were decided and planned. During a bomb attack in 1944, this imposing villa was gutted by fire. In the post-war era, it fell into ruin. Since the 1980s, only an abstract rusted steel sculpture by Richard Serra and an inscribed bronze plate set into the ground have remained to remind of the sad events. Temporary commemoration and art actions were regularly held to draw attention to this overshadowed area of the city, which has since been used primarily as a bus stop.

It was not until the new millennium that a persistent initiative group secured the building of a new, clearly visible memorial with an information area. An art and landscape architecture competition was held. Conversations took place. They were looking for solutions that would redefine the themes »monument« and »memorial«, embedded in a gentle landscape and plaza design. This is not a 19th century glorification, but the opposite: the representation of the moral aberrations of the elite Nazi leadership, and the lethal consequences for handycapped people.

The obvious motif of a »wall« had some negative connotations in Berlin because of the Berlin Wall. This makes it all the more surprising that the jury ultimately decided in favour of the blue glass wall proposed by the Berlin architect Ursula Wilms, her landscape architect husband Heinz W. Hallmann, and the Austrian artist Nikolaus Koliusis.

My proposal involved using grey concrete beams to create a suggestion of the destroyed building. For the interior of the plaza zone, I planned information boards showing historic photos, with names of the places where the killings took place. A row of weeping willows on the east side would have given the memorial site an appropriate natural note of melancholy. The solution created by the first-prize-winning group, realised in 2015, initially appeared alien to me – and to a number of critics – owing to its wordless minimalist, bare and yet almost Romantic beauty. I have since come to admire it. The transparency of the blue (sadly somewhat too low) glass wall and the alienating »separateness« created by the way the visitors and passers-by change colour as they pass behind it lends this work a quiet, profound metaphysical quality.

Incidentally, the information content is clearly separated from this »blue wall«, which features no writing. The information is documented on an accompanying media board running parallel to the wall. The competition winners dispensed entirely with tree planting and with other green elements. The Tiergarten forms a lush green horizon in the northerly direction.

T4-Gedenkplatz, Berlin, Wettbewerbsbeitrag, 2012. Ausschreibung und Auftraggeber: Stadt Berlin

Der bisher wenig beachtete Berliner Gedenkort liegt nördlich der Philharmonie an der Tiergartenstraße. Hier stand einst jenes Gebäude, in dem zur NS-Zeit die Euthanasie-Morde an geistig und körperlich behinderten Menschen beschlossen und geplant wurden. Bei einem Bombenangriff 1944 brannte die stattliche Villa aus und zerfiel in der Nachkriegszeit zur Ruine. Seit den 1980er Jahren erinnerten nur eine abstrakte Roststahl-Skulptur von Richard Serra und eine flach in den Boden eingelassene Bronzetextplatte an die traurigen Ereignisse. Temporäre Mahn- und Kunstaktionen machten immer wieder auf die belastete Stadtzone, die inzwischen vor allem als Bushaltestelle benutzt wurde, aufmerksam.

Erst im neuen Jahrtausend konnte sich eine hartnäckige Initiativgruppe für die Errichtung eines neuen, deutlich sichtbaren Denkmals mit Informationsbereich durchsetzen. Ein Künstler- und Landschaftsarchitekten-Wettbewerb wurde ausgeschrieben. Kolloquien fanden statt. Die gesuchten Lösungen sollten das Thema »Denkmal« und »Mahnmal«, eingebettet in eine sanfte Landschafts- und Platzgestaltung, neu definieren. Es ging hier nicht, wie im 19. Jahrhundert, um Verherrlichungen, sondern um das Gegenteil: die Darstellung moralischer Verirrungen einer NS-Führungselite mit tödlichen Folgen für behinderte Menschen.

Das naheliegende Motiv »Wand« und »Mauer« war in Berlin durch die Berliner Mauer etwas vorbelastet. Deswegen ist die Endentscheidung der Jury für den blauen Glaswand-Vorschlag der Berliner Architektin Ursula Wilms, ihrem Ehemann, dem Landschaftsarchitekten Heinz W. Hallmann und dem österreichischen Künstler Nikolaus Koliusis um so verblüffender.

Ich hatte bei meinem Vorschlag auf eine graue Betonbalken-Andeutung des zerstörten Gebäudes gesetzt. Im Inneren der Platzzone plante ich Informationstafeln mit historischen Photos und Namen der Tötungsorte. Eine Reihe von Trauerweiden an der Ostseite hätte dem Gedenkort die erforderliche Natur-Melancholie gegeben. Die 2015 realisierte Lösung der ersten Preisträger erschien mir – wie manchen Kritikern – zunächst befremdlich wegen der wortlos-minimalistischen, kahlen, trotzdem fast romantischen Schönheit. Inzwischen bin ich begeistert davon. Durch die Transparenz der blauen (leider etwas zu niedrigen) Glaswand und das umfärbende Verfremden der dahinter gehenden Besucher und Passanten in »Abgeschiedene«, erhält dieses Werk eine tiefgründig-verschwiegene Metaphysik.

Die Informationen sind übrigens von dieser schriftlosen »Blauen Wand« deutlich getrennt. Sie werden auf einem parallel zur Wand verlaufenden medialen Begleitbord dokumentiert. Auf Baumpflanzungen oder andere Grünelemente verzichteten die Wettbewerbsgewinner ganz. Der Tiergarten bildet Richtung Norden den üppigen grünen Horizont.

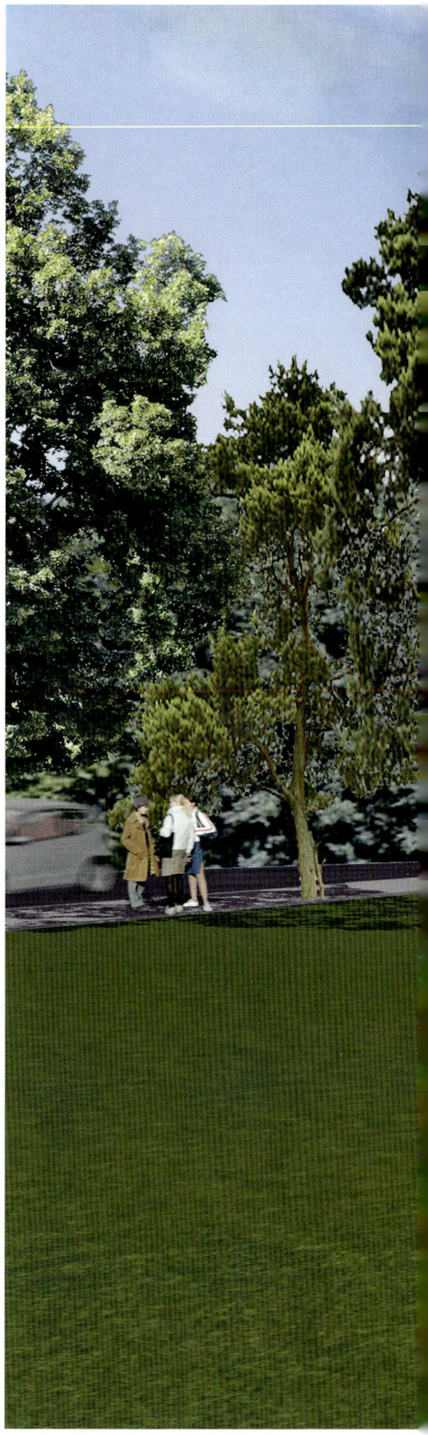

1. View from the Western position (from the Kunstgewerbemuseum) in an easterly direction. In the foreground is a broad meadow, with the Philharmonic on the right and the Tiergarten on the left. In the background of the proposed memorial site, there is a row of weeping willows. Digital representation.

1. Blick aus einer westlichen Position (vom Kunstgewerbemuseum aus) Richtung Osten. Im Vordergrund eine weite Wiese, rechts die Philharmonie, links der Tiergarten. Im Hintergrund des vorgeschlagenen Gedenkortes eine Reihe von Trauerweiden. Digitale Darstellung.

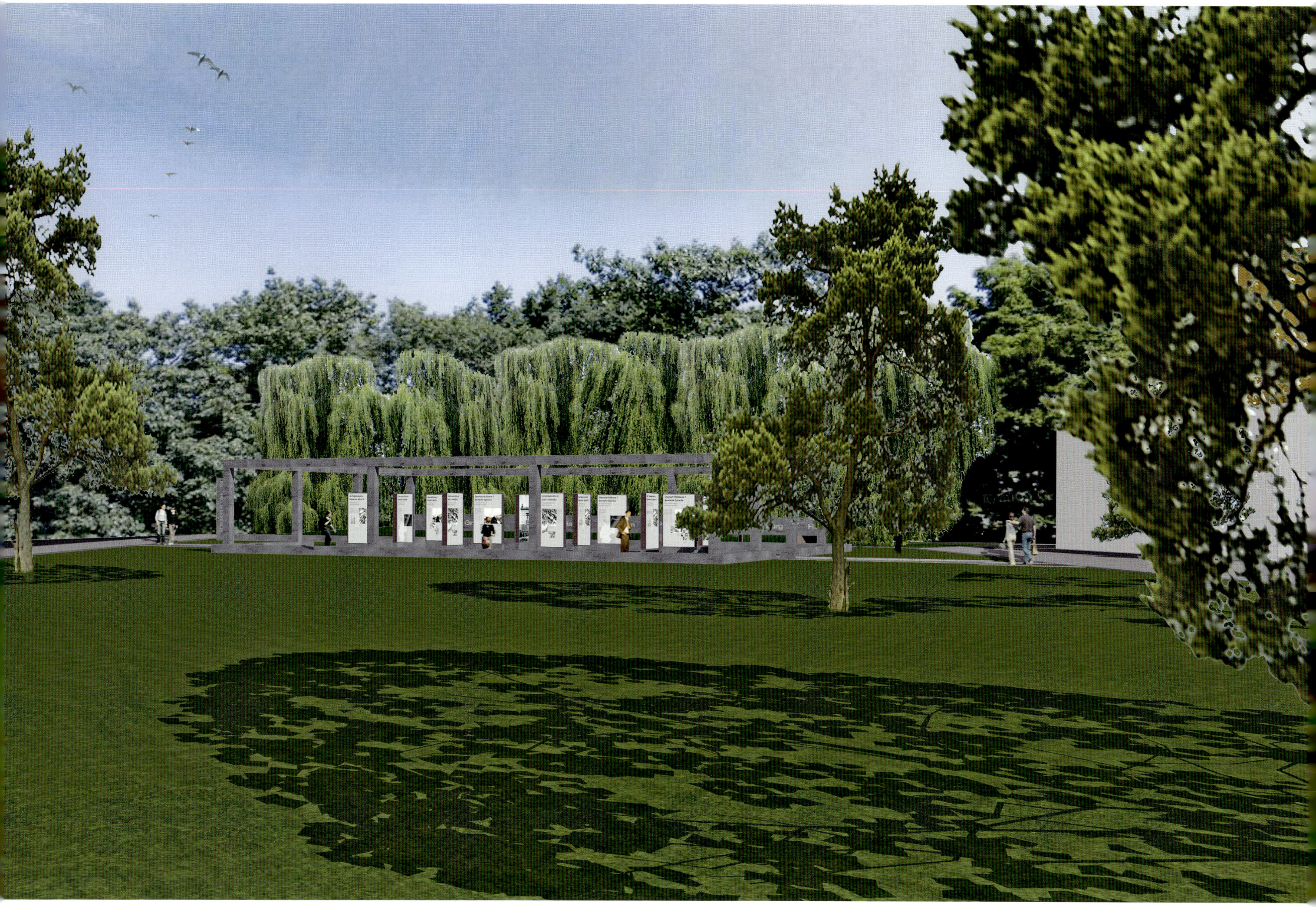

Mühldorfer Hart, landscape design competition, 2013. Commissioned by: Gedenkstätte KZ-Dachau (Dachau concentration camp memorial site)

This design is a competition entry by invitation, which was ultimately rejected by the jury without comment. Within a dense woodland nature reserve, a plan for new paths, plazas, and information panels was to be created to commemorate a huge factory building, camouflaged like a bunker, where, during the late Nazi era, the assembly of »war decisive« jet aircraft was planned. Ultimately, completion never took place. Since almost all the hall arches (made of meter-thick concrete) of the factory bunker were blown up by the Americans after the war, today, there are few authentic memory fragments left.

In itself, the idea of bringing the overgrown ruins to the attention of modern-day tourists by means of modern access paths, information panels, and unsupervised media stations, was questionable. As required by the competition conditions, I interfered too much with the existing natural elements, resulting in terraces and even a viewing tower. It would appear to make more sense to commemorate here only the thousands of slave labourers who were forced to live in damp and cold earthen huts during the construction work that started in 1944. Many died of cold, malnourishment, sickness, and hard construction site work. They were buried in mass graves next to their forest housing.

Incidentally, the competition was won by Peter Latz. He made only very cautious interventions into the terrain. We are left to wonder: has any of this been realised, and will any of this ever be realised in the future?

Mühldorfer Hart, Landschaftsgestaltungswettbewerb, 2013. Auftraggeber: Gedenkstätte KZ-Dachau

Bei diesem Entwurf handelt es sich um einen eingeladenen Wettbewerbsbeitrag, der am Ende von der Jury kommentarlos aussortiert wurde. Hier sollte in einem dichten Naturschutzwald mit neu geplanten Wegen, Plätzen und Informationstafeln an ein riesiges, bunkerartig getarntes Fabrikgebäude erinnert werden, in dem während der späten NS-Zeit die Montage »kriegsentscheidender« Düsenflugzeuge geplant war. Zur endgültigen Fertigstellung kam es nie. Da fast alle Hallenbögen des Fabrikbunkers aus meterdickem Beton von den Amerikanern nach dem Krieg gesprengt worden sind, gibt es heute nur noch wenige authentische Erinnerungsfragmente.

Schon die Idee, die zugewucherten Ruinen mit modernen Zugangswegen, Informationstafeln und unbeaufsichtigten Medienstationen ins Bewußtsein heutiger Touristen zu rücken, war fragwürdig. Ich griff in meinem Entwurf, gemäß der Ausschreibung, zu stark in den Naturbestand ein. Terrassen und sogar ein Aussichtsturm waren die Folge. Naheliegender wäre es gewesen, hier nur den Tausenden von Zwangsarbeitern zu gedenken, die während der Baumaßnahmen ab 1944 in feuchten und kalten Erdhütten wohnen mußten. Kälte, Unterernährung, Krankheiten und harte Baustellenarbeit führten bei vielen von ihnen zum Tod. Sie wurden neben ihren Wald-Unterkünften in anonymen Massengräbern verscharrt.

Der Wettbewerb wurde übrigens von Peter Latz gewonnen. Er hatte nur ganz vorsichtig in das Gelände eingegriffen. Ob etwas davon realisiert wurde oder wird?

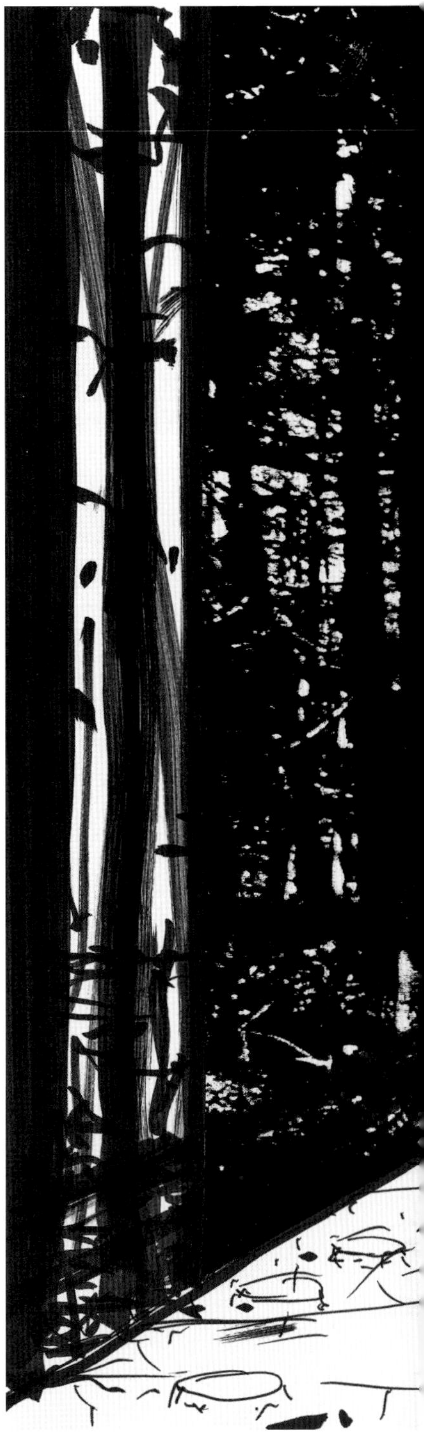

1. In the unmarked woodland grave area I proposed the felling of the trees to create a clearing. A weeping willow and simple memorial panels are intended as reminders of the suffering of the victims. Draft sketch with collage elements.

1. In dem unmarkierten Waldgräberbereich schlug ich vor, die Bäume zu fällen und eine Lichtung zu schaffen. Eine Trauerweide und schlichte Gedenktafeln sollten an das Leid der Opfer erinnern. Entwurfsskizze mit Collage-Elementen.

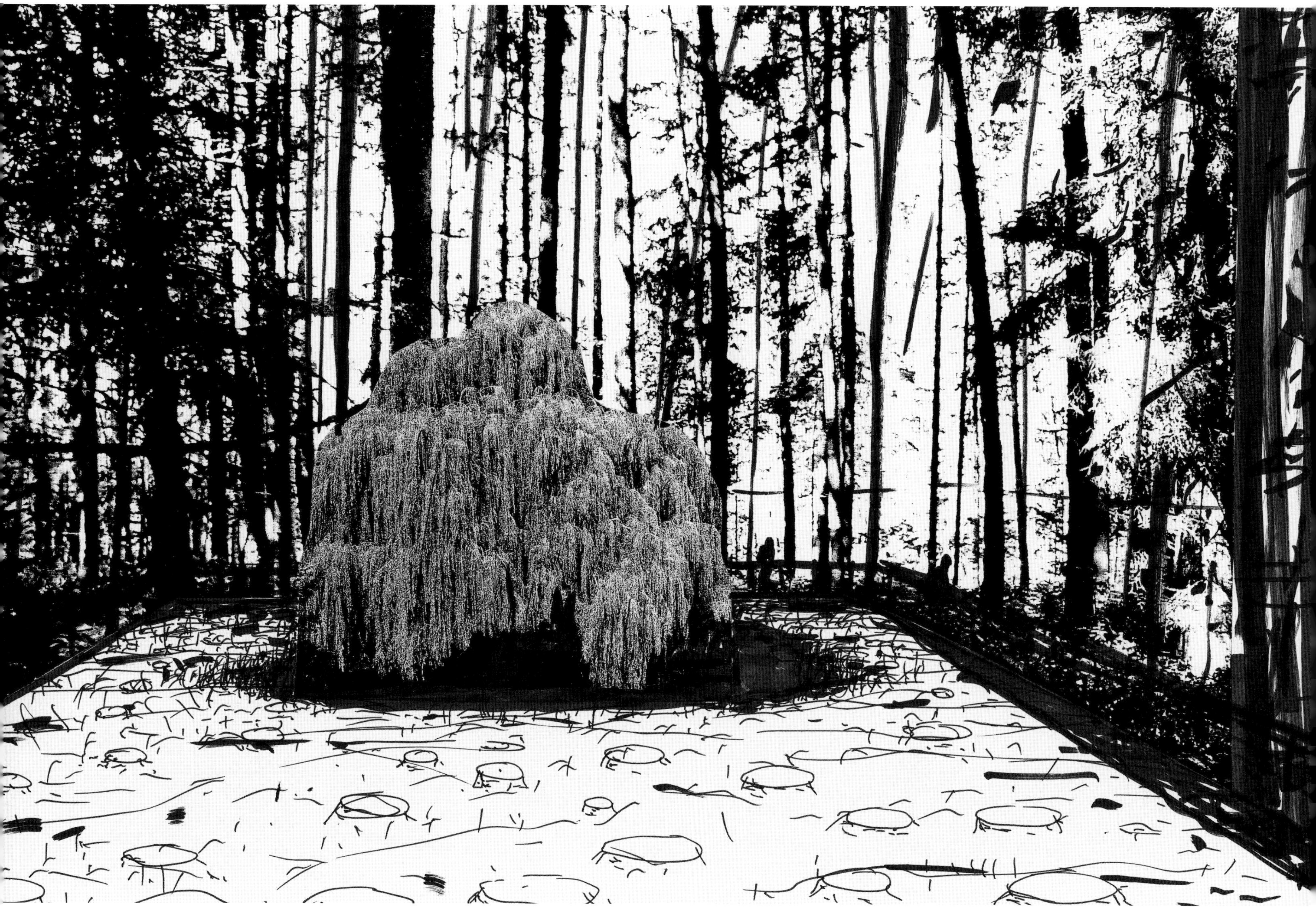

»Trauerweg« (path of mourning), Celle city cemetery, 2013/2014

For ten years – from 2002 to 2012 – I had to, or was permitted to, work as an exhibition designer, and sometimes as an architect, for memorial sites. All these projects involved memories of the crimes of the Nazi era. Unfortunately, all landscape design competitions relating to the outdoor areas of these memorial sites ended negatively – if I was invited in the first place. This applied to Bergen-Belsen, Mittelbau-Dora, and Sachsenhausen, but also to Brandenburg and Esterwegen.

The »Trauerweg« (path of mourning) in Celle city cemetery might have been a follow-up project commission for our concentration camp memorial in Esterwegen. Those responsible for the hospice at Celle saw our design work there and wanted something similar for their city cemetery. I went there, spoke to them, looked at the large, Romantic cemetery and, ultimately, got to work. What was wanted was a place, a garden, or a path, where the dying could prepare for their death, and where relatives could later say farewell to their dead – those »vanished forever«.

As so often with me, it turned into a whole book. I came up with too many thoughts and design ideas. The principal was approving and enthusiastic, but in reality – as I heard only after submitting the little book – they had no money to realise even one of my proposals. Thus, the design sketches, two of which are represented here, remained on paper only.

»Trauerweg«, Stadtfriedhof Celle, 2013/2014

Zehn Jahre lang – von 2002 bis 2012 – mußte oder durfte ich mich als Ausstellungsgestalter, manchmal auch als Architekt, mit Gedenkstätten beschäftigen. Alle Projekte erinnerten an die Verbrechen der NS-Zeit. Alle landschaftsgestalterischen Wettbewerbe für die Außenanlagen dieser Gedenkstätten verliefen für mich – sofern ich überhaupt eingeladen wurde – leider immer negativ. Das gilt für Bergen-Belsen, Mittelbau-Dora, Sachsenhausen, aber auch für Brandenburg und Esterwegen.

Der »Trauerweg« im Stadtfriedhof von Celle hätte ein Folgeauftrag unserer KZ-Gedenkstätte in Esterwegen werden können. Hospiz-Verantwortliche aus Celle hatten dort unsere Gestaltungsarbeiten gesehen und wollten etwas Ähnliches auf ihrem Stadtfriedhof haben. Ich fuhr hin, sprach mit ihnen, schaute mir den großen, romantischen Friedhof an und machte mich anschließend an die Arbeit. Gewünscht wurde ein Ort, ein Garten oder ein Weg, an dem sich Sterbende auf ihren Tod vorbereiten und an dem später die Angehörigen Abschied von ihren Toten – den »Für-immer-Verschwundenen« – nehmen können.

Wie so oft bei mir wurde ein ganzes Buch daraus. Mir fielen zu viele Gedanken und GestaltungsIdeen dazu ein. Die Auftraggeber waren zwar begeistert und angeregt, aber in Wirklichkeit hatten sie – wie ich erst nach Abgabe des kleinen Buches hörte – kein Geld für die Realisierung eines einzigen Vorschlags. So blieben die skizzenhaften Entwürfe, von denen ich hier zwei abbilde, nur auf dem Papier stehen.

1. Proposal for a small clearing. All around it are old trees and shrubs. A narrow path leads to a plaza paved in natural stone. To the left and right of the plaza space are two stelae with texts of poems by Novalis, Georg Trakl, Gottfried Benn, and Paul Celan. The plaza terminates at a wall (concrete or natural stone) with a large window. In front of it is a bench. Beyond are the old trees. This is nature as a transitional zone between our world and the beyond. Nature as a medium of meditation and calming.

1. Vorschlag für eine kleine Lichtung. Ringsum alter Baum- und Staudenbestand. Ein schmaler Weg führt zu einem mit Natursteinplatten belegten Platz. Links und rechts der Platzfläche stehen jeweils zwei Stelen mit Gedichttexten von Novalis, Georg Trakl, Gottfried Benn und Paul Celan. Den Abschluß des Platzes bildet eine Wand (Beton oder Naturstein) mit großem Fenster. Davor eine Bank. Dahinter alte Bäume. Die Natur als Übergangszone vom Dieseits zum Jenseits. Die Natur als Meditations- und Beruhigungsmedium.

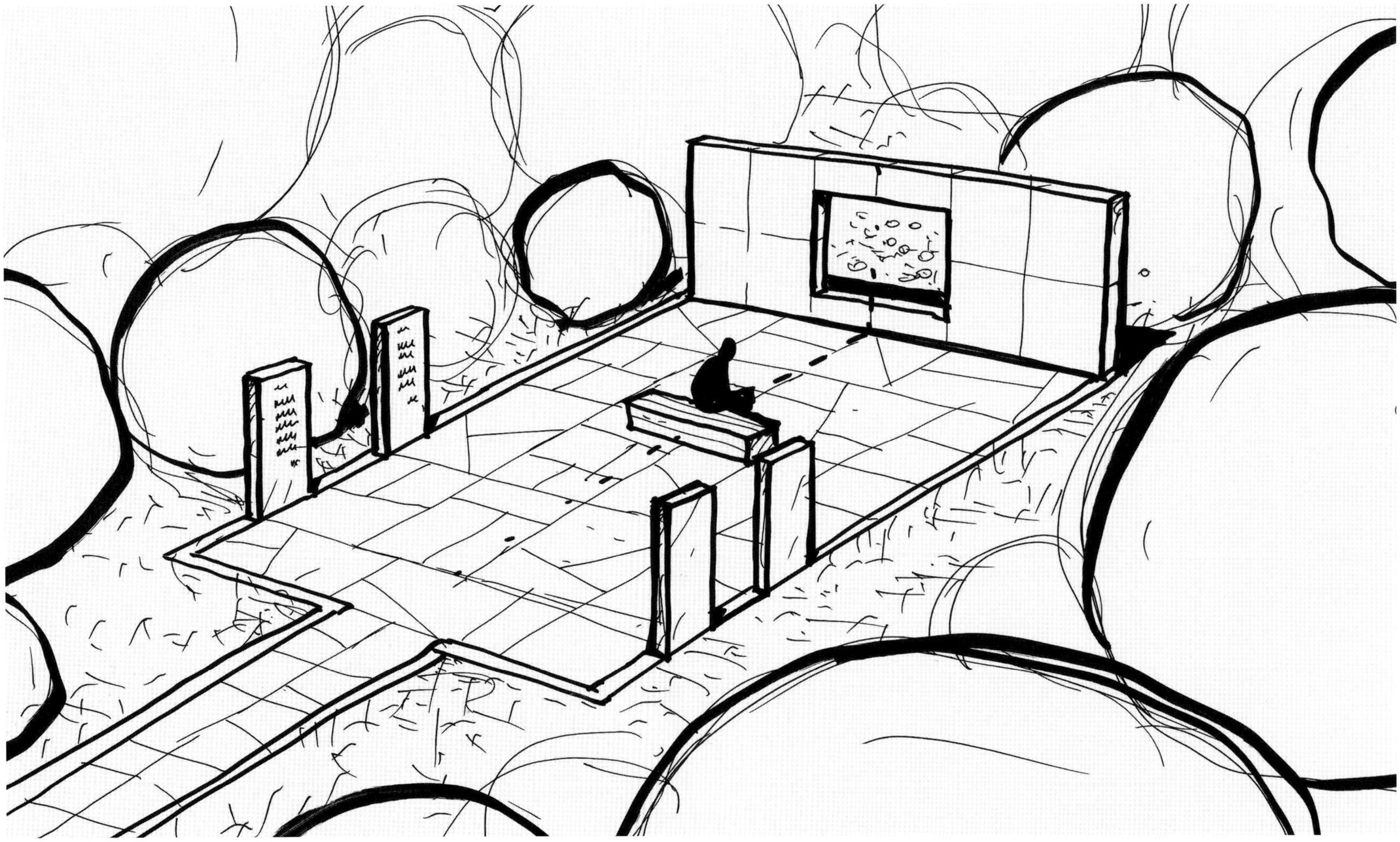

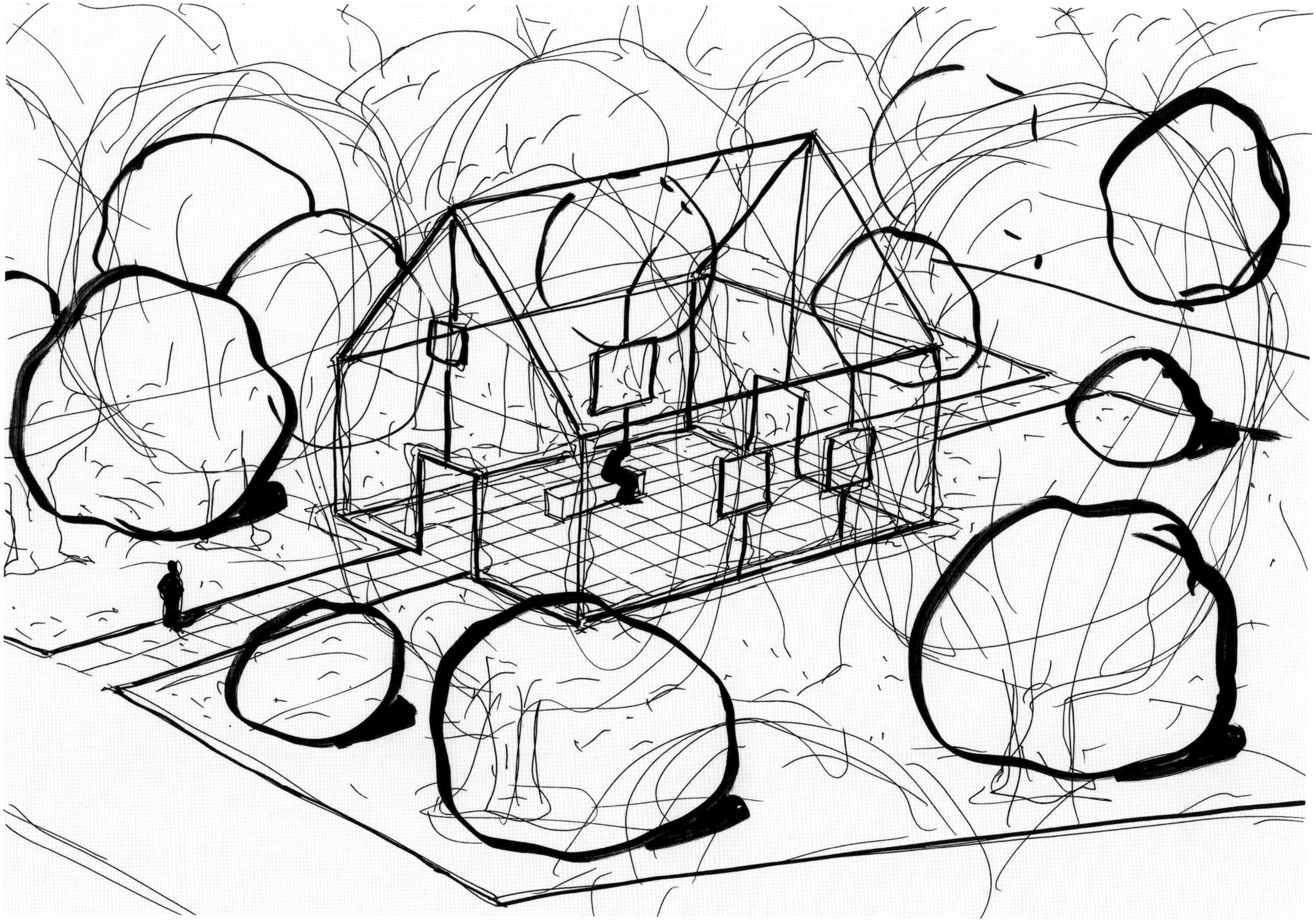

2. A suggestion of an arbour house. Unlike my Stuttgart-Vaihingen version, this house would have been built from steel profiles. It was intended to become covered with ivy and wild vines over time. Here, also, a suggestion of a transitional zone. At once in this world and the next. A fading memory of life, passing into vegetation. A dwelling house of the departed.

2. Ein angedeutetes Laubenhaus. Im Gegensatz zu meiner Version in Stuttgart-Vaihingen wäre dieses Haus aus Stahlprofilen gebaut worden. Es sollte mit Efeu und wildem Wein einwachsen. Auch hier eine angedeutete Übergangszone. Dieseits und Jenseits zugleich. Verblassende, in Vegetation übergehende Erinnerung an das Leben. Wohnhaus der Verstorbenen.

Hans Dieter Schaal

On my works. A retrospective

Just as every generation pursues their own ideals, every generation has its own landscape and nature images in their heads. Whilst our great-grandparents' landscape image was still influenced by paintings (Dürer, Rembrandt, Vermeer, Feuerbach, Böcklin, and later Nolde, Kirchner, Hodler and Klee) and by limited personal travel experiences, our great-grandparents and parents' image was darkened by catastrophes of war, destroyed cities and incinerated forests, flight and expulsion. During the peaceful 1950s, photos and films were added to this. Individual mobility (cars) widened individual experience of the image repertoire by enabling excursions and shorter trips.

From the 1960s onwards, air tourism meant that a lot of people had even more chances to experience landscapes. Additionally, from that point on, landscapes could also be experienced from above. When they were broadcast on television on 21 July 1969, the Apollo 11 mission images led to an explosion in this way of looking at the Earth. Most human beings were now aware that they lived on a sphere floating freely in space, and that they were hanging head downwards over endless space – along with the mountains, lakes, oceans, trees, and cities. Technology had made this possible. However, it also opened up a rift between personally spent world landscape experience, and world and landscape images supplied by the media. Today, these two image worlds are mixed together in our heads. Whether this means that the rift has vanished and been healed, or whether it has been widened and deepened by the longings for distant places thus evoked is a question that each of us must answer for himself or herself.

Born in 1943, I began my intensive involvement in designing landscapes, parks, and gardens in 1965, after I started my architecture studies in Hannover. Previously, I had been a contemplator of and visitor to landscapes and forests, fields, beautiful trees (there are no trees that are not beautiful!), the shapes of leaves, the courses of rivers and streams, reflective water surfaces, field paths, and the moods of the weather had inspired me to create sketches, drawings, images, and sometimes texts and poems, but I never saw myself as an intervening, reshaping designer of landscapes, parks, or gardens.

At the age of 16, in order to penetrate into nature and the wild landscape far more deeply than one would in everyday life, I began to look for a way to spend three weeks in an isolated mountain cabin. And a possibility did in fact turn up in the Alpine foothills. As my only companion, I took along the very well-behaved and anxious family dog. Our diet consisted of tinned foods and water from a nearby spring. I spent the long, lonely days rambling and drawing my woodland surroundings. I wanted a dialogue with virtually wild nature. My dialogue partner, however, was silent, apart from the rustling of leaves and needles, twittering, and the creaking and cracking of branches.

Only once did nature become extremely loud and intimidate me with a summer thunderstorm. All around me, a gale, rain, thunder and lightning. Sometimes, the bright glaring flashes of light struck my immediate surroundings. Not only myself, but the dog also was seized by fear and panic. At every crack of thunder, he barked, howled loudly, and crept whimpering beneath my bed.

Back then, there were no mobile telephones. If I had been struck, I would have been entirely abandoned to my fate. But this was the nature adventure that I had been looking for, and I survived it unscathed.

Beginning in 1965, during my journeys in my own car from my home city of Ulm to Hannover, I expanded my image of landscape relative to modern reality. It was sobering. I discovered the roads and motorways, including the natural images accompanying them, as new zones of liberation and inspiration for myself. Their geometric and functionalised uniformity fascinated me, as did the unambiguity of the motorway's vanishing point on the horizon. Space and time began to visibly flow, and to accelerate – and myself with them. Forests, trees, pieces of meadows, and road signs raced by like cars, trucks, and buses. I could co-determine the tempo, or I could get out of the flow and steer for a car park.

At that time, I tried to work this new feeling for life and reality into my drawings (and sometimes into my designs also). In the background, there was always my threatening experience of mountains and thunderstorms. There was also my experience with film. When I was at school, I used to see all the new films – important and unimportant – in Ulm's cinema. Thus, I got to know American, French, and Italian film landscapes, with their adventurous plots and love stories – sometimes better than my own German surroundings. First in black and white, later in colour.

In Hannover, I continued living the same life, and continued my search. Always, I was driven by the question: what kind of condition are we in? Where do I myself stand? What do nature, technology, and architecture mean to me? Should I join in the criticism of industrialisation, of the increase in environmental pollution, the growing artificiality and automation of our living environment and our life? As an architecture student, I had – or so I thought – taken a clear position: I was in favour of technology, of construction, and of continued building, of the ongoing project of »modernity«. In spite of this, it was plain to me that architecture embodied precisely the opposite of living natural landscapes that changed with the seasons: it does not live, it is dead, and like the rocks and mountains, it has a stony permanence. Every shell, every building structure: an immobile, hollowed-out brake block, a silent, obdurate enemy of nature offering protection and security?

The backdrop to my Hannover years was the fermenting of the unrest of 1968. In spite of the semester I had spent studying with Ernst Bloch in Tübingen in 1964, this was something that I did not really understand. The Berlin students were fighting against »the old musty odour under the gowns« (history, tradition?), they did not want to be patronised any longer (by the state, by architecture, by the powerful), they wanted to abolish capitalism and be free. Free, free, free. Like the American hippies and their peace movement against the senseless and absurd Vietnam war, like the Beatles and the Rolling Stones. They did not have much time for nature, the landscape, or even parks and gardens, and that included clipped hedges, lakes, the jets and basins of fountains. West Germany had no Woodstock concert to sink into the mire. The Berlin students liked to occupy houses, and preferred to provoke street fights with the police. There was a certain (grim and wet) irony in the fact that water cannons (the »fountains« of the state's defensive artillery) were deployed in these conflicts.

Some time when I had a free afternoon, in the weeks of the first lectures on architectural construction, the science of materials, statics, Palladio and Le Corbusier, I wandered through the neighbouring Georgengarten, admiring the open meadows and old trees. A typical English garden, designed freestyle and with no artificiality. Close to normal nature, but somewhat more boring. But suddenly the picture changed. I came under the spell of an endless alley of lindens, which led, guided, drove, and compelled me toward the Herrenhäuser Gärten. I had heard of these gardens, and had seen images on postcards.

When I finally reached the periphery of the wide, flat-as-a-carpet, geometrically-formed picture-book parterre, amid the baroque garden, I was overwhelmed and excited. At one stroke, I realised: this was precisely the image I was looking for! It all seemed to be spread out before me: the whole history of culture, its painstaking work, its beauty, its exaggeration, and its limits. Although it was clear to me that this ornamental style showed nature being violated and forced into forms that it would never take of its own free will, I also thought immediately of agricultural line structures, of tulip fields, and of pictures by Malevich, Mondrian, Kandinsky, Albers, and Max Bill. The idea of spreading these abstractions of nature, here much ornamented, out flat on the ground on a large scale, appeared to me to be a stroke of genius, but also irritating, visionary, and utopian. As I walked further, I thought about the recent and topical concepts and works of the American Land Art artists, which I knew from the Kassel documenta. Had Walter de Maria or Robert Smithson ever been here? Both men would probably have preferred a helicopter flight over the Herrenhäuser Gärten to the normal process of wandering around.

I walked onward, past clipped hornbeam hedges, flowerbeds, water basins, cascades, grottoes, springs, bastions, a labyrinth, and a garden theatre, stopping at the fountain and the round temples marking the termini of the large axes. There is no fence around the garden's three flanks and no wall, only a water-filled ditch, a kind of moat. This frames this artful landscape image, and also protects it from undesirable intruders. Once upon a time, aristocrats and princes would have wished to keep this place for themselves, and not to share their garden pleasures with the common people. Today, Herrenhausen belongs to everyone.

When I reached the white stone sculptures and scenic figure groups, I thought about the surreal absurdity of theatre, opera, and film. Strange, silent heroes with animal skins and swords, and naked women. Mythological abduction scenes, or the love stories of gods and nymphs? I was happier not knowing – the sensual poetic suggestions were enough for me. I was very enthusiastic. The idea of weaving scenes and narratives through a piece of manicured garden landscape lodged in my imagination. Immediately, I pictured modern gardens with mysterious features, hearing as I did so music by Mozart, Verdi, Puccini, Richard Strauss, John Adams, and Arvo Pärt, and sometimes also music by the Rolling Stones. Then I saw, in my imagination, boats on small, still lakes. Within them, celebrations were in progress. Suddenly, all the costumed figures froze, creating surreal figural groups. White marble dust fell on them. The music went on, and blue fog arose …

There were only a few hornbeam squares within which nature was permitted to run wild, within boundaries. Entering them, it was clear to any visitor to the garden that if the gardeners ceased their work of tending the garden, the geometric Herrenhausen composition would become an overgrown jungle within a few years. Every year, every tree and every plant in the whole world spreads millions of seeds, with only one goal: to multiply itself egoistically, unrestrainedly. Nature does not need us as human beings, and that includes gardeners. Culture means setting boundaries for nature, directing its anarchic drive to occupy the ground, and enabling it to be made use of by us as human beings. Thus, culture also means working against nature. It is for each generation – and, of course, for each individual garden owner – to decide how far this should go.

Due to my strong interest in landscape architecture, it might have made sense for me to begin a second course of study on the theme of »Landscape Design« in Karlsruhe or Weihenstephan in 1970, when I completed my architecture degree at the TH in Stuttgart, but I preferred to spend a number of years as an independent artist, formulating my questions and themes in images and drawings, and sometimes also in objects, landscape interventions, photos, and films.

In my little Stuttgart studio, I tried to interconnect everything in image form: the wild beauty of mountains, rocks, coasts, fjords, and beaches, the artful beauty of historic gardens, the ancient battle between land husbandry and free nature. Mixed in with these were the products of modern technology and architecture: apartment blocks, urban peripheries, industrial complexes, power stations, dams, allotments, car parks, parking garages, motorways, petrol stations, country roads, lay-by areas, rubbish dumps, transformer stations, and atomic power stations. I wanted to get an overview of the whole, not excluding the current landscape destruction and environmental problems.

The »Laubenhaus« (arbor house) in Stuttgart-Vaihingen represented my first entrance into the architectonic and landscape design in reality. The planning and implementation acquainted me with certain entirely routine problems with the principals – in this case, the university construction authorities – the bureaucracy, the licensing office, and the eventual users. I was spared nothing. Nor were the difficulties with the real world over after completion. Vandals made the »life« of the small unprotected building hard. I don't know whether the »Laubenhaus«, with its ironic/Romantic front garden, also had friends and gratified visitors. Its demolition in 2000 is a sad fact. Perhaps one should always cordon off experiments of this sort temporarily, and also protect them better. In our increasingly unthinking ego society, vandalism assumes ever more obtrusive forms and proportions.

In 1981, after my second scholarship period (lasting several months) in Rome's Villa Massimo, which I spent making a detailed study of Italian gardens from the Renaissance and baroque eras, I moved out of Stuttgart to a rural area. Our new domicile in Attenweiler near Biberach an der Riß was a strictly protected historic structure: a rococo manse (or rather the former summer residence of the abbots of Schussenried, with stucco work by Dominikus Zimmermann), built between 1727 and 1729. I also saw this move as a clear commitment to living in and with nature. Rural life, with all its advantages and disadvantages.

There was no historical garden. Only a larger kitchen garden. To commemorate my Herrenhausen experience, I planted – jointly with my wife – a 5 x 5 meter hornbeam square, with a paved green interior space and fountain basin. In front of this, there was a small kitchen garden with berry bushes, and a meadow with fruit trees. The yard area is occupied by a walnut tree, also planted by us, which has since attained a prodigious size.

I find it sad that, in the years that followed, in spite of numerous publications, exhibitions of my own drawings, and competition entry proposals, only very few larger scale garden and landscape architecture projects ever became a reality. I had to be content with stage sets and exhibition designs. With hindsight, the few highlights were provided by the urn cemetery in Singen am Hohentwiel, the two IGA-projects in Stuttgart, the Monopteros in Hohenheim, and the Wielandpark in Biberach. In any case, all five of these projects allowed me to realise fragments of my garden and park ideas –the »scenic gardens«.

Here, I will list only a few of the projects for compe titions that I did not win. In the 1980s: Stadtzeichen Hannover (Hannover city icon), the Gustav-Gründgens-Platz (plaza project) in Düsseldorf, the »Metallflußbett« (metal riverbed) at the new planetarium in Mannheim and the »Holzturm« (wooden tower) in Freiburg. In the 1990s: the Stadteingang (city entrance) in Freiburg (poplar plantings), plazas in Böblingen and Neu-Ulm, the Kunst-am-Bau (art for buildings) competitions in Hamburg, Munich and Stuttgart (with green spaces), the grounds around the Jahrhunderthalle (Century Hall) in Bochum, undertaken jointly with Jacques Blumer (Bern), Borja Huidobro (Paris), Helen Mayer and Newton Harrison (Del Mar, California), the Freibad (open-air swimming pool) in Biberach/Riß, the Fröbelplatz in Berlin (with sunbathing lawns, play areas, and green spaces), the »Mauerdenkmalspark« (wall memorial park), and the Lustgarten (pleasure garden, Museum Island) in Berlin. In the new millennium, these were joined by the Christliche Garten in Berlin-Marzahn and the Landesgartenschau in Sigmaringen (both jointly with Christof Luz), and the Gedenkstätten-Park in Esterwegen and the Gedenkstätten-Park of Dachau, both memorial park projects (Mühldorfer Hart and Hebertshausen).

The state of things today

Compared with our parents and grandparents' generation, we are living in an era of image saturation. Aside from our own travel experiences, this condition is contributed to by television reports on exhibitions into the Earth's most remote landscape zones. Almost all of us think that we know the Arctic, Greenland, Tierra del Fuego, New Zealand, Africa, India, America, Mexico, South America, Japan, Russia, China, Canada, Alaska, the South Sea, the oceans, the rainforests, and the deserts. Once, unknown, mysterious landscape realms existed, but today it is barely problematic to fly even to those places, to join safaris and adventure exhibitions, to interact with these landscapes by looking, photographing, and filming, or – if prevented by time and financial constraints – to collect information about them from Google Earth or from Wikipedia.

So, what bearing does this have on our subject? This general unrest, this continual and to some degree global state of being on the move (real or media-generated) has led to most people becoming increasingly alienated from their immediate landscape. The city inhabitant of today (below a certain age) sees these landscapes only when jogging with earphones, perceiving them as a sporty movement and fitness space with open-air scenery. City parks are seen as the green lungs of our high-density civilisation. Mountains serve hiking, climbing, hang-gliding, and skiing needs. Oceans are for sailing, surfing, swimming, snorkelling, or diving. Those with enough time and money fly to Ireland to play golf, to Portugal or Lanzarote to surf, to the Maldives to snorkel, and to Ibiza, Florida, or Hawaii to sunbathe. Quiet, contemplative encounters with nature and its manifestations are considered boring: there is barely any demand for them.

Some contemporaries who live on the city periphery do, however, have their own garden, or their own small park with a terrace, a pool, and a tennis court. In summer, the meadow is mowed with a lawnmower every week like a golf course or football pitch – for the sake of tidiness, watchful neighbours, and invited guests. The owners of terraced houses do likewise. They have long since been living in the kind of surreally clean world described in such a lovingly sarcastic way in Jacques Tatí's *Mon oncle*.

The old, somewhat prim garden romanticism – with a distinct tendency toward vegetable gardens – is abandoned to allotment gardeners. They also number among the enthusiastic visitors – generally getting on in years somewhat – to garden shows with abundant offerings of flowers.

At the same time, most people are aware of the major environmental issues. They sit in comfortable armchairs and watch, with curiosity, reports on wars and natural and environmental catastrophes, on screens that become ever larger, more high-definition, and colourful. They feel themselves to be innocent, and laugh complacently to themselves. But sometimes, when the dangers come closer, they shift around uneasily, even in a horrified manner, on their leather sofas, and feel fear and panic attacks coming on. Every magazine and TV programme, along with countless books – not to mention current catastrophe reports – describes apocalyptic images of the world coming to an end. What started in America in 1962 with Rachel Carson's *Silent Spring* and gradually became a certainty from 1972 onwards thanks to the admonitory books of the Club of Rome, has now become undeniable. The consequence of the world becoming industrialised has been, and continues to be, an unbridled consumption of energy. Natural resources have been exploited, the air has been polluted, and landscapes have been covered with rubbish tips. A critical endpoint had been reached. Even cynical contemporaries have realised that a rethink and change of direction is needed. Regardless, Buckminster-Fuller's assertion from 1970 continues to hold true: »Now there is one outstandingly important fact regarding Spaceship Earth, and that is that no instruction book came with it.«

Today, most governments of major industrial nations are working to reduce CO2 emissions, in order to protect the world climate, to reduce global warming, and to keep the air clean. Ecology, the end of overexploitation, recycling, and sustainability are the new magic words.

This notwithstanding, no government in the world has gone as far as the German government did following the Fukushima catastrophe by planning to totally phase out atomic energy. In general, one is struck by the fact that, in Germany, efforts to be environment and nature-friendly are somewhat overstated. For the »Greens« today, renaturation, wetland biotopes, bat bridges and toad tunnels are more important than problems among people (e.g. social issues). This might have increased love for landscape and nature, but in fact interest in these things has tended to dwindle. Priority is given to major decisions and plans such as the expanding of cycle paths in cities, wind energy and solar plants in the landscape and on roofs. It is true that there is a greater desire for green space within cities, but at the same time gardening arts and ambitious landscape architecture have become a fringe interest in Germany, where they are derided as zones of backward, superfluous expression – in contrast to other European countries. Meadows and forests, pure and simple, must suffice. High-maintenance gardens such as Herrenhausen, Schwetzingen, Veitshöchheim, and Nymphenburg gardens are only permitted to survive for the sake of historic monument preservation and promoting tourism. It is astonishing that »green history iconoclasts« have not long since turned up to forcibly help nature back to its original, wild appearance!

However, in spite of this, perhaps one fact can be numbered among the more welcome results of the increase in environmental consciousness and those »green tendencies« which, incidentally, have existed since the beginning of the 20th century in the form of rambling and naturist movements: today, there are more forests and green zones spread across Europe than ever before. In previous centuries, human beings tended to cut down whole forests and forested mountain ranges, without any replanting. The wood was needed for fires and heating, for housebuilding and shipbuilding. Today, every area of forest that is felled is re-forested with young trees, and this is safeguarded by forestry laws and forestry authorities.

Amid all these dimensions of development, has our image of nature and the landscape fundamentally changed? Certainly it has become more varied, and perhaps, thanks to more information and knowledge, more differentiated. At the same time – even for farmers – it has lost something of its original dusty, dirty, sometimes dangerous sensuality. Media images, computers, scientific insights, fertilisers, chemical anti-pest measures and machines have come between human beings and landscapes, between nature and our own hands.

For the dwellers in cities (which are now in the majority) there have always been two worlds: the day-to-day world and the Sunday world, the working world and the holiday world. Then there are the growing numbers of retired people who have been freed from work. The yearning for beautiful, but also restorative and usable and at the same time exciting natural places for weekends, on holidays, and during the boring life of the retired, grows ever greater. Our western socially safeguarded prosperity has also led to ever more people becoming isolated, tending more to empathy with pets, plants, and trees than with other human beings.

This is precisely the point from which my ideas for new (or old?) gardens and parks begin. In my opinion, these things are more important now than they ever were. Although it is true that they may always have possessed this particular importance: slowing us down, causing us to pause and – mixed with images from the known »culture world« – causing us to look inward, to the essence of nature. The »outside« has now been conquered, hacked down, researched, discussed, jogged through, raced through, flown through, and is for the most part known to us. Unfortunately, it continues to be much oppressed by noisy, hectic, constantly-growing cities, and by ongoing, if somewhat checked and slowed, environmental destruction.

Every garden or park, private or public – and, of course, every nature conservation area and every protected forest – speaks of the yearning for reconciliation and peace with nature. Just as in Pompeian house gardens, in Christian cloister gardens, or in the gardens of Chinese and Japanese temple complexes, it is today equally important to remind hyperactive, media-stressed people of »nature«, their zone of origin and of return. Max Weber once described the old creed of science thus: »The task of science is the disenchantment of the world«. I wish to achieve precisely the opposite.

All my previously developed and only very fragmentarily realised garden and park ideas – not excluding their architectural and artistic features – aim to lead back to »enlightened magic«, and thus also into the mysterious world of nature. Not entirely in the radically wild and humourless sense of Jean-Jacques Rousseau: the idea is that there should always be a hint of the historical, the cultural, the psychological, the narrative, and the futuristic. Contrary to the assertions of many scientists of today, we can presume that the mysteries of nature are by no means all explained. The mysteries prevail, and have taken on more cosmic dimensions. We, the visitors to the landscapes and new garden sites, constantly carry our experiences, our knowledge, our questions, our imagination, and our yearning within us, and we cannot be passively silent like trees, plants, flowers, and stones. Certainly we can take things in and feel things without words, but our consciousness, our understanding operates in words, sentences, explanations, imagery, and memories – and, more rarely, in mathematical formulae. In my proposals, I therefore try to prompt dialogues between nature and the visitors as individuals, by means of staged situations and path systems possessing dramatic tension.

Suddenly, trees begin to tell stories, leaves to speak, waterfalls to sing, and stones to dance. Spider webs transform into harps and bird's nests into caves from the grey dawn of time. Sometimes a cheeky garden gnome emerges between bushes and leaves, with cheerfully silly phrases to remind visitors not to leave the paths, and not to litter in the meadows. If this rule is broken, a poem by Ernst Jandl must be recited 10 times:

»We are the people in the meadows,
Soon to be people under the meadows,
We'll become meadows and we'll become trees,
An endless rural vacation it is.«

In my vision, it is important for all visitors to gardens and parks to be put in a certain state of mind. Among other things, this means that they should begin by passing through a gate (such as a cinema or theatre entrance). Each of the newly designed landscape areas – the scenic gardens – must be encompassed, framed, and protected by a wall, so that they are clearly set apart from the day-to-day world, with its noise and vandalism. This »secret of transformation« has always been known to all great garden and park designers all over the world. Apart from the Herrenhäuser Gärten, I am thinking of the famous Chinese gardens of Suzhou, of the gravel and rock gardens of the Toji Temple in Kyoto in Japan, of César Manrique's »Cactus Garden« in Lanzarote, but also of the »Disney-Worlds« in Los Angeles, Florida, and Paris.

Everyone who enters is one of the »transformed«, travelling within in search of his or her memories, hopes, and yearnings. At the same time, the visitor looks up to the sky and sees the clouds and birds with new eyes. To a visitor travelling here after dark, the cosmos opens up under new, planetary aspects. Aside from blazing meteors in forest clearings, such a visitor may encounter space travellers or strange extraterrestrial beings on mountain peaks.

I am not picturing religious sites, forest churches or places of pilgrimage, or landscape temples, but natural sites featuring peculiar scenes and architectonic elements: overgrown ruins and carousels, cages with floating rocking horses and remains of sculptures, wandering garden gnomes, beds spun in caves, school tables in a clearing, home furniture in a maize field, kitchen items half-buried between jagged rocks, old wine bottles, overgrown with ivy, on shelves, masks on tree trunks, stuffed animals in glass cases, television sets under water, water lily ponds with live goldfish, old gravestones, traffic lights in the thickets, armchairs in the crowns of trees …

Paths lead through artfully designed valleys of natural stone, past waterfalls and fern forests, to suggestions of rooms with windows but without roofs, to groves and lake shores with reed bed zones, to Romantic lakes with ducks and herons. But also to meadows where sheep, cows, horses, and goats graze. Sometimes one stumbles upon zoo enclosures with elephants and hippopotami. All around, peacocks spread their tails and make their strange cries.

Suddenly, there is a stone with writing by the side of the path (where crosses would once have stood). Colourful parrots are sitting on it, translating the chiselled questions into human sounds:

»How is it possible that a whole tree can come out of an apple seed, a plum stone, a walnut? How is it possible that all the leaves, blossoms, and fruits (which are fresh every year!) can be contained and preprogrammed in this seed?«

An additional stone, with the questions:

»What is the energy that allows our hearts to beat for the space of a whole lifetime? Is the sun the source of all life? Or are there other mysterious, hitherto undiscovered forces? Why are there positive and negative forces? Why do sicknesses exist? Why does life exist at all? Why is there a world, and a universe? Why is there something and not nothing?«

Hans Dieter Schaal

Zu meinen Arbeiten. Ein Rückblick

Wie jede Generation ihren eigenen Idealen nachjagt, so hat auch jede Generation ihre eigenen Landschafts- und Naturbilder im Kopf. War das Landschaftsbild unserer Urgroßeltern noch geprägt von Gemälden (Dürer, Rembrandt, Vermeer, Feuerbach, Böcklin, später Nolde, Kirchner, Hodler und Klee) und wenigen eigenen Reiseerfahrungen, verdüsterte sich das Bild bei unseren Großeltern und Eltern durch Kriegskatastrophen, zerstörte Städte und verbrannte Wälder, Flucht und Vertreibung. In den friedlichen 1950er Jahren kamen Photos und Filme dazu. Mit der individuellen Mobilität (Autos) ergänzten eigene Erfahrungen bei Ausflügen und kleineren Reisen das Bildrepertoire.

Der touristische Flugverkehr, der zu Beginn der 1960er Jahre einsetzte, ermöglichte vielen Menschen eine noch größere Landschaftserfahrung. Außerdem gehörte jetzt der Blick von oben dazu. Zu einer Explosion dieser Sehweise auf die Erde führten die Fernsehübertragungsbilder der Apollo-11-Mission am 21. Juli 1969. Den meisten Menschen wurde bewußt, daß sie auf einer frei im Weltall schwebenden Kugel leben und – wie die Berge, Seen, Meere, Bäume und Städte – kopfunter im unendlichen Raum hängen. Die Technik hatte es ermöglicht. Aber sie hatte auch gleichzeitig den Riß zwischen individueller, selbst erlebter Welt-Landschaftserfahrung und medial vermittelten Welt- und Landschaftsbildern geöffnet. Heute vermischen sich diese beiden Bildwelten in den Köpfen. Ob der Riß damit verschwunden und geheilt ist, oder ob er sich durch angestachelte Fernweh-Sehnsüchte eher verbreitert und vertieft hat, kann nur jeder für sich selbst beantworten.

Als 1943-Geborener begannen meine gestalterischen Auseinandersetzungen mit Landschaften, Parks und Gärten intensiver erst 1965, nachdem ich mit dem Architekturstudium in Hannover begonnen hatte. Davor war ich zwar auch Betrachter und Besucher von Landschaften und ließ mich durch Wälder, Äcker, schöne Bäume (und es gibt nur schöne Bäume!), Blattformen, Fluß- und Bachverläufe, spiegelnde Wasserflächen, Feldwege und Wetterstimmungen zu Skizzen, Zeichnungen, Bildern, manchmal auch zu Texten und Gedichten anregen, aber als eingreifender und umformender Landschafts-, Park- oder Gartengestalter sah ich mich dabei nie.

Um einmal tiefer, sehr viel tiefer als im Alltag, in die Natur und wilde Landschaft einzudringen, bemühte ich mich im Alter von 16 Jahren um einen dreiwöchigen Aufenthalt in einer einsamen Berghütte. Tatsächlich fand sich eine Möglichkeit im Voralpengebiet. Als einzigen Begleiter nahm ich unseren sehr braven und ängstlichen Familienhund mit. Unsere Ernährung bestand aus Doseninhalten und Wasser einer nahegelegenen Quelle. Die langen, einsamen Tage verbrachte ich mit Herumwandern und mit dem Zeichnen meiner Waldumgebung. Ich wollte in den Dialog mit der fast wilden Natur treten. Aber die Gegenseite schwieg. Außer Blätter- und Nadelrauschen, Zwitschern, Krächzen und Knacken von Ästen war nichts zu hören.

Nur einmal wurde die Natur sehr laut und schüchterte mich mit einem sommerlichen Gewitter ein. Sturm, Regen, Donnerschläge und Blitze ringsum. Manchmal schlugen die grellen Lichtstrahlen in meiner unmittelbaren Waldumgebung ein. Nicht nur ich, auch der Hund wurde von Angst und Panik gepackt. Bei jedem Donnerschlag bellte er, heulte laut auf und verkroch sich winselnd unter meinem Bett.

Es gab damals noch keine Mobilteleph-one. Wenn es mich getroffen hätte, wäre ich ohne Hilfe meinem Schicksal ausgeliefert gewesen. Aber genau dieses Naturabenteuer hatte ich gesucht und heil über-standen.

Ab 1965, während der Fahrten mit dem eigenen Auto von meiner Heimatstadt Ulm nach Hannover, erweiterte und ernüchterte sich mein Landschaftsbild Richtung moderner Realität. Ich entdeckte die Straßen und Autobahnen, einschließlich der begleitenden Naturbilder als neue Befreiungs- und Anregungszonen für mich. Ihre geometrisierte und funktionalisierte Gleichförmigkeit faszinierte mich genauso wie die Eindeutigkeit des Autobahnfluchtpunkts am Horizont. Raum und Zeit begannen sichtbar zu fließen und sich – gemeinsam mit mir – zu beschleunigen. Wälder, Bäume, Wiesenstücke und Verkehrsschilder rasten vorbei wie Autos, Lastwagen und Busse. Ich konnte das Tempo mitbestimmen oder aus dem Fluß aussteigen und einen Parkplatz ansteuern.

Damals versuchte ich, dieses neue Lebens- und Wirklichkeitsgefühl in meine Zeichnungen (manchmal auch in meine Entwürfe) einzuarbeiten. Im Hintergrund immer mein bedrohliches Gebirgs- und Gewittererlebnis. Außerdem meine Filmerfahrungen. Ich hatte mir in den Ulmer Kinos während meiner Schulzeit alle wichtigen und unwichtigen neuen Filme angeschaut. Dadurch kannte ich amerikanische, französische und italienische Filmlandschaften mit ihren abenteuerlichen Handlungen und Liebesgeschichten manchmal besser als meine deutsche Umgebung. Erst in Schwarzweiß, später in Farbe.

In Hannover setzte ich dieses Leben fort und suchte weiter. Immer von der Frage getrieben: In welchem Zustand befinden wir uns? Wo stehe ich selbst? Was bedeuten Natur, Technik und Architektur für mich? Soll ich teilnehmen an der Kritik gegenüber der Industrialisierung, der zunehmenden Umweltverschmutzung, der wachsenden Künstlichkeit und Automatisierung unserer Lebensumgebung und unseres Lebens? Als Architekturstudent hatte ich – meiner Meinung nach – eindeutig Stellung bezogen: für die Technik, für Konstruktion und Weiterbau, für das fortschreitende Projekt »Moderne«. Trotzdem wurde mir klar, daß Architektur genau das Gegenteil von lebendigen, sich mit den Jahreszeiten verändernden Naturlandschaften verkörpert: Sie lebt nicht, sie ist tot und wie Felsen und Gebirge auf versteinerte Dauer angelegt. Jedes Gehäuse, jeder Hauskörper: ein unbeweglicher, ausgehöhlter Bremsblock, ein sturer, schweigender, Schutz und Sicherheit bietender Naturgegner?

Im Hintergrund meiner Zeit in Hannover gärten die Unruhen der 1968er Jahre. Ein Thema, das ich trotz meines Studiensemesters 1964 in Tübingen bei Ernst Bloch nicht so richtig verstand. Die Berliner Studenten bekämpften »den alten Muff unter den Talaren« (die Geschichte, die Traditionen?), sie wollten nicht mehr bevormundet werden (vom Staat, von der Architektur der Mächtigen), sie wollten den Kapitalismus abschaffen und frei sein. Frei, frei, frei. Wie die amerikanischen Hippies, die sich friedensbewegt gegen den sinnlos-absurden Vietnamkrieg wehrten, wie die Beatles und die Rolling Stones. Mit Natur, Landschaft oder gar Parks und Gärten, einschließlich beschnittener Hecken, Seen, Brunnenbecken und Fontänen, hatten sie nicht viel im Sinn. In Westdeutschland gab es kein Woodstock-Konzert, das im Morast versank. Die Berliner Studenten besetzten gern Häuser und provozierten am liebsten Straßenschlachten mit der Polizei. Daß dabei Wasserwerfer als staatliche Gegenwehr-Fontänen eingesetzt wurden, birgt eine gewisse, wenn auch grausam-feuchte Ironie.

Irgendwann an einem freien Nachmittag, in den Wochen der ersten Vorlesungen über Baukonstruktion, Materialkunde, Statik, Palladio und Le Corbusier streifte ich durch den benachbarten Georgengarten, bewunderte die freien Wiesen und alten Bäume. Ein typisch englischer Garten, frei gestaltet ohne jede Künstlichkeit. Nahe der normalen Natur, nur etwas langweiliger. Doch plötzlich änderte sich das Bild. Ich geriet in den Bann einer endlos langen Lindenallee und wurde von ihr hinaus Richtung Herrenhäuser Gärten geführt, geleitet, getrieben, gezwungen. Ich hatte davon gehört und Abbildungen auf Postkarten gesehen.

Als ich schließlich am Rande des weiten, teppichflachen, geometrisch gefaßten Bilderbuch-Parterres, inmitten des Barockgartens stand, war ich überwältigt und verzaubert. Mit einem Schlag wurde mir bewußt: Genau dieses Bild hatte ich gesucht! Hier schien alles vor mir zu liegen: die gesamte Geschichte der Kultur, ihre mühsame Arbeit, ihre Schönheit, ihre Übertreibung und ihre Grenzen. Obwohl mir klar war, daß auf diese ornamentale Weise die Natur vergewaltigt und in Formen gezwungen wird, die sie freiwillig nie annehmen würde, dachte ich sofort auch an landwirtschaftliche Linienstrukturen, an Tulpenfelder und an Bilder von Malewitsch, Mondrian, Kandinsky, Albers und Max Bill. Die Idee, diese hier stark verschnörkelten Natur-Abstraktionen groß und flach auf den Boden auszubreiten, erschien mir genial, gleichzeitig auch irritierend, visionär und utopisch. Beim Weitergehen fielen mir die aktuellen Konzepte und Werke der amerikanischen Land-art-Künstler ein, die ich von der Kassler documenta kannte. Ob Walter de Maria oder Robert Smithson je hier waren? Beide hätten bestimmt einen Hubschrauberflug über die Herrenhäuser Gärten dem normalen Herumwandern vorgezogen.

Ich ging weiter, vorbei an den beschnittenen Hainbuchenhecken, an Blumenrabatten, Wasserbecken, Kaskaden, Grotten, Brunnen, Bastionen, einem Labyrinth, einem Gartentheater, bis zur Fontäne und den Rundtempeln, die den Abschluß der großen Achsen bilden. Rings um den Garten auf drei Seiten kein Zaun, auch keine Mauer, sondern ein Wassergraben, eine Gracht. Das künstliche Landschaftsbild wurde damit gerahmt und vor unerwünschten Eindringlingen geschützt. Früher wollten die Adligen und Fürsten hier unter ihresgleichen bleiben und ihre Gartenlust nicht mit dem gemeinen Volk teilen. Heute gehört Herrenhausen allen Menschen.

Als ich bei den weißen Steinskulpturen und szenischen Figurengruppen ankam, dachte ich an die surreale Absurdität von Theater, Oper und Film. Seltsame, verschwiegene Helden mit Fellen und Schwertern, dazu nackte Frauen. Ob es sich um mythologische Entführungsszenen oder Liebesspiele unter Göttern und Nymphen handelt? Ich wollte es nicht genau wissen, die lasziv-poetischen Andeutungen genügten mir. Ich war begeistert. Die Idee, ein Stück gepflegte Gartenlandschaft mit Szenen und Erzählungen zu durchweben, setzte sich in meiner Phantasie fest. Sofort stellte ich mir moderne Gärten mit rätselhaften Einbauten vor, dazu hörte ich Musik von Mozart, Verdi, Puccini, Richard Strauss, John Adams und Arvo Pärt, manchmal auch von den Rolling Stones. Dann sah ich in meiner Phantasie Schiffe auf kleinen, stillen Seen treiben. Im Inneren wurden Feste gefeiert. Plötzlich erstarrten alle Kostümierten zu surrealen Figurengruppen. Weißer Marmorstaub fiel auf sie herab. Die Musik spielte weiter und blauer Nebel kam auf …

Innerhalb weniger Hainbuchenquadrate durfte sich die Natur in Grenzen austoben. Beim Eintreten wird jedem Gartenbesucher klar: Würden die Gärtner und Gärtnerinnen ihre tägliche Pflegearbeit einstellen, entstünde aus der geometrischen Anlage in Herrenhausen innerhalb weniger Jahre ein zugewucherter Urwald. Jeder Baum und jede Pflanze auf der ganzen Welt verstreut jedes Jahr Millionen von Samen und hat nur eines im Sinn: sich hemmungslos egoistisch zu vermehren. Die Natur braucht uns Menschen, einschließlich Gärtner und Gärtnerinnen, nicht. Kultur heißt: die Natur in Grenzen zu weisen, ihre anarchische Okkupationssucht lenken und für uns Menschen nutzbar zu machen. Kultur heißt demnach auch: gegen die Natur zu arbeiten. Wie weit man dabei gehen darf und soll, entscheidet jede Generation – natürlich auch jeder einzelne Gartenbesitzer – anders.

Wegen meines starken Interesses für Landschaftsarchitektur wäre es nach Beendigung meines Architekturstudiums 1970 an der TH in Stuttgart vielleicht sinnvoll gewesen, ein zweites Studium zum Thema »Landschaftsgestaltung« in Karlsruhe oder Weihenstephan anzuschließen, aber ich zog es vor, einige Jahre als freier Künstler meine Fragen und Themen in Bildern und Zeichnungen, manchmal auch in Objekten, Landschaftsaktionen, Photographien und Filmen zu formulieren.

In meinem kleinen Stuttgarter Atelier versuchte ich bildhaft, alles miteinander zu verbinden: die wilde Schönheit von Gebirgen, Felsen, Küsten, Fjorden und Stränden, die künstliche Schönheit der historischen Gärten, den alten Kampf zwischen Landwirtschaft und freier Natur. Darunter mischten sich die Hervorbringungen der modernen Technik und Architektur: Wohnblocks, Stadtränder, Industrieanlagen, Kraftwerke, Stauwerke, Schrebergärten, Parkplätze, Parkhäuser, Autobahnen, Tankstellen, Landstraßen, Rast- und Müllplätze, Umspannwerke und Kernkraftwerke. Ich wollte das Ganze in den Blick bekommen und dabei auch die aktuellen Landschaftszerstörungen und Umweltprobleme nicht außer acht lassen.

Mit dem »Laubenhaus« in Stuttgart-Vaihingen stieg ich zum ersten Mal in die architektonische und landschaftgestalterische Realität ein. Bei der Planung und Durchführung lernte ich die ganz alltäglichen Probleme mit dem Bauherren, in diesem Fall dem Universitätsbauamt, der Bürokratie, dem Genehmigungsamt und den späteren Nutzern kennen. Nichts wurde mir erspart. Auch nach der Fertigstellung waren die Schwierigkeiten mit der realen Welt nicht vorbei. Vandalen machten dem kleinen, ungeschützten Bau das »Leben« schwer. Ob das »Laubenhaus« mit seinem ironisch-romantischen Vorgarten auch Freunde und beglückte Besucher hatte, weiß ich nicht. Der Abriß im Jahr 2000 ist eine traurige Tatsache. Vielleicht sollte man derartige Experimente immer temporär begrenzen, aber auch besser schützen. In unserer zunehmend rücksichtslosen Ego-Gesellschaft nimmt der Vandalismus immer bedenklichere Formen und Ausmaße an.

Nach meinem zweiten, mehrmonatigen Stipendien-Aufenthalt in der römischen Villa Massimo, den ich zum ausführlichen Studium der italienischen Gärten aus der Renaissance- und Barockzeit genutzt hatte, zog ich 1981 von Stuttgart aufs Land um. Unser neues Domizil in Attenweiler bei Biberach an der Riß stand unter strengem Denkmalschutz: ein Rokoko-Pfarrhaus (besser: der ehemalige Sommersitz der Äbte von Schussenried, mit Stuckaturen von Dominikus Zimmermann), erbaut zwischen 1727 und 1729. Ich sah in dem Umzug auch ein klares Bekenntnis zum Leben in und mit der Natur. Landleben, mit allen Vor- und Nachteilen.

Einen historischen Garten gab es nicht. Nur einen größeren Nutzgarten. In Erinnerung an mein Herrenhausen-Erlebnis, pflanzte ich – gemeinsam mit meiner Frau – ein fünf mal fünf Meter großes Hainbuchenquadrat, mit plattenbelegtem, grünem Innenraum und Brunnenbecken. Davor ein kleiner Nutzgarten mit Beerenstauden und eine Wiese mit Obstbäumen. Den Hofbereich besetzt ein ebenfalls von uns gepflanzter Nußbaum, der inzwischen schon eine bedenkliche Größe erreicht hat.

Daß sich in den Jahren danach, trotz zahlreicher Veröffentlichungen, Ausstellungen mit eigenen Zeichnungen und Wettbewerbsvorschlägen, nur wenige größere Garten- und Landschaftsarchitekturprojekte in der Realität ergaben, finde ich traurig. Ich mußte mich mit Bühnenbildern und Ausstellungsgestaltungen begnügen. Im Rückblick bilden der Urnenfriedhof in Singen am Hohentwiel, die beiden IGA-Projekte in Stuttgart, der Monopteros in Hohenheim und der Wielandpark in Biberach die wenigen Höhepunkte. Immerhin ließen sich in allen fünf Projekten Fragmente meiner Garten- und Park-Ideen – der »szenischen Gärten« – verwirklichen.

Von den verlorenen Wettbewerben will ich hier nur einige wenige aufzählen. In den 1980er Jahren: Stadtzeichen Hannover, Gustav-Gründgens-Platz in Düsseldorf, »Metallflußbett« beim neuen Planetarium in Mannheim und »Holzturm« in Freiburg. In den 1990er Jahren: Stadteingang in Freiburg (Pappelpflanzungen), Plätze in Böblingen und Neu-Ulm, Kunst-am-Bau-Wettbewerbe in Hamburg, München und Stuttgart (mit Grünanlagen), Gelände um die Jahrhunderthalle in Bochum zusammen mit Jacques Blumer (Bern), Borja Huidobro (Paris), Helen Mayer und Newton Harrison (Del Mar, Kalifornien), Freibad in Biberach/Riß, Fröbelplatz in Berlin (mit Liegewiesen, Spielplätzen und Grünanlagen), »Mauerdenkmalspark« und Lustgarten (Museumsinsel) in Berlin. Im neuen Jahrtausend kamen der Christliche Garten in Berlin-Marzahn, die Landesgartenschau in Sigmaringen (beides mit Christof Luz), der Gedenkstätten-Park in Esterwegen und die Gedenkstätten-Parks von Dachau (Mühldorfer Hart und Hebertshausen) dazu.

Zustand heute

Verglichen mit der Generation unserer Großeltern und Eltern leben wir heute in einer Zeit der Bildübersättigung. Neben eigenen Reiserlebnissen gehören auch Fernsehberichte über Expeditionen in die abgelegensten Landschaftszonen der Erde dazu. Fast jeder glaubt dadurch die Arktis, Grönland, Feuerland, Neuseeland, Afrika, Indien, Amerika, Mexiko, Südamerika, Japan, Rußland, China, Kanada, Alaska, die Südsee, die Meere, die Tropenwälder und die Wüsten zu kennen. Gab es früher noch unbekannte, rätselhafte Landschaftsbereiche, so ist es heute kaum noch ein Problem, selbst dorthin zu fliegen, an Safaris und Abenteuer-Expeditionen teilzunehmen, sich schauend, photographierend und filmend einzumischen oder sich zumindest – aus Zeit- und Geldmangel – bei Google-Earth oder Wikipedia darüber zu informieren.

Was bedeutet das für unser Thema? Die allgemeine Unruhe, das ständige, teilweise globale Unterwegssein (echt oder medial), hat dazu geführt, daß die nähere Landschaftsumgebung den meisten Menschen immer fremder geworden ist. Der heutige Stadtbewohner (bis zu einem gewissen Alter) nimmt sie nur noch joggend, mit einem Kopfhörer auf den Ohren, als sportlichen Bewegungs- und Fitneßraum mit Frischluftaufnahme wahr. Die Stadtparks gelten als grüne Lungen der verdichteten Zivilisation. Gebirge dienen zum Wandern, Klettern, Drachenfliegen und Skifahren. Meere zum Segeln, Surfen, Schwimmen, Schnorcheln oder Tauchen. Wer genügend Geld und Zeit hat, fliegt zum Golfen nach Irland, zum Surfen nach Portugal oder Lanzarote, zum Schnorcheln auf die Malediven und zum Sonnenbaden nach Ibiza, Florida oder Hawaii. Ruhige, betrachtende Auseinandersetzung mit der Natur und ihren Erscheinungsformen gilt als langweilig und ist kaum noch gefragt.

Manche Zeitgenossen, die am Stadtrand wohnen, besitzen trotzdem einen eigenen Garten oder einen eigenen kleinen Park mit Terrasse, Pool und Tennisplatz. Die Wiese wird im Sommer jede Woche mit dem Rasenmäher gestutzt wie ein Golf- oder Fußballplatz, schon der Hygiene, der aufmerksamen Nachbarn und der eingeladenen Gäste wegen. Auch Reihenhausbesitzer verhalten sich ähnlich. Längst leben sie in jener surrealcleanen Welt, wie sie Jacques Tatí in seinem Film *Mon oncle* so liebevoll-sarkastisch beschrieben hat.

Die alte, etwas spießige Gartenromantik – mit starkem Hang zum Nutzgarten – wird den Schrebergärtnern überlassen. Sie gehören auch zu den begeisterten, meist etwas betagten Gartenschaubesuchern mit ihren überquellenden Blumenangeboten.

Gleichzeitig sind den meisten Menschen die größeren Umweltprobleme bekannt. Sie schauen sich neugierig, im bequemen Sessel sitzend, die Nachrichten über Kriegs-, Natur- und Umweltkatastrophen auf immer größer, schärfer und farbenprächtiger werdenden Bildschirmen an. Sie fühlen sich unschuldig und lachen hämisch in sich hinein. Manchmal allerdings, wenn die Gefahren näher rücken, rutschen sie beunruhigt, gar entsetzt auf ihrem Ledersofa hin und her und fühlen sich Angst- und Panikattacken ausgeliefert. In allen Zeitungen und TV-Sendungen, aber auch in unzähligen Büchern werden – neben den aktuellen Katastrophenmeldungen – apokalyptische Weltuntergangsbilder beschrieben. Was 1962 mit dem *Stummen Frühling* von Rachel Carson in Amerika begann und sich mit den mahnenden Büchern des Club of Rome seit 1972 zur Gewißheit steigerte, kann heute niemand mehr anzweifeln. Die Industrialisierung der Welt hatte und hat einen unbändigen Energiebedarf zur Folge. Bodenschätze wurden ausgebeutet, die Luft verpestet und die Landschaften mit Müllplätzen überzogen. Ein kritischer Endpunkt war erreicht. Selbst den zynischsten Zeitgenossen wurde klar: Es muß umgedacht und umgesteuert werden. Allerdings galt nach wie vor Buckminster Fullers Feststellung aus dem Jahr 1970: „Nun gibt es noch eine äußerst wichtige Tatsache, die das Raumschiff Erde betrifft: Es wurde nämlich keine Bedienungsanleitung mitgeliefert.«

Heute arbeiten die meisten Regierungen der großen Industrienationen daran, den CO2-Ausstoß zu verringern, um das Weltklima zu schützen, die Erderwärmung zu reduzieren und die Luft reinzuhalten. Ökologie, Ende des Raubbaus, Recycling und Nachhaltigkeit sind die neuen Zauberworte.

Trotzdem ging keine Regierung der Welt nach der Fukushima-Katastrophe soweit wie die deutsche und beschloß den totalen Atomenergie-Ausstieg. Überhaupt fällt auf, daß in Deutschland die welt- und naturfreundlichen Bestrebungen etwas übertrieben werden. Bei den »Grünen« sind heute Renaturierungen, Feuchtbiotope, Fledermausbrücken und Krötentunnels wichtiger als die Probleme unter den Menschen (z.B. die sozialen). Obwohl dadurch die Liebe zur Landschaft und Natur hätte gesteigert werden können, verkümmerte das Interesse daran eher. Große Entscheidungen und Planungen wie der Ausbau der Radwege in den Städten, Windenergie- und Solaranlagen in der Landschaft und auf Dächern haben Priorität. Zwar wird mehr Grün in den Städten gewünscht, aber gleichzeitig rückten Gartenkunst und anspruchsvolle Landschaftsarchitektur in Deutschland – im Gegensatz zu anderen europäischen Ländern – an den Rand des Interesses und werden eher als rückständige, überflüssige Ausdruckszonen abgetan. Wiesen und Bäume an sich müssen genügen. Nur noch über die Aspekte Denkmalsschutz und Tourismusförderung (versteht sich: sanfter Tourismus!) können pflegeintensive Gärten wie Herrenhausen, Schwetzingen, Veitshöchheim und Nymphenburg überleben. Erstaunlich, daß hier nicht längst »grüne Denkmal- und Bilderstürmer« auftauchen und der Natur gewaltsam zu ihrem ursprünglichen, wilden Aussehen verhelfen!

Vielleicht gehört eine Tatsache trotzdem zu den erfreulichen Ergebnissen des zunehmenden Umweltbewußtseins und damit der »grünen Tendenzen«, die es übrigens schon seit Beginn des 20. Jahrhunderts (Wandervogel- und FKK-Bewegungen) gibt: Noch nie breiteten sich so viele Wälder und Grünzonen wie heute in Europa aus. In den Jahrhunderten davor neigten die Menschen dazu, ganze Wälder und bewaldete Gebirgszüge abzuholzen, ohne nachzupflanzen. Man benötigte das Holz zum Feuern und Heizen, zum Haus- und Schiffsbau. Heute wird jeder gefällte Waldbereich mit jungen Bäumen aufgeforstet. Dafür gibt es Forstgesetze und Forstämter.

Hat sich unter all diesen Entwicklungsaspekten unser Natur- und Landschaftsbild grundsätzlich geändert? Es ist vielfältiger, vielleicht durch Informationen und Wissen auch differenzierter geworden. Gleichzeitig hat es – selbst für Landwirte – etwas von der ursprünglich staubig-dreckigen, manchmal auch gefährlichen Sinnlichkeit verloren. Zwischen Menschen und Landschaften, zwischen Hände und Natur haben sich mediale Bilder, Computer, wissenschaftliche Erkenntnisse, Düngemittel, chemische Bekämpfungsmethoden von Ungeziefern und Maschinen gestellt.

Es gibt für die Städter – und sie sind inzwischen in der Mehrheit – nach wie vor die Alltags- und die Sonntagswelt, die Arbeits- und die Urlaubswelt, hinzu kommt die anwachsende Zahl der arbeitsbefreiten Rentner. Die Sehnsucht nach schönen, aber auch erholsamen und benutzbaren, gleichzeitig spannenden Naturstellen am Wochenende, im Urlaub und während des langweiligen Rentnerlebens wird größer und größer. Der westliche, sozial abgesicherte Wohlstand hat außerdem dazu geführt, daß immer mehr Menschen vereinsamen und eher zu Empathie mit Haustieren, Pflanzen und Bäumen als mit anderen Menschen neigen.

Und genau an diesem Punkt setzt meine Idee für neue (oder alte?) Gärten und Parks ein. Sie sind, meiner Meinung nach, heute wichtiger denn je. Allerdings in einem Sinn, den sie vielleicht schon immer hatten: Verlangsamen, Anhalten und – gemischt mit Bildern aus der bekannten Kulturwelt – wieder nach Innen, auf das Wesen der Natur schauen. Das »Außen« ist nun erobert, durchackert, erforscht, durchdiskutiert, durchjoggt, durchrast, durchflogen und zu einem großen Teil bekannt. Leider weiterhin sehr bedrängt durch lärmig-hektische, ständig weiter wachsende Städte und fortschreitende, wenn auch etwas gebremste Umweltzerstörungen.

Jeder private oder öffentliche Garten und Park, natürlich auch jedes Landschaftsschutzgebiet und jeder Bannwald, spricht von der Sehnsucht nach Versöhnung und ruhigem Frieden mit der Natur. Wie in pompejianischen Wohngärten, in christlichen Klostergärten oder in den Gärten von chinesischen und japanischen Tempelanlagen wäre es heute wichtig, die überaktiven, mediengestreßten Menschen an ihre Herkunfts- und Rückkehrzone Natur zu erinnern. Entgegen dem alten Wissenschaftler-Credo, das Max Weber einst mit den Worten beschrieb: »Die Aufgabe der Wissenschaft ist die Entzauberung der Welt«, will ich genau das Gegenteil erreichen.

Alle meine bisher entwickelten und sehr fragmentarisch verwirklichten Garten- und Parkideen wollen, einschließlich ihrer Architekturen und künstlerischen Ergänzungen, in den »aufgeklärten Zauber«, damit auch in die Rätselwelt der Natur zurückführen. Nicht ganz im radikal wilden und humorlosen Sinne von Jean-Jacques Rousseau, denn immer soll auch noch etwas Historisches, Kulturelles, Psychologisches, Erzählerisches und Futuristisches mitschwingen. Entgegen der Behauptungen vieler heutiger Wissenschaftler können wir davon ausgehen, daß bei weitem nicht alle Geheimnisse der Natur entschlüsselt sind. Die Rätsel überwiegen und haben eher kosmische Dimensionen angenommen. Wir, die Besucher der Landschaften und neuen Gartenorte, tragen unsere Erfahrungen, unser Wissen, unsere Fragen, unsere Phantasie und unsere Sehnsüchte stets in uns, und wir können nicht passiv schweigen wie die Bäume, Pflanzen, Blumen und Steine. Es ist uns zwar möglich, wortlos zu empfinden und zu fühlen, aber unser Bewußtsein arbeitet mit Worten, Sätzen, Bildern, Erklärungen, Erinnerungen – seltener mit mathematischen Formeln. Deswegen versuche ich in meinen Vorschlägen, mit inszenierten Situationen und dramaturgisch zugespitzten Wegführungen Dialoge zwischen der Natur und den einzelnen Besuchern anzuregen.

Plötzlich beginnen Bäume zu erzählen, Blätter zu sprechen, Wasserfälle zu singen und Steine zu tanzen. Spinnweben verwandeln sich in Harfen und Vogelnester in Höhlen aus grauer Vorzeit. Manchmal taucht zwischen Büschen und Blättern ein frecher Gartenzwerg auf und ermahnt die Besucher mit fröhlich-albernen Sätzen dazu, die Wege nicht zu verlassen und die Wiesen sauber zu halten. Bei Zuwiderhandlung muß ein Gedicht von Ernst Jandl zehn Mal aufgesagt werden:

»wir sind die menschen auf den wiesen
bald sind wir menschen unter den wiesen
und werden wiesen, und werden wald
das wird ein heiterer landaufenthalt.«

In meiner Vorstellung ist es wichtig, daß alle Garten- und Parkbesucher in einen besonderen Zustand versetzt werden. Dazu gehört, daß sie zunächst ein Tor (wie einen Kino- oder Theatereingang) durchqueren. Jeder der neu gestalteten Landschaftsbereiche – der »szenischen Gärten« – muß von einer Mauer umgeben, gerahmt und geschützt sein und sich so deutlich von der zu Lärm und Vandalismus neigenden Alltagswelt unterscheiden. Dieses »Verwandlungsgeheimnis« haben alle großen Garten- und Parkgestalter auf der ganzen Welt gekannt. Ich denke – neben den Herrenhäuser Gärten – an die berühmten chinesischen Gärten von Suzhou, an den Kies-und-Fels-Garten des Toji-Tempels im japanischen Kyoto, an den »Kakteengarten« von César Manrique auf Lanzarote, aber auch an die »Disney-Worlds« in Los Angeles, Florida und Paris.

Jeder Eingetretene ist ein »Verwandelter« und geht nach innen, auf den Spuren seiner Erinnerungen, seiner Hoffnungen und Sehnsüchte. Gleichzeitig blickt er auch nach oben zum Himmel und betrachtet die Wolken und Vögel mit neuen Augen. Ist er bei Dunkelheit hier unterwegs, öffnet sich der Kosmos unter neuen, planetarischen Aspekten. Vielleicht begegnet er – neben leuchtenden Meteoren in Waldlichtungen – Raumfahrern oder seltsamen außerirdischen Wesen auf Berggipfeln.

Mir schweben keine religiösen Orte vor, keine Waldkirchen oder Wallfahrtsorte, auch keine Landschaftstempel, sondern Naturorte mit eigenartigen Szenen und architektonischen Elementen: eingewachsene Ruinen und Karussells, Käfige mit schwebenden Schaukelpferden und Skulpturenresten, wandernde Gartenzwerge, eingesponnene Betten in Höhlen, Schultische in einer Lichtung, Wohnmöbel im Maisfeld, halbverschüttete Küchengeräte zwischen Felsbrocken, alte efeubewachsene Weinflaschen in Regalen, Masken an Baumstämmen, ausgestopfte Tiere in Glasvitrinen, Fernsehgeräte unter Wasser, Seerosenteiche mit lebendigen Goldfischen, alte Grabsteine, Verkehrsampeln im Dickicht, Sessel in Baumkronen. ...

Wege führen durch künstlich gestaltete Natursteintäler, vorbei an Wasserfällen und Farnwäldern, zu dachlosen Raumandeutungen mit Fenstern, zu Hainen und Seeufern mit Schilfzonen, zu romantischen Seen mit Enten und Reihern. Aber auch zu Wiesen, auf denen Schafe, Kühe, Pferde und Ziegen weiden. Manchmal stößt man auf Zoogehege mit Elefanten und Nilpferden. Pfaue schlagen Räder und rufen ihre fremdartigen Schreie in die Runde.

Plötzlich stehen Textsteine am Wegrand (wie früher Kreuze). Auf ihnen sitzen bunte Papageien und übersetzen die eingemeißelten Fragen in menschliche Laute:

»Wie ist es möglich, daß aus einem Apfelkern, einem Pflaumenkern, einer Walnuß ein ganzer Baum entsteht? Wie ist es möglich, daß alle Blätter, Blüten und Früchte (jedes Jahr neue!) in diesem Kern enthalten und vorprogrammiert sind?«

Daneben ein Stein mit den Fragen:

»Welche Energie läßt unser Herz ein Leben lang schlagen? Woher kommt die unerschöpfliche Kraft? Ist die Sonne die Quelle alles Lebens? Oder gibt es noch andere geheimnisvolle, bisher unentdeckte Kräfte? Warum gibt es positive und negative Kräfte? Warum gibt es Krankheiten? Warum gibt es das Leben überhaupt? Warum gibt es die Welt und das Universum? Warum gibt es etwas und nicht das Nichts?«

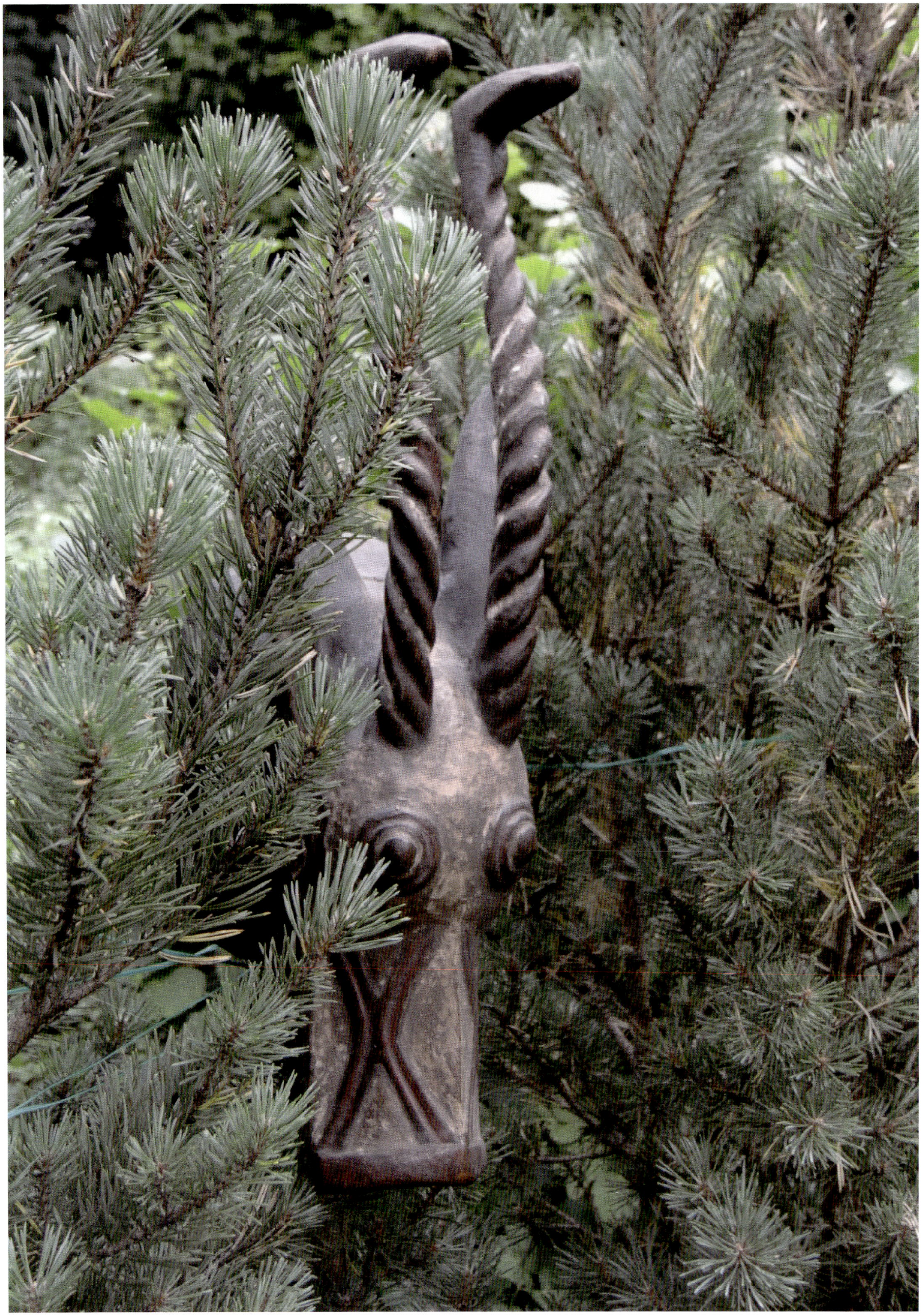

1. »African mask between pine trees«, 2016. A staged image within the new garden. (Photo: Hans Dieter Schaal.)
2. »Ancient marble footprint in the forest«, 2015. Photo collage. A picture to evoke memories of old stories.

1. »Afrikanische Maske zwischen Kiefern«, 2016. Inszeniertes Bild innerhalb des neuen Gartens. (Photo: Hans Dieter Schaal.)
2. »Antiker Marmor-Fußabdruck im Wald«, 2015. Photocollage. Erinnerungsbild an alte Geschichten.

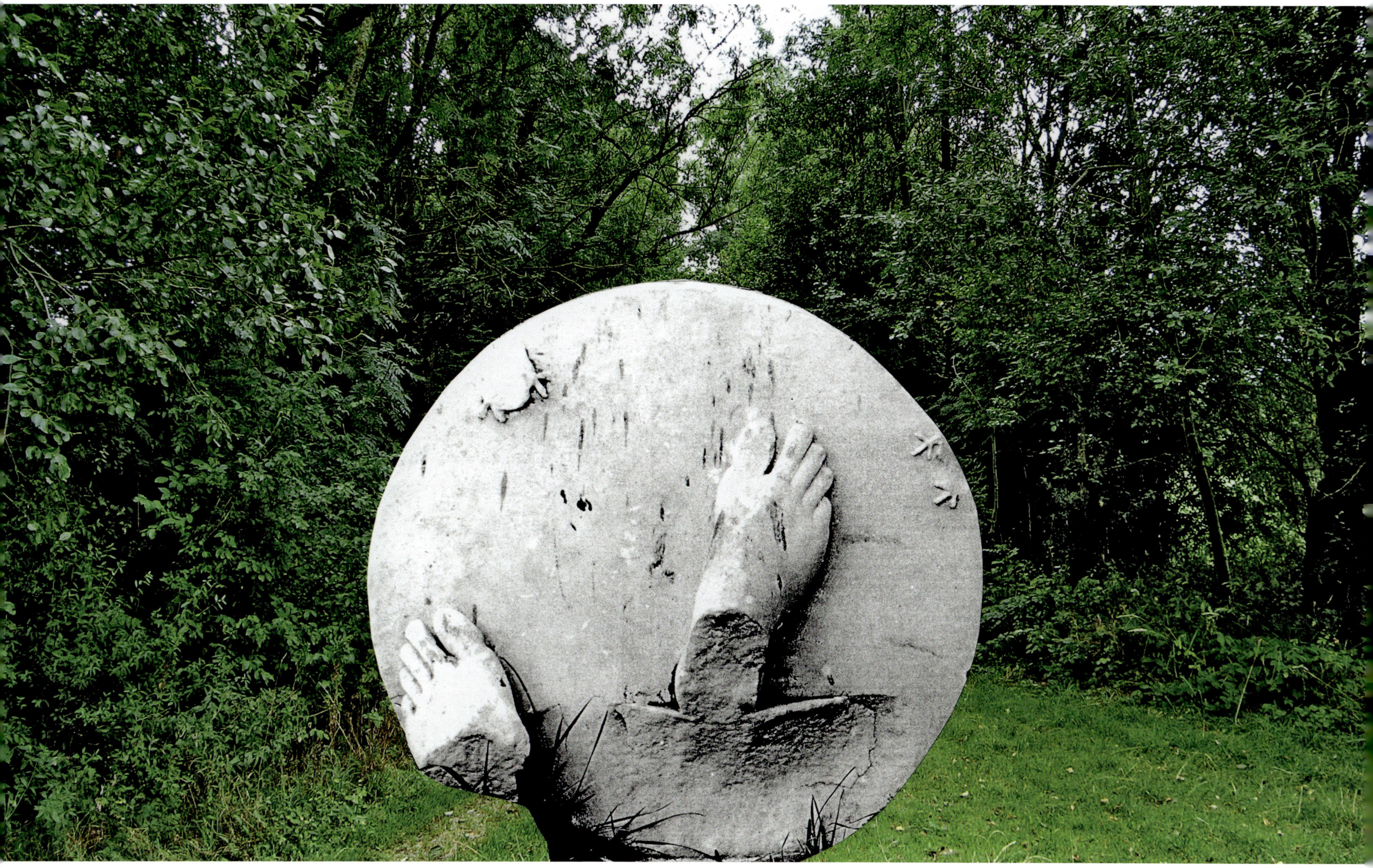

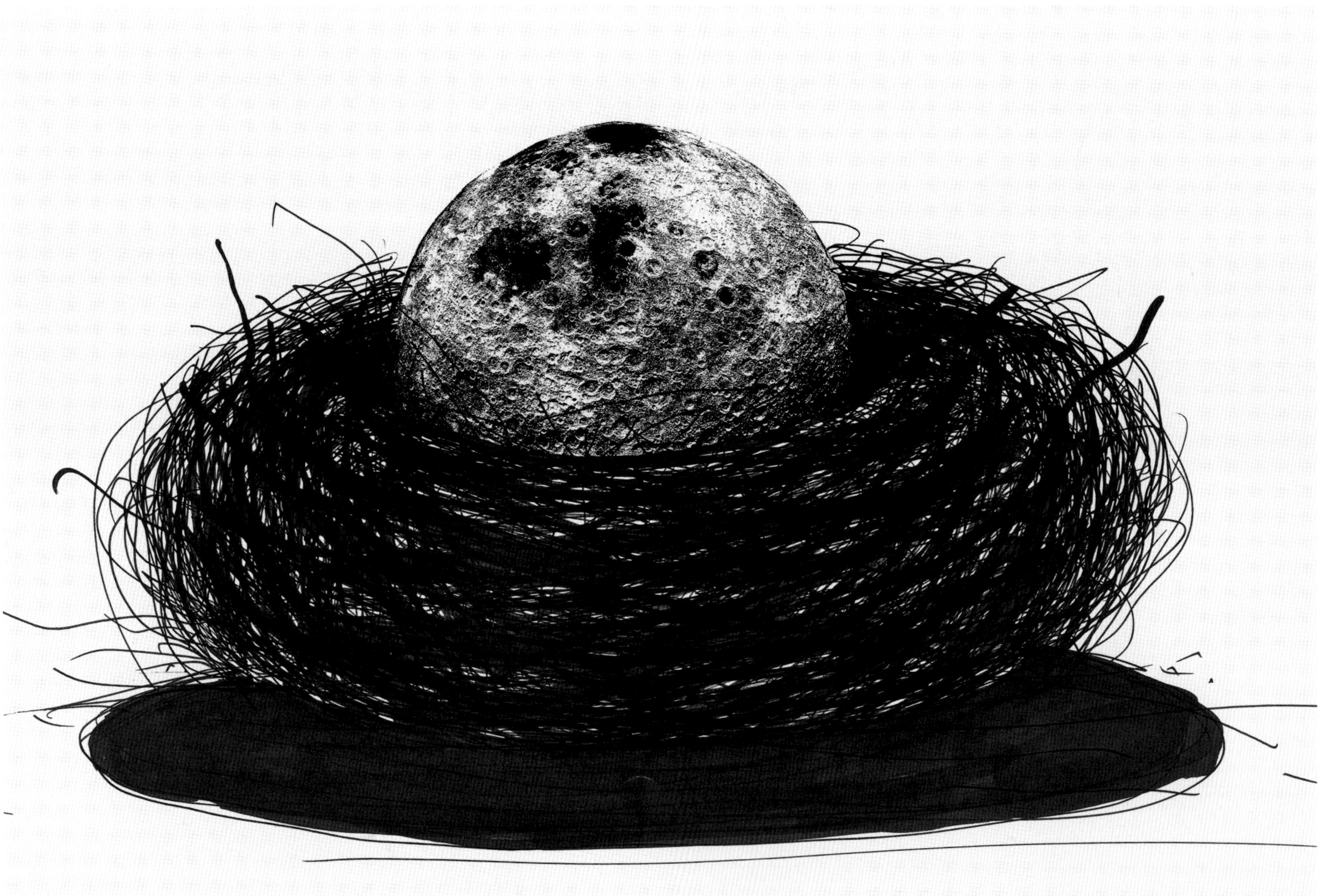

3. »Moon in enlarged nest«, 2013. Photo collage.
4. Nocturnal park-romanticism with full moon and film projection, 2015. Photo collage.

3. »Mond in vergrößertem Nest«, 2013. Photocollage.
4. Nächtliche Parkromantik mit Vollmond und Filmprojektion, 2015. Photocollage.

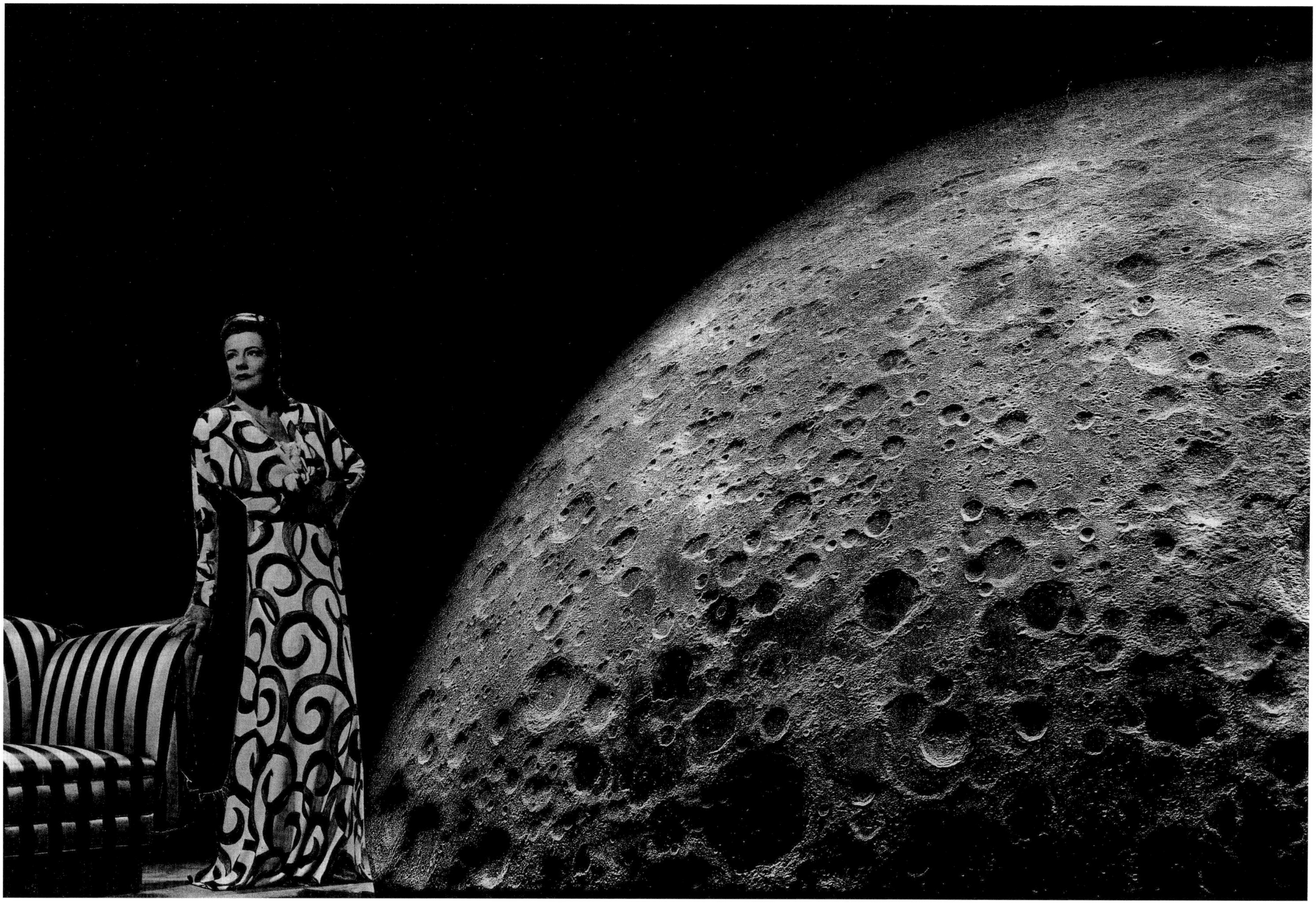

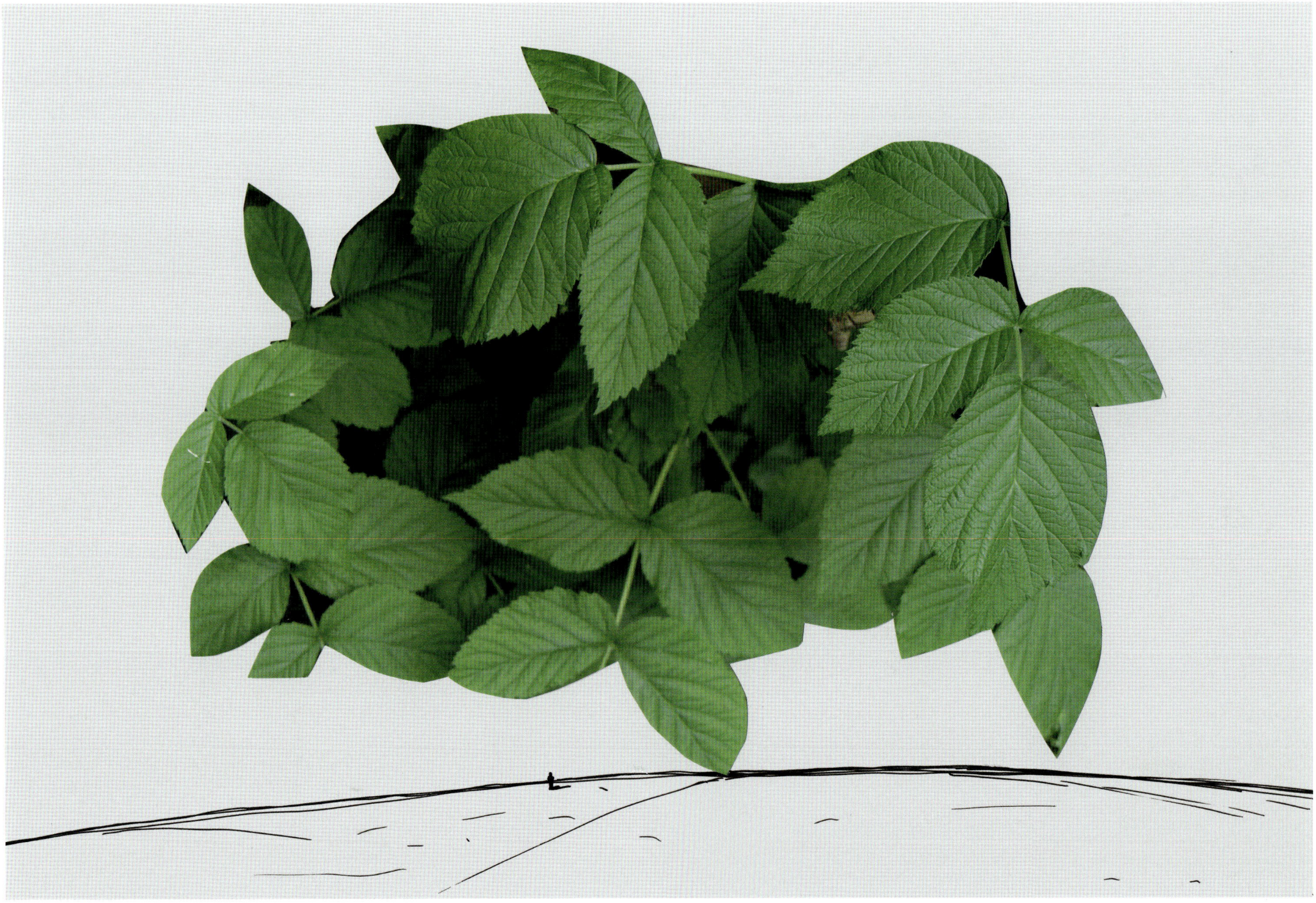

5. »Leaf cloud«, 2016.
6. »A garden gnome emerges in the new garden«, 2016. Unimpressed by the vandals in Berlin, Stuttgart, and Biberach, he defends his position with an indomitable smile. A staged situation within the new garden. (Photo: Hans Dieter Schaal.)

5. »Blattwolke«, 2016.
6. »Gartenzwerg taucht im neuen Garten auf«, 2016. Er hat sich von den Vandalen in Berlin, Stuttgart oder Biberach nicht beeindrucken lassen und verteidigt seine Stellung mit unerbittlichem Lächeln. Inszenierte Situation innerhalb des neuen Gartens. (Photo: Hans Dieter Schaal.)

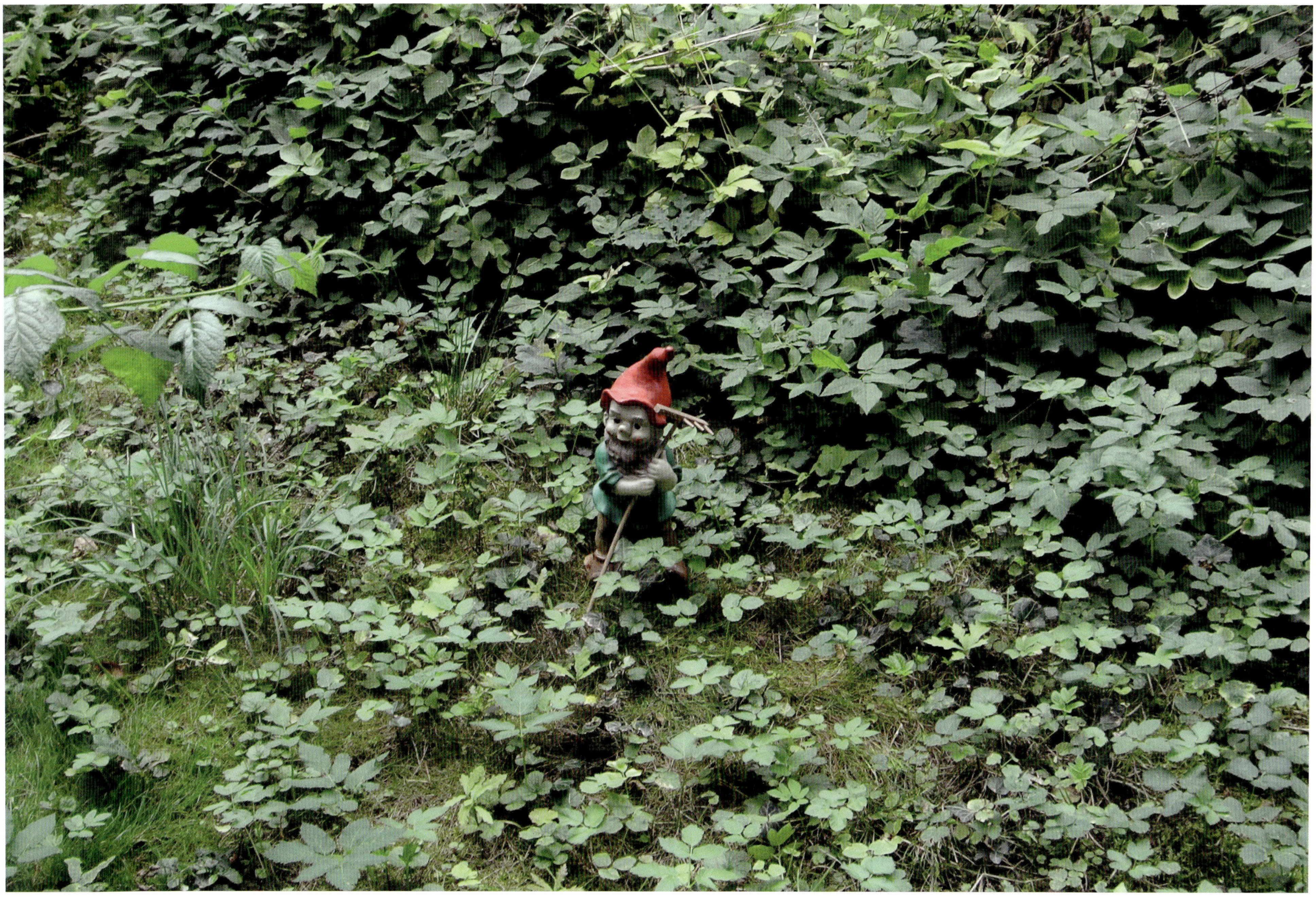